D1085379

COMPARATIVE MYTHOLOGY

COMPARATIVE MYTHOLOGY

Jaan Puhvel

The Johns Hopkins University Press
BALTIMORE AND LONDON

This book has been brought to publication with the generous assistance of the David M. Robinson Publication Fund and the Andrew W. Mellon Foundation.

The Johns Hopkins University Press
701 West 40th Street
Baltimore, Maryland 21211
The Johns Hopkins Press Ltd., London

The paper used in this publication meets the minimum requirements of American National Standard for Information Sciences—Permanence of Paper for Printed Library Materials, ANSI Z39.48-1984.

Library of Congress Cataloging-in-Publication Data

Puhvel, Jaan.
Comparative mythology.

Includes index.
1. Mythology. I. Title.
BL311.P84 1987 291.1'3 86-20882
ISBN 0-8018-3413-9

When features of resemblance, too strong to have been accidental, are observable in different systems of polytheism, without fancy or prejudice to colour them and improve the likeness, we can scarce help believing, that some connection has immemorially subsisted between the several nations, who have adopted them.

SIR WILLIAM JONES

Contents

Preface

This book is not so much a research treatise as a compendium born of pedagogy. Since a course in comparative mythology was introduced to the University of California curriculum in 1960, a whole generation of students has been exposed to my teaching of the subject, into which I myself was initiated by Georges Dumézil in Paris and Stig Wikander in Uppsala during my peregrinations in the fifties. Mindful of the fluidity of the subject, I stuck for a quarter century to instructional orality, recreating the course many times in words and thoughts, without benefit of text, anxious to eschew the premature staleness of a fixed version. Fortunately, such druidic restraint did not keep others from worthwhile summations of their own—for example, C. Scott Littleton's *New Comparative Mythology* or Donald Ward's *Divine Twins*. At length, however, after promises made over the years to students in want of study aids that "someday" there would be a tome they could use, the bulk that follows has taken on written form. I hope that it has shaped up as self-contained and lucid enough to be of some use to a wider educated public, those without the benefit of further oral exegesis.

The recommendations for further reading at the ends of chapters aim to include well-edited, up-to-date primary source editions in English whenever available, and a selection of more specialized handbooks and detailed materials chosen with a view to reinforcing the presentations of the book itself. This being a summary survey rather than a monographic grappling with every contrary issue and author, a subtext of notes has purposely been curtailed.

Evolving abstractly over the years, this book has assimilated, integrated, and refigured shifting strands and influences. It cannot pretend to be a summa of any kind; it is merely one man's view of a complex and somewhat amorphous mass of multimillennial tradition at a point when our own millennium is lurching to a precarious finish. Perhaps the material can contribute in some measure to a recovery of the lost intellectual horizons of Western man, to a realization that our concept formation and abstract patrimony extend beyond the confines that, since antiquity, have constricted the vision of a remoter past. May it inform and enlighten without ideological or sectarian prejudice.

COMPARATIVE MYTHOLOGY

Introduction

There are many notions that the ancient Greeks not only defined but named forevermore, such as "hybris," "irony," and "tragedy." Another such is "myth." No modern language has a substitute—the word comes with the concept. From the very start it is no mere technical or scholarly term but an everyday, colloquial one. Its origins are unclear—most probably it is based on the interjection *(mu)mû,* comparable in formation to English *(yak-)yak*. "Word, speech, talk" is the original sense, juxtaposed by Homer to *épos* (*épos kaì mûthos* 'word and speech') and opposed to *érgon,* as when Achilles was reared to be a speaker of words and doer of deeds (*múthōn te rhētêr' émenai prēktêrá te érgōn*). In Homer and the tragedians it can also mean "tale, story, narrative" without reference to truth content. But starting with prose writers such as Herodotus, the word *mûthos* takes on a polarized tinge of "fictive narrative," "tall tale," "legend." As such it contrasts with *lógos,* another term for "word," which came to denote "true story" to Herodotus; the father of history had no compunction about terming his own hodgepodge of legendry "Lógoi" and reserving the term *mûthos* for things that not even he could believe. From Plato onward a technical sense of "myth" begins to emerge in *mûthos,* while *lógos* takes on ever more rational, philosophical, and even transcendental overtones, from Aristotle's logic to the primordial Word that launches the Gospel of Saint John.

It is in retrospect ironic that modern usage has managed to defeat such exalted semantic monopolies and revert at least partly to the pre-Platonic colloquialism of the ancients. "It's a myth" means to the average American that there is not a shred of truth in it, that something is either a brain phantom originating in a group's collective neurosis or organized hokum foisted on the public by the "mythmakers" in government or the media or on Madison Avenue. More learnedly but with equal irreverence, verbal incontinence is dubbed "logorrhea." The latter compound is of modern man's making, whereas *mūthopoiīā* goes back to the ancients, as do *mūthologíā* and *mūthológēma,* which are attested from Plato onward. "Mythology" thus means originally and literally "storytelling" and is loosely used nowadays to denote a body of mythical narrative ("Greek mythology"), but technically its proper modern sense is "the study of myth," even as, for example, pathology studies the bulk of ailments. To say we study mythology is pleonasm. What we study is myth.

Myth in the technical sense is a serious object of study, because true myth is by definition deadly serious to its originating environment. In myth are expressed the thought patterns by which a group formulates self-cognition and self-realization, attains self-knowledge and self-confidence, explains its own source and being and that of its surroundings, and sometimes tries to chart its destinies. By myth man has lived, died, and—all too often—killed. Myth operates by bringing a sacred (and hence essentially and paradoxically "timeless") past to bear preemptively on the present and inferentially on the future ("as it was in the beginning, is now, and ever shall be"). Yet in the course of human events societies pass and religious systems change; the historical landscape gets littered with the husks of desiccated myths. These are valuable nonmaterial fossils of mankind's recorded history, especially if still embedded in layers of embalmed religion, as part of a stratum of tradition complete with cult, liturgy, and ritual. Yet equally important is the next level of transmission, in which the sacred narrative has already been secularized, myth has been turned into saga, sacred time into heroic past, gods into heroes, and mythical action into "historical" plot. Many genuine "national epics" constitute repositories of tradition where the mythical underpinnings have been submerged via such literary transposition. Old chronicles can turn out to be "prose epics" where the probing modern mythologist can uncover otherwise lost mythical traditions. Such survival is quite apart from, or wholly incidental to, the conscious exploitative use of myth in literature, as raw material of fiction, something that Western civilization has practiced since artful verbal creativity began.

A myth in its pristine state is by definition specific to a given human environment. How it fares from then on (its "life," "afterlife," survival, transposition, revival, rediscovery, or whatever) is a matter of historical accident. It follows that the study of any specific past body of myth has to be mainly a historical discipline employing written sources, whereas contemporary myth can be pursued by the methods of field anthropology. Comparative mythology of separately localized and attested traditions can be practiced on different levels of abstraction and generalization. "Universal mythology" is essentially reduced to explaining accordances (and, if relevant, differences or contrasts) by appeal to human universals or at least common denominators based on similarities of psychological patterning, environment, or levels of culture. Needless to say, it has to pursue the typical and usual at the expense of the specific and unique. "Diffusionary mythology" studies how traditions travel, charting the spread and transmission of myth. The trouble is precisely that myth does not "travel" very well and, when it does travel, frequently moves from its specific historical and geographical fulcrum into the international realm of legend, folktale, fairy tale, and other debased forms of originally mythical narrative.

It is not always easy to diagnose mythical data on a bipolar axis of polygenesis (spontaneous multiple generation based on broad factors of similarity) and diffusion. For instance, the notions that illness is caused by shamanistic soul loss on the one hand or by supernatural injection (elf-shot, etc.) on the other exist in a crazy-quilt pattern worldwide, often in complementary distribution. Which is more universal, and how may one or the other have spread? Seventeenth-century travelers to the New World were baffled by similarities between Greek and native Indian myths, and two books (by Helen Gayton and Åke Hultkrantz) have been written on the "Orpheus myth" in North America, especially Comanche and Pawnee traditions about a man's loss of his wife and his abortive attempt to recover her in the West (i.e., the Otherworld). Is this a universal datum, or had their ancestors picked it up at Coronado's campfires or from other temporal or spiritual conquistadors? The universality of the Oedipus complex has become a commonplace of our civilization, and yet Oedipus-type tales stretch in a continuous band from Europe through the Near East and South Asia into the Western Pacific, to the exclusion of other native mythologies (northern Asia, Africa, America, Australia). The "average hero legend" abstracted psychoanalytically by Otto Rank and ritualistically by Lord Raglan (see chap. 1) is based solely on European, Near Eastern, and South Asian exemplars, showing the same doubtful pattern of universality as the Oedipus story. In short, the polygenetic and diffusionary approaches not only are limited in themselves but also are subject to dubious conflations.

A third approach involves monogenesis, that is, tracing the mythical matter of disparate societies back to a common ancestry, one that includes language, society, and culture alike. Such inductive historical and prehistoric reconstruction of prototypes always yields fringe benefits of a deductional kind, as dislocations themselves come to appear separately meaningful after the inductive hypothesis has been verified. Such an approach, to be fruitful, needs width and depth in several dimensions and enough similarity and variety to allow both positive conclusions and negative controls. In the entire world, only the Indo-European language continuum attested for four thousand years throughout Europe, the Near East, and Central and South Asia offers an adequate laboratory for such an enterprise. That it impinges upon and overlaps with the so-called cradle of civilization in the Near East only enhances its value, because this very adjacency affords control data on diffusion as well.

Such will be the approach adopted in this work. But before proceeding, let us take a closer look at the history of mythology and its current state.

I · DIRECTIONS

1 · The Study of Myth

While "mythology" is the study of myth, a look at the history of mythology is a study of the study of myth, thus a sort of "metamythology" not unlike the history of science or the history of any other branch of scholarly endeavor.

Whereas mythical thinking underlies mythopoeia, man's reaction to myth constitutes the rudiments of mythology, and such response has tended to be revulsive rather than rational or dispassionate. Most of the recorded reacting before relatively modern times, and some of it up to this day, has been by partisans of philosophy and zealots of faith, thus by espousers of dogmatic thought that (in Alfred North Whitehead's words) "plays the devil with religion" and is not unknown to science either. The earliest Ionian Greek nature philosophers, Thales of Miletus, Anaximander, and Anaximenes, were each promoting a cosmological "first cause" (water, *tò ápeiron* = the infinite, and air respectively), which of course eschewed any mythical cosmogony. Their successors, Xenophanes, Parmenides, and Zeno of Elea, pushed the search for ontological immutables to the point of affirming the illusory nature of movement and change (Zeno's paradoxes, notably "Achilles and the tortoise"). In the interim the old theological apparatus had suffered much debasement at the hands of the oral epic poets with their worldly views on divine goings-on. The first recorded clash came in Xenophanes' attack on anthropomorphic religion:

> Homer and Hesiod have imputed to the gods all things that are a shame and a disgrace among men, stealings and adulteries and deceiv-

> ings of one another. . . . But mortals think that gods are begotten as they are and have clothes like theirs, and voice and form. But if oxen and horses or lions had hands and could draw with their hands and produce works as men do, horses would draw the forms of the gods like horses, and oxen like oxen. . . . The Ethiopians say their gods are snubnosed and black, the Thracians say theirs are blue-eyed and red-haired. . . . —One God . . . neither in form like mortals nor in thought. He sees all over, thinks all over, and hears all over. And without toil he sways all things by the thought of his mind.

Such no-nonsense moral earnestness and absolutist fervor were not quite characteristic of the opposite ontological camp, that of Heraclitus of Ephesus; but his seemingly nihilist slogan *pánta rheî* ("all is flux") also implied rejection of conventional mythology, and he elevated Logos to a kind of universal Reason that left little room for any conventional Mythos.

With the rise of Athens as the center of Greek culture during the fifth century B.C.E., moral philosophy became a professional pursuit, and reactions to myth took on new complexity. The sophist Protagoras, who claimed that man is the measure of all things (*pántōn khrēmátōn métron ánthrōpos*), also tossed off the following frank profession of agnosticism: "Of gods I have no knowledge, whether they exist or not, nor what their natures might be. Many things stand in the way of such realization, such as lack of certainty and the shortness of human life." Plato, on the other hand, did not make matters quite so easy: he had little use for the literary varieties of debased myth and banished the likes of Homer and Hesiod from citizenship in his ideal republic. He did not have much regard for raw folk tradition either, and yet some of his own mythopoeic creations, such as the story of Er the Pamphylian in the *Politeia* (*Republic*), are suffused with transmuted Orphic theories of metempsychosis that originate in mystery cults of a popular kind. To compound the contradictions, he had a pragmatic streak as well and in his *Nomoi* (*Laws*) was quite willing to tolerate popular myth as a clumsy but edifying expedient for popular consumption.

All such reacting was still short of the theoretical. But soon enough the phenomenon of myth as such also preoccupied the Greeks, and in short order it supplied explanatory trends and formulations that prevailed thereafter and have not lost their relevance. They learned to see myth as a matter of language on the one hand and as a problem of history on the other. Theagenes of Rhegium was the first to suggest that myth might be symbolic, that is, to be taken not as literal but as token truth, as a linguistic device of the rhetoric of ineffability, to express either natural elements or ethical principles. In due course allegory (literally "speaking in other terms," "putting it differently," "expressing figuratively") became the keynote of such myth interpretation (first attested in Cicero as a loanword from Greek, appearing in Greek literature only with Plutarch). The other concept, that of myth as a miscarriage of history, of tradition gone haywire, crops up in passing as early as Herodotus, implying that gods were in origin exceptional human beings such as kings or heroes, deified by the patina of ages in the minds of posterity. This is usually tagged euhemerism, after the Sicilian philosopher Euhemerus of the third century B.C.E.

Both of these theoretical insights were thenceforth selectively handy whenever a certain body of myth was to be exorcised by adherents of new and "better" philosophies or religions, even as Xenophanes had earlier scorned the way men created deities in their own image only to set up his own immutable God. A moralistic rationalist like Prodikos found uses for the trappings of myth, even launching the fable of "Herakles at the Crossroads" being wooed by feminine allegorical impersonations of Virtue and Vice, an incongruous scene for the club-wielding exterminator and skirt chaser of Greek hero saga. The Stoics, whose moral philosophy entailed transcendent notions of divinity that hark back to thinkers like Xenophanes, found in nature allegory an easy tool for dismantling and dismissing the Olympian apparatus. Most rationalists, such as Palaiphatos in his *Perì apístōn* ("On the Incredible"), were easygoing euhemerists in explaining away mythical matter as outgrowths of popular fancy, or priestly concoction, or historical garble. Euhemerism particularly suited the Epicureans, whose own metacosmic deities were wholly aloof ideals; a decent respect to mankind's more standard views of divinity induced them to find helpful ways of interpreting popular religion in the euhemeristic mode. Many historians of later antiquity—for example, Megasthenes, Polybius, and Diodorus Siculus—appear as routine euhemerists, while a great eclectic like Cicero, in works such as *De natura deorum,* is the perfect fence straddler spanning Platonic, Stoic, and Epicurean approaches.

With the advent of Christianity a new, deadly serious myth was sprung on the culture, and negative polemics by various church fathers also turned on the old mythic traditions, merely twisting the by now traditional twin theories of antiquity. Allegory could always be dismissed as arbitrary symbolic interpretation, whereas, in an era when monstrous Roman emperors were deified by decree, euhemerism was tailor-made to show that alleged pagan divinity was in reality anchored somewhere between unconscious corruption and intentional fraud. In their zeal to discredit, writers such as Eusebius, Hippolytus, Lactantius, Arnobius, and Firmicus Maternus sometimes played a valuable part as unintentional mythographers, recounting seamier traditions that normal circumspection would have caused to be lost to posterity. As an example, Arnobius transmits the Phrygian cult myth of Cybele and Attis from Asia Minor, the picturesque details of which would otherwise not have come down to us, despite the fact that Cybele's import worship on the Roman Palatine antedates the year 200 B.C.E.: Papas, the Phrygian Zeus, cohabited with a rock, Agdos, who bore a bisexual monster Agdistis; to tame the latter, the gods tied the sleeping Agdistis's phallus to a tree; as he started up from slumber the organ was torn off, thus reducing Agdistis to the female Cybele. From the blood-soaked ground sprung a pomegranate tree, the fruit of which was plucked by Nana (daughter of the river Sangarios); it disappeared in her lap and impregnated her; she subsequently bore Attis, who in due time castrated himself in his orgiastic devotion to Cybele (hence the self-mutilation of the eunuch priests of Cybele [the *Galli*] and similar goddesses such as Atargatis, recorded by Lucian in *De dea Syria*). Much of this is illuminating for the ancient myths of Asia Minor (for the detail of rock birth cf., e.g., chap. 2 below).

Whatever interest in classical myth lingered during the Middle Ages was usually cloaked in the protective garb of euhemerism. In latter-day imitation of Roman practice (tracing the *gens Iulia* back via Aeneas to Venus-Aphrodite-Cybele in the Troad), Geoffrey of Viterbo's *Speculum regum* in the eleventh century supplied genealogies for the likes of Charlemagne and the Hohenstaufen dynasty. But for the first time nonclassical myth received scholarly and antiquarian attention. Irish monks compiled the *Book of Conquests,* Saxo Grammaticus produced his *Gesta Danorum,* and Snorri Sturluson's *Prose Edda* and *Heimskringla* passed off the Norse gods as immigrants from the general direction of Troy. These writers were good Christian euhemerists, apparently believing that saga picked up where historical record left off and that pagan myth was merely a misguided idolatrous corruption of tradition that they felt free to rectify in the direction of "historical truth" (the irony is that in reality myth has been secularized into saga, as was touched upon in the Introduction above; cf. further chap. 2).

In the fourteenth century Giovanni Boccaccio, better known for his other literary efforts, composed a handbook of Greek mythology (commissioned by Hugo de Lusignan, king of Cyprus) titled *De genealogia deorum,* which was to remain an unsurpassed authority for a couple of centuries. In theoretical terms this final mythological monument of the Middle Ages had little to offer, coasting along on allegory in general and the kind of astrological myth interpretation that had enjoyed popular favor since Hellenistic (Alexandrian) Greek days. Boccaccio's influence lingered largely by default, because the Renaissance, for all its revival of classical learning and Greek studies in particular, did next to nothing for mythology, and this dormancy extended through much of the seventeenth century. Curiously, it was not the intellectual odysseys of the great Renaissance humanists but the voyages of discovery and the treks of conquistadors that ultimately widened the mythological horizon; paradoxically, adventurers like Pedro Álvares Cabral and Vasco Nuñez de Balboa proved more influential in the long run than Marsilio Ficino, Erasmus, and the Scaligers combined. As contacts with the East and colonization of the New World proceeded, commodities less tangible than worldly treasure gradually began seeping toward Europe on the route of the Manila–Acapulco–Vera Cruz galleons. Missionary intellectuals such as the Jesuits were confronted with traditions wholly alien to the circum-Mediterranean orbit. In time a data base was laid for new comparative evaluations. The eighteenth century with its rationalism and "enlightenment" was not likely to embrace myth with ease, and writers like Diderot and Voltaire were almost pathologically hypersensitive to "priestly deceit" in all manifestations of religion. Yet for the first time in the modern world probing minds were producing serious treatises on mythology. Bernard de Fontenelle in his *De l'origine des fables* (1724) pointed to notable similarities between Greek and Amerindian myths and proposed a theory of the worldwide polygenesis of motifs at given levels of culture. This was a concept far ahead of its time, implying that myth as such had meaningful, indeed universal, roots in mankind's past. In 1760 Charles de Brosses published *Du culte des dieux fétiches,* pointing out "primitive" traits in Greek religion and daring to dismiss both allegory and euhemerism as viable explanations. Giambattista Vico in his *Scienza nuova* (posthumous third edition 1744) was the first to grasp at last something of the complexity of myth, listing creative imagination, religious inspiration, impressions created by natural phenomena, and reflections of social institutions as alternative and coexistent ingredients of mythogenesis.

All this was still mere prefiguration. But something new finally broke in with great force with the advent of romanticism in the latter half of the eighteenth century. From being at best indifferent and at worst nefarious, myth was suddenly embraced emotionally and accorded not only respect but downright adulation. Voltaire's persiflage and Johann Gottfried Herder's veneration overlap in time. Via a great synthesis of mythology, poetry, and language, Herder aspired to understand the spiritual development of mankind, thereby affirming the religious significance and above all the intrinsic worth of myth. Herder's successors drew manifold consequences from this profound reorientation. In poetry Greek myth was idealized, as epitomized, for example, in Schiller's great outburst *Die Götter Griechenlands*. Mythopoeic minds like Goethe had the courage to follow Plato's example through millennia and to elevate new myths and symbols on the soil of antiquity. Jakob Grimm brought Germanic mythology into new focus, and professional philosophers found in the symbolism of myth a fruitful field for speculation. Among the latter, Friedrich Schelling with his *Philosophie der Mythologie* (published posthumously in 1857) set a new tone by rejecting all attempts to impose on myth a secondary "meaning," be it euhemeristic or allegorical. Instead he applied to myth the term "tautegorical," implying that it must be understood on its own terms as an autonomous configuration of the human spirit, with its own mode of reality and a content that cannot be translated into rational terms without an irretrievable loss of inner force. As a part of theoretical philosophy such an approach has undergone varied convolutions down to our own day; for instance, Ernst Cassirer (1874–1945) devoted the second volume of his *Philosophy of Symbolic Forms* to a redevelopment and reassessment of Schelling's approach under the title *Mythical Thought*. But the surpassing significance of Schelling's manifesto for mythology lay in its declaration of autonomy. Myth must be understood as myth, not as history or metaphor or any other substitute.

Outside the rarefied realms of theoretical philosophy, however, the ever-increasing body of mythic matter, pouring in from faraway climes and a dim and remote past alike, weighed down prosaic minds to much more mundane taxonomic tasks. Just when the intellectual fruits of the Age of Exploration had become abundant, they were compounded by the sudden yields of the Era of Archeology. Discovery and cultural penetration had provided access to a mass of material, from "primitive" data to the written riches of the high cultures of India and the Far East. Not only did the scholarly exploitation of the latter gather momentum in the early nineteenth century, but spadework of spectacular dimensions subsequently unearthed the ancient civilizations of Egypt, Syro-

Mesopotamia, Iran, and Asia Minor. Out of it all emerged one of the great discoveries of modern times, the realization that the languages of Europe, Iran, and India are genetically related, that they constitute a vast language "family" with an attested history of several millennia and a prehistory that is reconstructible in considerable measure by the precise methods of comparative historical linguistics. This Indo-European group of languages is unique in world history in terms of scope, diversity, spread, and length of written documentation; other groups, such as the Semitic or Sinitic, may rival it in time depth but not in diversity or areal extent. Crucial for the discovery was the British conquest of India and subsequent acquaintance with its ancient language of learning, Sanskrit, on the part of classically learned members of the colonial establishment.

It was a revelation, but one fraught with dubious consequences for mythology for the rest of the nineteenth century. Protolanguage implies protocommunity, protocommunity entails protoculture, and protoculture points to protomyth: thus historical reconstruction had suddenly become the task of a new comparative mythology, to match the triumphs of comparative philology. But herein lay a parting of ways: on the one hand a bookish discipline, beholden to comparative grammar, and on the other synchronic, contemporary fieldwork approaches to nonliterate traditions, and thus the beginnings of myth study allied with the nascent disciplines of anthropology, ethnology, and sociology. The latter partook of all the -isms that the century was heir to: historicism, positivism, evolutionism, materialism, and the rest, whereas the former withdrew into an ivory tower: Charles Darwin set sail for the Galápagos Islands, while Friedrich Max Müller withdrew to the library to edit the *Rig-Veda* and expound the nature of language and myth.

Alas, philological triumph became coupled with mythological disaster. The practitioners of the new comparative method were great linguists but innocents in theoretical mythology. Instead of Fontenelle, De Brosses, Vico, Herder, or Schelling, they took their cues from second-rate theoreticians such as Christian Heyne and Gottfried Hermann. Etymology, which since Plato's *Kratylos* had been one of the less savory mythological procedures, seemed newly habilitated by the progress of comparative philology and was applied with abandon to the matching of mythical names (e.g., Greek *Kéntauros* was identified with Sanskrit *Gandharvás, Erīnýs* with *Saraṇyū́s, Ouranós* with *Váruṇas,* etc.). Allegory remained the one mode of explanation (to the exclusion of euhemerism), specifically, nature allegory tinged with a monomaniacal reductionism to one single type; thus were born the storm gods of Adalbert Kuhn, the animal allegories of Angelo de Gubernatis, the fire mythology of Johannes Hertel, the moon myths of Georg Hüsing, and above all the solarism of Max Müller. Friedrich Max Müller (1823–1900), one of the great scholarly figures of the nineteenth century, in honor of whose sesquicentennial a postage stamp was issued by India in 1973, compounded the standard naturist tendencies with a peculiar theory about language that had been prefigured by Heyne and Hermann. According to him human language is a wretched device hiding and corrupting the purity of thought and is in constant danger of disintegration through the decay of metaphors. The creation of myth is a defense mechanism against the evanescence of metaphors, a kind of antibody formation to this "disease of language" (for rejuvenation of metaphors, cf. "*grasp* a concept" ['concept' being itself a paled Latin 'grasping'], "break of day," "crack of dawn," etc.). Thus Max Müller argued that, for example, the Greek and Indic mythologies were originally identical, as were the languages, but that subsequently in Greek the vivid meanings of the mythical names became obscured, and the new etiological stories devised to fill the void are what we know as properly Greek myth. Max Müller never satisfactorily explained why all the decay was confined to the Greek side (it was an extension of the view that practically identified Sanskrit with Proto-Indo-European) or why every myth had to be a sun myth. This preposterous approach enjoyed prolonged favor and had a number of disciples, for example, George Cox and Robert Brown, who transmuted Greek and Oriental myth into a jumble of solar allegories. But in fact solar mythology was notorious already in Max Müller's infancy, for in 1827 Jean-Baptiste Pérès published his *Grand Erratum: The Non-existence of Napoleon Proved* (English translation in H. R. Evans, *The Napoleon Myth* [Chicago, 1905]; cf. A. Sonnenfeld in *Yale French Studies* 26 [1960–61]: 32–36), showing that the emperor had been merely the allegorization of a sun-god; this spoof satirized Charles-François Dupuis, who in 1795 had declared Christ himself a solar myth and his apostles the twelve signs of the zodiac. Thus Max Müller was in the end just another practitioner of astrological allegory, this time in the guise of "Indo-European comparative mythology."

Max Müller had his detractors from early on, in particular Andrew Lang, a promoter of the new ethnology; their decades-long polemic became a kind of scholarly landmark of late Victorian England. When Max Müller was gathered to his sun-gods at the turn of the century, the sun had already set on his brand of solarism, and Indo-European comparative mythology had been dragged down with it into prolonged and utter discredit.

The rise of the ethnological sciences, under the heavy stimulus of Darwinism, had inevitably stirred new theorizing into the nature and origin of religion. Myth was not always the focal point of such researches, but the next important "schools" of mythology were clearly an outgrowth of these trends.

Two approaches to myth dominate the intellectual landscape during the first half of the twentieth century: the ritualistic and the psychoanalytic. The former, epitomized by the "myth and ritual" or Cambridge school beholden to the Oxonian E. B. Tylor's *Primitive Culture* (1871) and with James G. Frazer's *Golden Bough* as its central talisman, owes its theoretical underpinnings to Jane E. Harrison's *Prolegomena to the Study of Greek Religion* (1903) and *Themis* (1912). Harrison provided a strikingly simple and exclusionary definition of myth: myth is nothing but the verbalization of ritual, "the spoken correlative of the acted rite" (*Themis,* p. 328), *tà legómena* 'what is said' accompanying *tà drṓmena* 'what is being done', myth and ritual being accordingly but two sides of the same religious coin; thus in principle there can be no myth without ritual, although time may have obliterated the act and left the narrative free to survive as myth or its debased subspecies (saga, legend, folktale, etc.). Harrison and her peers (J. G. Frazer, A. B. Cook, F. M. Cornford, Gilbert Murray) were classical scholars, and through their efforts a healthy dose of ethnology and anthropology was administered to the study of antiquity: what Wilhelm Mannhardt had done for European peasant lore (*Die Korndämonen* [1868], *Wald- und Feldkulte* [1875–77]), the Cambridge classicists (and their Oxford ally Murray) did for ancient cultures, unraveling the patterns of cyclical year cults, vegetation demons, dying gods, and such (Harrison's *eniautòs daímōn* 'year spirit', Frazer's Adonis, Attis, Osiris). From such beginnings a wave of ritualism washed over the study of culture and literature, epitomized by Murray's comparative essay "Hamlet and Orestes" (written in 1914, published in *The Classical Tradition in Poetry* [Cambridge, Mass., 1927], pp. 205–40) and by Jessie Weston's *From Ritual to Romance* (with its echoes in T. S. Eliot's *The Waste Land*). The excesses of ritualism are blatant in the works of Margaret Murray (*The Witch-Cult in Western Europe* [1921]; *The God of the Witches* [1933]; *The Divine King in England* [1954]), who found remnants of a pagan "Dianic" cult rampant in Christianized Europe, complete with ritual human sacrifices thinly disguised as murders or legal executions (Joan of Arc and her contemporary Gilles de Rais, William Rufus and Thomas à Becket, and in fact instances about once every seven years of English history from William the Conqueror to James I; enough heads fell in the Tower of London and elsewhere to underwrite such selective juggling of history). Much more balanced and valuable work was done by Fitzroy Richard Somerset, fourth baron Raglan. Lord Raglan's *The Hero* (1936) was a bold plea for the proposition that pattern takes precedence over person, ritual formula over recorded history. For example, Robin Hood's historicity, besides being dubious, is not even important or interesting; what matters is his conformity to a type Raglan found attested in Oedipus, Theseus, Romulus, Herakles, Perseus, Jason, Bellerophon, Pelops, Asklepios, Dionysos, Apollo, Zeus, Joseph, Moses, Elijah, Watu Gunung (Java), Nyikang (Upper Nile), Sigurd-Siegfried, Lleu Llawgyffes (Wales), and Arthur. This pattern involves noble origin, unusual conception, threat of infanticide, rescue and youthful exile, return on maturity to claim his due, triumph over an obstructionist, marriage to a highborn local, successful reign, but ultimate downfall, exile, and mysterious end, often in a raised location, disappearance of mortal remains, and cenotaphic cult at holy sepulchers. The hero is thus a formula-bound bundle of themes only incidentally attributable to real persons. In the American edition of 1956 Raglan even rejected the historicity of Leif Erikson, showing his story to be a variation on Irish voyage myths, and suggested that the "Old World hero-god pattern" may have diffused via Asia to such figures as the Aztec Quetzalcoatl.

Raglan, writing his baronial opus "in the depths of the country" with a "limited knowledge of foreign languages," was apparently unaware that in 1914 the psychoanalyst Otto Rank had published his essay *The Myth of the Birth of the Hero* (English edition 1959), in which the dossier comprised Sargon (of Akkad), Moses, Karṇa (in the *Mahābhārata*), Oedipus, Paris, Telephus, Perseus, Gilgamesh, Cyrus, Tristan, Romulus, Hercules, Jesus, Siegfried, and Lohengrin. This plowing of the same ground points up the tangential and overlapping areas between ritualistic and psychoanalytic approaches to myth, including a reliance on a combination of ancient lore and anthropological material. Apart from his naming complexes after figures of Greek saga and the questionable theories of *Totem und Tabu* (1913), Sigmund Freud's main contribution to mythology was his parting shot *Moses und Monotheismus* (1939), significantly concerned with manipulations and inversions of the same kind of hero legend that had preoccupied Rank and Raglan.

The archetype of the hero has also occupied the Jungian branch of the psychoanalytic movement (Joseph Campbell's *The Hero with a Thousand Faces* [1949]), which in its pursuit of the collective unconscious and of racial memory, and in its preoccupation with astrology and alchemy, risks its own entry into the mystical and the occult. But for an appreciation of the sources of mythopoeia something can be learned from Carl Gustav Jung's own early clinical (as opposed to later purposeful) experiences with myth. The following paraphrases pages 50–52 of *The Archetypes and the Collective Unconscious* (1959): In 1906 Dr. Jung, himself as yet innocent of mythology, attended an uneducated paranoid schizophrenic who had been interned for many years and was considered incurable. One day he found the patient wagging his head and blinking into the sun, advising the doctor to do the same. When Jung could see nothing special, the patient retorted: "Can't you see the sun's penis? When I move my head it moves also, and that's where the wind comes from." Jung was none the wiser but made a notation in the patient's record. Four years later, having taken up mythology, he came upon Albrecht Dieterich's *Eine Mithrasliturgie* (issued after the patient had been committed), which published from a Greek papyrus a late classical mystagogic injunction of the Mithraic cult: "The path of the visible gods will appear through the disk of the sun, who is God my father. Likewise the so-called tube, the origin of the ministering wind. For you will see hanging down from the disk of the sun something that looks like a tube. And toward the regions westward it is as though there were an infinite east wind. But if the other wind should prevail toward the regions of the east, you will in like manner see the vision veering in that direction." The patient, some ten years older than Jung, was prone to religious delusions and believed he was God and Christ in one person. He treated Jung patronizingly, allowing him to share his vision as a neophyte. In the act of head wagging he performed as the sun-god himself creating the heavenly wind, undergoing in his mind a ritual transformation comparable to the Helios apotheosis Apuleius attests for the mysteries of Isis. The wind is the procreative *pneûma* that streams from the sun, and in association with the penis (or "tube") recalls medieval paintings that depict the impregnation of Mary via a hosepipe descending from the throne of God and passing into her body, with a dove symbolic of the Holy Ghost flying down it. Thus a late classical mystery liturgy, medieval iconography, and the spontaneous fantasy of an untutored schizophrenic seemingly had independently enacted the same archetypal panorama of sun, penis, movement, and divine *pneûma*. Such cases tend to support the notion that archetypal mythopoeia can be gleaned preferentially from "primitives"; in our society that includes the demented and young children. The true "savage" is still close to the ritual wellsprings of myth and performs with his body as well as his tongue, whereas in "civilization" ritual and myth are mostly left to professionals. The deranged religionist, on the other hand, not only intuits his own truth with exceptional force but senses a need to proclaim it to the world. If a child is allowed to develop his own worldview at the age of four or five without any premature infusions of Sunday school, he is apt to traverse in a year or two a slice of mythical ontogeny that uncannily replicates mankind's phylogenic millennial mythopoeia. I have heard a four-year-old visiting a national cemetery exclaim, "God was the first to die," matching the Vedic concept of Yama, the primordial colonizer and ruler of the Otherworld; the same child experiencing a thunderstorm asked, "Can lightning be seen under water?" in perfect harmony with the Vedic deity Apā́m Nápāt, who dwells in watery depths and shines forth "clad in lightning." A five-year-old inquired whether "George Washington was the first man," equating the father of his country with the father of mankind, even as in ancient Iran the primordial king equaled the first mythical man.

The twentieth-century search for universally applicable "patterns" that so clearly marks the ritualist and psychoanalytic approaches to myth is also characteristic of the trends that remain to be mentioned, the sociological and the structuralist. Whereas ritualism had its roots in England and psychoanalysis in the German cultural orbit, the French contribution is important here, starting with the sociological school of Emile Durkheim and Marcel Mauss. Durkheim's "collective representations," Mauss's seminal studies on gift giving and sacrifice, and Bronislaw Malinowski's views on myths as social "charters" all recognized the paramount role of myths as catalysts in cementing structured human coexistence. The structural study of myth, with Claude Lévi-Strauss as its most flamboyant paladin, also stresses the role of myth as a mechanism of conflict resolution and mediation between opposites in the fabric of human culture and society, not least in the great dichotomy of nature versus culture itself. But Lévi-Strauss's analytic method is one of binary oppositions influenced by structural linguistics (especially the work of Roman Jakobson) and folklore (starting with Vladimir Propp's *Morphology of the Folktale* [1928]), which themselves are but manifestations of the vast structuralist movement in science and scholarship. Lévi-Strauss's analysis intentionally overlooks cultural disparity and diachronic evolution alike ("all cultures are created equal," a myth is merely a sum of all its variants) and is content to view myth ultimately in terms of bundles of binary oppositions and their resolutions. These somewhat austere and sterile procedural principles are counterbalanced in Lévi-Strauss's case by a temperamental attachment to poetry and music, especially of the symbolist variety, resulting in a style and form that seem to oscillate (but not necessarily mediate) between the lucid and the enigmatic, the spare and the bombastic, the open-minded and the dogmatic, the refinedly analytic and the heavy-handedly synthetic (a dialectical Hegelian trait not unrelated to the author's Marxism). His multivolume magnum opus *Mythologiques* begins with a lengthy "overture" like a Wagnerian opera, and his views on the relation of myth to language and literature (especially poetry) are personal and controversial in the extreme (myth is an autonomous synthesis of the structural and statistical sides of language [Ferdinand de Saussure's *langue* vs. *parole*]; poetic language is at the opposite pole from mythic language, since it is often ruined in translation, whereas myth has a sturdiness that survives linguistic transposition). Mutatis mutandis, the figure of Lévi-Strauss in the second half of the twentieth century in many ways recalls that of Max Müller a hundred years earlier: the patent solution, the rhapsodic proclivities, idiosyncratic views on the relation between language and myth.

While Lévi-Strauss himself, after starting with the Oedipus myth, has for the most part resolutely ranged from Alaska to the Amazon, structuralist ideas have begun to seep into the study of classical myth and "historical" mythology in general. The obvious danger is that the approach is by nature generalist, universalizing, and ahistorical, thus the very opposite of text oriented, philological, and time conscious. Overlaying known data with binaristic gimmickry in the name of greater "understanding" is no substitute for a deeper probing of the records themselves as documents of a specific synchronic culture on the one hand and as outcomes of diachronic evolutionary processes on the other. In mythology, as in any other scholarly or scientific activity, it is important to recall that the datum itself is more important than any theory that may be applied to it. Hence historical and comparative mythology, as practiced in this book, is in the last resort not beholden to any one theory on the "nature" of myth or even its ultimate "function" or "purpose." But it is fully cognizant that myth operates in men's minds and societies alike, that it is involved in both self-image and worldview on an individual and a collective level (being thus tied to religion and its manifestations such as ritual and prayer, and to societal ideology as well), and that it creates potent tensions of language and history (speaking of timeless happening, narrating eternal events in the grammatical frame of tense forms for [usually] past or [rarely] future occurrences [as in the case of prophecy], never in the generalizing present).[1]

Thus the twentieth-century lessons of ritualism, psychoanalysis, sociology, and structural anthropology alike deserve to be heeded by the historical and comparative student of myth and religion, but only to the extent that they offer viable insights into a study that is by definition historical, and more specifically philological, rooted in the minute and sensitive probing and comparison of primary written records. Such a comparative mythology, centered on ancient Indo-European language groups and their accompanying cultures, has been gradually evolving over the past half-century, spearheaded by scholars such as Emile Benveniste, Georges Dumézil, Stig Wikander, Jan de Vries, and Jacques Duchesne-Guillemin.

Recommended Reading

De Vries, Jan. *The Study of Religion: A Historical Approach*. New York: Harcourt, Brace and World, 1967.

Feldman, Burton, and Robert D. Richardson (ed.). *The Rise of Modern Mythology 1680–1860*. Bloomington: Indiana University Press, 1972. Useful collection of texts, but commentary has numerous errors.

Peradotto, John. *Classical Mythology: An Annotated Bibliographical Survey.* American Philological Association Pamphlets. Reprinted Chico, Calif.: Scholars Press, 1981.

White, Lynn, Jr. "Christian Myth and Christian History." In *Machina ex Deo: Essays in the Dynamism of Western Culture*. Cambridge: MIT Press, 1969.

1. A sample of mythical style is Eccles. 9:11 ("I returned, and saw under the sun, that the race is not to the swift, nor the battle to the strong, neither yet bread to the wise, nor yet riches to men of understanding, nor yet favor to men of skill; but time and chance happeneth to them all"), which George Orwell ("Politics and the English Language," in *Shooting an Elephant and Other Essays* [New York, 1950,] p. 84) "translated" into nominalized modern sociological jargon: "Objective consideration of contemporary phenomena compels the conclusion that success or failure in competitive activities exhibits no tendency to be commensurate with innate capacity, but that a considerable element of the unpredictable must invariably be taken into account." Such rendering amounts to parody (retaining content but debasing form), whereas the transposition of myth to saga (quasihistorical narrative) technically constitutes travesty (retaining form but debasing content).

2 · Creation Myth in the Ancient Near East

Traditions of origin and creation tend to be the most mythical matter of all. Cosmogony purports to account for the universe and the world, while anthropogony purveys clues to the origin of man. All of this is assigned to mythical time, "in the beginning, of yore, *in illo tempore*." At the opposite chronological pole from such accounting of "first things" one finds in many mythical and religious systems some form of eschatology, a sketching of "last things," couched in terms of mythic prophecy. In the rectilinear time frame imposed on occidental cultures by the Judeo-Christian tradition, the entire world drama fits within a straight path between those two poles, as a dynamic, unique cosmo- and anthropohistorical process from start to finish, marked off by static, latent "time without end" on both sides. This contrasts with the cyclical time concept and worldview of many oriental and classical cultures, where not only the world but mankind at large is periodically rejuvenated and regenerated, and even individual men are reincarnated in terms of metempsychosis. Because such myth purports to deal with universal verities it invariably has supranational pretensions and can become export religion on a large scale; witness the provincial ancient Near Eastern variety of the Hebrew Genesis that still claims adherents in fundamentalist Judeo-Christian circles, or the spread of Indian Buddhism through much of Asia. On the other hand, creation myth can also become secularized in both international and national context. Both the Marxist vision of passage from "socialism" to the nirvana of true communism and the "National Socialist" dream of a "thousand-year Reich" are twentieth-century secular eschatologies, and the impending turn of the millennium will no doubt spur a spate of eschatological outpourings on all levels. In deeper historical perspective, however, creation myth has often been transmuted or transposed to foundation legend, and man's origin to stories of specific ancestral beginnings. In ancient traditions where the mythical boundaries of god and man are somewhat fluid, theogony, anthropogony, and dynastic saga could blend in varying proportions.

For the study of all this the ancient Near East offers a complex laboratory. Unlike Egypt, which constituted a specific remarkably self-contained, almost monolithic, ethnically and linguistically uniform tradition, the ancient Near East at large was not one civilization but many, more or less contiguous by geography and stretched out along a time span of several millennia. We must pick and choose among Sumerians, East Semites (Akkadians = Babylonians + Assyrians), Hurrians, and Proto-Indians in Mesopotamia, West Semites in the area of Syria, Lebanon, and Palestine (from Ebla in the third millennium to Ugarit in the second, to Phoenicians, Canaanites, and Hebrews in the first), Indo-European-speaking Hittites and Luwians in Anatolia (= Asia Minor), and likewise Indo-European Iranians in the whole vast territory between Asia Minor, Mesopotamia, and India. And it is not always easy to say where ancient Greece ends and the Near East begins, owing to extensive cultural interpenetration. Some of the above are themselves irreducible protocultures as far as our knowledge goes—for example, Sumerian or Hurrian—but mainly we have diverse exponents of two great language families, Semitic and Indo-European. Semitic is tight and reasonably uniform in its linguistic makeup, but any reconstruction of Proto-Semitic tradition is hampered by the heavy Sumerian influence on its Eastern, Mesopotamian component. The Indo-European language group is vastly more widespread and diversified. The three branches involved in the ancient Near East (Anatolian, Greek, Indo-Iranian) are the earliest attested forms of Indo-European, but they are linguistically distinct and of unequal value for the reconstruction of Proto-Indo-European myth and religion, since both Greek and Hittite traditions have undergone heavy substratal exposure and adstratal influence rather than being conservative repositories of Indo-European heritage: vertical diffusion from the local past and lateral diffusion from the contemporary vicinity have effected transformations and created new syntheses. One must be very careful about postulating any genetic Indo-European reconstruct based on, for example, Iranian, Hittite, and Greek material, since their mutual contiguities strengthen the probabilities of later contact, secondary interaction, and joint exposure to extraneous influences.

Hence diffusion is the key word in ancient Near Eastern mythology in general and creation myth in particular. Even the best-known specimen of the latter, the Hebrew Genesis, reeks of diffusionary regional motifs ultimately traceable to the Sumerians, who have left us their paradise myth of the pure and bright land of Dilmun, the tale of Dumuzi the petulant shepherd's antagonism toward Enkimdu the peaceful farmer, which is inversely reminiscent of the Cain-Abel conflict but does not culminate in murder, and the story of the flood hero Ziusudra, which has replicated itself in Utnapishtim of the Gilgamesh epic and Noah of Genesis. One important difference is that God himself has of course become transcendent in the Hebrew tradition, and by polarization the humanity and mortality of Adam, Cain, and Noah are not in doubt, whereas the Sumerian protagonists are still divine or at least semidivine; even at the level of heroic saga, Gilgamesh himself is at least a demigod and constantly wears the divine determinative in cuneiform spelling. This is understandable, since the notion of a dying god, a cyclical divinity whose life span could be (to use a very up-to-date word) recycled, attaches to the very figure of Dumuzi, who becomes the Babylonian Tammuz and is a first cousin to his Frazerian counterparts, Adonis in Syria, Attis in Anatolia, and Osiris in Egypt. In other words, the very notion of an insurmountable gulf separating divinity and humanity, the notion that the deity is the Wholly Other, *das Ganz Andere,* as a modern German theologian would put it, was alien to the ancient Near East at large; its emergence in the Hebrew orbit owes something to earlier monotheistic trends traceable as far back as Akhnaton's heresy in Eighteenth-Dynasty Egypt and to the emergence of a linear time concept that tends to fuse mythical and historical time and to stress uniqueness rather than cyclicity.

In spite of such ambiguities, specific theogony in the narrow sense is a hallmark of ancient Near Eastern tradition. Typical of it is a certain dynastic depth, as if the "current" layer of ruling divinity resulted from generations of succession, usurpation, conflict, and all the other time processes that human kingship might be heir to. The central and canonic document is the Babylonian creation epic, *Enūma Elish,* which is essentially an account of how the incumbent ruling god of Babylon, Marduk, came to achieve and consolidate his reign; the name of Babylon itself, *bāb ilim* 'gate of God', marks it as the holy city of Marduk. Let me summarize the plot of the *Enūma Elish:*

In the beginning there are a male/female pair, Apsu and Tiamat, or freshwater and saltwater deities respectively. Their bodies commingle and engender a host of deities, notably Ea, the god of wisdom and magic. When this new generation becomes unruly and troublesome for the old pair, Apsu wants to destroy it, but Ea is quicker and more decisive and slays Apsu first, leaving Tiamat widowed. Apsu remains from then on as an inert entity, the mythical sweetwater ocean beneath the earth that is the abode of Ea, where he sires Marduk. Meanwhile Tiamat seeks revenge by enlisting Ea's half-brother Kingu in a dynastic plot and engendering a brood of monsters. By then it is the grown-up Marduk who takes up the defense, eclipsing Ea. In a great struggle he slays Tiamat, wipes out the monsters, and consigns Kingu to the safekeeping of the death-god. Marduk and Ea then bisect Tiamat's body to form heaven and earth, and Marduk's rule is consolidated forevermore. In this myth extravagant curiosities abound: heaven and earth are formed from the body of the salt sea, who is the champion's grandmother, and his childhood home is identical with the watery corpse of his grandfather. But rather than worry about the fantastic aspects, let us fasten on the three-generational pattern of overthrow, usurpation, succession, challenge, and consolidation.

This official genealogy of Babylon's divine dynasty is relatively "civilized" compared with other, more provincial versions of the Mesopotamian tradition of divine succession. In 1965 Wilfred Lambert and Peter Walcot published in the journal *Kadmos* a local theogony of the obscure town of Dunnu, which they transcribed from a Babylonian tablet in the British Museum. Here the primal pair consists of an obscure male called Hain and the female Earth. They first engender the Sea with the help of a plow and subsequently give birth to a son, Amakandu. Earth seduces and marries this son of hers, who kills his father Hain and succeeds him as ruler. Amakandu next marries his sister the Sea, who bears a son, Lahar. Lahar kills his father Amakandu, marries his mother the Sea, and reigns. Lahar's daughter is the River, and he also has a son who kills both him and his mother-wife the Sea, marries his own sister the River, and reigns. And so it goes for at least a couple more generations, with increasingly deteriorating textual transmission. The pattern would seem Oedipal except that sons slay mothers as well as fathers and marry sisters as well as mothers. Again the salient trait is the string of overthrow and violent succession within the family, this time reeking of actual patricide, matricide, and incest.

This text is very late Babylonian, from the middle of the first millennium B.C.E. The next story is attested about a millennium earlier and comes from the Hittite archives at Boğazköy in north-central Asia Minor. It is in the Hittite language but is clearly a translation version from Hurrian and thus native to the northern reaches of Mesopotamia.

In the Hittite text there is a god Alalu who rules in heaven for nine years. His son Anu (identical with the Sumero-Akkadian god whose name means heaven) does him obeisance but then revolts and deposes him "down to the dark earth." Anu's son Kumarbi replicates this pattern by deposing his father in the ninth year. Anu tries to escape, but Kumarbi snatches him down from heaven by the feet and bites off and swallows his genitals. The emasculated Anu tells his son that by so doing Kumarbi has impregnated himself with five deities, most notably the storm-god Teshub and the river-goddess of the Tigris, whose name is Aranzah. At this point the text is badly mutilated, but it appears that Kumarbi tries to terminate his pregnancy by spitting out the sperm and, failing that, attempts to devour his offspring after they are born. But apparently all this is to no avail, for when the coherent stories pick up again Teshub reigns and Kumarbi has been superseded. Kumarbi then cohabits with a rock and sires a monster made of diorite, whose name is Ullikummi and who is to be Kumarbi's secret weapon against his son and usurper. Ullikummi is attached to the shoulder of a cosmic giant Upelluri in the sea, and he starts to shoot up. In no time at all he stands out of the water and reaches heavenward to threaten the gods. The sun-god spots him first and reports to Teshub, who weeps in despair. Teshub's sister Ishtar tries sex on Ullikummi, but the monster is less than receptive, since he is both deaf and blind. But this does not keep him from being a deadly threat in combat, forcing the gods to retreat from the battleground around Mount Hazzi on the Syrian seashore to Teshub's last stronghold of Kummiya. Still Ullikummi is in hot pursuit (how is not made clear, since he is supposed to be stuck all the time on Upelluri's shoulder). At this moment of utter peril, Teshub's brother and vizier Tashmishu has the bright idea that they should visit Ea for advice in his Apsu home. This they do, and Ea then goes to consult Upelluri; he asks if Upelluri knows what monstrosity is growing on his shoulder. This Atlas-like giant replies:

> When Heaven and Earth upon me they built, I knew nothing.
> But when they came and Heaven and Earth with a cutter they cut apart,
> this too I knew not.
> Now something makes my right shoulder hurt,
> but I know not who he is, this god!

And the Song of Ullikummi continues:

> When Ea the words heard,
> Upelluri's right shoulder he turned:
> and there the diorite on Upelluri's shoulder
> like a blade stood.
> Ea to the Former Gods again began to speak:
> "My words hear, O Former Gods,
> who the former words know!
> Again open them, the old ancestral storehouses!
> Again the Former Fathers' seal they shall bring,
> and with it again they shall seal them!
> And the former saw they shall bring out,
> with which Heaven and Earth they cut apart.
> And under Ullikummi's diorite feet we shall saw,
> Whom Kumarbi against the gods as a rebel raised!"

So the primeval cutting tool is dusted off, and Ullikummi's base is severed. One would have expected this act to render him mobile (which he was illogically anyway in his pursuit of the gods, as we saw before), but instead it seems to rob him of his power base, and the gods are able to rally and defeat him for good as the text peters out in fragmentation and illegibility.

These traditions, which have been known and understood for barely forty or fifty years, have come to be pivotal instances of myth diffusion in the ancient Near East. We can see that by the latter half of the second millennium B.C.E. they had already spread from northern Mesopotamia to Asia Minor. Their Hurrian source is clear though not directly attested. The wider Mesopotamian (i.e., Sumero-Akkadian) elements and influences are visible (e.g., the gods Anu and Ea), but the whole tradition is distinct from the Babylonian theogonies discussed earlier. We have here a very specific set of events: A shadowy first god is succeeded by one whose name means heaven. "Heaven" is deposed and castrated by his son, who in his turn feels threatened by his unborn or newborn offspring and tries cannibalism as a prophylactic. But nothing avails; he is overthrown by his son, who becomes the ruling storm-god. The deposed father creates a monstrous enemy as his last-ditch champion, but the storm-god and his cohorts eliminate this threat and consolidate their rule.

Daughter versions of this myth have been scattered around the periphery of the Mesopotamian-Anatolian core area ever since the second millennium B.C.E. By 700 B.C.E. we find it in the *Theogony* of Hesiod in Greece, by the first century of the common era in the fragments of the *Phoenician History* of Philo of Byblos and in the so-called *Library of Apollodorus,* by the fifth century in the *Dionysiaca* of Nonnos in Byzantine Greece, and by the end of the first millennium in the Persian *Book of Kings,* the *Shāh Nāma* of Firdausi. None of these versions match one another to the point where one might draw up a consistent stemma of transmissions, but all are clearly variants of the same protomyth whose earliest attested form is the Hurrian-Hittite one. Let us consider them briefly one by one:

While the incidental scraps of theogony in Homer name Okeanos 'Ocean' as the origin of the gods (*theôn génesis*), in Hesiod it is Earth (Gaia) who gives birth to Heaven (Ouranos) and then marries him; they engender the Titans, among them Okeanos and Kronos. Ouranos maltreats his offspring, and Gaia conspires with her last-born son Kronos, who emasculates his father from ambush with a jagged sickle, at the moment when Ouranos gets ready to cover Gaia in his primordial performance of the sex act. The severed genitals fall into the sea, and from their foam is born the goddess Aphrodite. This event is placed near Cyprus; Aphrodite is in origin an emanation of the Near Eastern great goddess of love (Phoenician Astarte, Akkadian Ishtar, Sumerian Inanna, Egyptian Isis, Anatolian Cybele, and so forth); all this points to Eastern origins even in such an incidental detail.

With his male powers gone, Ouranos is *eo ipso* dethroned, and Kronos reigns; Ouranos is henceforth just a pensioned-off *deus otiosus.* But he is not killed; this myth is not as explicitly sanguinary as the Mesopotamian ones.

Kronos (= Saturn in Roman interpretation) is married to his sister, the titaness Rhea, and lives in fear of his own offspring, lest he himself suffer the fate of Ouranos. He therefore eats his children at birth (graphically depicted in Goya's "black painting," *Saturno devorando a un hijo;* see fig. 1) until the youngest, Zeus, is whisked away by a trick and a swaddled rock is substituted, which Kronos, who is not particular, swallows without bothering to look. In a repetition of ultimogeniture, Zeus grows up in secret, comes of age, enlists various allies, and overthrows Kronos, making him regurgitate Zeus's siblings. Zeus thus becomes the ruling king of heaven, as cloud gatherer and thunder-god. The Titans are placed in maximum security in Tartaros, although an intrusive tradition also locates Kronos in the Happy Isles as an Elysian retiree.

Up to this point Hesiod and Apollodorus differ only in details, and

FIGURE 1. *Saturno devorando a un hijo* (Kronos Devouring a Son), by Goya. (Courtesy of Museo del Prado, Madrid.)

Nonnos has little to say. But when it comes to the episode of the final adversary, the three complement and supplement one another in significant ways. This enemy is Typhoeus or Typhon, the son of Kronos's mother and ally Gaia, who mated with Tartaros. Some scholiast also alleges that he was instead born in Cilicia of an egg impregnated by Kronos, and Apollodorus too places the birth in Cilicia, which is in southern Anatolia around the corner from Syria and Cyprus. In any event Typhoeus or Typhon was Kronos's last best hope of reversing his fortunes. Hesiod describes him as having a hundred heads of snakes growing from his shoulders, and Apollodorus and Nonnos also agree on his snakiness. But Nonnos also describes him advancing to battle in terms that are uncannily reminiscent of Ullikummi almost two millennia earlier: "There stood Typhon in the sea, his feet firm on the bottom, his belly in the air and his head crushed in the clouds." Hesiod makes short work of the monster: Zeus simply sears the snake heads with his lightning bolts and hurls Typhoeus in a heap down to Tartarus. Apollodorus, however, has Zeus wound the monster with a sickle (cf. the cutting off of Ullikummi's base), upon which Typhon flees to Mount Kasios in Syria (the very Hazzi of the Ullikummi myth). There Typhon wrests the sickle from Zeus and cuts the sinews of his hands and feet; he then dumps the incapacitated Zeus in the Corycian Cave in Cilicia. Here there is obvious intrusion by an aboriginal myth of Anatolia that is also preserved in Hittite, in which the dragon Illuyankas robs the storm-god of his heart and eyes. Zeus ultimately recovers his sinews through the intervention of trickster-gods (Hermes and Aigipan in Apollodorus, Corycian Pan in Oppian's *Halieutica,* and Kadmos in Nonnos). He is thus restored and ends up burying Typhon alive under Mount Etna in Sicily, where he continues to rumble and breathe fire from time to time.

We can thus see how ripples of tradition must have diffused from the East to Greece over a millennial time span, and also how the details shift: Typhon is a snaky monster whereas Ullikummi is stony; yet their posture is the same, especially in the latest Greek source, Nonnos. Ouranos's genitals are severed by a jagged sickle whereas Anu's are bitten off; but the primordial sickle also figures in the stories of both Ullikummi and Typhon. Kronos and Kumarbi are matched in their castration of their fathers and their cannibalism of their own offspring, but Kronos regurgitates them afterward whereas Kumarbi tries to abort them proleptically by spitting out Anu's seed. We can infer that we are dealing with parallel elaborations of the same basic myth in widely differing circumstances. Probably the Hesiodic version came to Greece via the Phoenicians in the eighth century B.C.E., and Apollodorus and Nonnos fortified it with subsequent filterings through Asia Minor. A later Phoenician emanation is found in the fragments of Philo of Byblos, which the church fathers Eusebius and Porphyry have preserved for us, embedded in their own works. Philo provides a Phoenician (i.e., West Semitic) theogony starting with Eliun, surnamed in Greek Hypsistos 'The Highest,' whose wife is Bruth (i.e., Beirut) and who settles at Byblos. Eliun is a figure matching the Hittite-Hurrian Alalu. He and Bruth give birth to Ouranos and Gaia, who marry and produce four sons, notably El, whom Philo also calls Kronos. In an ensuing conflict El and his brothers take Gaia's side; when Ouranos tries to destroy them, El makes some kind of sharp weapon and vanquishes his father, who leaves Byblos. El reigns, but he turns tyrannical and kills a son and a daughter. The exiled Ouranos sends three of his daughters to intercede with El, but El marries them incestuously instead and sires numerous offspring, notably Baal. Thirty-two years later El lures Ouranos back to Byblos and in an ambush castrates him. By and by Baal takes over the kingship without much trouble, and Typhon figures simply as one of the numerous offspring of El. As an afterthought, El also castrates himself thirty-two years after mutilating his father.

This looks very much like our myth gone haywire, even apart from being euhemerized, that is, presented as the dynastic history of a Phoenician city. Why the delayed castration unrelated to loss of ruling power? Why the anticlimactic positions of Baal and Typhon? We do not know. Philo's work is obviously a Hellenistic concoction by an educated Greek speaker and Greek writer whose culture knew Hesiod and who could freely syncretize West Semitic antiquities. But the Semitic El and the Hurrian Kumarbi were identified in Ugaritic texts as early as the second millennium B.C.E.; since we now know that Kumarbi equals the Greek Kronos via the Hurrian-Hittite route, we can close the circle of correspondences Kumarbi : El : Kronos without suspecting Philo of having invented it. A lot is obviously out of joint here; the second castration is reminiscent of the later Greek traditions current especially in Orphic theogony, that Zeus castrated Kronos as a form of tit-for-tat poetic justice. But there may also be some method in the madness, as we can glimpse when we look at the last remaining version of our myth, the one in the Iranian *Book of Kings*.

In Firdausi's treatment of the legendary kings of Iran the theme of heavenly dominion seems to be grafted onto the fourth, fifth, and sixth kings, Jamshid, Zohak, and Feridun. These kings are otherwise famous each in his own right, and there are no filial ties between them; but the way Firdausi's plot ties them together has many elements reminiscent of the heavenly kingship theme. Jamshid, the primordial king and culture hero, is ultimately brought down by pride and sinning, loses his regal nimbus, and is overthrown by the intrusive monster-warrior Zohak. Zohak has snakes growing from his shoulders, which is reminiscent of Typhon, but these snakes must be sated with children's brains, which again agrees more with the cannibalistic Kronos. Zohak waits a hundred years before hunting down the dethroned Jamshid and sawing him in two, in a delayed mutilation reminiscent of El's castration of Ouranos in Philo. Zohak also marries two sisters of Jamshid, which is another random and curious detail in agreement with Philo's version, where El marries three daughters of his predecessor Ouranos. Zohak is ultimately overthrown by Feridun, who is Jamshid's grandson and, like Zeus, must be shielded as a baby from the murderous attentions of Zohak. When he grows up, Feridun wields a cow-headed mace called *gurz* that corresponds to Zeus's thunder weapon; with it he overcomes Zohak and chains him high on Mount Demavend, to perish from exposure. Feridun then rules, but simply for a heroic royal life span. And the epic of kings continues.

All together it looks as if at this late date a potpourri of by now folkloristic and hence footloose motifs has encrusted a segment of a heroic sequence; the euhemerized nature of the kings, who are in origin demigods of pre-Islamic Iran, may explain some of the particular similarities between the Phoenician and the Iranian versions. This Iranian parallel was discovered in the late 1940s by the Swedish scholar Stig Wikander, who also drew the conclusion that the Kingship in Heaven myth is an Indo-European theme independently preserved in Greece, Anatolia, and Iran. I have already hinted at the flaw in such reasoning; in that case one would expect to find some trace of it in the older Indo-Iranian records, such as the Vedas or the Avesta, rather than in an epic of the Islamic period. Instead this myth is a textbook case of ancient Near Eastern diffusionism and entails a methodological lesson about proper procedure in comparative mythology. What can be reconstructed of Proto-Indo-European cosmogony and anthropogony proper is taken up in chapter 17.

Recommended Reading

Kramer, Samuel N., ed. *Mythologies of the Ancient World*. Garden City, N.Y.: Doubleday Anchor, 1961.

Littleton, C. Scott. "The 'Kingship in Heaven' Theme." In *Myth and Law among the Indo-Europeans,* ed. Jaan Puhvel, 83–121. Berkeley and Los Angeles: University of California Press, 1970.

3 · The Concepts "Indo-European" and "Indo-Iranian"

In each section so far, passing mention has been made of the term "Indo-European" as crucial to the diachronic study of myth. However, such fleeting reference was always incidental to another main topic. Before we proceed further the concept needs to be faced head-on.

The very notion "Indo-European" is both complex and diffuse. It is in essence a linguistic term denoting the comparativistically reconstructible protolanguage that underlies the Indic, Iranian, Tocharian, Anatolian, Armenian, Greek, Italic, Celtic, Germanic, Baltic, and Slavic language groups. These genetically derivable offshoots of the putative protoidiom have undergone very unequal and uneven attestational and evolutionary developments in the course of the past five millennia. In each case the advent of writing marks the borderline between prehistory and history. Some groups in early times nudged the Near Eastern cradles of culture and in consequence emerged onto the scene of world history much earlier than others; this is true of the Indic, Anatolian, and Greek branches, which are all attested from the second millennium B.C.E. During the first millennium B.C.E. the Iranian and Italic groups emerge from the penumbra of prehistory. Everything else is mainly attested later; thus northwestern and northern Indo-Europeans (Celts, Germanics, Balts, Slavs) achieved significant literacy only in the context of Christianization, in the case of the Balts as late as the middle of the present millennium. The same is true of the Armenians in the first millennium of the common era, while the Tocharians of Central Asia gained literacy from the spread of Indic Buddhism about the same time.

Spread and survival are different and separate matters, and here too there is a wide variety of vicissitudes. Ancient India created a great civilization and refined a language of learning and literature, Sanskrit, that lives on as a basic medium of culture to this day. It also spawned an export religion, Buddhism, that has spread Indic influence over much of the rest of Asia. The modern forms of Indo-Aryan such as Hindi are still spoken by hundreds of millions. Ancient Iranians launched great empires and a great religion, Zoroastrianism, both rather transitory in the main; nowadays the Iranian influence is pretty much confined to Islamic Iran proper. Tocharian is just a flash in a remote darkness, the brief records of a vanished people about 800 C.E. The Anatolian Hittites in Asia Minor created an important empire and an original though heavily derivative civilization in the second millennium B.C.E., only to be wiped off the map and almost out of man's memory before the millennium was over; they have been rescued from oblivion through archeology in our own century. Armenians have always been few in number and self-contained, in Armenia and more recently also diasporadically. The Greeks founded Western culture in many ways, only to retire to modest and marginal participation in its modern period. One minor subdivision of Italic took flight through a knack for political hegemony and imposed its onetime patois first on the rest of Italy and then on the entire western half of the known world. The linguistic offshoots of this Roman Empire live on in the Romance languages. The Celts dominated much of western Europe before the Romans and were major expansionists during the first millennium B.C.E., but their lack of political discipline, coupled with a druidical tabu against writing and other quirks of national psychology, led to their gradual and permanent decline. The Germanic peoples emerged relatively late but were to play a major role in more modern European and world history. The Balts were the last Europeans to be Christianized; their conservative and sedentary rural traditions constituted a major repository of linguistic and cultural archaism. The Slavs emerged only slightly earlier, mainly under Byzantine Greek rather than Roman Christianizing influence. They also had a long prehistory in close proximity of the Iranians who lived in what is now South Russia, such as the Scythians and Sarmatians.

In sum, then, the overwhelming majority of present-day Indo-European speakers around the world belong to one of four language groups: Germanic, Italic, Slavic, and Indic. Iranian, Armenian, Greek, Celtic, and Baltic are numerically insignificant, as are some other marginal survival languages such as Albanian; Tocharian and Anatolian are long since extinct. Other branches that once existed are little more than names to us, such as Illyrian, Thracian, and Phrygian, and still others may have perished with no trace.

The historically traceable movements of peoples that led to such linguistic spread are easy enough to enumerate. They begin with the great Celtic migrations about 500 B.C.E., coincident with the archeological Iron Age, when Celts not only settled large areas of central and western Europe (Gaul [= France], Britain, Ireland, Celtiberian Spain) but invaded northern Italy (= Cisalpine Gaul) and proceeded down the Danube into the Balkans and Asia Minor. The Gaulish sack of Rome in the early fourth century B.C.E. and the pillaging of Delphi in Greece in 279 B.C.E. are historical facts, as are purely Celtic place-names like Mediolanum (> Milan) and Vindobona (> Vienna). Some of Rome's greatest poets (Catullus, Vergil) were of Celtic extraction, and Saint Paul addressed an epistle to the Galatians (= Celts) in Asia Minor in the first century of that same common era he helped to launch. By that time, however, the Celtic force was spent. Gaul and Britain had been conquered by Rome, but Roman expansion itself (including the thrust into Dacia [= modern Romania], which lasted from the emperor Trajan to Aurelian [ca. 105–275 C.E.]) was being tempered and turned back by the Germanic migrations that finally overran much of the western Roman Empire (Ostrogoths and Langobards in Italy, Visigoths and Vandals in Spain, Anglo-Saxons in Britain, Franks in Gaul). By 500 C.E. the next wave, the Slavs, was pushing westward into central Europe and southward into the Balkans, reaching the heart of what is now Germany and penetrating Greece, to recede only slightly in subsequent pullbacks. After a relative hiatus during the High Middle Ages, marked by the westward movements of the non-Indo-European Turks out of Central Asia into lands of the eastern Roman (= Byzantine) Empire, and the limited, quixotic activities of the Christian Crusaders (significant only in the Teutonic thrust into eastern Europe), modern migrations into the Americas, the belated settlement of the Terra Australis, and the eastward penetration of Siberia were essentially accomplished by speakers of the Germanic, Romance, and Slavic language groups. Of the early historical migrant forms Celtic is absent in these later expansions, but it lingers on indirectly, for Spanish and especially French have become what they are by virtue of being Latin superimposed on a Celtic substratum, with characteristic changes (e.g., Latin *secūrus* > *sicuro* [Italian], but *seguro* [Spanish] > *segur* [Provençal] > *seür* [Old French] > *sûr* [French]). In short, French is the descendant of a broken-down import Latin in the mouths of Gaulish speakers, a patois related to Classical Latin about as Haitian creole is to Standard French, subsequently refurbished with learned Latinisms through the bookish efforts of scholars.

By contrast, the prehistoric migrations of the Indo-Europeans, of which horrified observers or recorders have left no written record, are much harder to chart. We note a general westward and southward movement of Celts, Germans, and Slavs, but from precisely what prehistoric holding tanks were they unleashed at half-millennium intervals? When and how did the Italics get to Italy, the Greeks into Greece, and the Hittites into Asia Minor? And at the far end, what propelled the Indic speakers down the Indus and Ganges valleys, with the Iranians in their wake? When did it all begin, and where, and how, and why?

A judicious juggling of archeological and linguistic data can supply some answers here. The debate has raged for nearly two centuries, placing the protohabitat at first in the interior of Asia (the traditional *vagina gentium* 'womb of nations'), then moving it westward to eastern Europe and the confines of Germany (not unrelated to the nationalistic and racist tinge of German-inspired scholarship of certain periods), and lately again pushing it out to the Eurasiatic steppe region north and east of the Caspian Sea, between the Volga River and the Altai Mountains. Archeology of recent vintage points to a specific cultural presence in that area and its dynamic spread westward during the third millennium B.C.E. Some of the characteristics of this culture are inhumation burials in barrows, horse and cattle breeding, and the use of wheeled vehicles. This was clearly a culture on the move, and radiocarbon dating helps pinpoint its astonishing expansion into Europe, the Caucasus, and Anatolia in the second half of the third millennium. The reconstructed vocabulary of Proto-Indo-European has protolexemes for 'horse' (**ekwo-*) 'cow' (**g^{w}ow-*), and 'wheel,' whereas, for example, the contemporary Sumerian in southern Mesopotamia lacked a primary word for 'horse,' calling it 'mountain ass' instead (*anšu kurra*), thus assigning indigenous cultural primacy to the donkey. The 'wheel' term is especially interesting, since it can be further analyzed into components: Sanskrit *cakrám* and English *wheel* (Old English *hweol;* cf. also Greek *kúklos*) jointly point to a protoform **k^{w}ek^{w}ló-,* which is a noun derived from a verb **k^{w}el-,* meaning 'to turn around a pivot', a sense still seen in Greek *pólos* 'pivot, axis' (< **k^{w}ólos*) and in Lithuanian *kãklas* 'neck' (on which the head turns). 'Wheel' shades over metonymically into 'chariot' (cf. 'get some wheels' = acquire a car), and such is the meaning of Tocharian *kukäl,* even as an alternative Indo-European 'wheel' word,

Latin *rota,* Irish *roth,* German *rad,* and Lithuanian *rãtas* (from a verb seen in Old Irish *rethim* 'I run', Lithuanian *ritù* 'I roll') appears in Sanskrit and Old Iranian as *rátha-* 'chariot.'

When we postulate such a third-millenium trans-Caspian starting point for the Indo-European migrations, many linguistic elements fall into place. Western Indo-European (Italic, Celtic, Germanic), which in many ways forms a distinct subunit, must have moved away (perhaps in several successive waves) and gradually overlaid numerically negligible substrata in thinly populated Europe (of which Basque is the sole surviving remnant). Tocharian figures as an eastern outcropping that was locked in the mountain fastness of Chinese Turkestan and thus preserved in isolation. Anatolian must have become severed from the remaining main body of Indo-European and crossed the Caucasus into the relative isolation of Asia Minor. Next to separate was Greek, moving southwest into the Balkans and the Mediterranean basin, along with Armenian, which instead crossed the Caucasus southward. The final breakup was that of the Indo-Iranian and Baltic-Slavic complex, which resulted in respective migrations to the south and northwest, the former toward the very cradles of ancient high cultures, the latter into an environment that doomed it to the archaism of a prehistoric illiteracy for several more millennia.

Such a tableau is arrived at by a balanced weighing of presumed old or new isoglosses (matching linguistic features) among these various separate "dialects" of the onetime postulated protolanguage. But these language groups were bearers of cultures, including such language-based nonmaterial cultural manifestations as religion, myth, epic, saga, folk song, and other forms of oral or (later) written literature. In this sphere too, the crucial question in each instance involves the degree of retention versus innovation, much as with the purely linguistic material; but there is a different emphasis, since cultural change can and does outstrip purely linguistic evolution. We must therefore pose certain specific questions of both principle and procedure. What does it take to reconstruct an Indo-European protomyth? It means recapturing via the comparative method a piece of the onetime living religion of a hypothetical protosociety. The procedure is to evaluate in relation to one another such survival versions as can be judiciously isolated and identified. Naturally the least-changed varieties would best reflect the prototype, and hence there is a premium on the conservatism of the tradition. The most retentive societies would tend to be those that are the most sedentary, self-sufficient, and self-enclosed, while conversely migratory groups, with rapid changeover of environment and exposure to alien ways, usually undergo much change. The latter is true especially if the contact element is culturally superior, as was the case with the various Indo-Europeans who reached the Aegean basin and the Near East. A new synthesis resulting from the fusion of an energetic Indo-European conqueror with a superior entrenched civilization may be essentially Indo-European in language, as in ancient Greece or Hittite Asia Minor, but its nonlinguistic component tends to reflect a profound change away from the inherited Indo-European pattern. These generalities are valid in the main, and indeed Greece and Anatolia contribute relatively little to the reconstruction of Indo-European religion and myth. But additionally, more refined angles of analysis must be adopted whenever we judge the relative archaism of any society. There is something that is not very predictable, namely the power of preservation that may be inherent in a hieratic tradition and the specific dynamics and emphases that may have fueled that tradition. Such underpinnings, largely hidden from our reconstructive eye, may have prevailed in the evolution over any generalizations we can formulate.

The study of hieratic entrenchment is indeed a basic tool of Indo-European comparative mythology. There is a great amount of specific social, religious, and legal terminology the eastmost and westmost branches of Indo-European have in common. These accordances between Indic and Iranian on the one hand and Italic and Celtic on the other reflect independent survivals of Proto-Indo-European lore. Examples are 'king' (Latin *rēx,* Old Irish *rī,* Vedic Sanskrit *rāj-*), 'law' (Latin *iūs,* Vedic *yoṣ,* Old Iranian *yaož-*), 'holy' (Old Irish *noib,* Old Persian *naiba*), 'believe' (Latin *crēdō,* Old Irish *cretim,* Sanskrit *śrad-dhā,* Old Iranian *zrazdā*). It is hardly accidental that those same branches exhibit the most notoriously powerful priestly establishments, such as the brahmin class in India, the high priesthood in Iran, which was still in power in the Sasanian empire and persecuted Christians and Manicheans alike, the pontifical and flaminical colleges in Rome, and the druids of ancient Gaul and Britain. The brahmins and flamens not only are probably etymologically related in name but have in common a unique and intricate set of tabus (see further chap. 9). The brahmin transmission of Vedic text through millennia by word of mouth has its parallel in the druidic sanctification of orality, the obverse of which was the proscription of writing.

Those same branches—Indic, Iranian, Italic, and Celtic—are also mainstays of reconstructed Indo-European myth, but Iran less than India, owing to the dislocations and overlays of the Zoroastrian reform, and the Celts much less than Rome, owing to the lateness and Christianized bias of the main attested sources. To India and Rome should be added as a third anchor the Germanic peoples, especially Scandinavia, and most peculiarly its colonial cranny of Iceland, where the pre-Christian tradition was preserved through the Eddic literature.

Myth can be transmitted either in its immediate shape, as sacred narrative anchored in theology and interlaced with liturgy and ritual, or in transmuted form, as past narrative that has severed its ties to sacred time and instead functions as an account of purportedly secular, albeit extraordinary happening (cf. the Introduction). This transposition of myth to heroic saga is a notable mechanism in ancient Indo-European traditions, wherever a certain cultic system has been supplanted in living religion and the superannuated former apparatus falls prey to literary manipulation. Thus in classical India the superseded Vedic myth finds its epic use in the *Mahābhārata* and *Rāmāyaṇa,* in Islamic Iran the Zoroastrian and pre-Zoroastrian divine lore becomes the stuff of royal beginnings in Firdausi's *Book of Kings,* the Norse gods appear as Trojan immigrants in the works of Saxo and Snorri, and the old Celtic divinities figure as pre-Celtic mound dwellers in the Irish *Book of Conquests*.

In India, Iran, and Scandinavia all such "literary" matter is merely a belated sideline to the direct transmission of living or at least embalmed myth. In Rome, however, it plays a more central role, because myth as such is not present as sacred lore in the native tradition. Rome has ritual stripped of discernible myth on the one hand and quasi-historical epicized narrative with a patriotic tinge on the other. Yet these remaining ingredients are so archaic and basic that Rome is nevertheless, paradoxically, crucial to Indo-European comparative mythology.

Apart from this overall Indo-European umbrella with its vast space-time dimensions, there exists as a self-contained subunit the Indo-Iranian group. It affords a simpler, two-dimensional laboratory for initial testing of the tenets of diachronic myth study on the monogenetic model. It is abundantly evident, on formal and substantive linguistic grounds alike, that Indic and Iranian are parallel offshoots of a joint Indo-Iranian prototype, a distinct subunit subsequent to Proto-Indo-European itself, somewhat in the manner that the Gaelic-Irish and British-Welsh branches of Celtic are ultimately reducible to Proto-Celtic unity. The historical divergences are great indeed, but the oldest Vedic Sanskrit and the earliest attested form of Iranian, the *Gāthās* of the

Avesta, are so close in language and in poetic and formulaic style as to allow a glimpse of the prototype not far below the prehistoric horizon. The same is true of religion and myth. Scraping off the barnacles of the Zoroastrian sea change, we reach a readily inferrable Proto-Iranian level that in most essentials closely matches Vedic tradition. Far from overlooking or downplaying the individuality and evolving originality of each, the comparison of the oldest traditions of India and Iran helps understand them in toto by uncovering their common starting point and joint prehistory, and hence the preconditions of their separate evolutions. A firm Indo-Iranian prototype is also a doubly secure foundation for further cross-Indo-European comparison.

Aside from the Indo-Iranian reconstruct, however, recapturing the earliest concrete individual data on the Indians and Iranians entails peculiar complications. Like all other Indo-European subgroups, they were originally inherently illiterate and hence inched closer to history only as they came to impinge on the culture cradles of the Near East. The earliest attestation is extraordinary on several counts. It comes from neither India nor Iran but northern Mesopotamia and became known only with the discovery and interpretation of the Hittite royal archives in the early part of the twentieth century. About 1400 B.C.E., Mitanni on the upper Euphrates was a kind of buffer state between Egypt in the south, the Semites to the east (Babylonia, Assyria), and the Hittites to the north, becoming a Hittite dependency during the early fourteenth century. Its population was in the main Hurrian (an indigenous people of unknown linguistic affinity), and the Hurrian element also exerted much dynastic and religious influence in the later stages of the Hittite empire. But around Mitanni it was apparently overlaid with a horse-breeding ruling aristocracy whose language was essentially Old Indic, seen in the names of rulers (Artatama, Tushratta) and perhaps of the country itself (Mitanni), a word designating the warrior elite (*maryanni*), various hippological technical terms in Hittite horse-training manuals written by Mitannians (*aikawartanna, tierawartanna, panzawartanna, sattawartanna, nāwartanna* expressing in the distortion of cuneiform syllabic spelling Old Indic *vartana* 'turn' and the prefixed numerals *aika-, tri-, pañca-, sapta-, nava-* '1, 3, 5, 7, 9'), and the names of certain deities. When about 1380 the weak Mitannian king Sattiwaza (or Mattiwaza or Kurtiwaza, depending on cuneiform reading) sealed by treaty his allegiance to his new liege lord and father-in-law Suppiluliumas, great king of the Hittites, he listed among the divine guarantors of his loyalty (or punishers of his potential oath breaking) a set of Old Indic deities (Mitra, Uruwana/Aruna, Indara, Nasattiya) who are none other than the canonic Vedic Indic grouping of the gods Mitra, Varuṇa, Indra, and the twin Nāsatyas (or Aśvins).

This lost tribe had no linguistic future, but the Near Eastern tradition of archival deposition of nonperishable cuneiform records made possible its rediscovery thirty-three hundred years later. How it strayed and briefly flowered in the Near East is a mystery; thousands of miles of mountain and desert, including the vast expanse of Iran, separate Mitanni from India. It is important to note that the Mitanni data are already specifically Indic, no longer Common Indo-Iranian in kind, and thus Indo-Iranian linguistic and cultural unity must have become sundered well before the Indic component bifurcated en route, ultimately to reach its ephemeral Mesopotamian and permanent subcontinental habitats. It is also likely that the Indic contingent was the first to move south across the general area of Iran and that the Iranians represent a somewhat later migratory wave in their wake. Ethnic and linguistic Iranians of the early historical period still occupied vast reaches of territory north and east of Iran proper, stretching from Scythia in South Russia across the Transcaspian lands (Sogdia, Chorasmia) deep into Central Asia (Khotan), and even in modern times the Afghans and Tadjiks are Iranians in the wider sense.

Tracing and dating of the Indic settlement and early history on the subcontinent are also complex and brittle. The initial penetration of the Indus valley must be roughly synchronous with the Indic appearance in Mesopotamia (ca. 1500 B.C.E.), and the flowering of Vedic culture in the "seven river land" (*Sindhu* [> *Iranian *Hindu* > Greek *Indos* 'Indus'] + *Sarasvatī* + *pañca āpas* [> Punjab] 'five waters') is roughly datable to the period 1200–800 B.C.E. From there the Indic penetration proceeded eastward down the Yamunā-Ganges river system, with the bulk of the indigenous (mostly Dravidian) population being squeezed southward ('to the right' [*dakṣiṇa* > Dekhan]).[1] All this is inferential rather than supported by primary records or even a firm native tradition. Writing did not come to India before the sixth century B.C.E., and then it came from Near Eastern, Aramean models; the "Proto-Indic" third-

1. The Old Indic terms for east and west similarly mean 'in front' and 'in back'. That a similar eastern orientation in determining cardinal directions may have been Common Indo-European is indicated by the Germanic word for north, which is cognate with Old Italic (Umbrian) *nertru* 'left[hand]' and with Greek *nérteros* 'pertaining to the netherworld' (the Germanic land of the dead [Old Norse *Hel*] lay in the north, and Odysseus had to sail to the northern ends of Ocean to gain access to Hades).

millennium scripts of the Mohenjo-Daro and Harappa civilizations had long since entered the sands, and cuneiform—despite undoubted cultural contacts with Mesopotamia—never gained a hold in Vedic India. Vedic civilization was thus essentially preliterate but was sustained at least in its hieratic aspects by an entrenched tradition of oral preservation and transmission that in effect obliterated a time gap of many centuries: when Vedic literature was finally consigned to written form (sixth century B.C.E.), at least its older parts were in fact faithfully preserved linguistic petrifacts of perhaps 1200 B.C.E. There is a certain parallelism with the secular oral aoedic tradition in Greece, which transmitted to posterity a dialect many centuries older than the Peisistratean recension of Homer from the sixth century B.C.E.

The gravest obstacle of all is the complete lack of a native sense of chronological history. A cyclic worldview with vague concepts of recurrent and self-rejuvenating "ages" had little concern for the linear ordering of events. Firm synchronisms with occidental events begin only about 300 B.C.E., when Megasthenes was the Seleucid Greek ambassador to the court of Chandragupta at Pāṭaliputra in Magadha (Patna in present-day Bihar). Vedic tradition thus appears to us concretely suspended by a later and much changed culture against a backdrop of prehistoric haze, without chronology and via the rote memorizations and pious mouthings of many generations bent on flawless transmission of sacred lore.

II · TRADITIONS

4 · Vedic India

Still another factor complicates the study of Old Indic tradition—the nature of the documents themselves. Vedic literature is religious in kind and as such tends to reflect the worldview, spiritual preoccupations, and social attitudes of the brahmin (*brahmán-*) or priestly component of Old Indic society. The social structure that was later to become rigid and subspecialized in the caste system already existed in main outline during the Vedic period, comprising the classes of *brāhmaṇá-, kṣatríya-* (or *rājanyà-*), *vaíśya-,* and *śūdrá-*. The first three were deemed *ā́rya-*, whereas the śūdras were *an-ārya-* 'non-Aryan', referring to the darker-skinned indigenous elements of the populaton (the Sanskrit term for 'caste', *várṇa-*, means 'color'). *Ā́rya* as a term for the Indo-European in-group goes back to Indo-Iranian (**Āryānam* > *Iran*) and Proto-Indo-European, for it recurs in Celtic in the Indo-European Far West (Old Irish *aire* 'free, noble') and occurs as a common noun in Hittite (*ara-* 'social equal, peer'). Vedic society proper was thus tripartite, composed of 'formulators, word manipulators, idea men, intellectuals' (*bráhman-* originally meant roughly 'effective verbal construct, formula, prayer'), 'power types, warriors, royal entourage' (*kṣatrám* 'rule, dominion', *rāj-* 'king'), and 'villagers, economic classes,' that is, herders, cultivators, artisans (*viś-* '[tribal] village', *véśa-* 'house[hold]' = Greek *oî-kos*).

Not only did Vedic literature have a brahmanic bias, but there is a further warp in its genres themselves. The basic texts are the *Saṁhitās* ('Collections') of the four Vedas (literally 'knowledge', but etymologically cognate with 'wisdom'), verse compilations of hymns to and about deities: *Rig-Veda* (for recitation), *Sāma-Veda* (for chanting), *Yajur-Veda* (for liturgy), and *Atharva-Veda* (named after a kind or group of priests). The *Rig-Veda* is the oldest, judging from language and style (ten books [*máṇḍala-*], just over a thousand hymns, in bulk similar to the *Iliad* plus the *Odyssey*); it is also corpuslike, comprehensive, whereas the *Sāma-Veda* and *Yajur-Veda* are mostly derivative, handbooklike distillates for cultic purposes (the *Yajur-Veda* including prose formulas as well as hymns). The *Atharva-Veda,* later than and partly derivative from the *Rig-Veda,* also contains much separate folkloristic and magical lore at variance with the more "high church" tenor of the *Rig-Veda*. In the later Vedic and early classical period a whole mass of secondary exegetic literature grew up around the four Vedas: theological treatises (*Brā́hmaṇa-* 'Priestly Books', *Āraṇyaka-* 'Forest Books'; later *Purāṇa-* 'Antiquarian Books'), handbooks on ritual (*Sū́tra-*), philosophical speculations (*Upaniṣád-*), and philological commentaries (e.g., Yāska's *Niruktá-* 'Etymology'). Such secondhand matter often constitutes a valuable (and sometimes invaluable) supplement for understanding the basic Vedic texts, while at the same time introducing the views and judgments of a later era that was evolving away from Vedic culture in radical fashion and at great speed.

Indeed classical Hinduism, with its elaboration of philosophical doctrines (*darśana-*) such as Sāṁkhya, Yoga, and Vedānta, its Buddhist heresy, its theological Brahmanism with the sectarian bifurcation into Viṣṇuism and Śivaism, and the general tenor of its spiritual life, is worlds removed from the culture of the early Vedic period. The chief document of that period, the *Rig-Veda,* is, however, a body of hymns, relatively short pieces of lyrical verse, addressed to or speaking of a deity or deities in the particular intimacy of religious communion and communication. The bald facts and details of the theological situation are implicitly known to author, communicant, and godhead alike, allowing allusiveness to dominate both prayer and narrative. Since physical monuments of the Vedic period do not survive and archeology is of no help, the situation is analogous to being handed a church hymnal in a vacuum and trying to construct from it a comprehensive overview of the spiritual (and if possible temporal and material) culture of a Christian society.

Nor is the bulk distribution of the *Rig-Veda* conducive to a balanced appreciation of the Vedic pantheon on its operative terms, especially its historical and comparative reconstruction. More than half the hymns invoke just three top-rated gods of the moment (Indra [250], Agni [200], Soma [100+]), while occasional stabs at internal systematization put the number of deities at thirty-three, sometimes broken down as 3 × 11. A further classification is found in *RV* 10.125.1–2: "I [i.e., *Vāk* or 'Word' (etymologically = Latin *vox*); cf. the evolving *Bráhman* = 'Formula'] go with the Rudras and Vasus, with the Ādityas and the all-gods. I carry both Mitra and Varuṇa, both Indra and Agni, and both Aśvins. I carry the swelling Soma, and Tvaṣṭar, Pūṣan, and Bhaga."

The closeness of the divine dual pairs (*devatā-dvandva*) *Mitrā́-Váruṇā, Índrā-Agnī́,* and *Aśvínā* to the Mitannian oath list (discussed in chap. 3) is patent and must represent ancient canonic lore. Equally significant are the generic terms *Rudrá-, Vásu-,* and *Ādityá-* that match them, while the catchall designation "all-gods" (*víśve devā́ḥ*) subsumes the assorted divine debris that spills over the bounds of the central formula. Mitra and Varuṇa are in fact the chief Ādityas (brood of *Áditi-*, an opaque ancestress), Indra (here secondarily coupled with the omnipresent popular fire-god Agni) was associated with the plural *Marút-* or *Rudríya-* (sons of the god Rudra, whose name also serves as a generic term for war- or storm-gods), and the Aśvins as Vasus epitomize the wealth-bestowing aspects of such benign and beneficent divinities (*dātā́ vásūnām* = Homeric *dotḗr eáōn* 'giver of goods' as divine epithet). The order of terms in this passage (Rudras, Vasus, Ādityas) is scrambled for metrical reasons, unlike parallel canonic lists; for example:

RV 5.51.10: Ādityas, Indrā-Vāyū, Vasus
AV 8.1.16: Ādityas, Indrā-Agnī, Vasus
AV 6.74.3: Ādityas, Maruts, Vasus
AV 5.3.9: Ādityas, Rudras, Aśvins

Thus, penetrating beneath the statistical hit parade of Indra, Agni, and Soma, we glimpse three pantheonic nuclei that have clear relevance to the three ārya social classes and their combined societal and religious concerns. The Ādityas, abstract deities bearing the marks of theologians' speculations, are clearly the special purview of the brahmins, war-gods of the kṣatriyas (cf. the name *Marút-* with the Mitannian *Maryanni* 'Young [Warriors]'), and the Vasus of the wealth-producing vaiśyas. Brahmin attitudes naturally arrogated the apex (they, after all, formulated what we have), and while looking down on mere kṣatriyas, nevertheless made common cause with the sources of temporal power and protection in lording it over those who did the work and produced the goods that made praying and fighting possible. Other deities swarm about these nuclei, not fully compartmentalized holdovers or relics from less systematic and more freewheeling pre-Vedic and Indo-Iranian polytheism, and hence of high interest to comparative study but doomed to disappearance in later Brahmanism. The following sketches attempt to sum up the essence of the deity involved and also to provide some preliminary intimation of his/her relevance to the comparative studies that will follow.

The major Ādityas are *Mitrá-* and *Váruṇa-* (the dvandva compound is always *Mitrā́-Váruṇā* with double dual, or elliptically *Mitrā́* 'Mitra and the other one' [i.e., his well-known dvandva mate Varuṇa]). Mitra as an independent figure has paled badly in the *Rig-Veda,* having only one hymn to his name (*RV* 3.59), but his lingering onomastic pride of place in conjunction with Varuṇa attests to his erstwhile importance, as does the continuing eminence of his Iranian counterpart *Mithra*. The name is an original abstract neuter noun *mitrám* with instrument suffix *-tra-* (cf., e.g., Latin *arātrum* 'plow[ing tool]'), either from the root *mi-* 'set up, fix, settle', or from *mī-* 'exchange', meaning 'contract, covenant, compact', either as 'instrument' (cf. 'instrument of a treaty', and Latin *pax* 'peace[-treaty]' from *pangō* 'make fast; fix') or as 'means of interaction', stressing mutuality. The personification of 'Contract' as a god has shaded over semantically into 'Contractor' and thence 'Friend' (Classical Sanskrit masculinized *mitrá-* 'friend', not in the English root-sense seen in Gothic *frijōn* 'to love', Sanskrit *priyá-* 'dear', but rather the friend of convenience with whom you have contracted not to kill each other). Mitra appears as basically benevolent, the god who 'regulates' (*yātáyati*) the tiller folk (*kṛṣṭī́r, carṣaṇī́r* [*RV* 3.59.1, 6] and vouchsafes *kṣéma-* 'settlement, security' (*RV* 7.82.5), which is underwritten by a *mitrám* 'internal peace compact' (*RV* 2.11.14 *rā́si kṣáyam rā́si mitrám asmé* 'give us settlement, give us peace!').

Varuṇa, by contrast, is the important Vedic god who upholds *ṛtá-*, the cosmic moral norm, and guards against all sinful deviation. This ṛta (approximately 'arrangement, order') is also known as *dhā́man-* ('law', literally 'what is set' [cf. German *Gesetz* 'law'], cognate with Greek *thémis* 'divine law'), and to enforce it Varuṇa employs spies (*spáśaḥ*). He is generally remote, devious, and mysterious, a somewhat sinister figure who instills fear and whose forgiveness is craved, very unlike the "open" and well-intentioned advocate of social man that Mitra seems to have been. Varuṇa has "snares" in which he catches and binds the guilty, who include the untruthful in general and the perjured in particular, whom he afflicts with crippling enteric distress which the *Atharva-Veda* describes as dropsy (*jalodararoga-,* literally 'water belly'). It can be lifted by priestly prayer medicine (story of *Śúnaḥśépa-* in *Aitareya-Brāhmaṇa* 7.13–16),[1] which underlines the extent to which this god is a creature of brahmin theology and imagination. His function as oath protector is old and basic, related to the Indic custom of swearing by water (cf. the gods swearing by Styx water in Hesiod's *Theogony* [775–806], with yearlong coma and nine-year ostracism as punishment for the forsworn); his watery connections range from the Vedic dropsy angle to his becoming a pensioned-off sea-god in later Brahmanism. The name *Váruṇa-* is palpably derived from the root *vr̥-* 'enclose, confine, restrict' (in *RV* 7.82.6 Varuṇa actually *prá vr̥ṇoti* 'confines'; cf., e.g., *dharúṇa-* 'holding' from *dhr̥-*). It is in origin an epithet of *Ásura-* 'Lord', thus 'Lord Confining', much like his Iranian counterpart Ahura Mazdāh 'Lord Wise' (conversely *Váruṇa-* has become the name, and *ásura-* is Varuṇa's frequent Vedic epithet). As such he may indeed personify the Oath, the magical pendant and reinforcement of the Contract; the semantic link is similar to that of Greek *hórkos* 'oath' beside *hérkos* 'enclosure'. The often-repeated cognate relationship to Greek *Ouranos* 'Sky' is illusory and spurious (*Ouranós* goes back to **Worsanós,* cognate with either Sanskrit *varṣám* 'rain' or *várṣman-* 'height, summit').

The "minor" Ādityas are *Aryamán-, Bhága-, Dákṣa-,* and *Áṁśa-*. They are a motley lot of abstractions, of varying chronological age and clearly lumped together by systematizing theologians. *Aryamán-* is originally a neuter abstract, something like "Aryanness," the deified embodiment of social self-identification. Within the social contract he is specialized as the patron of the institution of marriage. His Indo-Iranian ancestry is proved by his Avestan counterpart *Airyaman,* concerned with both marriage rites and the institution of healing rituals. *Bhága-* is literally 'Portion', thence 'Apportioner' (cf. 'Contract' > 'Contractor'), epithet of various gods but here typically on a brahmin level of abstraction as the personification of the divine handout, thus the

1. Childless King Hariścandra vowed to sacrifice to Varuṇa any son he might have, but when Rohita was born he temporized, until finally Varuṇa pressured him into compliance. Rohita, now grown up, escaped to the forest, while Varuṇa seized the king, and his belly swelled up. After years of wandering, Rohita at length found a starving brahmin who sold him one of his three sons, Śunaḥśepa 'Dog's Tail', as a substitute victim. When Rohita offered to redeem himself and his father with this victim, Varuṇa was pleased to accept, because "a brahmin is better than a kṣatriya." Śunaḥśepa was bound to the sacrificial stake, but with his brahmin knack for prayer he began invoking various deities in succession. As each verse was uttered by him, "a bond [i.e., Varuṇa's 'snare'] was loosened," and Hariścandra's belly started shrinking. When the last verse was done, the last "bond" was removed, and the king was cured. The story is alluded to also in *RV* 1.24.12–13 and 5.2.7.

determiner of dues, the arbiter of good fortune, rather than a random distributor of goods in the manner of Vasus. In part of the Iranian area, spilling over into Slavic, the cognate word has become the generic term for "god" (Old Persian *baga-*, Old Slavic *bogŭ*). *Dákṣa-*'Ability, Efficiency' and *Áṁśa-* (another term for 'Portion') are more obscure but may be equally ancient, chiastically comparable with Greek *Aîsa* 'Lot, Share' and *Póros* 'Effectiveness' (opp. *aporíā* 'quandary'), whom Alkman in the *Partheneion* called "the oldest of the gods." To Dakṣa attaches the mythical paradox that he is both son and father of Aditi (*RV* 10.72.4; cf. the Roman Fortuna in chap. 9). *Á-diti-* herself means 'unbinding', thus 'being set free, deliverance', an abstraction that need have signified no more than 'Delivery, Childbirth', thence 'Childbearer, Mother' (cf. 'Contract' > 'Contractor'); alternatively it may denote 'Liberation, Liberty' as an antidotal goddess to *áṁhas-* 'narrowness, constriction', which obsessed the Vedic mind and from which it ever craved surcease (etymologically cognate with Latin *angus-tus* 'narrow' and German *Angst*). "Deliver us from *aṁhas*" is indeed a leitmotif of Vedic prayer lore, whether it relates to being boxed in by enemies, or being cramped in living space by natural obstacles, or simply being beset by spiritual blight.

The Ādityas, being personified abstractions, were almost by definition devoid of or deficient in action myth. Not so the gods of the warrior class, and most especially the preeminent one, *Índra-* (of uncertain etymology, perhaps 'Strong'; cf. Slavic **jędrŭ* 'strong'). Indra is the great macho deity of the Vedic pantheon (*sahásramuṣka-* 'thousand-testicled') who behaves like a rutting bull and prepares for his pivotal deed by ingesting prodigious amounts of psychotropic soma. That deed, however, unlike others in Indra's repertory, is not primarily sexual in kind but involves the slaying of a monstrous adversary, a creature named *Vṛtrá-*. Vṛtra's name is an original abstract noun (cf. *Mitrá-*) from the same root that yields *Váruṇa-*, thus literally 'Confinement', and thence actively 'Confiner, Obstructor'. Unlike Varuṇa, whose activity involves positive sanctions in the interest of moral order, Vṛtra is the roadblock on the path of Aryan progress, a demonic impediment whose elimination by Indra is celebrated over and over in the lyrics of the *Rig-Veda*, accounting in large measure for Indra's high frequency ranking in the hymns. The cognate derivation of names such as Varuṇa and Vṛtra is not surprising: 'confinement' can be for good or evil, depending on whether you are on the side of the jailer or the jailed; similarly, both Varuṇa and Vṛtra use *māyā́*, supernatural magic ability to change the appearance of things (and hence to deceive), but when Varuṇa or other gods do so it is a condoned practice (an all-too-human rationalization), whereas Vṛtra's *māyā́* boils down to dirty tricks.

Indra *Vṛtrahán-* has become a focal figure for the ingathering of mythical matter, a centerpiece around which various levels of abstraction and elaboration have coalesced. It is possible (cf. Iranian materials discussed in chap. 6) that the relatively abstract epithet *Vṛtrahán-* 'Obstruction-smiter', attested with several mythical figures, attached itself specifically to the action-god Indra, a dragon killer of enormous appetites who shades over into a storm-god with a thunder weapon (*vájra-*), and that the dragon hence came by his name *Vṛtrá-* by secondary concretization, being otherwise known as *Triśirás-* 'Three-Headed' or *Viśvárūpa-* 'All Shapes' (alluding to protean *māyā́*-qualities). The storm-god in turn controls precipitation for pastoralist and agriculturalist alike, polarizing the foe into a demon of drought who needs to be vanquished in order to make the rains (and hence the rivers) flow. On a more earthly level the enemy takes on traits of a cattle rustler who (along with other demonic beings such as the *Paṇí-*) absconds with the herds of the Aryans and sequesters them in a mountain cave. This cave, *Valá-*, once again shows the same root of 'confinement' as does *Vṛtrá-* (*r* and *l* have coalesced into a single phoneme in Indo-Iranian, which may appear as either *r* or [more rarely] *l*). Indra's tracking down the cows with the help of his bitch *Sarámā,* and freeing them, is a heroic deed that somehow meshes with the release of the pent-up rainclouds (the breaking of the monsoon), so that in lyric diction it is sometimes hard to tell where thunderheads leave off and bellowing herds take over. Such poetic conflations and allusions and even more esoteric ones have woven a many-layered texture of myth about Indra; *RV* 1.32 is among the clearest and most straightforward of the Indra hymns:

> 1. Let me say right out the heroics of Indra, the first that he did, the *vajra*-holder: He slew the snake, broke open the waters, and split the bellies of the mountains.
>
> 2. He slew the snake who reclined on the mountain. Tvaṣṭar ['Fashioner', smith-god] had forged for him the whizzing bolt. Like lowing cows, the flowing waters went swiftly down to the sea.
>
> 3. In bullish fashion he ordered up a soma, on a three-day binge he imbibed the brew. The Generous One took the bolt for his missile and slew that firstborn of snakes.
>
> 4. As you, Indra, slew the firstborn of snakes, as you moreover outtricked the tricks (*māyā́ḥ*) of the tricksters, producing sun, sky, and

dawn, from that time on you never found a foe to match you!

5. This shoulderless Archobstructionist (*Vṛtrám vṛtratáram*) he slew, Indra with his big murderous bolt. Like tree branches split with an ax, the snake lies flat on the ground.

6. Like a nonwarrior who can't hold his liquor, he provoked the hard-pressing, lees-quaffing super champion. He did not withstand the onslaught of his weapons. He was crushed for having challenged Indra, his features smashed.

7. Without feet or hands he waged battle against Indra. The latter hit him in the back with his bolt. A castrato aspiring to match the macho, Vṛtra lay shattered in many places.

8. As he lies there like a broken reed, the rising waters of Man go past him. Those whom Vṛtra had blockaded in his heyday, under their feet the snake has come to lie.

9. Vṛtra's dam had a fit of fainting as Indra bore down on her with his weapon. Above was the mother, beneath her the son—Dānu lay like a cow with her calf.

10. Amid ever-moving, restless courses, waters rush over Vṛtra's deposited, hidden corpse. In long darkness he came to lie for having challenged Indra.

11. Dominated by the demon, watched over by the snake, the waters stood sequestered like cows by the Paṇi. But he that slew the Obstructor tapped the reservoir that had been bottled up.

12. You turned into a horsehair [a piece of *māyā́*!], Indra, when he bashed you in the fangs, you, the one god. You, hero, won the cows, you won the soma, you set free to flow the Seven Rivers!

13. Neither lightning nor thunder availed him, nor the mist and hail he spread around [Vṛtra's *māyā́s*]. When Indra and the snake fought, the Generous One won a victory even for the future.

14. Whom did you see as the snake's avenger, Indra, that fear came to your heart after the kill, that you crossed the ninety-nine streams, even as a frightened falcon traverses the skies?

15. Indra is the king of the moving and the unharnessed, of the hornless and horned, he with the bolt in his hand. He as king rules the folk; like the felly the spokes, he encompasses them.

In addition to this overworked mythologem, other frequently obscure scraps of Indra lore rate attention. While the above panegyric reflects a pinnacle of Indra worship, other pieces tend to hint at a less heroic, more controversial troublemaker. This prototypical divine aggressor's Oedipal traits are patent in the obscure allusions to attempted infanticide and retaliatory parricide (*RV* 4.18.12: "Who made your mother a widow? Who wanted to kill you latent [in the womb] or moving [down the birth canal]? What god was in your good graces as you grabbed your father by the foot and wasted him?") and his resentment against his own offspring as potential rivals (*RV* 10.28). His rather blurry consort is referred to simply as *Indrāṇī́* 'Mrs. Indra', later as *Śacī́* (a feminine noun meaning 'Might'). He fights and feuds with assorted fellow deities (e.g., Uṣās, Sūrya, Aśvins). The *Rig-Veda* narrates with great gusto how Indra outsmarted Vṛtra and smote him in the back, but later tradition came to view him as a dirty, unfair, and treacherous fighter, less than a paragon of the warrior ethic he was supposed to patronize. Late Vedic and post-Vedic tradition, where Indra's godhead progressively declines with the onset and elaboration of Brahmanism, is still replete with increasingly submythological, epic, and folkloric Indra lore, some of it in direct succession and elaboration of the Vedas, other parts purveying potentially important ancient para-Vedic tradition, still others probably reflecting the fictional impulses of a later age.

The story of Triśiras or Viśvarūpa as an alternative to Vṛtra has been shunted to a Rig-Vedic sidetrack but reflects ancient and persistent tradition. *RV* 10.8.8–9 tells how *Tritá Āptyá* (literally 'Third Āptya' [the latter a mythical clan name meaning 'Watery']), a henchman of Indra, struck down Triśiras ['Three-Headed'] and set free his cows. Indra himself also partook of the slaying, drove home Viśvarūpa's cows, and cut off his three heads. Triśiras's father was Tvaṣṭar, who not only forged Indra's bolt but whom later tradition claimed to be the very object of Indra's parricide in *RV* 4.18.12 (Tvaṣṭar does in fact figure in *RV* 4.18, though not explicitly as father of Indra). This made Indra and Triśiras half-brothers, breaching the brahmanic injunction against killing of kin and adding fratricide to the criminal record.

As this tradition shows, the opposition of gods (*devá-*) and demons (*ásura-*, *dā́sa-*) was somewhat less than polarized. Rather than irreconcilable extremes, they were more like rival and antagonistic supernatural "parties" or factions continuously at loggerheads with each other, but with possible interactions other than purely hostile ones. Tvaṣṭar sired Triśiras on a demoness, while Indra's mother was presumably a goddess; but they had the same divine father. Triśiras was semidemonic and monstrous, yet he held a contradictory priestly position as chaplain of the gods. Thus Vṛtra's unrelieved snakiness in much of the *Rig-Veda* contrasts with Triśiras's relative theomorphism. Indra could proceed against Vṛtra with impunity as an anguicidal maniac, but his liquidation of Triśiras was fraught with grave religious and legal implications.

On top of violating the bonds of kinship, Indra also broke his contractual agreements, such as his nonaggression pact with the demon *Námuci-*, who through such a compact had become his *sákhā* ('friend', of convenience, to be sure, but a kind of ally nonetheless). After a serious provocation by Namuci, who incapacitated Indra by plying him with *súrā* (alcohol, a vile brew in Vedic India, in contrast to the psychedelic *sóma-*), Indra managed to recover and circumvented the spirit of the agreement by finding a loophole in its verbiage that let him slay Namuci by a trick. No wonder Namuci's severed head branded him a *mitradrúh-* 'covenant breaker, friend betrayer'; such censure further compromised Indra's dubious standing as the supernatural paragon of the kṣatriyas. These traditions, hinted at in the Vedas, are fully developed in the Brāhmaṇas and echo down to the epics, where the *Mahābhārata* (book 5) has a lot to say about Indra's (or his allonym *Śakrá*'s 'Mighty One') underhanded dealings with an adversary conflated out of Triśiras and Vṛtra, and epic rogues find in Indra's casuistry welcome support for their own Machiavellian doings. The *Rāmāyaṇa* has the story of Indra's seducing Ahalyā while disguised as her husband Gautama and of his castration by the latter (at a curse from this brahmin, Indra's testicles fell to the ground [just two, not the thousand he is credited with in the Vedas], to be replaced later by transplants from a ram). Thus compounded with sexual villainy, Indra's kin killing and contract breaking add up to a catalog of misdeeds that has become a traditional theme down to the late *Purāṇas:* Indra the triple sinner. Although its grafting onto Indra may involve bad-mouthing of the superannuated kṣatriya patron by disparaging brahmin theologians, the theme itself reflects an ancient Indo-European tradition about the social and moral ambiguities of the heroic warrior figure, one reflected also in Epic Indic, Old Norse, and Greek tradition, as will be discussed in chapter 13.

Indra's multivalent role as warrior-deity, dragon killer, storm-god, and by extension water bringer makes him a pivotal figure in Indic myth. As a great god of an elaborate and creative mythology, he displays agglomeration and innovation of traits rather than isolated survivals. His very centrality at the warrior level makes it expedient to discuss other deities of this class with reference to him. It is noteworthy how many other names form dvandva pairs with Indra in the *Rig-Veda,* more than with any other deity: *Índrā-Marútas, Índrā-Vāyū́, Índrā-Víṣṇū, Índrā-Agnī́, Índrā-Sómā, Índrā-Pūṣán-, Índrā-Bṛhaspáti* or *Indra-Brahmaṇaspáti* ('Lord of the Formula', the divine magician), and other, minor figures.

The Maruts are essentially the cohorts of the war-gods, thus supernatural reflections of the rank and file of fighting men of Vedic and pre-Vedic times, probably more in the nature of warrior bands pledged to fraternal allegiance and attachment to individual warlords than any formal military setup. The Maruts are involved in atmospheric activities as Indra's storm troopers but, as mentioned earlier, are alternatively called Rudras or Rudriyas (sons of Rudra) or sons of Vāyu ('Wind'; *RV* 1.134.4) and occur also in the company of Trita, Parjanya, and Viṣṇu. Like Indra's, their doings are marked by a certain willful independence expressed by the term *sva-dhā́* 'self-law' (= Greek *auto-nomíā*) or *priyám dhā́ma* (etymologically English *free-dom*), leading to such tense and recriminating exchanges as *RV* 1.165.5–6:

> Maruts: "Indra, you have always been agreeable to our *svadhā́*."
> Indra: "Where was that *svadhā́* of yours, Maruts, when you left me alone at the snake-slaying?"

Such self-centered, strong-minded proclivity to do one's own thing, take the law into one's own hands, was apparently a trait of the Vedic (and by inference Indo-European) warrior's "ethic" (etymologically Greek *éthos* goes back to a cognate Indo-European **swe-dhos*), being further reflected in the Latin word *sodālis* (Old Latin *suodālis* < **swe-dhā-lis*) 'member of a band', later 'boon companion, comrade'. This volatility of the warrior (protector : menace, team player : lone wolf, model officer : berserk) is an important facet of early Indo-European social history (see further chap. 13).

Vāyú- or *Vā́ta-* 'Wind' is properly of atmospheric origin, a gale-god whose Indo-Iranian age is proved by his more important Iranian counterpart *Vayu*. *Parjánya-* (once [*RV* 1.164.51] in the plural [cf. *Rudrā́ḥ*]) is a related rain-god figure cognate in name with the Baltic (Lithuanian) thunder-god *Perkū́nas* and his Slavic (Old Russian) counterpart *Perunŭ;* in that case he is an ancient variant of the type, shunted to the Vedic periphery by the ascendancy of Indra.

Such pruning leaves the two difficult, contradictory figures of *Víṣṇu-* and *Rudrá-*. Both are medium-rank deities in Vedic times, with clear associations to the warrior class, but otherwise they are poles apart. The polarization becomes absolute in classical Hinduism, where Viṣṇu and *Śivá-* (propitiatory euphemism 'Kind, Friendly' for Rudra) have become the eponyms of the two main contrary sects of Brahmanism, *Vaiṣṇava* and *Śaiva,* the former more rational, enlightened, and intellectual, the latter tending toward the mystical, instinctual, and orgiastic; a broad comparison with the binary Apollinian and Dionysiac strands of Greek psychohistory may be apposite. The disparateness can already be sensed in the fragmentary and allusive Vedic context: Viṣṇu is Indra's ally and helpmate; Rudra is conspicuous by never forming a dvandva pair with Indra, but on the other hand he is the father of the Maruts and has a name that, as we saw earlier, also serves as a designation for the entire group of warrior-gods. Viṣṇu is called in the *Rig-Veda adveṣá-* 'without hatred', whereas the terrifying Rudra is typically styled *nr̥hán-* 'man-killing'. Viṣṇu is the constructive, positive deity whose human incarnations of the classical period (Rāma, Kr̥ṣṇa) are brought on by the need to countervene demonic forces. In the *Rig-Veda* Viṣṇu is repeateadly praised as the "three-stepper," or "wide-strider," for taking his crucial primordial three strides that somehow measured out and affirmed the habitable universe for gods and men alike (fig. 2). He is thus the deity who created living space and elbowroom, a primeval figure whom Indra the precocious *aṁhas* fighter enlisted on his side soon after being born (*RV* 4.18.11: *átha abravīd Vr̥trám Índro haniṣyán: sákhe Viṣṇo vitarám ví kramasva* 'then Indra spoke as he set out to kill Vr̥tra: "Friend Viṣṇu, stride forth most widely!"'). There is a remarkable onomastic and mythical parallel to Viṣṇu in the Germanic god Vīðarr of Norse tradition, whose very name also contains the exhortation 'wider!' (*Vīðarr = vitarám;* see chap. 11), even as *Víṣṇu-* is plausibly analyzable simply as 'Wide' (beside *víṣu-*, *víṣvañc-* 'apart, different'; cf., e.g., *dhr̥ṣṇú-* beside Greek *thrasús* 'bold').

Rudra's name may be equally revelatory. Rather than the old storm-related connection as 'Howler' with the verb *róditi* 'weep, cry' (cf. Latin *rudere* 'howl, bellow', Russian *rydát'* 'weep'), the plausible tie-in is with Latin *rudis* 'coarse, rough, wild' and *rullus* 'ruffian' (< **rud-lo-*); the Roman cognomen *Rullus* may in fact be identical with *Rudrá-* as 'Wild'. Less clear is an affinity to a noun **ródas-* (cf., e.g., *ugrá-* 'mighty' beside *ójas-* 'might'), attested in the dual number *ródasī* denoting heaven plus earth, possibly an elliptic dvandva for 'earth and the other [half of the universe]'; then **ródas-* might mean 'earth' and **rudrá-* 'earthy' (but by the same token **ródas-* could have meant 'heaven', or nonelliptically simply 'half'; then **rudrá-* would be 'heavenly', or *ródasī* 'the two halves [of the universe]'). Whatever the basic sense of **ródas-*, it may even have been Rudra's original, abstract-noun designation (later replaced by the derivative adjective **rudrá-*), for Rudra's wife is known to the *Rig-Veda* as a feminine singular derivative *Rodasī́* from **Ródas-* (cf. *Indrāṇī́, Varuṇānī́, Agnā́yī, Aśvínī*). Perhaps

FIGURE 2. Wide-Striding Viṣṇu. Tenth century C.E. Archeological Survey of India, New Delhi.

**ródas*- meant in the beginning 'raw state, roughness, unfinished condition', and the dual *ródasī* denotes the two unfinished world halves, imperfect in themselves, joined into an ordered universe. Rudra is indeed the god of the wild, of chaos before cosmos, of nature antedating culture, of all that as yet, or ever, eludes control. Viṣṇu is the land surveyor who measures and expands the regulated domain, while Rudra is the unseen archer whose lethal arrow, or elf-shot laden with poison, darts from the wilderness that surrounds the Vedic homestead. Attempts to propitiate this fearsome agent of untamed nature include incantatory appeals to his mercy and goodness, turning the plague shooter into a healer (e.g., *RV* 1.114.10 and 1: *āré te goghnám utá pūruṣaghnám . . . yáthā śám asad dvipáde cátuṣpade* 'away with your killings of cattle and men . . . that there be blessing for biped and quadruped!'). Finally in classical Hinduism the euphemistically named and evolved god Śiva replaces both Rudra and his allonym *Śarvá*- meaning 'Archer' or 'Destroyer' (cf. *śáru*- 'arrow' or *śar*- 'destroy'; this name is Indo-Iranian, attested also for the Avestan demon *Saurva*-). Rudra has deep roots in the Indo-European past, stretching all the way via the Greek Apollo to the great Germanic god exemplified by the Norse Odin (see chaps. 8 and 11).

While the near-abstract Ādityas were at best localizable in some vague "heaven," the more anthropomorphically conceived kṣatriya deities operated closer to man's habitat, "atmospherically" in their naturistic storm-god aspect, but also in cave and woodland, where they directly intervened in the life of the Vedic pastoralist or homesteader. The line between war-gods and vaiśya divinities (or Rudras and Vasus) is in fact a fluid one, for Indra himself releases both rain and cows, Trita Āptya leans strongly toward the third estate, Rudra is also *Paśupati*- or 'Lord of Animals', and Viṣṇu's prevalent benevolence and lack of "storminess" underline his atypicality.

The term *Vásu*- likewise straddles down-to-earth and more "cosmic" spheres. It is literally 'Goods, Wealth' and by extension 'Giver of Good Things', but the root *vas*- signified basically 'shine, be radiant', and the meaning 'be beneficial, be good' is a semantic outgrowth thereof. This duality is clear in the nature of the Aśvins. The dual *Aśvínā* means literally 'Pair of Horsemen'. On an earthly level their legendry details feats that in our own culture are ascribed to Coast Guard helicopters, sheriff's rescue posses, human or veterinary paramedic teams, and physicians dealing in restorative and rejuvenative cures. Hymns such as *RV* 1.112 and 1.116–19 give extensive lists of their interventions, some well known in Vedic lore, others wholly obscure: for example, saving Bhujyu and Rebha from drowning at the hands of enemies, rescuing Atri from a fire pit, restoring eyesight to Ṛjrāśva, fitting the mutilated racehorse Viśpalā with a prosthetic iron shank, and stripping the crumpled skin from the aged Cyavāna, making him once again attractive to young women. Their conveyance is an airborne chariot (*rátha-, RV* 7.68.3), and they are clearly no mere earthbound horsemen. Their allonyms are *Nā́satyā* (interpreted as 'Rescuers', or perhaps rather 'Nose-Born', referring to a peculiar birth myth), *Divó nápātā* '[Grand]sons of Dyaus', and *Dasrā́* 'Wonder Workers'. Although they are regularly invoked in unison in the hymnic style that submerges their individualities, it is possible that one or another name was originally peculiar to one twin only and that the duals are actually elliptic dvandvas ('the so-and-so and his brother'); thus *Nā́satya-* (matching the Avestan single *Nāñhaithya-*) may be the original Aśvin, while his brother Dasra was descended from the god Dyaus (one mythical twin often has a divine father, witness in Greek saga Herakles [father: Zeus] vs. Iphikles [father: Amphitryon] or Polydeukes [father: Zeus] vs. Kastor [father: Tyndareus]).

The Aśvins are hence much more than man-oriented do-gooders. They are the Divine Twins, sprung at least partly from the Vedic *deus otiosus Dyaús* (genitive *Divás,* from a root meaning 'be bright'), the ancient Indo-European sky-god who has been shunted aside in Vedic theology but whose Greek and Roman counterparts *Zeús* (genitive *Diós*) and *Diēs-piter* (or in the vocative case *Ju-piter*) have retained heavenly and added atmospheric dominion. Dyaus's remaining mythic function is his primordial mating with *Pṛthivī́* 'Earth' (dual dvandva *Dyā́vā-Pṛthivī́*), reminiscent of the Greek coupling of Ouranos and Gaia (chap. 2), or of Zeus's hierogamy with Hera in *Iliad* 14.346–51. As offspring of Dyaus, the Aśvins are thus ancient figures of Indo-European myth, despite the alternative descent from Vivasvat that Vedic India invented for them (see below). They are in fact closely matched by the Greek *Dióskouroi* 'Zeus's boys' (Kastor and Polydeukes) and by the Baltic (Latvian) *Dieva dēli* 'Sons of God' (see chaps. 8 and 12). In the oldest versions (e.g., *RV* 4.43.6, 1.119.5) the Aśvins are the joint husbands (*pátī,* in the dual) of *Sūryā́,* the sun-maid daughter of the sun-god *Sū́rya-,* also known as *Duhitā́ Sū́ryasya* 'Daughter of the Sun'. Typically, the Vasu level is concerned with temporal well-being in a comprehensive sense, not just shiny goods but "radiance" in all human forms, good living, good health, good looks, good sex, and marriage. This brings us to the status of Vedic goddesses. The first lady of Varuṇa's heaven was as obscure a denizen of the Vedic pantheon as a Russian leader's wife used to be in the Soviet hierarchy, Mrs. Varuṇa on a par with Mrs. Chernenko. Indrāṇī is at least also known later by her own name *Śacī,* and in a bawdy dialogue-hymn not only accuses a lecherous simian family friend Vṛṣākapi 'Male Monkey' of having insulted her sex appeal but is downright unladylike in flaunting it in words (*RV* 10.86.6): "There is no woman more fair-assed than I, nor better lubricated, nor more counterthrusting, nor a better thigh spreader." But only the Vasu circle offers a variety of more distinctive female deities, being the one segment of the overly male Vedic pantheon that somewhat prefigures the "strong goddesses" of later Hinduism (Devī, Kālī, Gangā, Durgā, etc.). In addition to Sūryā there is the dawn-goddess *Uṣā́s-,* the etymological cognate of the Greek *Ēṓs* and the Latin *Aurōra* (Indo-European *[*A*]*usṓs-,* from the same root as is seen in *vas-* 'shine'). Quite often referred to in the plural (as if she were somehow multiple), she is not quite like Eos with the latter's nymphomanic taste for young mortals (Tithonos, Kephalos, Kleitos, Orion), but she does afford the Vedic poets plenty of opportunity for rapturous description of sensuous, breast-baring feminity. Uṣās is notably the sister (*svásar-*) of the night-goddess *Nákt-* or *Rā́trī* and occurs in the devatā-dvandvas *Uṣā́sā-Náktā* or *Náktoṣā́sā,* or sometimes elliptically *Uṣā́sā* or *Náktā.* Together they are said to nurse a baby (or "calf") who is implicitly their joint son, or alternatively Night's son being nursed by Dawn, and who can only be the young sun-god, Sūrya, being nurtured and prepared for rapid daily maturity by his maternal aunt. This myth, which has important parallels in ancient Roman ritual (see chap. 9), lets us see a mythic genealogy: Uṣās (and presumably Rātrī) is the daughter of Dyaus (*Divó duhitā́),* Sūrya is Rātrī's (or her and Uṣās's joint) son, Sūryā is Sūrya's daughter, and Sūryā marries the *Divó nápātā,* the (grand)sons of her great-grandfather Dyaus. We glimpse here ancient and complex solar myth with sociotheological implications, even as in Indra's instance warlike and atmospheric figurations coalesced. Another important part of the mythologem is the theme of Uṣās's transitoriness, her daily welcome being predicated on her not overstaying it (*RV* 5.79.9: "Shine forth, daughter of Dyaus, do not drag out the task!"). Her tendency to temporize can turn her into a menace by holding back the day, and Indra the demon chaser has to intervene by shattering her chariot and driving her from the scene (*RV* 4.30.8–11). This "darker side of Dawn" is of Indo-Iranian and Indo-European age, for it survives in Roman ritual as well, and on the Iranian side in the Zoroastrian demoness *Būšyanstā* 'Futurity', that is, "What Will Be Will Be," the laissez-faire creature who sabotages daily progress by lulling people to sleep late and to put things off, to temporize and lapse into a *mañana* mentality; she has to be counteracted by the crowing of the sacred rooster Parōdarš and neutralized by the club of the war-god that Mithra has become in Iran upon the demonization of Indra (see chap. 6). The enmity of Indra toward Uṣās is paralleled by the hostilities of Indra and Sūrya, alluded to several times in the *Rig-Veda* (1.175.4, 4.28.2, 4.30.4, 5.29.10), where Indra prevails over Sūrya by removing or damaging a wheel of the solar chariot. Finally, Indra's antagonism vis-à-vis the Aśvins is a well-known theme, told at length in the *Mahābhārata* (Poona edition, 3.121–25) in the course of the story of the Aśvins' rejuvenation of Cyavana: Indra holds the Nāsatyas to be unworthy of partaking in the Soma ritual, but the grateful, reinvigorated Cyavana challenges him, defies his bolt, and by his ascetic power (as son of the great seer Bhṛgu and a brahmin magician in his own right) conjures up a demonic monster *Mada* 'Drunkenness, Intoxication', who coerces Indra into admitting the Aśvins, whereupon peace is made and Mada is neutralized by being parceled out over liquor, women, dice, and hunting, the four cardinal vices of ancient India to which he properly belongs anyway. This myth is of course colored by its classical rather than Vedic setting, involving the debasement of Indra and the stress on brahmin influence. But at its core may be discerned very ancient elements. The erstwhile blackballing and subsequent agonistic incorporation of the Aśvins into the ritual circle of the high gods is the paled Indic version of a well-known Indo-European theme of the "war of the divine classes," opposing the third-estate deities to those of the priestly and warrior levels, variously attested in Roman, Celtic, and Germanic traditions. The creation of Mada has a noteworthy counterpart in Norse myth in the figure of Kvasir (see further chap. 11).

Indra's successive run-ins with Uṣās, Sūrya, and the Aśvins are symptomatic of his general ascendancy, which reached its apogee during the high Vedic era only to decline thereafter. The naturists of the nineteenth century were unable to take a balanced view of these conflicts, instead resolving them in a dominant solar (Max Müller) or storm-god (Adalbert Kuhn) direction. They reflect tensions of the warrior class with both priests and cultivators but were misunderstood instead solely on the more symbolic level as sunlight versus storm clouds.

Aside from the "solar" ladies, only one goddess matters further, namely *Sárasvatī* 'Rich in Waters', identical with the mythical river of the same name. Her Vedic dossier is slight and unrewarding, but she is significant as a great female soil-based, fertility-oriented deity who seems to transcend the class-conscious male gods and to extend her patronage to the society at large, a kind observable in many other Indo-European mythologies starting with the Iranian. I shall call her the transfunctional goddess.

Apart from the obvious circle of Dyaus-descended divine characters discussed above, a vague tinge of "solarity" attaches to a number of deities. This is due to certain generalizing and syncretistic trends in Vedic theology itself, tendences that fatally beguiled Max Müller and his cohorts. Since the Vedic religion is predominantly "heavenly" and light oriented rather than chthonian and soil based, daylight and its chief source are naturally dominant in divine prosopography and iconography. Hence it is not difficult to find in hymnic lyricism sun-related descriptions of such generally beneficent gods as Mitra or Viṣṇu, or even of the Ādityas at large. There is the important divine figure *Savitár-* (literally a masculine agent noun 'Birther', from the same root as the noun *sū́s* 'bearer, birth giver, mother', denoting Vṛtra's dam in *RV* 1.32.9; cf. English *sow*), whom scholarship generally describes in solar terms. He in fact often appears syncretized with the sun-god and connected with Uṣās (e.g., *RV* 5.81), but in the same hymn and same breath he is identified with both Mitra and Pūṣan, in the very beginning of the following hymn he is called Bhaga (*RV* 5.82.1), and elsewhere he is counted among the Ādityas (*RV* 8.18.3). He further resembles the Āditya marriage patron Aryaman, for it is he who delivers the prototypical bride Sūryā to her mate in the great nuptial hymn *RV* 10.85(.9). His brahmanic importance is still visible in the invocation of him (*RV* 3.62.10) that is employed liturgically to this day in orthodox Hinduism. Thus the "solarity" is mostly a gloss and a poetic conceit; Savitar is rather a theologically induced beneficence originating with the Ādityas.

In *RV* 10.85.36, Bhaga, Aryaman, and Savitar are credited by the groom as bride givers, while Pūṣan (ibid., 37) is called upon to arouse the woman and prepare her for marital intercourse. Pūṣan has been artificially drawn into the fringes of the family of Dyaus, figuring occasionally as winning Sūryā's hand (*RV* 6.58.4), but his true nature is elsewhere. He recalls Aryaman by his involvement in roads and journeys (including bridal processions), with a gradual shift from hymeneal to psychopompous concerns (guiding the dead to the Otherworld). He is Sūrya's messenger (*RV* 6.58.3), bears the exclusive epithet *ā́ghṛṇi-*

'glowing', carries a cattle prod, and patronizes both livestock and wayfarers on ongoing as well as terminal journeys (*RV* 10.17.3, 6):

> Pūṣā́ tvetáś cyāvayatu pra vidvā́n ánaṣṭapaśur bhúvanasya gopā́ḥ. Sa tvetébhyaḥ pári dádat pitṛ́bhyaḥ.
>
> Let Pūṣan move you hence, the knowing one whose cattle perish not, the shepherd of creatures. He shall deliver you to these [fore]fathers.
>
> Prápathe pathā́m ajaniṣṭa Pūṣā́, prápathe diváḥ prápathe pṛthivyā́ḥ.
>
> On the far path of paths was Pūṣan born, on the far paths of heaven, on the far paths of earth!

Much in Pūṣan's dossier resembles the various functions of the Greek god Hermes (messenger, wayfarer, cattleman, psychopomp) and of Hermes' son Pan; the latter's name (*Pā́n* < *Pāṓn* < **Pāusṓn*) is related to *Pūṣán-* as, for example, *Ēṓs* 'Dawn' (< **Ā́usōs*) is to *Uṣā́s;* cf. the adjective *pūṣaryà-* (describing a bull in *RV* 10.106.5), cognate with Greek *pûar, pūós* 'beastings, colostrum', thus perhaps 'milkfed'. This would make *Pūṣán-* etymologically 'Nourisher', who brings cows to calving and into milk, even as he is called *puṣṭimbhará-* 'nurture bringer' in *RV* 4.3.7. The Indic-Greek parallel points here to an ancient Indo-European cattle-god whose role has come to transcend rangeland concerns and take in far-ranging nomadic horizons. Here is a true pastoralist's deity, and any "solar" traits are strictly secondary.

Not only are secondary sun-gods created, the rosters of real ones tend to change by retirement and replacement. In Greek myth there is the Titanic Hyperion eclipsed by Helios (cognate in name with *Sū́rya-* and English *sun*), but later on Apollo becomes more and more of a sun-god in syncretism with Helios. Behind Sūrya lurks the senior solar deity *Vivásvat-* (root *vas-* again!), of at least Indo-Iranian date (Iranian *Vīvahvant-*). He has mainly an ancestral role, collateral to that of Dyaus. In a famous myth, touched on in the *Rig-Veda* (10.17.1–2) and elaborated in later sources, Vivasvat married Tvaṣṭar's daugher *Saraṇyū́-* (sister of Triśiras) and begot twins, *Yamá-* 'Twin' and *Yamī́-* (feminine of same), a "first couple" who in *RV* 10.10 discuss the advisability of primal incest, which Yamī advocates but Yama rejects, thereby forgoing an anthropogonic role and instead ending up as ruler of the Otherworld; as the first mortal to colonize the place for all to follow, he is invoked in the funeral hymns (e.g., *RV* 10.14). An almost identically named Iranian male-female anthropogonic pair is attested, but there also the female twin soon evaporates into thin air, while Yama as the first man and first king is slated for much wider mythic glory than his Indic counterpart (see chap. 6). It seems that this Indo-Iranian male-female twin myth is of a trite and transitory anthropogonic kind, with the female a mere folkloristic foil to her brother; we are dealing basically with a primal mythic figure called "Twin" (whose twin, and why, will be speculated upon in chap. 17). As Vivasvat's and Saraṇyū's romance continues, she creates a double of herself, *Savarṇā* 'Same Looks', leaves the twins in her care, turns herself into a mare, and leaves. Vivasvat at first cannot tell the difference and begets *Mánu-* 'Man', the ancestor of mankind. Later he gets wise, turns himself into a stallion, sets out to find the equiform Saraṇyū, and sires on her the twin Aśvins, thus providing the latter with an alternative lineage to that from Dyaus, implying not only horsemanship but actual hippomorphism, a trait also found in the Greek Dioskouroi and such other horse-men as the Indic *Gandharvá-* and the Greek *Kéntauros*. The former were semidivine males with equine heads and human bodies, the latter were beings with a human head and torso mounted on the body of a horse. Both kinds were known for their unrestrained sexual appetites (Nessos, the ravisher of Herakles's wife, was a Centaur). The Gandharvas had as their female playmates the Apsarases (*a-psarás-* 'shameless, immodest'), a famous specimen being the fairy bride *Urváśī* 'Widely Lustful', who lived with the mortal Purūravas until the Gandharvas tricked him into breaking the tabu against letting her see him nude, and thus losing her. When he later espied the nymph in a lake, they exchanged recriminations, and she even ungraciously suggested that he was the oversexed one (*RV* 10.95.5: "Three times daily you stabbed me with your prick, and you filled me even when I had no desire"). Much of this is folklore rather than myth, but interestingly the birth story of the Centaurs involved Ixion mating with the Hera-double *Nephélē* 'Cloud' (cf. *Chāyā́* 'Reflection, Shadow' as the Saraṇyū-replica in post-Vedic tradition) and siring Kentauros, who then mated with mares to produce the Centaurs. We are here touching the borderline where true myth leaves off and frequently internationalized and diffused folktales take over.

We have now worked our way through the Vedic pantheon, with the exception of the two great gods who belong more in the cultic than the purely mythical sphere of tradition, Agni and Soma. Myths of any kind, and especially comparativistically significant ones, about these much-hymned cultic deities are few. Nor do they figure to any overriding extent in the great Vedic consecrational rituals (*aśvamedha, rājasūya, vājapeya*) that will be mentioned later in comparative contexts (see chaps. 9 and 15). They are, however, basic to the Vedic sacrificial rites, where the liturgy has encrusted them with an immense mass of symbolic and esoteric lore.

Agní- is one of the common Indo-European words for 'fire' (Latin *ignis,* Old Slavic *ognĭ,* Lithuanian *ugnìs*), the other being an ancient neuter noun seen in Hittite *pahhur,* Greek *pûr,* and English *fire*. Curiously it does not survive in Iranian, despite the prominence of fire worship. The myths associated with Agni's ritual are rarefied ones about his birth, loss, and recovery. Ancient matter may lurk in the crannies of this creative agglomeration by seer-poets, ranging from ritual detail (round altar for domestic fire, square for public worship—*aedes rotunda Vestae* [goddess of domesticity] in Rome vs. the normal *templum quadratum*) to side figures eclipsed by the greatness of the creatively inflated Agni. Such is notably *Apā̊m Nápāt* 'Offspring of the Waters', who in *RV* 2.35 and 10.30 is hymned as the fiery guardian spirit immanent in waters, who gives off light without fuel (*dīdā̊ya anidhmáḥ*), who shines forth (*ví bhāti*) clad in lightning (*vidyútaṁ vásānaḥ*), and who must be properly approached and propitiated by successful priestly drawers of water. The corresponding figure on the Iranian side, *Apam Napāt,* has considerable relevant myth, and the tradition of the fire-god in water also lives on in the Roman *Neptūnus* and the Irish god *Nechtan* (see chap. 16).

Just as Agni is both actual fire and the god embodying it, *Sóma-* is both a pressed liquid and its great inherent divinity. Iran has a cogent match in *Haoma* (see chap. 6). It is some kind of psychotropic, hallucinogenic plant extract, as the trancelike imagery of its numerous cult hymns clearly shows (the entire ninth mandala of the *Rig-Veda* is made up of Soma hymns). Colorful and violent visions are common, as are heightened feelings of omnipotence and immortality, the kind that fortified Indra for his great deeds. Concrete myth is scarce, the most notable being the story of the birth of Soma in a high (heavenly or mountainous) locale, to which an eagle carries Indra in order to acquire it for god- and mankind, losing only a feather in the process to its demonic guardian archer *Kṛśānu* (*RV* 4.26–27). This story has various vague parallels, such as Odin's aquiline recovery of mead (chap. 11) or Prometheus's theft of fire from heaven, but is especially reminiscent of the Mesopotamian tale of Etana, attested from Old Akkadian down to Neo-Assyrian sources (third and first millennium B.C.E.). It tells of Etana's blight of infertility, to be alleviated by a birth plant available only in heaven. Etana rescues an eagle from a snake pit and rides the bird to heaven in adventurous fashion, with a lost but inferentially successful outcome. Such parallels may not be sufficient to postulate Near Eastern diffusion to India, but they are more convincing than attempts to construct a putative Indo-European mythologem of heroic theft of a life elixir out of assorted "sun-birds" and "ambrosia cycles."

What was soma? After more than a century of modern research and a long series of plant candidates from rue to rhubarb, plus drugs ranging from alcohol to cannabis, the ethnobotanical investigations of R. Gordon Wasson have suggested a plausible answer (*Soma: Divine Mushroom of Immortality* [1968]; *Soma and the Fly-Agaric* [1972]). He identified the plant as the poisonous toadstool *Amanita muscaria,* which grows homorrhizally on the roots of birch trees at higher latitudes and elevations in Eurasia and is found only in some northwestern parts of North America. Its hallucinogen muscimol causes trance in flies and Siberian shamans alike; there are reports since the sixteenth century of shamans' not only using it for cultic purposes but of heightening the effect by drinking urine in which the substance has been excreted. Similarly there are Vedic references to Indra or men as pissing soma (*RV* 8.4.10, 9.74.4), and in 1978 Prime Minister Morarji Desai of India boasted on American television that he stayed healthy at an advanced age (next best thing to immortality!) by daily drinking his own urine. We have here a cultural phenomenon brought down to the subcontinent from the Eurasian north. No wonder the real thing became harder to obtain when the center of Indic culture moved southward from the Indus valley to the Yamunā-Ganges river system; already in the *Brāhmaṇas* there is much discussion of substitutes.

Apart from stray references to the likes of Indra and Viṣṇu, creation myths are clustered in the tenth (least ancient) mandala of the *Rig-Veda* and wax increasingly speculative and philosophical, from the most primitive, the sacrificial dismemberment by gods of the cosmic giant *Púruṣa-* 'Man' (*RV* 10.90), via *Viśvákarman-* 'All-maker' (*RV* 10.81–82) and the 'Golden Germ' or 'Lord of Creation' (*Hiraṇyagarbhá-, Prajā́pati-, RV* 10.121) to refined epistemological paradoxes on the relationship of being and nonbeing (*RV* 10.129). The *Puruṣasūkta* and the relevant anthropogonies of Yama and Manu are considered in chapter 17. Epicization of onetime inherited eschatology is treated in chapter 5.

Recommended Reading

O'Flaherty, Wendy D. *Hindu Myths: A Sourcebook Translated from the Sanskrit*. Baltimore: Penguin Books, 1975.

———. *The Rig Veda, an Anthology: One Hundred and Eight Hymns, Translated and Annotated*. New York: Penguin Books, 1982.

5 · Epic India

The five-century time span of roughly 800 to 300 B.C.E. effects the transition from Vedic to classical culture. Its early stages fit such tags as "later Vedic" or "post-Vedic," and the latter centuries qualify as "preclassical" or "early classical." It is punctuated by a series of crucial cultural events. About the sixth century B.C.E. India becomes literate. By 500 Gautama Siddhārtha preaches in Magadha and has launched Buddhism, in considerable measure beholden to post-Vedic Sāṁkhya and Yoga philosophies and thus presupposing the earlier rise of the latter. About 400 the activity of grammarians (notably Pāṇini) starts the codification of Sanskrit, which in the course of the next few centuries renders it both "classical" and literary or "dead," in favor of the varieties of folk speech (Prākrits, 'natural' or 'common' languages, vs. *saṃskṛtā* 'done over, contrived, refined'); among the Prākrits, Pāli was preferred by the lower-class missionary zeal of southern Buddhism. By 300, finally, India has entered history with the coming of the Greek ambassador to the Maurya court in Magadha. During the third century the Maurya emperor Aśoka extends his Buddhist rule over much of the subcontinent, leaving his edicts on rocks and pillars all over the realm (mostly in Prākrit; but even a Greek-Aramaic bilingual version has been found in Afghanistan).

Those centuries also mark the rise of the great epics. Although the *Mahābhārata* and the *Rāmāyaṇa* may not have reached their full-blown preserved shapes and scopes before the early centuries of our common era, the staging of their action and their basic creation antedate the middle of the first millennium B.C.E., as do the pre-Pāṇinean linguistic traits of Epic Sanskrit. The locales differ: the *Mahābhārata* takes place in the North Indian plains between the Yamunā and the Ganges, whereas the *Rāmāyaṇa* is centered farther to the east and is symptomatic of more advanced Indo-Aryan penetration of the subcontinent, with the action reaching all the way to Lankā (Ceylon). The *Mahābhārata* is more specifically "national" ("Great Bhārata", the latter an ancestral designation; cf. *Bhārat,* the Hindi name of India), while the *Rāmāyaṇa* has the kind of universal folkloristic appeal that has made it a staple of narrative, pictorial, and theatrical art all over Southeast Asia (but much of the *Mahābhārata,* too, was translated into Old Javanese about 1000 C.E.). Certain broad parallels can be drawn to the character of the *Iliad* versus the *Odyssey,* as a war epic centered on a showdown event in contrast to the far-flung and fantastic adventures of a name-hero. But the differences predominate, for the *Mahābhārata* in particular is always something more, something larger and more diffuse than any one definition can encompass.

It is the largest epic known to world literature, comprising anywhere from 78,000 to more than 100,000 couplets (depending on recension), mostly *ślokas* of thirty-two syllables (the Greek hexameter normally has fourteen to seventeen syllables, and the *Iliad* and the *Odyssey* have about 27,800 hexameters between them; hence the size ratio is about 6.5:1). Its eighteen *parvans* or "books" (plus the appendix *Harivaṁśa*) are of very unequal length, with some of the later ones verging on sketchiness. The climactic central event, the great battle of Kurukṣetra, with its preparations and cleanup operations, accounts for books 5–11, but even here there is room for lengthy excrescences, such as the *Bhagavadgītā,* which is a dialogue fitted into book 6. Book 3 is for the most part a vast collection of tales (including a mini-*Rāmāyaṇa*), and books 12–13 are an agglomeration of assorted encyclopedic advice and wisdom from the mouth of a slowly dying battlefield hero. Otherwise books 1–4 deal with the prelude of the main action and books 14–18 with its aftermath, ranging pretty nearly from Creation to posthumous paradise. The whole is cast within frame stories and narrated by various speakers, with overall authorship attributed to Kṛṣṇa Dvaipāyana, called Vyāsa 'Compiler' (on whom the Vedas are also foisted for good measure), himself paradoxically a figure in the epic. Thus we hear the entire battle sequence as described to the sidelined blind old king by his "eyes" Saṁjaya, who is preternaturally equipped with wide-angle, zoom, and infrared vision as well as long-range eavesdropping and recording devices, so that he can convey panoramic vistas, close-up detail, nighttime accounts of battlefield happenings, and long verbatim dialogues between distant participants.

What is the relevance of this monstrosity to mythology in general and comparative mythology in particular? In the most general terms, granted the encyclopedic nature of books 3, 12, and 13, it is bound to incorporate incidental matter of relevance. Unlike the Vedas it is secular in genre, which does not preclude the inclusion of a Viṣṇuite minibible, the *Bhagavadgītā*. All together it is a repository of enough ancient para-Vedic material to have earned in Indic antiquity the nickname "Fifth Veda" (in chap. 4 I had occasion to use its account of Cyavana and the Aśvins' admission to the Soma ritual). Along with the earlier *Brāhmaṇas* and the later *Purāṇas,* the *Mahābhārata* is an important link in the post-Vedic preservation, transmission, and elaboration of Indic mythical lore.

But even as we strip away all the padding, it remains to be determined where the main line of characters and story should be pegged on the scale of myth versus history. The setting is "real" enough, centered on the tribal kingdom of the Kurus in the northern plains of the "Indic Mesopotamia," the riverine interspace formed by the Ganges and Yamunā as they flow nearly parallel south from the Himālaya ('Abode of Snow'), subsequently turn southeast, and ultimately converge into an enlarged Ganges; downstream (east) from the confluence lay Kāśi (present-day Banaras), and farther down was the land of Magadha, scene of the Buddha and Megasthenes alike. To the south of Kuru country were the Vṛṣṇis or Yadus (with their stronghold of Mathurā on the Yamunā), west of them across the Yamunā the Matsyas, east of them on both banks of the Ganges were the Pañcālas, and farther south, beyond the now east-flowing Yamunā, lay the kingdom of Cedi.

Although the locale is firm, the "Book of Beginnings" (*Ādiparvan*) typically takes its time getting the protagonists into place and the action going. The authors of the *Mahābhārata* did little to deserve Horace's praise of Homer for plunging right in (*in medias res*) and not starting the *Iliad* from the 'twin egg' (*gemino ab ovo,* i.e., the birth of Helen and the Dioskouroi from Leda and the Swan back in Sparta). The *Mahābhārata* dawdles for well over a hundred pages of preface matter, summary descriptions of content, little previews, and frame stories with their own incrustations of legend, before getting down to the ancestral tales, tracing the line of the protagonists through the ages. This middle third of the *Ādiparvan* is a sort of self-contained chronicle-epic, where generations and happenings are lined up on a time axis rather than all being spread out in a vast synchronic tableau of events; thus the great action epic incorporates into its boundlessness even a specimen of the other genre, the chronicle type that we shall meet in Iran, Italy, Ireland, Scandinavia, and Russia.

But even here the narration proceeds jerkily, not as a true chronicle but spaced by the contrived queries of the frame story, at times in speedy summation, then again in detailed and leisurely episodic fashion, studded with repetitions and not in strict chronological order. With typical measurelessness we are provided comprehensive theogonies, demonogonies, and anthropogonies of Brahmanism, a host of incarnations, and a plethora of semidivine or miraculous births of the ancestors, down to the contemporaries of the main action of the *Mahābhārata*.

In the cradle of transmigration (*saṁsāra*) that is classical India, the device of incarnation assumed a life of its own, far beyond any Vedic inheritance. It was a convenient theological (and by extension literary) device for projecting divinity onto an earthly plane, individualizing a piece of godhead for its "human interest" value, causing avatars (literally 'descents') that mesh with mortality and yet retain their immanence and transcendence for repeated revelation. Thus the great god Viṣṇu was incarnated either theriomorphically (fish, tortoise, boar) or as a freakish (man-lion [Narasiṁha], dwarf) or relatively normal human being (Paraśurāma, Rāma, Kṛṣṇa), and a mighty demon might go through several careers as an earthly evildoer (e.g., Hiraṇyakaśipu, Rāvaṇa, and Śiśupāla, killed by Narasiṁha, Rāma, and Kṛṣṇa respectively). Such avatars are wholly apart from the folkloristic animal or human disguises gods occasionally don, usually for purposes of sexual coupling (Vivasvat or Poseidon turning into a stallion, Indra or Zeus impersonating the husband of Ahalyā or Alkmene). The incarnations provide important figures of the *Mahābhārata* (e.g., Bhīṣma, Kṛṣṇa, Draupadī), but the dynasty itself is explained on the whole as being merely of ultimate divine descent (not unlike Roman or "Holy Roman" emperors of other climes), liberally interspersed with additional lateral infusions of divine genes through the generations, usually on the male side (as in Greece), but with occasional childbearing by goddesses (e.g., Urvaśī with Purūravas, like Aphrodite with Anchises).

The line descends from Manu (son of Vivasvat and Savarṇā) via his daughter/son Iḷā 'Libation', claimed to be both mother and father of Purūravas, whose ultimately unhappy union with his fairy bride Urvaśī (see chap. 4) produced six sons, notably Āyus who begot Nahuṣa who begot Yayāti. Here the story expands into an elaborate body of legendry surrounding King Yayāti, his turbulent marriages to Devayānī (daughter of Kāvya Uśanas, sorcerer in service of the demons) and Śarmiṣṭhā (daughter of the demon-king Vṛṣaparvan), his five sons, the youngest of whom, Pūru, shoulders his father's old age for a millennium and therafter, restored to youth, succeeds Yayāti, Yayāti's subsequent posthumous fall from heaven into the company of his four grandsons, and his restoration to salvation by their pooled virtues. How he came by those grandsons, who were born to his here-unmentioned virgin daughter Mādhavī, is explained later in an incidental tale of book 5, a story of wide ramifications for the mythoepical underpinnings of Indo-European kingship (see chap. 14). There was clearly a wide body of folklore around Yayāti, ultimately of mythic origin, centering on the notion of a primeval sovereign who fell because of pride (hints of hybris attach also to Purūravas and, in the garbled tale of Indra's sinnings in book 5, involve Yayāti's father Nahuṣa as well).

After the eponymous Pūru, his Paurava line descends through a dozen or so gap-filling "begats" to Duḥṣanta, and here the epic expands once more into the tale of Duḥṣanta and Śakuntalā, anachronistically placed just ahead of Yayāti's chapter by the makers of the *Mahābhārata*. Duḥṣanta is described as an ideal ruler of the earth in an idyllic era. During a hunt he comes upon the forest hermitage of the renowned ascetic Kaṇva, in whose absence he is received by a young girl who introduces herself as Kaṇva's daughter. Duḥṣanta challenges her, because he is certain that the holy man "has never spilled his seed." The girl then recounts the true story of her parentage, which she had once overheard as Kaṇva told a fellow hermit. It epitomizes an ever-recurring theme of the *Mahābhārata* and classical India, the place and nature of brahmin asceticism in the total culture. Unlike Western monasticism, the stress is not on continence and mortification per se, but on a kind of creative tension. Indic ascetics are true athletes of austerity; they store up *tapas* 'heat' amounting to an accumulation of spiritual power that can even threaten the gods. But they stockpile sexual energy as well, and this pent-up force can on proper stimulation explode into gross eroticism and sensuality. Sex-crazed ascetics impregnating young girls are stock characters in this culture. Conversely, there is arrogant pride in abstinence; the same Prime Minister Desai who disclosed urine drinking as his recipe for longevity also boasted of not having had sex for many decades. Here is the girl's account: Viśvāmitra, an upwardly mobile ascetic (he was one of the rare men ever to be promoted from kṣatriya to brahmin), performs such awesome austerities that Indra himself feels threatened and sends the Apsaras Menakā to take him down a peg by seducing him. The nymph feels intimidated by the terrible-tempered holy man but finally agrees to perform a wind-assisted striptease in front of the sage. In no time the "bull among brahmins" lusts for the "good-assed nymph," as this "strictest of seers" sees her nude and clutching at her skirt. And so he begets a girl, whom the Apsaras abandons on a riverbank, where the saintly Kaṇva finds her. He names the foundling Śakuntalā and raises her at the hermitage.

King Duḥṣanta is overjoyed to hear all this, for the girl is by male bloodline a kṣatriya like himself, and he is hence eligible to marry her. He offers to do so on the spot and, when Śakuntalā temporizes for Kaṇva's return, delivers a lecture on various types of wedlock, informing her that marriage by free consent of the couple without the presence of a third party is legal for kṣatriyas. She consents, being promised that any son born will be Duḥṣanta's heir, they consummate the marriage, he leaves, and the returning, all-knowing Kaṇva blesses the match as proper. At the end of a protracted pregnancy of three years Bharata is born at the hermitage, and after assorted troubles he ultimately gains acceptance by Duḥṣanta and the right to royal succession. The freewill marriage of Śakuntalā points back all the way to Indo-European antiquity on the one hand (cf. the Old Roman marriage practices discussed in chap. 9), and her story has also become renowned in subsequent Indic literature (as in Kālidāsa's drama). Here, however, it points the dynasty forward via the eponymous Bharata. Several gap-filling Bhārata generations lead down to Saṁvaraṇa, who marries Vivasvat's daughter Tapatī (another side-infusion of divinity, right back to the beginnings!) and sires another eponym, Kuru. Thereupon half a dozen Kauravas bring the line to Śaṁtanu.

Here the lineage is approaching "contemporaneity" and gets more complicated. Śaṁtanu's father arranges for him to meet and marry the river goddess Gangā (= Ganges), on condition that he not question her identity or actions. Gangā had earlier promised Dyaus and seven other Vasu deities, who had been cursed by the wronged sage Vasiṣṭha (Varuṇa's son) to become incarnated as men, that she would bear them in her womb and then promptly drown their incarnations in her own waters, thus expeditiously shortening their humiliation. Gangā duly killed her sons by Śaṁtanu, but relented with the eighth (or, as a variant, bore a ninth), thus giving Śaṁtanu the son Devavrata, who came to be known as Bhīṣma. It was all foreordained: Gangā had so contracted with the Vasus, and it was contingent on Vasiṣṭha's curse itself, for he had doomed Dyaus alone as the chief culprit to undergo a lengthy incarnation as a man, yet without siring human offspring. Thus long-lived Bhīṣma, the old wise warrior of the *Mahābhārata,* is the explicit incarnation of the old sky-god Dyaus (see chap. 4).

After this intermezzo, Old Girl River just kept on flowing along, and Śaṁtanu turned toward the parallel stream of Yamunā for his sexual needs. On the Yamunā he smelled an overpowering perfume, and thereby hang other tales. The source of the fragrance was Satyavatī, with a history of her own. Her father was Vasu Uparicara, whose story is told earlier in book 1. He was not some Vasu divinity but a hero of the Paurava line, who with Indra's help had become king of Cedi. When he showed ascetic tendencies and retired to the forest, the gods worried about the potential power of his *tapas*. Rather than sending him a seductive Apsaras, however, Indra personally negotiated his return to worldliness with a set of divine gifts; besides a fadeproof lotus garland and a bamboo pole as talismanic ritualistic tokens of Indra's trust, he was given an airborne crystal chariot that he put to good use (hence the nickname Uparicara 'High-Flyer'). The rest of his life story casts him as a "universal monarch" (*samrāj*) who parallels Yayāti in several respects (five sons whom he spreads around other kingdoms and especially, as told in books 12, 13, and 14, his later sinning and fall from grace, not however from pride but rather for having truck with untruth, and not posthumously from heaven to earth but rather from his aeronautic conveyance into the ground; he too is saved, not however by any grandsons but by Viṣṇu). The story of Vasu, like that of Yayāti, is important for the reconstruction of a coherent Indo-Iranian **Yamá-,* as will be seen in chapter 6.

Here, however, we catch Vasu at an early stage of his career, as the young king of Cedi. His wife is Girikā, born of Vasu's hometown river, who had been raped by a nearby mountain. Once, when he is about to cohabit with Girikā, his apparitional ancestors interrupt him and inconsiderately order him to go hunting. (The dead are hungry!) He complies, but he ejaculates during the hunt and collects his semen on a leaf. An obliging kite is to fly it back home to Girikā but is attacked by another en route, and the leaf drops into the Yamunā, where it is swallowed by a curse-ridden Apsaras in fish form. She conveniently conceives, for only by bearing twins can she be freed from her pisciform predicament. Ten months later she is caught and opened up by fishermen, who find a boy and a girl and present them to the king. The Apsaras is off the hook, literally and figuratively, and Vasu unknowingly takes in his own brood. The son Matsya 'Fish' will become the eponymous founder of the Matsya tribe to the west, but the beautiful girl smells so fishy that she has to be turned back to fisherfolk. As a nubile oarswoman she is seen on the river by the saintly ascetic Parāśara, who is touring the local hermitages. He imperiously desires her; like Poseidon in Homer he creates a misty boudoir for their privacy, vows to restore her virginity (lest father find out), promises to deodorize her, and has his way. As he departs for his next devotional appointment, she is left perfumed and pregnant and gives birth the same day to Vyāsa, the great Compiler who is to become the maker of the *Mahābhārata*. It is after this incident that Śaṁtanu smells the fragrance and tracks down its source. Satyavatī's fisher-father will consent to a marriage only if Satyavatī's son will have exclusive rights to royal succession. Śaṁtanu cannot do this to his son Devavrata and grieves instead, whereupon the son himself magnanimously negotiates the match, not only forgoing his primogeniture but vowing to remain without offspring who might later challenge the succession (not knowing that the pact of Gangā and the Vasus had barred him from having progeny anyway). For these superhuman renunciations he is dubbed Bhīṣma 'Awesome', and Śaṁtanu grants him the boon of dying only by an act of his own will, something that Bhīṣma makes good (ab)use of later in the *Mahābhārata*.

Śaṁtanu and Satyavatī, at the ancestral seat of Hastinapura on the Ganges, had two sons, Citrāngada and Vicitravīrya. Both died young and childless, but Vicitravīrya left two widows. Under the rules of the levirate a dead man's brother could beget children in his name. The paternal half-brother Bhīṣma having taken a vow of celibacy, Satyavatī enlisted the maternal one, her son Vyāsa. Before the great ascetic could compose the *Mahābhārata,* he had to buckle down to siring its protagonists! He was glad to oblige, but the two widows were aghast at their hairy and smelly partner: one shut her eyes and the other blanched during the enforced insemination. In the true tradition of old wives' pregnancy lore, one bore the blind son Dhṛtarāṣṭra and the other the pale-faced Pāṇḍu 'Pallid'. When mother-in-law Satyavatī tried to breed the first widow a second time, she stealthily substituted as proxy a śūdra girl who bore the half-breed Vidura. The three half-brothers were accordingly not dynastic mainliners at all, being descended from the Pauravas only through their paternal grandmother Satyavatī, the daughter of Vasu Uparicara, whose sperm had landed inside on ichthyomorph Apsaras. They were brought up by Bhīṣma as regent. Pāṇḍu excelled in archery, Dhṛtarāṣṭra in physical strength, and Vidura in law and sagacity. Pāṇḍu was designated to become king, the others being disqualified by blindness and by half-caste status.

Consulting with Vidura, who early on acquired a reputation as a wise and discreet adviser in general and marriage consultant in particular, Bhīṣma set out to find wives for the other brothers. For Dhṛtarāṣṭra he negotiated the princess Gāndhārī, who resolved always to wear a blindfold out of sympathy for her husband's disability. She had been endowed with the boon of bearing a hundred sons. Pāṇḍu first married the Yadu chieftain's daughter Pṛthā, better known as Kuntī. Her story is told repeatedly, first in book 1 and later at length in book 3. As a young girl she had well pleased an "awesome and dreadful brahmin of strict vows," who in appreciation supplied her with a spell for summoning up gods at will to beget children on her. Out of girlish curiosity she had called upon the sun-god Sūrya, who had come in all his splendor and, despite her terrified second thoughts, gotten her with child. A son was born with a miraculous gleaming breastplate and earrings, to be known as Karṇa 'Ear'. Kuntī disconsolately floated the baby downriver in a basket, whence it was rescued by a coachman's wife, to grow up around Dhṛtarāṣṭra's court as a foundling of unknown (hence suspect) parentage. Despite this youthful indiscretion, Kuntī now became Pāṇḍu's virginal bride, her maidenhead having been restored by Sūrya. Bhīṣma also bought Pāṇḍu a second wife, Mādrī. After a series of punitive military expeditions Pāṇḍu retired to an idyllic life as a woodsman in the company of his two wives, running his kingdom by remote control. Gāndhārī, meanwhile, after a two-year pregnancy, aborted a huge blob of flesh that was divided into one hundred pieces and hatched in individual pots. Thus were born the hundred sons of Dhṛtarāṣṭra, notably Duryodhana and Duḥśāsana, the archvillains of the plot to follow (many of their names have the pejorative prefix *Duṣ-*, antonymic to the usual *Su-* 'good, well'). Bad omens attended Duryodhana's birth, and sages advised doing away with the child, but Dhṛtarāṣṭra, with an irresolution that was to become characteristic, demurred. Pāṇḍu, meanwhile, had shot a buck in the act of copulation, who turned out to be a mighty ascetic in theriomorphic disguise; with his dying breath he condemned Pāṇḍu himself to perish if he ever engaged in sex. Thus reduced to impotence on pain of death, Pāṇḍu had to find other means of perpetuating his dynasty. Here Kuntī's spell came in handy; in close consultation with her husband she conceived Yudhiṣṭhira 'Steady in Battle' by the god Dharma, Bhīma 'Terrible' by Vāyu, and Arjuna 'Shiny, White' by Indra. She then lent her mantra to her cowife Mādrī, who invoked the Aśvins to father the twins Nakula and Sahadeva. Pāṇḍu thus put together a happy family, but one spring day in the woods he was overcome with lust for Mādrī, forgot himself, forcibly penetrated her, and fell dead. Mādrī dutifully committed suttee on his funeral pyre.

With the five Pāṇḍavas and the hundred Kauravas now in place, the action proper of the epic begins, starting with the boyhood stories of the two sets of cousins as they are brought up together by Dhṛtarāṣṭra, who now rules despite his blindness with the help of the ageless Bhīṣma. Childish horseplay soon takes vicious turns, as Duryodhana tries to drown and poison Bhīma. Great tutors are engaged for the unruly boys—Kṛpa and Droṇa, whose birth tales continue the litany of lecherous holy men ejaculating at the sight of heavenly nymphs. The Pāṇḍavas make good athletic progress—notably Bhīma in wrestling and Arjuna in archery—but animosities increase, and Arjuna and Karṇa have a tense showdown during a tournament after Bhīma insults Karṇa about his supposed low-class origin, as Indra and Sūrya shower rain and sunshine on their jousting sons in a supernatural show of paternal support. The Pāṇḍavas are clear popular favorites, but Duryodhana engineers their temporary sojourn away from the seat of power and even plots to cremate them and their mother Kuntī in combustible lodgings. Saved by Vidura's providential warnings, they escape to the woods. A minor "forest book" is intercalated here, comprising encounters with demons and retrospective tales (Tapatī, Vasiṣṭha), until our heroes make their way, in brahmin disguise, to the "self-choice" (*svayaṁvara,* i.e., husband selection) of the Pañcālas princess Draupadī. Arjuna alone of the assembled wooers passes the crucial bow-shooting test and, after an incognito run-in with Karṇa, walks off with the bride, who becomes the joint wife of the five Pāṇḍavas (with daily renewable virginity). A weak folkloristic explanation (inadvertent and misspoken but binding words by Mother Kuntī) is given for such *an-ārya* polyandry. The brothers also make the acquaintance of the Yadu (or Yādava) princes Kṛṣṇa and Balarāma, sons of Kuntī's brother Vasudeva. After the wedding in Drupada's kingdom word gets out that the Pāṇḍavas are well and are maritally allied to the Pañcālas. Duryodhana and Karṇa are frantic, and the weak-willed weathervane Dhṛtarāṣṭra is as wishy-washy as ever, but Bhīṣma, Droṇa, and Vidura advocate recall and conciliation. The Pāṇḍavas return and are awarded half the kingdom, where they found Indraprastha, the future Delhi, on the banks of the Yamunā, some sixty miles southwest of Hastinapura. Yudhiṣṭhira rules, while Arjuna has assorted forest adventures and ends up marrying (on top of his 20 percent share of Draupadī) Kṛṣṇa's sister Subhadrā, on whom he sires Abhimanyu. Book 1 ends with a kind of theomachy, in which Arjuna and Kṛṣṇa confront gods and demons in the frame of a great forest fire.

Book 2 is much shorter and more schematic. Yudhiṣṭhira constructs a great palace at Indraprastha and plans a royal consecration (*rājasūya).* Kṛṣṇa advises him that one more threat exists to his sovereignty, King Jarāsaṁdha of Magadha, who with the help of his marshal Śiśupāla, has become *samrāj* and has in fact captured and imprisoned a large number of lesser kings, intending them as human sacrifices to his divine patron Śiva. An expedition is mounted, Bhīma kills Jarāsaṁdha in an extended wrestling match, the kings are freed, and Yudhiṣṭhira's path to world sovereignty is open. His four brothers secure the allegiance of the four corners of the earth, and all kings are summoned to the consecration. The laws of hospitality require the designation of a guest of honor, and on Bhīṣma's nomination the award goes to Kṛṣṇa, whom Bhīṣma knows to be Viṣṇu incarnate. At this Śiśupāla of Cedi, who was born with the marks of Śiva, demurs vehemently, because Kṛṣṇa is not even a king, and escalates the quarrel to a point of no return, until Kṛṣṇa (alias Viṣṇu) decapitates him with his discus and, as Universal God, absorbs his essence into his own being. These extraordinary traditions about Jarāsaṁdha + Śiśupāla reflect transmuted ancient Indo-European warrior myths attested also in Greece and Scandinavia, in the figures of Herakles and Starkaðr in their dealings with gods (see chap. 13). After this incident the ceremony goes off as scheduled. Back home the envious Duryodhana, abetted by a crooked gambler friend, prevails on his ever-vacillating father to invite the Pāṇḍavas for a "friendly" visit. Once there, the "Law-King" (Dharmarāja) Yudhiṣṭhira succumbs to his one tragic flaw, the gambling urge that was one of the cardinal vices of ancient India (starting with the "Gambler's Lament," *RV* 10.34). As the dice game proceeds, the king succesively loses his wealth, his kingdom, his brothers, and in the end Draupadī, whereupon Duḥśāsana drags her by the hair into the hall, despite her protestations that she is having her period. He rips off her garment, which is magically replaced, shielding her nakedness, while Bhīma vows that he will drink Duḥśāsana's blood. Upset by the brutality, Dhṛtarāṣṭra has a momentary fit of willpower and declares the crooked game void, allowing the guests to depart. Yet still bitten by the gambling bug, Yudhiṣṭhira heeds a later repeat invitation and loses on lesser stakes: twelve years' exile and one further incognito year. Amid portents of disasters to come, the Pāṇḍavas depart for a forest on the river Sarasvatī.

In book 3 (*Vanaparvan*, 'Forest Book'), despite its length (about 17,500 couplets), there is hardly any action (except for a brief abduction of Draupadī), the twelve-year exile being filled with assorted excuses for story telling such as the tales of the lovers Nala and Damayantī, of the great sage Agastya (already in *RV* 1.179; a match for Viśvāmitra and Vasiṣṭha) with his unique digestive capabilities, of Ṛśyaśṛnga (a precursor of the unicorn legend), of Cyavana and Sukanyā (mentioned in chap. 4), and of the Fish, the Flood, and Manu, and of Rāma and Sītā.

For their year of disguise (book 4) the brothers choose the court of the Matsya king Virāṭa, where they pass themselves off as itinerant, unemployed sometime household staff of the Pāṇḍavas. The king engages Yudhiṣṭhira as a brahmin gamester, Bhīma as butcher-cook and athlete, Arjuna as a transvestite dance teacher, and Nakula and Sahadeva as horse groom and cattleman respectively; Draupadī becomes maidservant to the queen. They manage to get by well as humble folk, supplementing their wages by secondhand dealings in food and clothing. Virāṭa's marshal and brother-in-law Kīcaka importunes Draupadī but is wrestled and killed by the mayhem specialist Bhīma, who pushes his limbs into his trunk, which leads to assorted unpleasantness involving Kīcaka's kinsmen. Soon the Matsya country suffers two invasions, the second by the cattle-raiding Kauravas themselves, and the Pāṇḍavas (still in disguise) mount a valiant defense of their master Virāṭa in a battle scenario that is a kind of abbreviated dress rehearsal for the big event to come, especially pitting Arjuna successively against Kṛpa, Droṇa's son Aśvatthāman, Karṇa, Bhīṣma, and Duryodhana. When it is over, the victorious Pāṇḍavas shed their disguises, and the grateful Virāṭa offers Arjuna his daughter Uttarā, whom Arjuna reserves as bride for his son Abhimanyu.

Book 5 is heavily laced with incidental tales (such as those of Yayāti and Mādhavī and of Indra's misdeeds, mentioned earlier) but also lays the groundwork for the showdown. The Pāṇḍavas lay claim to their erstwhile holdings while starting war preparations. Kṛṣṇa joins them as a noncombatant, and they can count on the Pañcālas and the Matsyas, on Cedi and Magadha, among others. The more remote easterly, northerly, and westerly tribes side with the Kauravas. There follow protracted negotiations, with embassies back and forth, interspersed with lengthy soul-searchings and consultations by the troubled and weak-willed

Dhṛtarāṣṭra, since he and the moderate party (Vidura, Bhīṣma, Droṇa) are up against the increasingly maniacal intransigence of Duryodhana and Karṇa. Kṛṣṇa as the Pāṇḍavas' ambassador conducts a final climactic peace mission to Hastinapura, complete with pleadings, threats, and even an awesome vision of himself as the avatar of the Universal God, but Duryodhana's terminal fatuity stays unshakable. With the help of Kuntī, Kṛṣṇa tries to sway Karṇa by revealing his true origin as a half-brother of the Pāṇḍavas, but the stubborn solar son merely promises his mother to fight only Arjuna, while sparing her other Pāṇḍava sons. Kṛṣṇa then reports back that war is inevitable. Bhīṣma is installed as Kaurava supreme commander, while Yudhiṣṭhira appoints Draupadī's brother, the Pañcāla Dhṛṣṭadyumna. The book ends with Bhīṣma's declared resolve not to fight the strange figure of Śikhandin (a woman transformed into a man), the complex tale that has brought him to this tabuistic refusal, and the marching of the vast armies toward the battlefield of Kurukṣetra.

Books 6–10 describe the eighteen-day battle, as reported to the blind Dhṛtarāṣṭra by his confidant Saṁjaya. For all its ferocity, it remains a gentleman's war, observing banker's hours of combat and with considerable civility during the intervals. Even before the start, Arjuna turns fainthearted in the face of this intrafamily massacre, and it takes his charioteer Kṛṣṇa's lengthy sermon of the *Bhagavadgītā* "Blessed's Song" to restore his resolve, including a terrifying vision of Kṛṣṇa-Viṣṇu as "like unto a thousand suns" and as "death, ripe to bring ruin to the world." Ten days under Bhīṣma's command end when the ageless one himself spills to Yudhiṣṭhira the secret of Śikhandin, after which he is cut down by a shower of arrows. He thus makes use of his privilege to die on his own terms, and emphatically so, for he is not yet through: propped up on the arrows that penetrate his body, he watches the rest of the battle like a reclining Saint Sebastian and waits for his turn to fill up books 12–13 with his interminable Mirror for Royalty; compared with this longest deathbed sermon on record, Homer's long-winded old man Nestor was a paragon of laconism.

Droṇa assumes command in book 7 but, disconsolate over faked news of the death of his son Aśvatthāman, drops his guard and is killed by Dhṛṣtadyumna. Karṇa takes over in book 8 and is slain after a great duel with Arjuna. Mādrī's brother Śalya succeeds but is killed in book 9, after which Bhīma confronts Duryodhana and fulfills his earlier vow to crush his thighs, having also had the satisfaction of clubbing down

Duḥśāsana, cutting open his chest, and drinking his blood. With this the Pāṇḍavas have triumphed.

But not quite. In book 10 three surviving enemy warriors, led by Droṇa's son Aśvatthāman, who is inspired by and practically an incarnation of Śiva, invade the Pāṇḍava camp accompanied by a host of phantasmagoric monsters and butcher the sleeping warriors, including Dhṛṣṭadyumna and the five sons of the Pāṇḍavas by Draupadī. The Pāṇḍavas themselves and Kṛṣṇa escape by being elsewhere. After reporting his success to the dying Duryodhana, Aśvatthāman is confronted in the forest by our surviving heroes and neutralized in the course of a showdown that pits the beneficent might of Kṛṣṇa-Viṣṇu against the malevolence of Aśvatthāman-Śiva.

In the remaining books, Dhṛtarāṣṭra and the Pāṇḍavas are reconciled, the dead are buried, and Yudhiṣṭhira is persuaded to reign at Hastinapura, is subjected to the dying Bhīṣma's endless sermons, and celebrates the great horse sacrifice (*aśvamedha*) that is one ritual form of regal consolidation. After helping him for many years, the old uncles Vidura and Dhṛtarāṣṭra, along with the latter's wife Gāndhārī and Queen Mother Kuntī, retire to the forest. Vidura, dying, transfuses his being into Yudhiṣṭhira (a mystical operation that would hardly raise an eyebrow in India), while the others perish in a forest fire. Kṛṣṇa (who had been cursed by Gāndhārī at the close of the war) and his Yadu tribe also fall on evil days, with internecine killings topped off by Kṛṣṇa's being shot in the woods by the hunter Jarā 'Old Age'. When Yudhiṣṭhira himself is ready to retire, he installs as ruler Arjuna's grandson (Abhimanyu's son) Parīkṣit and sets out with his brothers and Draupadī on a long march beyond the Himālaya, toward the mythical Mount Meru and Heaven (*svarga*). Draupadī, Nakula, Sahadeva, Arjuna, and Bhīma successively collapse en route, but Yudhiṣṭhira makes it, accompanied by a faithful dog who turns out to be his father Dharma in disguise. Posthumous recognition scenes and celestial bliss conclude the epic. Parīkṣit's son Janamejaya is instrumental to the frame story within which the *Mahābhārata* is recited by the sage Vaiśampāyana, who had learned it from Vyāsa.

After this summary of the main line of the story we can better assess its mythological significance, both in the ancestral tales and in the action epic proper. We have clearly glimpsed ancient, embedded myth of Indo-European or Indo-Iranian relevance in and around such figures as Yayāti, Duḥṣanta, Vasu Uparicara, Bhīṣma, and Jarāsaṁdha. We have also been exposed to an inordinate number of miraculous boons, amorous ascetics, recyclable virgins, metamorphoses of all sorts, in short, the stock-in-trade of India's imaginative folklore. The somewhat cozy, even symbiotic Vedic opposition of gods and demons has passed from the stage of live religion, being replaced by a sectarian Vaiṣṇava : Śaiva antagonism. The *Mahābhārata* is in the main a Viṣṇuite work, and hence the only truly religious incarnation is that of Kṛṣṇa or, in a negative vein, of Śivaistic badmen such as Śiśupāla or Aśvatthāman. The other explicit incarnations like Bhīṣma, the many "sons of deities," and the superannuated gods themselves such as their "king" Indra are part of an epic, not a religious apparatus. But what is the genesis of this "epic apparatus"? Is it a historical tale of early dynasts in the Ganges-Yamunā riverland, overlaid with generous helpings of folklore, encrusted with a secularized divine setup in the manner of Homer, and further complicated by the omnipresence of avatars and incarnations in classical India? If it were so, any mythological interest would be late and secondary. Such a historicist approach has long been and is still prevalent but is worthless for the student of myth. While it is perfectly valid to study the *Mahābhārata* synchronically, as a self-contained expression of a certain period of Indic culture, diachronic historicism seems delusionary. Instead the *Mahābhārata* as a whole, in its genealogical structure, its protagonists, and its main action, points back to a mythic inheritance of Vedic, para-Vedic, pre-Vedic, Indo-Iranian, and ultimately Indo-European provenance.

The basic structure of the Pāṇḍavas bears this out. Though they themselves are "historically" kṣatriyas, their roster of divine fathers—Dharma, Vāyu, Indra, and the Aśvins—recalls the Vedic god lists of the three varṇas (e.g., *RV* 5.51.10, Ādityas, Indrā-Vāyū, Vasus) and thus comprehensively covers the Vedic pantheon (with the substitution of the classical abstraction Dharma for the obsolete Mitra). There is even a hint of pre-Vedic archaism in the placing of Vāyu over Indra, which is supported by Iranian data; Indra's ascendancy at the expense of Vāyu was a Vedic phenomenon that did not affect this para-Vedic structural relic of Indo-Iranian date. Here alone is proof that the *Mahābhārata* preserves mythical petrifacts that cannot be secondary incrustations, for later mythologizers would not have imposed obsolete structures that eluded them. A second blow to the historicist view is administered by the "scandalous" polyandry of Draupadī. A "sociological" interpretation invoking Dravidian influence is ruled out by the epic tradition itself, which found it intrinsically incomprehensible and resorted either to accidental sanction through word tabu or to convoluted theological explanations via the "sins of Indra" (the Pāṇḍavas were born of the shattered pieces of Indra's total glory,[1] which were deposited in several gods and reinvested in the wombs of Kuntī and Mādrī; thus they were piecemeal incarnations of the one Indra, and there was no real polyandry in Draupadī's [herself an incarnation of either Śrī 'Lady Luck' or of Mrs. Indra] marrying them jointly). The real explanation is again via theology of Indo-Iranian and Indo-European date, where the transfunctional goddess whom Draupadī reflects (see on Sarasvatī in chap. 4) spans the whole range of the compartmentalized male deities. Thus we have in reality an old pantheonic structure transposed to the level of heroic saga through the device of divine fatherhood. This is simply an Indic way of transposition through time, alternative to outright incarnation, unlike, for example, Greek heroes who may have divine fathers (Herakles) or be heroicized divine sons (Dioskouroi) but who do not serve as allonymous vessels for the epic transfusion of their divine originators.

Once this principle is established, it is possible to investigate figures and plot alike for the mythic prototypes of character and action, and optimally even to reconstruct elements of these prototypes back to the mythical level.

Yudhiṣṭhira's right-minded self-control and "saintliness," the club-wielding Bhīma's near-mindless brutality, the archer Arjuna's adventurous high-mindedness, the good looks and modest helpfulness of Nakula and Sahadeva all point to type concepts rather than individualized personalities. They are bundles of Vedic (or pre- or para-Vedic) theologems about the spheres of Mitra, Vāyu, Indra, and the Aśvins, secularized and epicized in a later milieu and fitted into the literary frame of a changed culture. They are kṣatriya brothers who act out roles ancestral to the brahmin and vaiśya classes as well, with all the tensions inherent in such cross-cutting (brahmin : kṣatriya rivalries, but also their basic solidarity as against the "lower class," seen in the maternity of Kuntī [marriage by *svayaṁvara*] vs. Mādrī [bartered wife in *vaiśya* fashion], and in the deferential attitude of the twins toward the older brothers). In

1. According to the *Mārkaṇḍeya-Purāṇa* (chap. 5) Indra lost his *tejas* 'sheen' for killing Triśiras, his *bala* 'strength' for treacherously slaying Vṛtra, and his *rūpa* 'looks' for impersonating Gautama in his seduction of Ahalyā (cf. under Indra in chap. 4). This triple set of transfunctional boons resembles such brahmin-inspired stock lists for the three varṇas as *dharma* 'law', *kāma* 'love', *artha* 'wealth', or *sattvam* 'truth', *rajas* 'passion', *tamas* 'dullness'.

their year-long masquerade at Virāṭa's court the brothers actually "sort out" their intrinsic natures in some degree: Yudhiṣṭhira readily chooses the disguise of a brahmin, while the twins easily dress up as vaiśyas; Bhīma and Arjuna must also hide their inherent kṣatriya nature, but they choose vocations that are only travesties of their true caste characteristics: "butcher" is after all a fit sobriquet for a brutal warrior, and Arjuna has merely exchanged his military finery, which harks back to his Vedic father Indra and his prancing Maruts, for the fancy drag of a eunuch dance master. Episodes of transvestism occur with other warrior figures as well, for example, the Greek Herakles at Omphale's court, Achilles on Skyros, and the Norse Thor dressing up as "bride" of the giant Thrymr.

It was noted in chapter 4 that the peculiar hymnic style of the *Rig-Veda* tended to invoke the Aśvins jointly and without differentiation, with only scant and allusive reference to their separate characteristics. The *Mahābhārata,* on the other hand, provides in its discursiveness data on the individualities of Nakula and Sahadeva that are not novelistic "character development" but reflect traits matched elsewhere (Iran, Greece) by the Indo-European Divine Twins. Nakula hires on as a horse specialist (just as the Greek Kastor was *hippódamos* 'horse tamer'), whereas Sahadeva is cattle oriented (even as Polydeukes was the sole victor in the twins' Arcadian cattle raid). When differentiation is in order Nakula is better looking, more warlike, more kṣatriya oriented, while Sahadeva is gentle, wise, and benevolent—in short, a kind of lower-echelon understudy of Yudhiṣṭhira himself (already *RV* 1.181.4 called one Aśvin [the original Horseman!] "victorious," while the other, the son of Dyaus, rated the epithet *subhága-* 'fortunate, blessed'). In such instances the evidence of the *Mahābhārata* either supplements or skirts Vedic information and points back to more remote Indo-Iranian and Indo-European vistas.

We glimpsed above snatches of the story of Karna—his miraculous birth as son of the youthful Kuntī by the sun-god Sūrya, his childhood as a foundling, his early antagonisms with the Pāṇḍavas and with Arjuna in particular ripening into mature hatred on the side of Duryodhana, hatred that neither Kṛṣṇa's nor Kuntī's representations could deflect, and his death at the hands of Arjuna in the great duel of book 8. He is an overt son of the sun, born wearing the stigmata of his sire (golden earrings and breastplate) and rendering him frequent and open homage. Sūrya beams down on him in his initial youthful joust with Arjuna, even as Indra showers rainy refreshment on his opponent. In short, Karṇa is the epicized transposition product of Sūrya. Sūrya, however, for all the solarity that permeates parts of the Vedic pantheon, is curiously deficient in myth. Just about the only item is the allusion to the hostilities of Indra and Sūrya mentioned in chapter 4, how Indra "stole" a wheel of Sūrya's chariot (*RV* 1.175.4, 4.30.4), how he "tore forward one wheel" and "made the other free to run" (*RV* 5.29.10), and how he "pressed down" the wheel (*RV* 4.28.2), all in the course of helping his heroic client Kutsa Ārjuneya. Similarly, in the climactic showdown between Karṇa and Arjuna in book 8, after many vicissitudes and the deployment of miraculous panoplies, after Arjuna shoots a magic arrow at Karṇa's chariot, Death (Kāla) announces that "the earth swallows the wheel," whereupon the left wheel falls into the ground and cripples the chariot. Karṇa exits, tries in vain to wrench the wheel loose, confronts Arjuna on foot, and is decapitated by another arrow. His death scene is bathed in the poetic imagery of the setting sun. This accordance is a splendid instance not only of mythic characters but also of actions transferred into epic narrative. Whether other traits of Karṇa reflect further lost Sūrya myths is less clear, but in his dual maternity there may lurk (under the typical Raglan type of hero legend) a hint of the joint motherhood of Sūrya by Night and Dawn (see chap. 4). Karṇa's epic character traits include stubbornness, boastfulness, and above all a boundless generosity, in itself a reflection of the sun that shines on the good and evil alike. In one episode, when Indra asks for his golden earrings and breastplate as alms, he unhesitatingly tears off these live parts of his anatomy and hands over the bloody specimens, thereby robbing himself of vital battlefield protection against Arjuna. Such matter may well be mythic reminiscence rather than epic invention.

In the explicit divine "paternity cases" or outright incarnations considered so far the Vedic Ādityas are notably absent (except for Dharma as reflecting Mitra), no doubt as a result of the swift decline of these abstractions in post-Vedic theology and tradition (Varuṇa had become a sea-god of little account). But it is still possible to discern transpositions, without the benefit of name tags. Thus Pāṇḍu reflects Varuṇa by his punitive inflictions, his remote-control government, his pallor, and his impotence (compare Varuṇa's vindictiveness, far-off cosmic abstractness, and ritual allusions to pallor and impotence alike, the latter probably afflictions symbolic of a shamanistic magician figure). Pāṇḍu is succeeded by the "Law King" Yudhiṣṭhira, even as in other chronicle-epics to be studied later (e.g., Roman, Russian) the peacemaker (Numa,

Oleg) follows upon the turbulent Magic Sovereign (Romulus, Rurik); thus in epicization the Varuṇa-Mitra pair is projected onto a diachronic dynastic plane.

Vidura, that specialist in interpersonal relations whom Bhīṣma consults early on about his brothers' marriages, who tries long and hard to mediate the quarrels of the cousins and to avert war, and who serves as a kind of minister of social harmony in Yudhiṣṭhira's postwar government, is an equally evident epic projection of Aryaman, the personification of Aryan family solidarity. When he finally fuses himself into Yudhiṣṭhira, piece by piece, this Yogic miracle is a mystic affirmation of an old truth of Vedic and pre-Vedic theology: Aryaman was a "satellite," a spin-off of Mitra, a "minor" Āditya hypostasized from the "major" one, and what was spun off can in the fullness of time be spun back into the Whole. Vidura is said to be an incarnation of Dharma;[2] since Dharma as a new abstraction (and father of Yudhiṣṭhira) replaced Mitra and his "satellites," this identification of Uncle Vidura is merely old wine in a new bottle.

Symmetry (Vidura : Aryaman as Dhṛtarāṣṭra : *x*) would now indicate an identification of Dhṛtarāṣṭra with the "minor" Āditya Bhaga, and the data bear this out. Bhaga the Vedic "Apportioner" is reflected in the preconflict and postwar role of Dhṛtarāṣṭra when he serves as a sort of chief disburser of handouts and honoraria under Pāṇḍu and Yudhiṣṭhira respectively. In para- and post-Vedic tradition, however, Bhaga was something more sinister than the divine paymaster of the Vedas; he was blind, thus Blind Fortune, the personification of inexorable fate and random chance alike, either evil, indifferent, or too weak to act. This aspect of Bhaga's theology is reflected in Dhṛtarāṣṭra's demeanor in crisis, when he pathetically vacillates between wrong and right, summons up an occasional modicum of willpower, but for the most part lets Duryodhana have his way and laments the tyranny of fate. This concept also paves the way for his rehabilitation after the debacle of Kurukṣetra and his reconciliation with the Pāṇḍavas, since in the last analysis it is futile to thwart the workings of Fate, incarnate or otherwise.

2. The story parallels Vasiṣṭha's curse on Dyaus to take mortal shape as Bhīṣma. The great ascetic Māṇḍavya, framed by criminals and unable to defend himself because of his vow of silence, was impaled by royal authority but stayed alive by might of austerity. Freed at length by the impressed king, he hied to Dharma and asked what karma or past act had caused his suffering. Informed that as a child he had stuck stalks up the rectums of locusts and in retribution had now himself suffered impalement by the anus, the outraged holy man cursed Dharma to a half-breed incarnation and legislated religious immunity from karma for childish misbehavior.

We saw above that Bhīṣma incarnates Dyaus, that Vedic *deus otiosus* who has a barely ancestral role but behind whom lurks the important Indo-European figure of the sky-god (see chap. 4). The strange story of Bhīṣma—birth from a great water deity, primordial avuncular role through three generations as procreation manager, guardian, and counselor rather than king or father, curious detachment in the great battle, despite being enemy commander, to the point of disclosing to Yudhiṣṭhira the means of killing him, voluntarily suspended death for observation and disclosure—all this bespeaks mythic matter presumably original to a para- and pre-Vedic Dyaus who had not yet been stripped of his mythical patrimony in the Rig-Vedic manner. The mythologems involved are in fact of Indo-European age, judging from their Germanic parallels involving the Norse god Heimdalr (see chap. 11). Thus the *Mahābhārata*'s epic matter can in given instances bypass the silence of the Vedas and tie in directly with other Indo-European mythic traditions.

The central plot of the *Mahābhārata* also has clear implications that transcend dynastic squabbles of early kingdoms. The enmity between the essentially noble Pāṇḍavas and their demonically infused Kaurava cousins has features of Vaiṣṇava-Śaiva sectarian strife, epitomized in the last-resort magical showdown between Kṛṣṇa and Aśvatthāman as Viṣṇu and Śiva incarnate in book 10, where they contend over the future embryos, and thus the very perpetuation, of the Pāṇḍava line. One is the preemptive Destroyer, the other emerges as the Savior who shall reanimate Arjuna's stillborn grandson Parīkṣit. Aśvatthāman bears the marks of the classical Śiva, while Kṛṣṇa, for all his Vaiṣṇava trappings, is older and more basic than merely the latest avatar of Viṣṇu: in the services he renders Indra's son Arjuna as the latter's charioteer there are echoes of the *Índrā-Víṣṇū* duality of the *Rig-Veda,* where the wide-striding Viṣṇu is the helpmate of Indra (see chap. 4). On a synchronic level, however, it is safe to say that the central plot is an epic transposition of he classical doctrine of the *yugas* or world ages, and especially of the eschatological turning point of their nadir, the *Kāli-yuga,* whose horrors cry out for cyclical annihilation and regeneration. But since, as we saw, various main actors (especially the Pāṇḍavas, Kṛṣṇa, and Bhīṣma) have clear preclassical mythical pedigrees, it is plausible to search for earlier roots of the showdown as well.

Vedic tradition is silent on eschatology. Bu there is good reason to push beyond India by the para-Vedic route and to view the climactic battle of Kurukṣetra as a transposition of an Indo-European myth of the final confrontation of the gods and their evil counterparts, an epicized equivalent of what appears in full cataclysmic authenticity elsewhere, in the Old Iranian one-to-one end struggle between divine and demonic entities, when the world is purified and transfigured in molten metal (see chap. 6), and in the Old Norse world-end story of Ragnarök (chap. 11). The latter resembles the *Mahābhārata* in protagonists, plot, and outcome. It is significant that two crucial divine actors of the Ragnarök-drama, Vīðarr and Heimdalr, were singled out above as the specific comparands of the Vedic Viṣṇu (incarnated as the Epic Kṛṣṇa) on the one hand (see chap. 4) and of the Epic Bhīṣma (as reflecting the para- and pre-Vedic Dyaus) on the other.

The structured similarities between the *Mabābhārata* and Old Norse traditions extend even further, involving the story of the battle of Brāvellir as told in Icelandic sagas and especially in books 7 and 8 of Saxo's *Gesta Danorum*. The accordances intimate not merely that mythical battle material was capable of separate epicizations in India and Scandinavia (while also surviving as world-end myth in Iran and Iceland), but that saga-epics had existed already in Indo-European times, complete with genealogical and action-related patterns, prehistoric common denominators handed down independently via Indo-Iranian and Germanic traditions. Of this kind are the warrior legends relating to Jarāsaṁdha + Śiśupāla (*Mahābhārata,* book 2, mentioned above), compared with the saga of Starkaðr in Saxo and Icelandic sources (see chap. 13). Such also are the complex, parallel three-generational tangles that precede and include the battles of Brāvellir (Swedish Bråvalla, allegedly fought between Swedes and Danes ca. 700 C.E.) and of Kurukṣetra:

Gesta Danorum: Drot was the mother of Hildiger by Gunnar and of the bastard Haldan by Borkar. Hildiger died. The princess Gurith had to perpetuate the Danish dynasty. She first rejected the ugly Haldan with his chronic ulcerated facial sore, but ultimately she married him. They had a son Harald.

Mahābhārata: Satyavatī was the mother of (Citrāngada and) Vicitravīrya by Śaṁtanu, having earlier given birth to the bastard Vyāsa, fathered by Parāśara. Vicitravīrya (like his brother) died. His two widows had to perpetuate the Kaurava dynasty. They were aghast at their hirsute and ugly partner Vyāsa but submitted to the insemination. Each bore a son, Dhṛtarāṣṭra and Pāṇḍu.

Gesta Danorum: Harald rebuilt Danish might, but in blind old age he had the great showdown of Bråvalla against his nephew (sister's son) Ring of Sweden. Great marshaling of forces and allies. Cataclysmic, apocalyptic battle description ("one might have thought that the whole of creation was in turmoil and had returned to ancient chaos . . ."). On the Danish side the great Frisian champion Ubbi was riddled with 144 arrows. Harald's retainer Bruni (Odin in mortal disguise) forsook him, swung the battle luck to Ring, and clubbed Harald to death with his own mace.

Mahābhārata: Pāṇḍu conquered widely but died, leaving blind old Dhṛtarāṣṭra to a great conflict with his nephews the Pāṇḍavas. Monstrous levies and battle sequences even beyond the call of martial hyperbole. On the Kaurava side, the great champion Bhīṣma was cut down and left suspended by a shower of arrows. Battle luck deserted Dhṛtarāṣṭra (himself the helpless embodiment of blind fate), and his two principal sons were clubbed down by the mace-wielding Bhīma, son of the god Vāyu.

Apart from a palpable Indic tendency to duplicate and proliferate characters, as opposed to the spareness of the Scandinavian framework, and various nonessential details, the only significant difference in the two accounts relates to the role of Odin at the end. This trait is anchored in Germanic martial theology, where Odin was the fickle and underhanded dispenser of war, as opposed to the more fatalistic "luck would have it" approach of the *Mahābhārata*. It thus seems that the ultimate sources of Indic epic take us back to rarefied, prehistoric Indo-European levels, where plots capable of independent survival were current as early as the fourth millennium B.C.E.

Tracing the descent of the *Mahābhārata* to an Indo-European past may seem somewhat like tracking the course of the river Ganges back to the heavens. But nothing is too fanciful in India, and the Ganges legend actually gets told in book 1 of the *Rāmāyaṇa*. Compared with the mind-boggling scope of the *Mahābhārata,* the *Rāmāyaṇa* is far more compact and cohesive, a mere 24,000 ślokas in seven books, attributed to the sage Vālmīki. Its somewhat more easterly locale (the Ikṣvāku tribe living in Kośala with its capital Ayodhyā east and north of the Ganges, and Videha even farther east) and "international" ramifications stretching down to Ceylon do not preclude rough contemporaneity with the *Mahābhārata,* and as a self-contained entity it may have been rounded out earlier; as I said above, the agglomerated *Vanaparvan* (book 3) of the *Mahābhārata* actually incorporates a summary, rather divergent Rāma epic. At least the nucleus comprising books 2–6 of the *Rāmāyaṇa* constitutes an ancient unit by itself, while the first and last books are somewhat awkward pre- and postfixes that stamp the work in the Vaiṣṇava mold and launch Rāma on his subsequent career as an important avatar of Viṣṇu. While there is, as we have seen, some evidence that Kṛṣṇa's identification with Viṣṇu is anchored in theology of the Vedic period and that he may hence have been an epic avatar of Viṣṇu before waxing great under the new theology, there is none for Rāma. His mythical background before "Viṣṇuization" was different. The name itself is commonplace: just like the frequent *Kṛṣṇá-* (cf., e.g., Kṛṣṇa Dvaipāyana, the real name of Vyāsa the Compiler), *Rāmá-* meant 'Black' and was the name of various heroes (we met above Paraśurāma, Viṣṇu's avatar before Rāma, and Kṛṣṇa's brother Bala-rāma), though perhaps equated with the adjective *rāma-* 'pleasing, charming' in folk-etymological association.

The beginnings of the *Rāmāyaṇa* are expectably laced with Viṣṇuite legendry, such as the tale, known also from various Purāṇic sources, of how Viṣṇu in his earlier dwarf avatar tricked a demon who had taken over the universe into allowing him a mere three steps and then instantly reinflated himself to retake the "three worlds" by his famous three strides. The cast of preliminary characters includes those two awesome ascetics mentioned earlier, Vasiṣṭha and Viśvāmitra; we are treated first to the story of their early conflict, also told repeatedly in the *Mahābhārata,* how King Viśvāmitra offended Vasiṣṭha by trying to rob him of his wonder cow, and how by mighty millennial austerities he ultimately won promotion to brahmindom and made his peace with Vasiṣṭha. Vasiṣṭha's eugenic ministrations relieve the barrenness of King Daśaratha's three wives Kaikeyī, Kausalyā, and Sumitrā, so that the sons Bharata, Rāma, and Lakṣmaṇa + Śatrughna are born respectively. Rāma and Lakṣmaṇa quickly hit it off, and they are entrusted by the king to Viśvāmitra, at whose hermitage Rāma first wins his spurs in demon slaying and is invested by the sage with hereditary weapons that go back to a legendary Kṛśāśva 'Lean Horse' (son-in-law of the creator figure Prajāpati), obscure but significant as the validator of the Indo-Iranian origin of the important Old Iranian hero Kṛsāspa (see chap. 6). Under Viśvāmitra's tutelage Rāma attends the *svayaṁvara* of the Videha princess *Sītā* 'Furrow', who had been born to King Janaka from the earth in the wake of his plow, and wins her in a bow-stringing contest (shades of Arjuna and Draupadī). Back home Rāma is designated heir apparent, only to see his hopes dashed on the eve of his consecration as a result of harem intrigue, when coqueen Kaikeyī retires to the "anger chamber" and by her sulking forces weak old Daśaratha to cancel the ceremony. On the basis of some old promise, Kaikeyī's son Bharata is to succeed instead, and Rāma gets fourteen years of exile (a baker's dozen compared with the Pāṇḍavas' twelve or thirteen). Ever the perfect Boy Scout, Rāma says "Yes, Father" and starts packing. Accompanied by Sītā and Lakṣmaṇa, he moves to the demon-infested Daṇḍaka forest, while back home Daśaratha grieves and dies, and Bharata, nobly refusing the succession but unable to induce Rāma's premature return from exile, places Rāma's shoes on the empty throne and rules as regent in his brother's name.

Back in the forest Rāma gears up for some serious demon hunting, after assembling an arsenal from Indra on the advice of Agastya, the great austere digestion champion chronicled in the *Vanaparvan*. His mass exterminations, and finally the indignities visited on a demoness named Śūrpaṇakhā, at length attract the attention of the latter's brother Rāvaṇa, the powerful archdemon of Lankā whose lecherous character sees possibilities in an abduction of Sītā. Rāvaṇa devises and executes a scheme to draw Rāma and Lakṣmaṇa away from the hermitage, gain access to Sītā in confidence-inspiring disguise, and spirit her off to Lankā in his airborne conveyance. The grieving Rāma now concludes a pact of assistance with the monkey-king Sugrīva and helps him vanquish his usurper-brother Vālin by shooting Vālin in the back. Sugrīva's henchman Hanuman carries out aerial surveillance of Lankā, and in the course of much extravagant folkloristic derring-do even manages a clandestine interview with Sītā. Bounding back to the mainland he briefs Rāma, who resolves to build a causeway to the island and attack Rāvaṇa head-on. There follows an extended free-for-all, less majestic than the ponderous goings-on at Kurukṣetra but even more bathed in the magic aura of martial fairy tales. In the finish Rāma kills Rāvaṇa at the end of a twenty-four-hour duel and recovers Sītā. Instead of a happy reunion, however, the priggish paragon finds her stained by her demonic surroundings, questions her fidelity, and pompously rejects her; such selfish cruelty resembles the treatment that Śakuntalā, the mother of Bharata, suffered at the hands of Duḥṣanta in book I of the *Mahābhārata*. The heartbroken Sītā, solemnly proclaiming her fidelity by an "act of truth," is vindicated by a fire ordeal; Agni himself certifies she is untainted, and the gods hail Rāma as Viṣṇu incarnate who has delivered them from Rāvaṇa. Rāma takes Sītā back, they pilot Rāvaṇa's airship to Ayodhyā, and Rāma is consecrated by Vasiṣṭha and reigns happily ever after.

Or almost. The final, tacked-on book 7 indulges in assorted flashbacks and irrelevancies involving Rāvaṇa and also spins on about Rāma and Sītā. Sītā has become pregnant, Rāma's pathological suspicions return, and he dismisses her once more. In a kind of frame story she bears twins at the hermitage of Vālmīki, who teaches the boys the *Rāmāyaṇa*, which they subsequently recite at a public ceremony. Rāma learns their identity and is about to put Sītā through a second public ordeal, when by another desperate "act of truth" she induces the ground to part and disappears in the arms of her mother the earth-goddess. (The Furrow returns to the soil!) Rāma, too, winds up his earthly career and reverts to the godhead of the all-encompassing Viṣṇu.

The self-righteous, humorless Rāma in all his virtue and purity resembles not a little the *pius Aeneas* of another clime and epic. The *Rāmāyaṇa* has made a great literary and artistic fortune in and beyond India, with innumerable spin-offs in the arts throughout Southeast Asia. It combines to perfection outlandish exotic appeal with the homely satisfaction of seeing the dragon get his due from an upright and noble paragon.

But what does it mean to the mythologist? I said above that the Vaiṣṇava trappings are a secondary gloss. A historicist would see in Rāma, as in Kṛṣṇa, another quasi-real tribal hero encrusted with legend. In fact, however, the personalities and the story of the *Rāmāyaṇa* are closely analogous to the Vedic myths of Indra. Rāma's closeness to Indra is even superficially palpable, for example, in Indra's magic weapons that Rāma stockpiles and in the war chariot he gets from Indra at a crucial juncture of the duel with Rāvaṇa. Rāma's underhanded, behind-the-back slaying of Vālin and his killing of Rāvaṇa are reminiscent of Indra's sneaky assault on Namuci and his murder of Triśiras. In Rāma's unchivalrous treatment of Śūrpaṇakhā and in his disgraceful repudiation of Sītā there are echoes of sexual villainy as well, thus completing the triple-sinner pattern. Hardly coincidentally, at Sītā's *svayaṁvara* Rāma stumbles over a rock that turns out to be Ahalyā, whom her husband Gautama had thus petrified for her adultery with Indra, and whom Rāma's kick liberates (see chap. 4). Rāma seems to be a folk version of Indra in a post-Vedic, agricultural milieu, unlike the patron of the Vedic pastoralists. Sītā appears in the *Rig-Veda* as the deified Furrow, and in later Vedic texts she is the genius of the plowed field, wife of Indra or

Parjanya. Rāvaṇa matches Vṛtra or Triśiras (Rāma actually kills a three-headed Triśiras in the poem), and significantly his son is called Indraśatru 'Indra Challenger', which is also an epithet of Vṛtra. Rāvaṇa's abduction and confinement of Sītā the Furrow are agriculturalist analogues to Vṛtra's and the Paṇis' rustling and sequestering of cattle. The high-flying and far-bounding Hanuman is called Māruti, being the son of the wind-god, an ally of Indra. Even as in the *Rig-Veda* Indra's emissary Saramā crosses the river Rasā to track down the hoard of the Paṇis, Hanuman crosses the sea to Lankā to find Sītā. All together, it appears that the prosopographic and topical models of the *Rāmāyaṇa* are transmuted replications of Vedic Indra myths, and that its primary relevance to Vedic and by extension Indo-Iranian mythology is hence without question.

As we have seen, post-Vedic India, particularly in its epic dimension, is just as crucial for comparative mythology as is the chronologically earlier and more archaic Vedic period. Vedic data provide the oldest theology, but the epics supply the narrative. The unique significance of Old India for comparative mythology lies in the triple preservation of myth, ritual, and saga as much as in its anchor position at one end of the Indo-European continuum. The treatments to follow will build their comparativistic dimension in large measure on the foundations laid in chapters 4 and 5.

Recommended Reading

Dumézil, Georges. "La terre soulagée." In *Mythe et épopée,* 1: 31–257. Paris: Gallimard, 1968 and later editions.

The Mahābhārata. Translated and edited by J. A. B. van Buitenen. Chicago: University of Chicago Press, book 1, 1973; books 2–3, 1975; books 4–5, 1978.

The Rāmāyana of Vālmīki. Introduction, translation, and annotation by Sheldon I. Pollock. Princeton: Princeton University Press, book 1, 1986.

6 · Ancient Iran

As I said above (chap. 3), Iranian habitation patterns have from earliest historical times spilled over the bounds of Iran. The recent preferential use of "Iran" over "Persia" actually entails a gain in comprehensiveness, for Iran (< **Āryānam*) potentially and etymologically covers Iranian-populated lands at large, whereas Persia is merely a pars pro toto term expanded from a single province (ancient Pārsa, modern Fars), even as Asia and Europe started out as names for small districts in western Anatolia and mainland Greece respectively. In the Indo-Iranian continuum, the Indic branch was soon confined to the subcontinent, whereas Iranians ended up occupying vast reaches extending from South Russian to Trans-Caspian steppes and from eastern Anatolia across the Iranian plateau and the Hindu Kush into the heart of Central Asia. Our information is of necessity haphazard and chronologically and topographically diverse. Those areas that abutted cradles of culture drew earlier historical notice. Political power first appeared in the sixth century B.C.E. in Pārsa in southwestern Iran (the modern Shiraz area), whence the Achaemenian dynasty, headquartered at Persepolis and Susa, operated an imperial string of satrapies for the next two centuries. These stretched to the Aegean and the Nile and used an adapted version of cuneiform writing in official inscriptions in the Old Persian language (jointly with other idioms of the multilingual empire: Akkadian, Elamite, Egyptian, Aramaic, Greek, Lycian). The monuments range in time from before Cyrus down through the several Artaxerxeses, and in spread from the great trilingual rock inscription of Darius I at Bisitun to the quadrilingual one found at Suez, where Darius commemorates his canal from the Nile to the Red Sea. As contemporary physical objects and documents they are exempt from transmissional corruption other than weathering, but in their often stereotypical formality they contain only limited information; the one on the sheer rock wall at Bisitun may have been intended for gods' eyes only, for it can be readily read only from a hovering aircraft.

In the Iranian northwest, the Scythians in South Russia had contacts with the Greek colonies on the north coast of the Euxine (Black) Sea and were chronicled in some depth by Herodotus in the fifth century B.C.E.; they even named that notorious body of water forever after (Old Iranian *axšaina-* 'dark blue', which the ancient Greeks folk etymologized as [Pontos] *A-xeinos* 'Inhospitable [Sea]' and appeasingly euphemized into *Eu-xeinos* 'Hospitable' [but Modern Greek again has *Mavri Thalassa* 'Black Sea']). A remnant of these ancient northern Iranians survives in the North Caucasian Ossetes, whose language and culture have preserved in the *Nart* epic a rich and comparativistically significant heroic lore.

Those Iranians deeper in the Eurasian interior had a longer road to literacy or literate notice by others. Cultural seepage started only in the wake of Alexander, with Indo-Greek and Indic Buddhist influences. During the Parthian (Arsacid) and Sasanian (third to seventh century C.E.) dynastic eras the political and by implication cultural center of gravity lay in western Iran, and it has stayed there during the Islamic period, creeping in the past millennium northward from Shiraz to Isfahan to Teheran up against the Elborz range, whose northern side (Mazandaran) slopes down to the Caspian.

And yet the wilds of (north)eastern Iran in the early first millennium B.C.E. spawned the most crucial cultural event of early Iranian history, the reforms of Zarathuštra, which changed the old religion. "The magus Zoroaster" (in Greek shape; also Zathraustes in Diodorus Siculus) was not unknown to the classical tradition (the word "magic" originates from the Iranian priestly title) but gained new popularity when the Zoroastrian holy writ, the *Avesta,* was published in France in 1771. Voltaire promptly dubbed it "execrable balderdash," but Zarathuštra's place in occidental culture was fortified, from Schikaneder's Sarastro in the libretto of *The Magic Flute* to Nietzsche's would-be superman-prophet. The "real" Zarathuštra is difficult to pin down in time and place, and the pious legendry of the *Avesta* is of limited help. The oldest parts of the *Avesta,* the *Gāthā* 'Song' hymns, are ascribed to his authorship, and their archaic dialect points to eastern Iran. His compound name, *Zarath-uštra-,* has 'camel' as its second part and may mean 'Camel Driver' (literally 'Drive Camel', a compound of the "spoilsport" type) or 'Old Camel'; his father and royal patron (Pouruš-āspa and Vištāspa) both bore typical compound Indo-European "horsey" names ('Dappled Horse' and 'Ready Horse'), like Sanskrit Bṛhad-aśva 'Great Horse' or Greek Agathippos 'Good Horse'. Scholars have seen in him everything from a hashish-using witch doctor of the shamanistic east to a polished courtier of the Achaemenian west (the father of Darius I also happened to be named Vištāspa [Greek Hystaspes]). Yet a sixth century B.C.E. date is much too late, in view of the Vedic-like linguistic and stylistic archaism of the *Gāthās,* the post-Zarathustrian compromise development of the reformed religion, and the fact that the Achaemenians were seemingly lackadaisical rote followers of the creed rather than having a fire-breathing prophet as court chaplain.

Nothing much is known of the early history of the *Avesta*. It was edited only in the Sasanian empire, in a defective script and abominable orthography of Aramaic origin, when Zoroastrianism was the aggressive state religion that persecuted Christians and Manicheans alike. Merely a quarter of the original has been preserved, comprising (apart from minor appendixes and remnants) three main divisions: *Yasna* 'Cult' or 'Liturgy' (seventy two chapters, including the *Gāthās* [= *Yasna* 28–34; 41–51, 53]), the twenty-one *Yašts* or 'Sacrificial Hymns' addressed to single (or occasionally multiple) deities, and the *Vidēvdāt* 'Anti-Demon Law', the only complete book (*nask*) of the *Avesta* to be preserved. Around this canonic text the Sasanians evolved their own secondary literature that lasted into the early Islamic period; preserved specimens include the encyclopedic *Dēnkart* 'Work of Religion' and the *Bundahišn* 'Foundation, Creation', which is a treatise on cosmology and eschatology.

Zarathuštra's world in eastern Iran (Bactria, Chorasmia) was one of nonurban pastoralism, not unlike the social background of the Vedic period in northwestern India. The society was divided into priests (*āthravan-*), warriors (*rathaeštar-*), and "herder-cattlemen" (*vāstryō-fšuyant-,* more "nomadic" sounding than the Vedic *vaíśya-,* which smacks of homesteading), with the later addition of an artisan class (*hūiti-*); but it never rigidified on the caste lines of India. The previously mentioned (chap. 3) linguistic, stylistic, poetic, and formulaic near matches between Rig-Vedic and Gāthic texts let us postulate an essential similarity of prereform religion as well. Testing such inferences requires a deconstruction of the Zoroastrian reforms and thus in the first place an understanding of the latter. The old religion of proto-Iranian and

Indo-Iranian heritage can be glimpsed through cracks in the Zoroastrian facade, inconsistencies, backtrackings, and compromises of its evolution that allow some measure of rollback, with Vedic tradition as a parallel data bank for control purposes.

The *Gāthās* are an exceedingly opaque extremist document by the prophet himself, one who (like Gautama the Buddha) may have come from the warrior class but had typically broken with the structure and was not afraid to take on the system by components or in its entirety. In his attack on the cruder aspects of the *haoma-* (Vedic *sóma-*) ritual he ranted at priest and warrior alike (*Yasna* 48.10): "When, O Mazdāh, will the warriors get the message? When will you crack down on this booze-urine whereby the mumbler-clergy wickedly bring on vomiting, as do the willfully evil rulers of the lands?"

One is reminded here of the soma-pissing (and presumably reingesting) Vedic priests (end of chap. 4). Zarathuštra's revulsion extended to the entire polytheistic setup of the old pantheon. In its place he constantly invokes his one god, Ahura Mazdāh 'Lord Wise', and constructs a new theological setup based on a dualistic opposition of Aša 'Truth' and Drug 'Lie' (cognate with German *Trug* 'deceit'), that is, true and false religion, or good and evil for short. The pairing itself is of Indo-Iranian age, for it matches the Vedic opposition of *ṛtá-* and *drúh-* (cf., e.g., *RV* 1.133.1, *ubhé punāmi ródasī ṛténa drúho dahāmi mahī́r* 'I cleanse both world halves by truth, I burn the great lies' [described as sorceresses]); but Zarathuštra polarized it and made it pivotal. In his system Aša and Drug were championed by Spənta Mainyu 'Beneficent Spirit' (cf. Lithuanian *šveñtas,* Old Church Slavic *svętŭ* 'holy', originally 'powerful', like Sanskrit *iṣirá-* 'strong' vs. Greek *hierós* 'sacred') and Angra Mainyu 'Evil Spirit' respectively; in later Zoroastrianism Spənta Mainyu faded, and Angra Mainyu was pitted against the supreme god directly, as Ohrmazd versus Ahriman. Other subordinate creatures of Ahura Mazda included a set of apparently new abstractions, called Aməša Spənta or 'Deathless Beneficents', sometimes referred to as "Archangels"; this is their canonical sequence, starting with characteristic attributes:

Cattle:	Vohu Manah	'Good Mind'	(= Sanskrit *vásu mánaḥ;* cf. Vedic *sumatíḥ* 'good thought, benevolence')
Fire:	Aša Vasišta	'Truth the Best'	(cf. Varuṇa's Ṛta and his seer-son Vasiṣṭha)

Metal:	Xšathra Vairya	'Rulerdom the Excellent'	(= Sanskrit *kṣatrám váryam*)
Earth:	Ārmaiti	'Right Thought'	(= Vedic *Arámati-*, called *gnā́ devī́* 'woman-goddess' in *RV* 5.43.6)
Waters and	Haurvatāt	'Wholeness, Health'	(= Vedic *sarvátāt,* Greek *holótēs* 'wholeness')
plants:	Amṛtāt	'Deathlessness, Long Life'	(cf. Vedic *amṛtatvám,* Greek *ambrosíā* 'immortality')

The *Gāthās* embroider endlessly on these abstract entities in disconcerting fashion, for example, *Yasna* 51.7:

Dāidī mōi yə gam tašō apasčā urvarāsčā
Amṛtātā Haurvātā Spəništā Mainyū Mazdā
təvīšī utayūiti Manaṅhā Vohū sənnhē

Give me, you who made the bovine and waters and plants,
Long Life and Health through the Most Beneficent Spirit, Wise One,
strength and endurance through the Good Mind, at the judgment

What, in the interim, happened to the old deities this list supplanted? Their eclipse was for the most part temporary, for the bulk of them are right back in there in the post-Gāthic *Yašts,* being hymned one by one. There were, however, some who never recovered from Zarathuštra's proscription and ended up in that pandemonium that is a mandatory part of any dualistic setup. The demonization took in especially two gods of the warrior class, Indara and Saurva (= Vedic Indra and Śarva, allonym of Rudra), and also Nāṅhaithya (= Vedic Nāsatya, one of the Aśvins). Other denizens of the pandemonium included Būšyanstā 'Temporizer' (the "Tarrying Dawn" we met in chap. 4) and such inherently evil abstractions as Drug 'Lie', Aēšma 'Fury', Āzi 'Greed', Apaoša 'Drought', Dužyāirya 'Crop Failure' (literally 'Bad Year'), and Nasu 'Dead Matter'. Still others were ambivalent demigods of Indo-Iranian ancestry, for example, Gandarəwa (= Sanskrit Gandharva). They are all known generically as *daēva-* 'demon', versus *ahura-* 'god, lord', whereas in India the development was exactly the opposite, *devá-* 'god' versus *ásura-* 'demon'. In Vedic *ásura-* was still a honorific designation of such great gods as Varuṇa, while *devá-* (= Latin *deus*) was more characteristic of the Indra type. The post-Vedic decline of the Ādityas must have promoted the pejoration of *ásura-,* while conversely

Zarathuštra's dim view of Indra's ilk precipitated the semantic decline of the term *daēva-*. In the Old Persian dialect of the Achaemenians *daiva-* was firmly 'demon', while the generic term for 'god' (such as Ahura Mazdāh) was *baga-* (cf. Vedic Bhaga and Old Church Slavic *bogŭ* 'god').

By implication it seems that Zarathuštra ought to have had a softer spot for the gods of the priestly class, the Iranian equivalents of the Vedic Ādityas, for these were already relatively abstract in kind, in line with the prophet's own proclivities. Such is in fact the case. One might even speak of their partial exaltation, for Ahura Mazdāh himself is the Iranian counterpart of the Vedic Varuṇa. No specific common name is attested, but both share the term *Asura, and Varuṇa is described as *médhira-* 'wise' in *RV* 1.25.20 (= Avestan *manzdra-*, Old Church Slavic *mǫdrŭ*, Russian *múdryj* 'wise'; Avestan *mazdā-* 'wise' formally matches Vedic *medhā́-* 'wisdom' < Indo-European **mn̥s-dhē̋-* 'mind setting' [adjective or noun], similar in kind to *k̂red-dhē̋-* 'heart setting' > Avestan *zrazdā-* 'trusting, faithful', Vedic *śraddhā́* 'trust, faith', Latin *crēdō* 'I place trust'). Aša (< Gāthic *arəta-* < Indo-Iranian **r̥tá-*) as his sublimated essence is the equivalent of the Vedic R̥ta, the cosmic order or norm or truth tended to by Varuṇa, but who is also (despite the neuter gender, R̥tam) listed as a god among gods (*RV* 1.75.5, 10.66.4). It occurs already theophorically in Mitanni names (Artatama, Artamanya) and quite possibly is the original Indo-Iranian abstraction out of which the deity has been theomorphized. Fire is Ahura's element, owing to the hypertrophy of fire worship in Iran (strangely, the old term for 'fire' [Sanskrit *agní-*] has vanished and been replaced by *ātar,* as in *āthravan-* '[fire–]priest').

Unlike Varuṇa, the Vedic Mitra has an exact onomastic counterpart in the Avestan Mithra. The basic sense of "Contract[or]" was established above in chapter 4. Much as in India the rather faded Mitra took on some solar characteristics and later came to be an appellative 'friend', in Modern Persian *mihr*, *mehr* still means both 'sun' and 'friendship'. Mithra is one of the most important Old Iranian divinities, the subject of *Yašt* 10 but unknown to the *Gāthās*. Zarathuštra has sublimated his essence into Vohu Manah, whose name embodies his essential benevolence and whose element was cattle, just as Mithra was the patron of the wide cow pastures (*vouru-gaoyaoiti-*) of the eastern Iranians. The ancient dvandva of the Vedic *Mitrā́-Váruṇā* survives on the Iranian side in the Avestan *Mithra-Ahura,* in the Old Persian **Miśa-Auramazdāh,* which is attested by Plutarch in Greek as a fossilized theonym *Mesoromasdēs,* and by such doubly theophorous later Persian names as *Mihrhormuz*. It shows (1) that Ahura Mazdāh does indeed belong in the slot of Varuṇa, (2) that the sequence of the Aməša Spəntas (Vohu Manah, Aša Vasišta) is not random but still reflects the canonic order of the Indo-Iranian gods, and (3) that Zarathuštra's exaltation of Ahura and onomastic suppression of Mithra were symptomatic of his henotheistic fervor that did not survive the reformer. It looks as if Mithra was fleetingly demonized by the prophet's reductionist and abstractionist zeal but reemerged once the religious revolution had run its course. Outside the onomastic formulas, the conjunction/contrast of Mithra and Ahura had of course collapsed, for Ahura was now a kind of pantheonic board chairman increasingly frozen in his polarized stance vis-à-vis Angra Mainyu, while it was left to Mithra to do the mythical dirty work. His roles have in fact expanded: on top of guarding human settlements and social compacts, he employs spies like Varuṇa and punishes perjurers and contract breakers, champions warriors, wields the thunderbolt and makes the rain fall (largely by default of the demonized Indara), and generally evolves toward a solar-tinged warrior-god not without connotations of cattle and fertility. When in the first century B.C.E. the Hellenized Mithras burst in on the Roman Empire, he was the centerpiece of a secret cult that extended its subterranean sanctuaries from Rome to Gaul to Germany to England. Mithras, born of a rock at the winter solstice, the Sol Invictus of the Roman legions and of the emperors Aurelian and Diocletian, in fact gave the rival sect of Christianity stiff competition until Constantine tipped the scales in the early fourth century C.E. Even so they remained wobbly through the reign of Julian the Apostate, and compromise or accommodation equated the Savior's birthday with that of Mithras (25 December). The cult images of the mithraeums depicted the young warrior-god seizing a bull by the nostrils and stabbing him in the heart, ears of grain sprouting from the wound and the tail, a dog lapping the blood, a scorpion attacking the bull's scrotum, and two mannikins with raised and sunken torch flanking the scene, which was often framed in zodiacal symbolism (see fig. 3). Despite all the differences, elements of the Iranian Mithra are present: warrior character, solarity, cattle relatedness, and promotion of growth. It may be that this Western Mithraism originated not in Zoroastrianism proper but rather among sects of *daēva* worshipers, for Mithraic iconography includes lion-headed statues sometimes dedicated (in Latin) *Deo Arimanio,* that is, Ahriman.

Of the Iranian counterparts of the Vedic "minor Ādityas" Aryaman

FIGURE 3. Mithraic cult scene from the Esquiline, Rome. Vatican Museum. (Reproduced by permission of Martinus Nijhoff Publishers, Dordrecht, The Netherlands.)

and Bhaga, Airyaman is absent from the *Gāthās* proper but does figure in an archaic Avestan prayer addressed to him repeatedly (*Yasna* 27.5, 54.1; *Vidēvdāt* 20.11), wherein he is invoked to help "Zarathuštra's men and women' with aid from Vohu Manah. Airyaman must thus have been allied with Mithra, for Vohu Manah is Zarathuštra's sublimate of Mithra. He was in charge of rituals of marriage and healing, mundane institutions of social welfare, but his cathartic function reached cosmic proportions in the eschatology, where he helps fire melt the metals for the purifying bath leading to transfiguration. *Baga-* survived only as a generic term for god, but Airyaman and *Baga may be further hidden under Zarathuštra's abstractions Sraoša 'Obedience, Discipline, Enforcement' (*Yašt* 11) and Aši 'Requital, Recompense, Retaliation' (*Yašt* 12). In *Yašt* 10 Sraoša escorts Mithra on the right, while on his left there is Rašnu (in itself a commonplace of areal mythology, for the Babylonian sun-god Šamaš and his syncretized Hittite counterpart both had viziers Mišaru 'Justice' and Bunene striding by their sides). *Rašnu-* is also a possible sublimate, a "meliorative" recasting of **Višnu-*, with a "constructive" prefix *ra-* 'aright' replacing the seemingly disruptive segment *vi-* 'asunder'. With the falling away of Indara and the moving of Mithra into the warrior slot, the wide strider's attachments were readjusted. The threesome Mithra, Sraoša, and Rašnu also figure as judges of the souls of the dead, with the "righteous Rašnu" as the special weigher of men's deeds.

While the gods of the priestly estate survived Zarathuštra's reforms fairly well, either directly or via sublimation (whereas the Vedic Ādityas later fell prey to such new abstractions as Dharma and Brahman), Zarathuštra's distaste for the warrior class caused him to subsume this entire level in one Aməša Spənta, Xšathra Vairya. Indara and Saurva were demonized, and we have picked up some of the other pieces (Mithra invading the vacuum, *Višnu > Rašnu cleaving to him instead of the discredited Indara). But two other warrior-gods, Vṛthragna (*Yašt* 14) and Vayu (*Yašt* 15), managed to make it past Zarathuštra. Vṛthragna or Vṛthragan 'Obstruction Smiter' was the god of victory (> Sasanian Vahrām or Bahrām; also borrowed as Armenian Vahagn and appearing in Hellenistic Greek as Artagnes), with ten mostly animal avatars. The name matches the Vedic *Vṛtrahán-* (occasional epithet of the Aśvins, Sarasvatī, Agni, and Soma, but especially of Indra as dragon killer, with Vṛtra abstracted as a secondary sobriquet for the three-headed monster Triśiras; cf. chap. 4). In Iran, too, the slayer of the three-headed dragon Dahāka was dubbed *vṛthraǰa taxmō Thraētaona 'vṛthra-*smiting heroic Thraētaona' (*Yašt* 5.61), which shows that the monstrous enemy was easily dubbed 'obstruction, obstacle', thus 'impediment, nuisance' (*vṛthragan-* occurs also with Sraoša, Haoma, Saošyant ['Savior'], and other triumphant entities on the side of the good creation). Presumably the pre-Zoroastrian Indara, too, rated this title. When Indara was demonized, his redeemable attributes were variously redistributed. His *vazra-* (= Indra's Vedic *vájra-*) and rainmaking fell to Mithra, the epithet Vṛthragna (formally a neuter noun, 'Obstruction Smiting', besides the agental *Vṛthragan* 'Obstruction Smiter') provided a new quasi-abstract deity, a pale slice of the "good Indara" perpetuating his qualities of animal metamorphosis, while dragon slaying was left to heroes such as Thraētaona (who also had the *vazra-*, for it reappears as the *gurz* of Thraētaona's epic self, Feridun; see chap. 7).

Vayu is also ambiguous. Of the eminence of the Indo-Iranian *Vāyu among the warrior-gods there is a hint in the Bhīma-Arjuna birth sequence of the *Mahābhārata* (see chap. 5), which transmuted into natal anteriority a para-Vedic hierarchic ranking of their divine sires Vāyu and Indra (unlike the Vedic dvandva *Índrā-Vāyū́)*. Indra clearly ascended at Vāyu's expense in Vedic India, whereas in Iran Vayu's pristine eminence shielded him from Zoroastrian condemnation. Vayu's stature is in fact astonishing; he is the first to receive sacrifices, and Ahura Mazdāh himself leads the list of his offerants in *Yašt* 15. As befits the wind, he is somehow in midair, between earth and heaven, neither here nor there, straddling this world and the Otherworld, traversing and filling the void between opposites. Such ambivalence was clearly at loggerheads with the Zoroastrian obsession for dualistic choice, and later theology saw to it that he was duly carved up between Ohrmazd and Ahriman, a good Vayu counterbalanced by an evil double.

The fourth Aməša Spənta, Ārmaiti, with the earth as her element, is the sublimate of the great Iranian goddess known as Anāhitā (Anaïtis in Greek). In fact she bore the triple name Arədvī Sūrā Anāhitā 'Moist, Heroic, Immaculate', embodying in her triplicity all three class divisions of society—soil based, warlike, and priestly. She is hymned in *Yašt* 5 as the furtherer of procreation, purifying the sperm of males and preparing the wombs of women, at the receiving end of a set sacrificial litany of a hundred stallions, a thousand cattle, and myriad sheep, offered by a long line of mythical heroes. Her appearance is, however, not that of midwife or amazon but rather of "a lovely young maiden whose girdle is raised high about her waist," "so that her breasts shall look well shaped and appear appealing." She matches the Vedic Sarasvatī and may in fact conceal beneath her triple epithets the Iranian equivalent Harahvaiti. The meaning is 'Rich in [Pools of] Water', which in India designates a river but in Iran is the name of a fertile province (Arachosia in Greek). Thus the female deity may appear as a great river or as the land itself (cf., e.g., the Russian Máti Syrá Zemljá 'Mother Moist Earth', or the Irish Ēriu). When about 60 B.C.E. King Antiochus of Commagene (son of Mithridates) set up his hierothesion or tomb ensemble on the conical top of the seven-thousand-foot mountain Nemrud Dagh in southern Turkey (see fig. 4), he traced his paternal ancestry to a Darius and his maternal descent to Alexander and ended up with colossal statues of syncretized Persian-Greek deities as follows:

Zeus *Ōromasdēs*
Apollōn *Mithras* Hēlios Hermēs

Artagnēs Hēraklēs Arēs
Emē Patris Pantotrophos Kommagēnē

Ahura Mazdāh, Mithra, Vṛthragna, and "My Fatherland All-Nourishing Commagene" appear here in rejuvenated Parthian-Hellenistic shape, with the Land itself occupying the slot of the goddess Anāhitā.

The last two Beneficents, the pair Haurvatāt-Amṛtāt, are Zarathuštra's substitutes for the Divine Twins. Of the latter, Nāṅhaithya, presumably the more warlike one (cf. the Vedic Nāsatya vs. Dasra, and Nakula vs. Sahadeva in the *Mahābhārata*), suffered explicit demonization. The water-and-plants association of Haurvatāt-Amṛtāt recalls the relation of the Vedic Aśvins to herbal cures and healing waters in the native Indic medical tradition (*āyurveda*). Unlike the other Aməša Spəntas, this pair with its jinglelike ring had a post-Gāthic future, as new names for the old Divine Twins, showing the thinness of Zarathuštra's overlay. There must have been enough myth even for export, since borrowed legends occur in Judaic and Arabic folklore, such as the story in the Koran (2.96) about a young woman who is pursued by the angels Hārūt and Mārūt and raised to the heavens by Allah as the planet Zohra (Venus). Other variants give her name as Anahīd, the planet Venus in astralized Iranian myth (Anāhitā having star associations as early as *Yašt* 5.85). The source is in Iranian myths about the Divine Twins, lost to us but matched by Indic parallels. The Aśvins not only jointly wooed Sūryā but were notorious for their pursuit of young women, as when they attempted to abduct Sukanyā from her decrepit ascetic husband Cyavana (instead they brought about Cyavana's rejuvenation and their own admission to the Soma ritual by Cyavana's forceful intercession with Indra; story told in chap. 4). It was Cyrus the Achaemenian who terminated the Babylonian captivity of the Jews; considerable Iranian influence is discernible also in postexilic Hebrew tradition, not least in the structuring of the archangels as Michael 'Like God', Gabriel 'Strong as God', and Raphael 'Healing as God'. So much so that Jeremiah (Jer. 9:23) had to warn his people against tripartition of the gifts of the Lord: "Let not the wise [*hāḵām*] glory in his wisdom, neither let the mighty [*gibbōr*] glory in his might, let not the rich [*ʿāšīr*] glory in his riches" (in other words, don't follow alien ways; let the Persians compartmentalize according to their triple structures; the God of Israel is one). Such formulas were current in both India and Iran, for example, *Rigvidhāna* 1.2.3: "A kṣatriya shall overcome misfortunes . . . by the strength of his arms, a vaiśya and a śūdra by their wealth, the chief of the twice-

FIGURE 4. Zeus Oromasdes at Nemrud Dagh. (Courtesy of *Aramco World Magazine*. Photograph by Alice and Robert Arndt.)

born [= brahmin] by muttered prayers and burnt offerings." In an apotropaic vein, the Achaemenians' standard prayer to Auramazda craved surcease *hačā haināyā hačā dušiyārā hačā draugā* 'from [hostile] army, from poor [harvest] year [cf. the daēva Dužyāirya], from the Lie [cf. the daēva Drug]', that is, from invasional, agricultural, and spiritual blight. The same type of afflictions are grouped in *RV* 8.18.10 as *ámīvām, srídham, durmatím* 'disease, ritual failure, enmity'. Similar old Indo-European structures are found in Rome (prayer to Mars in chap. 9), among the Celts, and in Scandinavia, where, conversely, a Norse king had to be both *sigrsäll* and *ārsäll,* blessed with victory and (good harvest) year (*ār*), on top of having runic wisdom.[1]

Other divinities corresponding to Indic counterparts are harder to come by in Iran. Uṣas's opposite number has been debased into Būšyanstā, the demoness of sloth (see chap. 4); there is no night-goddess, no real sun-god (although *Yašt* 6 is dedicated to Xvar Xšaēta 'Splendid Sun' > Modern Persian *xoršīd* 'sun'), nobody matching Savitar or Pūṣan. Dyaus had faded enough in India; in Iran he is no longer there. Fire worship is central, yet Ātar, for all the rituals, has even less real myth than does the Vedic Agni. Some Vedic fringe figures with fire associations, such as Apām Napāt 'Offspring of the Waters' (see chap. 4) and *Nárāśáṁsa-* 'Praise-of-Men'[1] have precise counterparts in the Avestan Apam Napāt and Nairyōsanha, and both occur in myths concerning assorted tugs-of-war between Ahura Mazdāh (or Spənta Mainyu) and Angra Mainyu. One of these myths, in *Yašt* 19, involves the *Xvarənah* (Old Persian *farnah,* Modern Persian *farr*), meaning roughly 'halo, nimbus, glory' and derivable (as 'solar matter') from the word for 'sun' (*xvar-,* Vedic *svár-,* Latin *sol,* etc.). It was the hallmark of the duly consecrated *airya* ruler of Iran, and its withdrawal was tantamount to downfall. Other speculation on its fiery essence identified it with ejaculate and sperm (cf. Danae and Zeus's "golden shower" in Greek tradition). Still other Iranian deities without clear Indic counterparts were Tištrya (*Yašt* 8), an astral figure whose battle against the demon of drought Apaoša (< **Apa-vṛta-* 'Water Obstructor') may have picked up some of the slack in the wake of Indra's demonization, and the time-god Zurvan, who represents a Zoroastrian heresy that tried to

1. The hunt for them can, however, be overextended. Thus *RV* 1.111.4 reads *sātáye dhiyé jiṣé,* which, if taken as juxtaposed asyndetic datives, seems to mean 'for gain, prayer, and victory', thus three structured blessings paralleling the three blights. But in reality the syntactic construction makes each word interdependent, and the meaning is 'for the hymn to win the prize'.

bridge the dualism by inventing a common parent for Ohrmazd and Ahriman.

There remains the strange case of Haoma, which also affords a transition from the divine to the heroic level of Iranian myth. We saw above Zarathuštra's rough attack upon the Haoma ritual in *Yasna* 48. But earlier in the same book, the younger *Yasna* 9–11 constitutes the *Haoma Yašt* that is a celebration engaging Zarathuštra himself. Haoma was alive and well in spite of the prophet, who was put to work posthumously hymning him, regardless of his own stated distaste (*Yasna* 9.1–3): "At pressing time Haoma came to Zarathuštra, who was consecrating the fire and reciting the *Gāthās*. Zarathuštra asked him: 'Who are you, man, the splendidest I have seen of all bodily being, in your own brilliant deathless life?' Then he spoke back to me . . . 'Zarathuštra, I am Haoma the true death dispeller. Take me, Spitama [Zarathuštra's allonym], press me for drinking, praise me for praise, even as future Saviors shall praise me!' Then spoke Zarathuštra: 'Glory to Haoma!'" Zarathuštra then asks Haoma who the first mortal haoma pressers were and what favors had befallen them. Haoma lists them in order:

1. Vīvahvant, who was favored with a son, Yama Xšaēta, "he of the good herds, most glorious of those born, looking like the sun among men, who in his reign made cattle and men undying, waters and plants undrying, food for eating unfailing. In the reign of the lordly Yama neither cold was nor heat, neither old age was nor death, nor demon-spawned envy."

2. Āthwya, who was rewarded with the son Thraētaona, who slew the three-headed Aži ('Snake, Dragon') Dahāka, a creature of Angra Mainyu (with *Dahāka* cf. Vedic *dāsá-*, *dásyu-* 'foe, infidel, demon', the antonym of *ā́rya-*).

3. Thrita, who was granted two sons, Urvāxšya the law giver and Kṛsāspa, another monster exterminator.

4. Pourušāspa, who became the father of Zarathuštra.

This piece of legendry sketches the outline of a broad cross section of Iranian heroic saga, the stuff that in due course culminated in the *Book of Kings*. The preserved *Avesta,* liturgical and prescriptive in kind, affords only incidental and allusive snatches and glimpses of such matter, much as do the Vedic hymns and sūtras.

Apart from Zarathuštra at the lower end, all the figures mentioned have significant Indo-Iranian mythic backgrounds. Yama (or Yima), son of Vīvahvant, is the equivalent of the Vedic Yama 'Twin', son of the solar Vivasvat (chap. 4). Vivasvat and Vīvahvant also have in common an ancestral position as "first sacrificer." But whereas the Vedic "king" Yama is confined to his role as the first man to die and as colonizer and ruler of the Otherworld (in association with Varuṇa), Yama Xšaēta is by contrast the first king of this world, not a semidivine funereal potentate but a culture hero whose rule was an antidote to decay and demise. Whereas the Vedic Yama's mythical career was circumscribed by being frozen in the "hereafter," Yama Xšaēta's dossier remained fraught with mortal vicissitudes. There are two separate myths about how his "golden age" ended. One is the story of his pride and consequent fall from divine grace. He was branded a sinner by Zarathuštra in the *Gāthās* (*Yasna* 32.8), and *Yašt* 19.31–36 details his collapse as he "lied" and lost his xvarənah in three staggered portions, which were seized by Mithra, Thraētaona, and Kṛsāspa. This myth is reminiscent of the story (in chap. 5) of how Indra's glory was shattered by sinning and reassembled in the wombs of Kuntī and Mādrī to produce the five Pāṇḍavas, with the totality of the king's essence portioned out over figures symbolic of the three social divisions (Mithra: priests; Kṛsāspa: warriors; Thraētaona: third estate). Yet though Indra was a triple offender, successively losing his sheen, strength, and looks, Yama Xšaēta compromised his halo all at once by the one overriding sin of his religion, having truck with the Lie. After the fall his end came at the hands of his brother Spityura and henchmen who sawed him in two.

The second myth contains features closer to the Vedic Yama's otherworldly concerns. In *Vidēvdāt* 2.20–41 and in later texts such as the *Bundahišn* there occurs the theme of Yama Xšaēta's *vara,* a subterranean enclosure Ahura Mazdāh orders him to build to shelter choice specimens and germs of human and other species against an impending "cosmic winter," an eschatological crisis resembling the Old Norse *fimbulvetr* that precedes the ending and regeneration of the world. This myth is strange on several counts. The *vara* is described as complete with waters and grasslands, at the very least a fantasy hothouse that would put any superdome to shame, nothing like cramped quarters to ride out a short-term crisis in the manner of Noah's Ark. The contradiction of being underground yet green and watery is the same that opposes the Greek Happy Isles or the Elysian Fields to the subterranean (or otherwise gloomy) Hades, with the result that Hades also exhibits horse-breeding meadows (see chap. 8). It is further remarkable that Yama

Xšaēta, given the task of setting up this comfortable elitist survival camp, seems to be merely its builder and founding organizer; Zarathuštra and his reformist ilk appear as the social directors who guide the further fortunes of this community of the elect. It appears that two separate notions have been thoroughly crossbred here. One is that of a shelter for the chosen during a temporary crisis, more an igloo type than the floating kind, for the simple reason that the geography and climate of the Iranian plateau differ from those of the Mesopotamian lowlands. The other is that of an idyllic Otherworld staked out and settled by Yama Xšaēta for the ingathering of the departed for the open-ended sojourn of afterlife. The latter would match the description of the Vedic Yama with his cow pastures as _saṁgámanam jánānām_ 'ingatherer of people' (_RV_ 10.14.1), and of the Greek Hades < Indo-European _*Sm̥widās_ (Homeric _A[w]id-_ < _*Sm̥wid-_) as 'Uniter' (_sam̊-gam-_ 'get together', _sam̊-vid-_ 'find [one another]' are the Vedic terms for the reunion of the dead with their [fore]fathers; cf. Russian _s-vídet-sja_ 'meet again', _do svidánija_ 'au revoir').

To summarize, the reconstructed dossier of an Indo-Iranian *Yama 'Twin' had *Vivasvant as his father, equipped him with a transitory twin sister (Vedic _Yamī́-_ who rejected incest, Middle Persian Yamīk who on the contrary consummated it), endowed him with pastures (Vedic _gávyūti-_; Yama Xšaēta 'with good herds'), and had him as a founding king in an otherworldly context. This is all the Indic Yama permits. The Iranian Yama Xšaēta is infinitely richer in story, in fact the most spectacular figure of Iranian myth and still (in the modern form Jamshid) the foremost hero of Persian folklore. His brilliant worldly career and its calamitous end seem to have no counterpart on the Indic side. Has Iran expanded the prototype, or has India contracted it? Chances are the latter is the case, although further embroidery of a popular figure on the Iranian side is of course also possible. Elements of Indo-European "Primeval Twin" mythology (chap. 17) are detectable in the birth tales and renunciation death of the Vedic Yama (chap. 4) and in the downfall of his Iranian counterpart, proving at least that Yama Xšaēta's catastrophe is not a purely new Iranian accretion. Yama's earthly career has parallels in Indic epic, indicating that it goes back to an Indo-Iranian prototype. Notions of hybris attach to several of the ancestral _samrāj_ types in book 1 of the _Mahābhārata,_ such as Purūravas and Nahuṣa, but they are all epitomized in Yayāti, who appears in both book 1 and book 5 of the _Mahābhārata_ and in chapter 5 above and chapter 14 below. After his long and glorious reign and an even longer well-deserved posthumous sojourn in the company of gods, Yayāti had a sudden fit of pride and was bounced out of heaven. But providentially he landed back on earth into the company of his four grandsons, who with their traits epitomized the three social classes, just as the Pāṇḍavas did later in the epic. These descendants pooled their merits and restored Yayāti's sovereign tripartite virtue, enabling him to reenter eternal bliss. Unlike the tragic Yama of the Iranian myth, we have here the epicized Indic counterpart with a novelistic happy ending. Yama Xšaēta's sin cost him his whole stockpile of *xvarənah,* which was splintered among several successors: Yayāti acted similarly but via his genes had taken out a multipartite insurance policy against this kind of loss. Yayāti's worldly and otherworldly careers combined seem to cover the maximum spectrum of a reconstructible Indo-Iranian *Yama. Yayāti's thousand-year rejuvenation (mentioned in chap. 5) is also reminiscent of the suspension of aging and death in Yama Xšaēta's golden age.

A somewhat different but equally unmistakable Indic epic "hypostasis" of the Indo-Iranian *Yama is present in Vasu Uparicara, that "high-flying" Paurava father of Satyavatī whose story was told in chapter 5. His remarkable similarities to Yayāti were noted there, especially his downfall from on high. But other very specific traits connect him with Jamshid directly, as told in post-Avestan sources down to the early Islamic period: both had airborne crystal chariots and each founded a great New Year festival (Indramālā in India, Nō Rōz 'New Light' in Iran). Vasu Uparicara was brought down specifically by untruth (rather than generalized pride), just as was the Avestan Yima Xšaēta. He was not saved by any successors, merely (almost as an afterthought) by Viṣṇu. Here is a summary:

Vedic Yama: Ruler of happy Otherworld.

Avestan Yama: Ruler of golden age, founder of otherworldly shelter, falls from grace, glory shattered.

Yayāti: Ruler of happy kingdom, then sojourner of heavenly Otherworld, falls from grace, shattered glory restored.

Vasu Uparicara: Ruler of happy kingdom, falls from grace, glory restored.

Thraētaona and Kṛsāspa both fought monsters, one the three-headed Aži Dahāka, the other various ones including a horned dragon and the demon Gandarəwa. The names of their respective fathers Āthwya and Thrita in reverse combination equal the Vedic Trita Āptya,

Indra's associate in slaying the three-headed Viśvarūpa, often called either Trita or Āptya alone (cf. chap. 4). Āptya-Āthwya being merely a clan name ('Watery') proper to an Indo-Iranian *Trita ('Third' [besides two obscure but obnoxious brothers of little account], slayer of 'Triple'), it looks as if the double name has been sundered to supply a patronym also for the genealogically more obscure Kṛsāspa. Āthwya has no other role, but Thrita is attested with a medical function, as the original herbalist who mobilized a pharmacopoeia against the host of illnesses the world owes to Angra Mainyu (*Vidēvdāt* 20.1–4). It is not (Thrita) Āthwya but his son Thraētaona who (as Frētōn) figures as the founder of agriculture and medicine in the *Dēnkart* (and later sources) and occupies the central slot of dragon slayer throughout the tradition (Thraētaona > Frētōn > Feridun). Apart from the similar name, Traitāna, of an obscure, lowly character in *RV* 1.158.5, Vedic tradition knows only Trita Āptya, whose functions include cleansing from the taint of necessary bloodshed and (in *RV* 8.47.13–17) dispelling nightmares. It looks as if the Vedic pattern is the conservative one and Iran has committed not only a patronymic but also a generational split.[2] The latter may be a corollary to the haoma-assisted "heroic reproduction" described in *Yasna* 9; just as haoma when excreted in urine gained in potency over the original product, with its help heroic seed could be upgraded to fiery xvarənah, producing an improved heroic son in whom the xvarənah blazed forth in visible form and who overshadowed his sire.

While Thraētaona is distinctly a culture hero who straddles the warrior and economic (third estate, commoner) strata, Kṛsāspa 'Lean Horse' is more of a pure fighting man, a reckless club wielder who has cultic ties to the god Vayu and resembles the Indic Bhīma, the son of Vāyu, in general brutishness and in sexual liaisons with demonic females. For all his prominence in the hero lists and (as Garshasp) down to the *Book of Kings,* there is little comparativistically significant myth apart from the one piece that connects him with his opaque Indic namesake Kṛśāśva (chap. 5). In *Rāmāyaṇa* 1.21.13–14 Rāma is promised by Viśvāmitra victory-bringing throw weapons once used by the ancestor Kauśika but descended from Kṛśāśva, who begot them with the daughters of Prajāpati (according to the *Viṣṇu-Purāṇa* Kṛśāśva had as off-

2. What may have happened is that the original *Thrita Āthwya was supplanted by *Thraētaona Āthwya, and that Āthwya was subsequently misunderstood as patronymic ('son of Āthwya') instead of gentilic; this left the original Thrita isolated and susceptible to secondary attachment.

spring fifty *śastradevatāḥ* 'weapon deities' with his wives Jayā and Vijayā, both 'Victory'). After Rāma proves his mettle by slaying the monster Tāṭakā, his tutor Viśvāmitra invests him with the "sons of Kṛśāśva" (*Rāmāyaṇa* 1.27.10). In the *Book of Kings* the young Rustam, the great white hope of Iran, after such preliminary deeds as killing a white rogue elephant, is formally invested by his father Zāl with the club of his grandfather Sām, whose ancestors had received it from Garshasp. The Indo-Iranian prototype of the two was thus at the very least a primordial supplier of thenceforth hereditary weapons to princely families.

We have seen repeatedly that the Old Iranian inventory of gods and heroes, for all the dislocations and reforms, hews just as close as does the Old Indic one to a classificatory principle that corresponds to the three strata of society. Even the more-or-less mythical lands enumerated in the beginning of the *Vidēvdāt* seem to adhere to the same scheme: of sixteen, the first thirteen are *airya,* comprising Iran proper (the domain of Ahura Mazdāh once ruled by Yama Xšaēta) and Gava (i.e., Sogdiana, a cattle land under Mithra's patronage); then *sūra* ('heroic') Margiana, Bactria, Nisāya, Haraiva, and Vaēkṛta (warlike places all); and finally Urvā *pouruvāstra* 'much-pastured', Xnənta 'Hyrcania', Harahvaiti 'Arachosia' (cf. Vedic Sarasvatī, and see under Anāhitā above), and other fertile places. The *Vidēvdāt* is a surprisingly rewarding document for comparative mythology, considering that much of it is a dreary, even revolting piece of preoccupation with uncleanness and pollution, with vicious beatings as a cure-all for most aberrations, including a woman's irregular menses. The main source of its horror is dead matter, which can contaminate the sacred fire, earth, and water alike, so that disposal of the dead is restricted to carrion birds at aeries called "towers of silence" (see fig. 5), a contemporary problem for the Zoroastrian Parsis of Bombay, India, where smog has decimated the vulture population and high-rise concrete-and-steel towers increasingly look down into the "silent" kind. *Vidēvdāt* 3.38–39 prescribes a triple set of penalties for permitting incursions of the demoness Nasu (cognate with Greek *nékus* 'corpse'): *čithā* 'restitution, fine', *āpṛtis* 'corporal punishment', and most important *yaož-dā-* 'weal setting' (cf. *mazdā-* and *zrazdā-* discussed above). The last constitutes ritual purification, where *yaož-* matches Vedic *yóṣ-* 'welfare' and Old Latin *ious* (> *iūs*), the latter having come to mean the 'justice' that is derived from it but originally denoting religiously tinged acts, as in *iūrāre* 'swear', *iūs iūrandum* 'oath', and *iū-dic-* 'law pointing' replacing **yows-dhē-* 'weal setting',

FIGURE 5. Tower of silence at Yazd, Iran. (Photograph by Roger Wood.)

and in the reshaped *iusta facere* 'perform funeral rites' (involving the *denicales feriae,* which cleansed the survivors of the taint of death, thus **de-nec-*, undoing the *nex* or dead matter, cognate with Nasu). All together Roman and Iranian pollution tabus have a good deal in common, and tripartite lists of crimes and punishments are attested also in archaic Roman laws, where the crimes *malum carmen* 'evil spell', *membrum ruptum* 'mayhem', and *furtum* 'theft' were punishable by fatal flogging, talion, and fine respectively.

The threefold division lingers also in the surviving traditions of the northern Iranians, such as the Scythian foundation legend in Herodotus (4.5–6) and Quintus Curtius (7.8.18–19): "Zeus" and a daughter of the river Borysthenes (the Dniepr) engendered Targitaos, who had three sons, Lipoxais, Arpoxais, and Kolaxais. In their reign three golden objects fell from the sky, a plow with yoke, a war ax, and a cup. The brothers one by one sought to capture these treasures, but the gold started to burn at the approach of the two older ones, only to yield to the young Kolaxais, thus validating his rule by ultimogeniture. From the three brothers were descended in chronological order the three "tribes" (in reality social classes) of the Scythians, *Aukhátai* or warriors (cf. Avestan *aogah-* = Vedic *ójas-* 'might', Latin *augus-tus* 'mighty'),

Tráspies and *Katíaroi,* herder-cultivators perhaps mirroring *Drvāspiya 'with fine horses' (cf. the Avestan horse-goddess Drvāspā of *Yašt* 9) and something like *Gaučahra 'with cow pastures', and *Paralátai,* thus the consecrated power elite whose name (with *l* < *d*) recalls the Avestan Paradāta, title of Haošyanha, one of the shadowy mythical sovereigns preceding Yama Xšaēta whom we shall meet in the *Book of Kings* (cf. the Vedic *puró-hita-* 'priest in charge' and Latin *prae-fectus* 'placed in front, put in charge, chief'). This is a folkloristic foundation myth of a widespread type, but its precise structure reflects an Indo-Iranian and Indo-European heritage: three golden objects embodying sacrality (cup), power (ax), and sustenance (plow with yoke) respectively, combined in the ruler's hands to constitute his sovereignty, and the three social classes sprung from a set of three anthropogonic ancestors. Such traditions survived with special tenacity among the northern Iranians, for the three main Nart families of the Ossetic epic were the wise, magically oriented Alägatä, the brave, warlike Äxsärtägkatä, and the cattle-rich Boratä.

Old Iranian cosmogony and anthropogony have been heavily colored by the Zoroastrian revamping, and the record is further obfuscated by its lateness, with the *Bundahišn* as the main source. By that time (ninth century C.E.) a millennium and a half of Zoroastrianism had had time to interact with Indic, Greek, and Judaic cultures, not least in the Hellenistic and Sasanian cauldron of cults and philosophies that spawned Christianity, Gnosticism, and the Manichean heresy. Proto-Iranian tradition may have had something comparable to the Vedic Puruṣa figure (see end of chap. 4), but the mythologem of the dismembered primordial man was sublimated and abstracted by Zarathuštra into a mere colorless *Gaya* 'Life' (*Yasna* 30.4). As in the case of Haurvatāt and Amṛtāt, the new name became a fulcrum for mythology that survived in spite of Zarathuštra, as Gaya Marətan 'Mortal Life' in the later *Avesta,* and as Gayōmart in the *Bundahišn*. This "remythologized" Gayōmart is described as slain to make metals and men, but the new dispensation assigns the deed not to the gods but to Ahriman, thus to the evil pole of creation. The killing of a primal bovine is also attributed to Ahriman, of the animal whose soul cries out to the gods against the cruelty of warriors in Zarathuštra's *Gāthā* 'Plaint of the Bovine' (*Yasna* 29); the prophet's advocacy proved transitory, however, for any notion of protected sacred cows was overridden in the Iranian orbit by the ritual passion that finds its iconographic expression in the Mithraic tauroctony.[3] The later tradition also knows a first human couple, Mašya and Mašyānag, sprung from the preserved semen of the slain Gayōmart; in the Manichean variant the first couple were instead Gēhmurd and Murdyānag, identical with Gayōmart and Mašyānag. Older traces of Indo-Iranian anthropogonic myth are present in Yama and his female foil Yamīk, and significant remains of the Indo-European myth of the Primeval Twin may linger in the "moral dismemberment" of Yama (piecemeal loss of his xvarənah) and his bisection by his brother Spityura (see chap. 17).

Preoccupation with "last things"—destiny of man's soul, fate of the world—is likewise rife in the Mazdean tradition. Zoroastrian soul terminology is complex and subtle, having considerable parallels with post-Vedic Indic speculation. There is not only the soul proper (*urvan*) but also its *Fravaši* (< **pra-vṛti-* 'protection, protector'), a kind of genius or daimon or "guardian angel" who is a higher, celestial replica of each creature, its preexistent module, and part of its postmortem *urvan* (*Yašt* 13 celebrates the Fravašis of the righteous from Gaya Marətan down to the last Saošyant or future Savior). Equally strange is the term *Daēnā,* formally identical with Vedic *dhénā* 'lactating female [cow or woman]', another heavenly double of the human soul, which is molded for beauty or ugliness by man's earthly demeanor and confronts him for good or ill at judgment. At the *Činvatō-pṛtu* 'Requiter's Bridge' the soul faces the tribunal of Mithra, Sraoša, and Rašnu and, if he passes Rašnu's weighing, proceeds onto the broad span, where his Daēnā welcomes him as a beautiful young woman of fifteen (the optimal Iranian age for sex appeal) and leads him to divine presence and celestial light. Those who flunk the test face their earthly deeds in the form of a hideous female and are dragged by demons into the realm of Ahriman.

Iran preserves a grandiose tableau of world-end eschatology, rivaled in attested Indo-European traditions only by Ragnarök. This is

3. The *Bundahišn* speaks of "Bovine and Gayōmart" as being afflicted by Ahriman in this order, even as Old Iranian has the set dual-dvandva *pasu-vīra* 'beast [and] man', which reverses the normal "chain of being" sequence 'man and beast' seen in the Italic Umbrian *uiro pequo,* or in *dupursus peturpursus* 'to biped[s] and quadruped[s]' on the same *Iguvine Tables* (cf. Vedic *virapśá-* and *dvipáde cátuṣpade;* Latin *pecudesque virosque* [Ovid, *Metamorphoses* 1.286] is dictated by metrical cadence). From the ejaculate of this dying bovine sprouted grains and healing herbs, and the semen was used to create all useful animals, starting with a male-female pair of cattle. In Iran the pastoralist preoccupation with cattle has hypertrophied into joint zoogonic creation myths of beast and man.

not Sasanian speculation but is repeatedly referred to from the *Gāthās* onward. Zarathuštra speaks of an ordeal by molten metal (*Yasna* 30.7, 32.7, 51.9) and of the *fraša* or *ākṛti* 'invigoration, perfection, transfiguration' that will ensue; this miraculous consummation is called *frašō-kṛti* in the later *Avesta* and *fraškart* in Middle Iranian, and the word has passed into Armenian (*hrašakert* 'marvelous'). *Yašt* 19.11 rhapsodizes about the rejuvenated and reborn world with strings of adjectives that recall Yama's golden reign at the earlier beginning. The *Bundahišn* and other late texts lay out the scenario: In one-to-one combat the divine entities will tackle and rout the daēvas, with Ohrmazd's showdown against Ahriman as the main event. When the good creation triumphs, bodily resurrection of the saved and damned alike is effected by the Saošyants (preprogrammed progeny of Zarathuštra in the far future); all are subjected to a three-day ordeal by molten metal that tortures and destroys the damned but is like a soothing milk bath to the righteous; and a draught of hom (haoma) seals the restoration of the saved to immortal life in a transformed world of eternal prosperity and progress. This Zoroastrian blueprint for the millennium points back to Indo-European antiquity on the one hand and at the same time forward to extremist soteriologies from the Christian Apocalypse to the Communist Manifesto.

Recommended Reading

Boyce, Mary. *Textual Sources for the Study of Zoroastrianism*. Manchester: Manchester University Press, 1984.

Duchesne-Guillemin, Jacques. *The Hymns of Zarathustra*. Boston: Beacon Press, 1963.

———. *Religion of Ancient Iran*. Bombay: Tata Press, 1973.

———. *Symbols and Values in Zoroastrianism*. New York: Harper and Row, 1966.

Gnoli, Gh. *Zoroaster's Time and Homeland*. Naples: Istituto Universitario Orientale, 1980.

Zaehner, R. C. *The Teachings of the Magi: A Compendium of Zoroastrian Beliefs*. London: Oxford University Press, 1976.

7 · Epic Iran

The Islamic conquest of Iran in the seventh century C.E. put an end to the official Zoroastrianism of the Sasanian empire but not to antiquarian preoccupation with the native tradition. Cultic religion fell into abeyance and gradual permanent decline, being nowadays restricted to Yazd and Kerman in the central desert and the Parsi émigré colony centered in Bombay. But such works as the *Bundahišn* were composed in the ninth century, and the new Arabic influence during its cultural apogee fructified rather than stunted Iran-related historiography. The great official Sasanian chronicle *Xvatāy Nāmak* (lost to us) fueled the works of various Arabic writers such as the *Chronicle of Tabarī* (with Persian version by Belʿamī) and al-Thaʿālibī's *History of the Kings of the Persians*. A prose *Book of Kings* (*Shāh Nāma*) had also been compiled in eastern Iran during the tenth century. The material of such now-lost works inspired a flowering of versified epic between the years 1000 and 1300, starting with the fifty-thousand-plus rhymed couplets of the *Shāh Nāma* of the poet Firdausi, composed between 975 and 1010 C.E. and followed by a number of other, sometimes very lengthy and increasingly epigonic works. These involve mostly heroes of the Sistan cycle, a "side epic" to the main line of the *Shāh Nāma,* with titles such as *Garšāsp Nāma* and *Sām Nāma*. This bulk is barely edited and hardly known in the West. Its imitative character detracts from its value as a source for primary tradition.

The *Shāh Nāma* is a "national epic," and as such it has helped mold Persian culture for the past thousand years as well as being itself a reflection of it. It is by definition a chronicle-epic, a history of the kings of Iran from Creation to the end of the Sasanian period, and hence has historical as well as literary pretensions. It is also a vast repository of international folktale motifs. Purely at random, there is an echo of Potiphar's wife or Phaedra in the attempted seduction of Siyavosh by his stepmother Sudaba, and of Siegfried's weak spot or Achilles' heel in Esfandiyar's vulnerability in the eyes, despite having bathed in the blood of the wonder bird Simorg. Both Feridun in the national tradition and Zāl in the Sistan cycle replicate the "average hero legend" postulated by Otto Rank and Lord Raglan, and the unwitting slaying of Sohrab by his father Rustam matches the Germanic Hildebrand-Hadubrand motif and its Celtic and Slavic parallels.

In order to appreciate the *Shāh Nāma* as a source work for comparative mythology, this chapter concentrates on the interplay of myth and history. The matter of historicity never bothered the practitioners of the art of epic poetry. For them the question of myth versus history was still blissfully neutralized; they were neither conscious euhemerizers nor aware of the potential of myth transposition to heroic saga. Modern scholarship, however, is squarely faced with this issue. The elaborate treatment of the Sasanian kings at the lower chronological end and the briefly sketched Arsacid or Parthian period preceding them are essentially historical in kind, although enmeshed in legend even here, as in the romance of Khosraw Parviz, the Sasanian ruler of about 600 C.E., and the Armenian princess Shirin. But essentially this latter part of the *Shāh Nāma* is a meticulous account of the Sasanian dynasty in its attested vicissitudes, its wars with Byzantium, its persecutions of Manicheans and Christians, and the usurpation of Bahram Chobin. Equally evident is the mythical nature of the "Pishdadian" kings of the beginnings, ranging dynastically from Keyumars via Siyamak 'Black' (who is a bleak gap filler) to Hushang to Tahmuras to Jamshid, then past the usurper Zohak to Feridun and his sons, only to peter out in internecine killings. This sequence is anchored not in Iranian history but in myth that partly antedates Iranian tradition proper and can be traced to Indo-Iranian and even Indo-European levels. The figures involved have Avestan counterparts that help trace their origins. The first king, Keyumars, is none other than Gaya Marətan or Gayōmart, the abstract and subsequently "remythologized" anthropogonic ancestor we met in chapter 6. Keyumars is thus a secondary replicate of the "first man," caught in the web of mythical logic that equated the first man with the first king, and stuck at the top of the list. The next king, Hushang, matches the Avestan Haošyanha, whose epithet Paradāta means 'put in front' and underlies the term "Pishdadian," which characterizes these kings as a group. Tahmuras is the Avestan Taxma Urupi 'Valiant Urupi', a demon smiter who in *Yašt* 15.12–13 and 19.29 is mysteriously said to have ridden Angra Mainyu as a horse for thirty years, from one end of the earth to the other. Only a late Parsi commentary elaborates on the allusion: Taxmoruw had somehow managed to lasso Ahriman and kept him tied up, saddling him three times daily for a worldwide ride. After thirty years of submission Ahriman devilishly bribed Mrs. Taxmoruw with jewelry into disclosing her husband's horsemanly shortcomings, especially his propensity to acrophobia at an elevated spot on the trail. He then took advantage of the rider's dizziness, threw him, and swallowed him. Taxmoruw's brother Jamshid undertook a search and finally learned the truth from Srosh (= the Avestan Sraoša, abstraction of Airyaman and associate of Mithra). To extricate the body from the devil's bowels, Srosh advised Jamshid to play in turn on Ahriman's weaknesses, particularly his homoerotic proclivities. Having aroused Ahriman with the prospect of anal penetration, he instead inserted his hand deep enough to extract his brother's corpse and then fled, eluding Ahriman's frustrated pursuit. Jamshid built the original "tower of silence" and exposed the body. His own hand, however, had withered and stank from contact with the diabolic innards. As this leprotic condition worsened he withdrew to solitude in the desert, until by chance the hand was urinated on by a bovine during his sleep and miraculously healed. This etiology of the renowned *gōmēz* or bull-urine remedy of Mazdean Iran competes with that of *Vidēvdāt* 22, where at the very end of the preserved *Avesta* the *gaomaēza-* is attributed to the founding ministrations of Airyaman, thus to purposeful divine myth rather than fortuitous heroic saga. The story as told is also clearly epic in kind, an almost burlesque outwitting of the Evil One. Elements of the tale (binding of an evil being by the ruler figure, thrusting of a hand into the monster's orifice in heroic trickery by a close associate, affliction of the inserted limb, devouring of the ruler by the demonic adversary) are close in kind to the Old Norse myth of the cosmic wolf Fenrir's being bound on the initiative of the chief god Odin, the god Týr's pledging and losing his hand in the wolf's maw as the price of the duping involved, and the swallowing of Odin when the wolf escapes at Ragnarök. The Iranian sequence differs, however, with the swallowing intercalated between the binding and the trickery, thus losing the link between the latter two and advancing another rationale for the dupery and loss of hand, namely the pious need to rescue a Zoroastrian corpse from the digestive tract of Ahriman. A different eschatological outlook dictates the discrepancy: the Norse Fenrir remained bound until Ragnarök and then destroyed Odin, whereas Ahriman (apart from a piddling thirty-year misadventure) stays active and potent through world history, to be vanquished by Ohrmazd in the final struggle. Thus clearly the epic tales concerning Tahmuras utilized ancient mythic material in Zoroastrian saga adaptation.

The Parsi tradition presented Jamshid as Tahmuras's brother, whereas the diachronically poised *Book of Kings* projects a filial pattern instead, equally at variance with the *Avesta,* where Yama Xšaēta is the son of Vīvahvant. Jamshid is the glorious all-round sovereign who ruled a golden age but was brought down by hybris and lost the farr or solar nimbus that marked the Elect of God, to be replaced by the intrusive dragon-king Zohak, the Aži Dahāka of the *Avesta.* Zohak was subsequently overthrown by Feridun, the Avestan Thraētaona, in whom a portion of Yama Xšaēta's lost xvarənah (in Firdausi's language Jamshid's vanished farr) had been reinvested.

While the Keyumars-to-Jamshid layer of the *Book of Kings* covers epicized anthropogony, in Feridun's victory over Zohak there is instead a reflection of the demon- or dragon-killer myth exemplified by Thraētaona versus Aži Dahāka in the *Avesta,* Trita Āptya versus Triśiras or Indra versus Vṛtra in the Vedas, Thor killing giants or fishing for the Miðgarð-serpent in Norse tradition. Such a myth usually attaches to a warlike bolt wielder who is also a rain bringer and thus furthers vegetal productivity: Indra releasing waters, Trita Āptya belonging to a watery clan, Frētōn in Sasanian and later texts as the patron of agriculture, Thor as the friend of Scandinavian *karlar,* the peasant class. The champion carries a weapon that embodies thunder, be it Indra's *vájra-* or Thraētaona's *vazra-* or Feridun's cow-headed mace *gurz* (going back to Avestan *vazra-*) or Thor's hammer. The Feridun figure is hence firmly anchored in Old Iranian, Indo-Iranian, and Indo-European tradition, although Firdausi's treatment of the entire Jamshid-Zohak-Feridun sequence exhibits some overlay of the diffusionary Near Eastern "Kingship in Heaven" myth (see chap. 2).

With the division of the world between Feridun's three sons Salm, Tur, and Iraj, the *Book of Kings* becomes a bit more attuned to diffusionary folklore and geographical reality. Salm gets Rum (i.e., Byzantium and the West), Tur gets the East, and Iraj inherits Iran itself by ultimogeniture. Salm and Tur gang up on Iraj and murder him, but in due time are killed in turn by Iraj's daughter's son Manushchihr. Amid all this unpleasantness other dimensions are added to the work. Turan enters the scene as an ever-present invasive eastern archenemy of Iran, with its long-lived persistent chieftain Afrasyab. It would be wrong to look for historical background in all this, for the Iranian-Turanian tug-of-war bears the hallmarks of myth. Afrasyab is already present as Franrasyan in the *Avesta,* where he performs in the company of gods, for example, in *Yašt* 19 trying in vain to capture the xvarənah of Iran that had been deposited by divinity for safekeeping in the mythical lake or sea named Vourukaša. There he is clearly labeled foreign, emitting barbarous gibberish, but in the *Book of Kings* a degree of symbiosis seems to exist between Iran and Turan, as when Siyavosh defects and marries Afrasyab's daughter and their son Khosraw later ascends the throne to Iran. The situation is similar to the ambivalent state of hostility that obtains in the Irish *Book of Conquests* between the Tūatha Dē Danann, the ruling mythical stratum, and the Fomoire, who are both an external archenemy and yet woven into the tribal fabric by various means including intermarriage.

At this point the Sistanian "side epic" intrudes as well. This is a provincial heroic cycle of Sistan and Zabulistan north of Baluchistan. Firdausi's hometown of Tus was farther to the northwest in the province of Khorazan. These eastern areas were the locale of both the Zoroastrian reform and the consolidation of the mythical tradition. The two centuries of Achaemenian imperial power in the southwest were not quite enough to effect a transfer of the cultural heartland to the Persepolis-Susa regions across a thousand kilometers of the central desert, and only with the Sasanian empire was this shift completed. Nor does Persia proper (the province of Fars) figure as the legendary scene of the early dynasts, unlike the north, where Zohak was chained by Feridun on Mount Demavend in the Elborz range and Rustam led fighting expeditions against the demons of Mazandaran. After the Islamic conquest the east remained a kind of backwater where the national tradition was relatively sheltered under a thin veneer of Islamic rule. The gentry of Khorazan not only kept alive the pre-Islamic heritage but made it thrive in a robust flowering of epic poetry, coterminous with the golden era of Persian literature.

Firdausi had to compromise. He had for his main topic the rectilinear national tradition, but he would not wholly neglect the rich store of the Sistanian cycle. So he forced a solution. While the Kayanid kings rule Iran, their Sistanian parallels intervene in multiple, usually supportive ways in the *Book of Kings,* so that they frequently dominate the action and attention of the epic.

This Sistanian dynasty is also of patently mythical origin, descended from Garshasp, that is, the Avestan Kṛsāspa, who figures besides Thraētaona and Mithra as the coequal recipient of one-third of Jamshid's lost nimbus. The Sistan epic is replete with spectacular episodes, such as Zāl's being born with snow-white hair and reared as a foundling in the aerie of a Simorg, the great romance of Zāl and Rudaba, parents of Rustam, and the Rustam : Sohrab tragedy of filicide that Matthew Arnold learned about in Sainte-Beuve's review of Jules Mohl's translation of the *Shāh Nāma* and that inspired one of the great English poems of the nineteenth century. Rustam has a preternatural life span that stretches through and beyond the entire Kayanid dynasty and obviously has nothing to do with any kind of actual historical synchronism.

The Kayanids are a major problem of Iranian studies. The *Avesta,* both in the list of Fravašis in *Yašt* 13 and in the rundown of possessors of the xvarənah in *Yašt* 19, provides a list of eight: Kavi Kavāta, Kavi Aipivohu, Kavi Usa(da)n, Kavi Aršan, Kavi Pisinah, Kavi Byaršan, Kavi Syāvaršan, and Kavi Haosravah. Anecdotal legendry about the first two, as Kay Kobād and Kay Apivēh, is found in Sasanian and Arabic sources. But the *Shāh Nāma,* apart from a short section on Kay Kobād, knows in essence only three successive father-son Kayanids,—Kay Us, Siyavosh, and Kay Khosraw—that is, numbers 3, 7, and 8. The remaining 4, 5, and 6 are unexplained padding, certainly without any generational impact. Rustam is the real hero, and Kay Us frequently serves as a mere prop for his derring-do. Kay Us is an unstable character, alternately good king and reckless fool. He subdues the demons of Mazandaran and has them build him bejeweled palaces in the Elborz Mountains, where gracious living and rejuvenation reign, almost an echo of Yama Xšaēta's golden age in the *Avesta*, when heat and cold, old age and death alike were suspended. But then again Kay Us gets in trouble with the same not-so-subservient demons and indulges in hybristic stunts such as trying to conquer heaven in a contraption powered by eagles, and it takes Rustam to extricate or rescue him. Yet he somehow has a charmed life, and God always pardons him in the end. His son Siyavosh 'Black Stallion' never rules, defects to Turan, and is killed there after begetting Khosraw. Khosraw grows up in Iran, succeeds his grandfather, has a reign still intertwined with assists from Rustam, and finally disappears into a snowstorm.

All this is another massive helping of myth and folklore. And yet, amazingly, historicist bias has mounted a serious effort to declare the Kayanids a real dynasty, most importantly in Arthur Christensen's 1931 book *Les Kayanides*. The title *kavi* itself matches the Vedic *kaví-*, which designates a kind of priestly magician and has no truck with royalty. The Kayanids are a purely legendary grouping concocted around the figure and kind of Kay Us, who corresponds to the shadowy Avestan Kavi Usan and in Indo-Iranian terms matches the Indic Kāvya Uśanas, who in the first book of the *Mahābhārata,* among the ancestral tales, is the resident sorcerer of the demons, professional colleague of the god Bṛhaspati, who in a similar manner sells his services to the gods. Kāvya Uśanas is thus in league with the demons and at one point becomes their master, even as Kay Us is the conqueror and sometimes the dupe of the *dīvs* of Mazandaran. Kay Us's jeweled Elborz palaces are matched by the riches Kāvya Uśanas has stashed on the mythical Mount Meru. Kāvya's arsenal of sorcery includes the power to resurrect the dead and to manipulate age, even as Kay Us possesses an elixir for healing mortal wounds (which he callously withholds from the dying Sohṛab) and institutes rejuvenation procedures in his Elborz palaces. And so forth. All told, it is clear that we have here a divine sorcerer figure of Indo-Iranian date who has been sucked into saga and secondarily dynasticized already in the *Avesta*. Such transposition may have to do with the Zoroastrian upheaval that not only demonized patron deities of the warrior class but extended the halo of rulership to priestly manipulators (witness the recent Iranian parallel of 1979). Firdausi simply utilized and rearranged preexisting material.

The artificiality of the Kayanids is mirrored indirectly in their successors. We cannot readily see, nor did the national tradition itself understand, where these came from. Suddenly there is Luhrasp (allegedly designated by Kay Khosraw much against the grain of his nobles), followed by his son Gushtasp. These are both "horsey" names, like Garshasp, and the *Avesta* knows a similar pair, Aurvataspa and Vištāspa. The latter, the exact preform of Gushtasp, partakes of an aftermath of the "Kavi" tradition in the *Avesta,* where Kavi Vištāspa is the patron of Zarathuštra, even as in the *Shāh Nāma* Gushtasp accepts the teachings of Zardosht. It seems that here at last the epic might approach reality, for Zarathuštra's historicity is not in doubt.

Yet even here the mythical intrudes. Luhrasp is such a pale nonentity out of nowhere that Gushtasp seems the dominant member of what is really a pair. His wife's name, Nahid, reflects that of the great goddess Anāhitā of the *Avesta*. Here may lurk an epic reflection of the Divine Twins, a saga projection of the Iranian equivalent of the Indic Aśvins in association with a goddess figure (cf. under Haurvatāt-Amṛtāt in chap. 6). Thus once more it is vain to look for history in this segment of the tradition.

At this point it is clear, however, that the mythical part of the epic is winding down. Afrasyab has already been killed by Kay Khosraw, and the Turanian dimension peters out. Gushtasp's son Esfandiyar fights with and is slain by Rustam in a sequence studded with supernatural intervention by assorted Simorgs. Rustam himself is finally dispatched by his own brother Shaghad. Esfandiyar's son Bahman has a daughter Humay (already known to the *Avesta* as Humāyā associated with a Vištāspa), also known as Chehrzad (Scheherazade), and father and daughter combine incestuous efforts to produce Darab. Darab had two sons, Dara and Sekandar.

This is how the *Shāh Nāma* crash-lands in history. Darab and Dara reflect the name of Darius, and Sekandar is none other than Alexander. We find a compressed, syncopated, elliptic representation of what to the West at least was *the* great period of Persian history, that of the Achaemenians. Not a word about the founders of the dynasty, nor of Cyrus or Cambyses, Xerxes or the several Artaxerxeses. Darab and his son Dara probably hark back not to the great Darius but to Darius II and Darius III Codomannus, who was overthrown by Alexander, although three generations separate them historically. The influence of the classical *Alexander Romance* is palpable in Firdausi's material, but the turning of the last Darius and his external nemesis Alexander into brothers, and of the showdown into a family feud, must be native to Iran. Iranian folk tradition does in fact exhibit a curious blind spot where the Achaemenians are concerned. However such a *damnatio memoriae* is to be explained, Persepolis is known to folk memory as *Taxt-e-Jamshid* 'Throne of Jamshid', and the royal necropolis near it, with the colossal rock-wall tombs of Darius the Great and his successors, is called *Naqsh-i-Rustam* 'Pictures of Rustam'. Possibly the contrived fraternization of the last Darius and Alexander the Great in the *Shāh Nāma* owes something to the Helleno-Persian syncretism of the Parthian period, with Hellenistic monarchs such as Antiochus of Commagene in the first century B.C.E., who in his hierothesion on top of Nemrud Dagh in southern Anatolia (mentioned in chap. 6) not only syncretized Hellenistic Greek and Iranian deities but traced his paternal ancestry to a Darius and his maternal descent to Alexander. Against these trends, such latter-day Western-inspired efforts as the late shah's celebration of the twenty-five hundredth anniversary of the Persian empire have been unavailing.

Thus the great epic of Iran is no clue at all to the actual early history of Iran, and scholarly efforts in this direction have been misguided. But it is a treasury of myth and legendry, a final gathering of a millennial epic-heroic tradition. It also displays Iranian national psychology in its wondrous as well as its deleterious aspects. Heroism and sacrifice are there, as is an acute sense of the poetic and the miraculous, but so are fanaticism and xenophobia, with a disquieting stress on revenge and martyrdom. The *Shāh Nāma* is in fact a sourcebook for comprehending the dynamics of distressing events, from High Priest Karter's martyring of the prophet Mani in the Sasanian empire to the Ayatollah Khomeini's persecution of the Bahai in the Islamic Republic, from the mob lynching of Aleksandr Gribojedov in the streets of Teheran in 1829 to the kamikaze madness of contemporary Iranian assassins. The influence of the *Shāh Nāma* on the Iranian nation has been profound. The popular first names of present-day Iranians are not the Islamic staples Mohammed, Ali, or Ahmed; they are rather Hushang, Tahmuras, Jamshid, Manushchihr, Khosraw, Dariush, and Ardashir. In the midst of Islamic overlay and the Arabic impact, the epic has contributed vastly to the preservation of linguistic purity, national consciousness, and native culture. To the comparative mythologist it points away from the measureless formats of the Indic epics, and in its tidy sequencing of events it recalls 40ther the chronicle patterns of the West.

Recommended Reading

Dumézil, Georges. *The Plight of a Sorcerer.* Edited by Jaan Puhvel and David Weeks. Berkeley and Los Angeles: University of California Press, 1986.

The Epic of the Kings. Translated by Reuben Levy, abridged. Chicago: University of Chicago Press, 1967; London: Routledge and Kegan Paul, 1985.

Sháhnáma. 9 vols. Translated by A. J. Warner and E. Warner, full verse translation. London: Trübner, 1905–.

8 · Ancient Greece

Greece is a special case for the comparative mythologist. Being somehow the central reference point for mythology at large, Greek myth tends to carry disproportionate weight in any comparison. Scholars speak of "the Orpheus myth in North America" or "Oedipus-like tales in Oceania" rather than of a "Coyote-type trickster in Greece." This book indulges in typological allusions to the likes of Ixion and Danae, Phaedra and Achilles, not in the sense of precise pairings with extra-Greek traditions, but as a means of evoking broad parallelism between the frankly "exotic" and what the educated reader in our culture can relate to from his own experience in art and literature. A double-digit percentage of the population in a Western country have probably heard of Aias or Herakles (or at least their Latinized equivalents Ajax or Hercules, if only from commercial brand names), while in the case of Indra or Mithra permillage might be too optimistic a unit of measurement. To the average educated person, myth remains above all Greek myth.

For the purposes of this book, however, Greek myth must be stripped of its unfair advantage and placed squarely into the frame of our study. That it happens to land near the middle of the volume implies a certain "centrality" without its necessarily being pivotal in the total picture. Greece was quite simply in the middle, at the crossroads of prehistory and history, at the interface of Asia and Europe, at the point where continentality and insularity, land mass and sea vistas met and interacted, where autochthon, northern invader, and eastern trader effected a complex interculturation. Greek culture is a matter not of preserving but of becoming, not so much of interrelation as of fusion, in short, a new synthesis. This streak of originality complicates the tracing of antecedents, whether diffusionary or genetic.

There are subsidiary complications as well. Unlike India or Iran, there are few early documents of a religious or even purposefully antiquarian nature. The Mycenaean inscriptions of about 1200 B.C.E. are prosaic palace inventories that incidentally record names of deities as recipients of tribute commodities. Epic poetry is essentially irreligious in outlook, the divine apparatus that overhangs the action is already a bit operatic in character and reflects a warrior-class (rather than sacerdotal) mentality, and the economy of the poems allows no mythographic expatiations in the profligate fashion of the *Mahābhārata*. The Homeric poems are instead interlaced with tantalizing scraps of allusive myth in the manner of the *Rig-Veda,* such as how the other gods plotted to bind Zeus but were thwarted by the hundred-handed Briareos whom Thetis summoned as a bodyguard (*Iliad* 1.396–406), how Ares was shut up for thirteen months in a brazen jar by Otos and Ephialtes and would have perished but for the timely intervention of Hermes (*Iliad* 5.385–91), how Hephaistos was hurled from Olympus on an all-day dive down to Lemnos for trying to protect Mother Hera from Zeus's wife beating (*Iliad* 1.590–94), how Hera herself tossed away her deformed baby Hephaistos, whom Thetis then saved in the Ocean (*Iliad* 18.394–99), or how Zeus strung Hera up in the clouds with arms tied and anvils dangling from her feet, flinging down to earth any fellow deity who tried to intervene (*Iliad* 15.18–24). Such snatches are clearly more than mere Homeric horseplay, yet their cultic and mythic content is often hopelessly opaque. Later literary consumers of myth, such as the "Homeric" hymnographers, lyricists (especially Pindar), and tragedians, were already operating with a considerably homogenized product, for the beginnings of conscious and purposive myth processing, sketched in chapter 1 above, tended to impose Panhellenic leveling on local and tribal peculiarities. The standard versions of Greek myth and saga that are a commonplace of Western culture are hence twice removed from their component wellsprings: once by the innovative genius of the early Greeks, and once more by the systematizing zeal of the later mythographers.

The three main ingredients of ancient Greek culture in general, and of myth in particular, may be described as substratal ("Aegean," "Pelasgian," "Minoan" in Crete), superstratal (Indo-European Greek), and adstratal (the steady seepage from Asia Minor and points farther east).

Indeed, the substratum and early adstratum may have been in considerable measure a continuum, for the same type of prehistoric place-name suffixes occur in Greece and in Asia Minor (Parnassos : Halikarnassos, Athēnai : Priēnē, Korinthos : Alabanda). Onto this base was superimposed from the north a gradual settlement of Indo-European Greek-speakers, starting about 2000 B.C.E. and completed by the coming of the Dorians about 1200 B.C.E. By 1600 B.C.E. mainland Greece was ruled by a Greek-speaking warlike aristocracy out of fortified strongholds such as Mycenae, fit to withstand land-based siege, while in Crete sprawling seaside and hillside palaces enjoyed the peace afforded by a carefree thalassocracy. By 1400, however, the mainland Greeks were maritime-oriented enough to have gained a foothold or beachhead in Crete; when the palace of Knossos was wiped out by the fallout from the explosive collapse of the volcano on Thera to the north, the chancery language of its accidentally baked and preserved clay tablets was already Greek (while the rest of Crete still wrote hitherto unintelligible "Minoan"). The same "Mycenaean Greek" syllabic script and language (based on "Minoan" models, deciphered about 1950) occurs in the palace archives of Pylos and Mycenae in the Peloponnesus, and at Thebes north of Athens, proving that toward the end of this "Helladic" era, when incendiary Dorians wrecked the palaces, southern and central Greece shared a uniform, though limited, form of official literacy. During this period both Minoan thalassocrats and Helladic Greeks must have settled Cyprus a thousand kilometers farther east, for "Cypro-Minoan" writing occurs both on the island and on the neighboring Syrian coast, and Cypriot Greeks of the classical period persisted in using their own version of a Cretan-inherited syllabary, despite being right on the transmission route of the Phoenician alphabet toward Greece. Archeology likewise proves Greek settlement of the west coast of Asia Minor. The Dorian upheavals overran all of western Greece and all of Peloponnesus except the isolated Arcadian interior (where an "Achaean" dialect related to Cypriot Greek was still spoken later), reached the borders of Attica and took in many of the southern islands (including Crete) all the way to Rhodes and the southwest corner of Asia Minor. The eastern Greeks, subdivisible into Ionians in Attica and Aeolians farther north, were largely driven overseas to the Cyclades and those islands hugging the coast of Asia Minor (Samos, Chios, Lesbos) as well as reinforcing the settlement of the coast. After a few centuries of the "dark ages," this colonial Ionia became the cradle of classical Greek culture, made up of city-states and marked by a rush to new colonization reaching all the way to the Black Sea (Crimea), southern Italy (Magna Graecia), and the southern coast of Gaul (= the French Riviera).

Through all this chronological, geographic, and communal splintering the Greeks stayed resolutely Greek in language and culture, and they even reestablished a great measure of internal uniformity during the Hellenistic period, a millennium after the acme of the Helladic era. The ethnogenesis, once effected, proved a powerful one: the Greeks and their language have remained stable, in place, and homogeneous for three millennia, and Greek is still profoundly Indo-European, next to Lithuanian the most archaic form of living Indo-European language. The substratum was bound to contribute some vocabulary, especially cultural terms with telltale suffixes (e.g., *asáminthos* 'bathtub', a tribute to Minoan plumbing, *labúrinthos* 'maze'). There is sometimes subtle evidence of its impact. The old terms for 'father' and 'mother' (*patḗr, mā́tēr* > *mḗtēr*) remain, but 'brother' and 'sister' have disappeared from use (*phrā́tēr* surviving only as 'member of a brotherhood, clansman'); instead there is *a-delphós,* literally 'womb mate, couterine', or *kasígnētos* 'jointly born', thus tracing filiation through the mother, clearly a terminological deviation from the Indo-European norm but in accordance with surviving practices in classical Greek times in Lycia (southwestern Asia Minor, home of the Iliadic hero Sarpedon, an ally of the Trojans).

Unlike language, however, Greek religion crucially reflects the interaction of overlay and substratum. In contrast to the relatively easy comparison of Vedic and Old Iranian deities, the Greek pantheon in its standardized form is a creation sui generis, a unique setup more notable for originality than preservation. It was not constituted during the "dark ages," since the Mycenaean inscriptions, for all their ledger-type brevity, supply an almost complete set of correspondents to the classical roster of the twelve Olympian deities: *di-we* (= *Diweí* 'to Zeus') *e-ra* (= *Hḗrāi* 'to Hera'), *po-se-da-o-ne* (= *Poseidaónei* 'to Poseidon'), *e-ma-a*$_2$ (= *Hermáhāi* 'to Hermes'), *a-re* and *e-nu-wa-ri-jo* (= *Árēi* 'to Ares' and *Enualíōi* 'to Enyalios', names of the war-god), *a-ta-na-po-ti-ni-ja* (= *Athā́nāi Potníāi* 'to Lady Athena'), *a-te-mi-to* (= *Artémitos* 'of Artemis'), *a-pa-i-ti-jo* (= *Hāphaistios*, man's name derived from Hephaistos), *di-wo-nu-so-jo* (*Diwonúsoio* 'of Dionysos'). Apollo is represented by his *pa-ja-wo-ne* (= *Paiāwónei* 'to Paean', while Demeter (< **Dā-mātēr*) as 'Earth Mother' (and doubtless her daughter Persephone as well) lurks under the plural *Pótniai* 'Ladies'. The only frankly missing major deity is Aphrodite, quite expectably, for this goddess is but the diffused outcome of the Semitic Astarte, spread to Greece via Cyprus by the seafaring Phoenicians during the "dark ages" (see chap. 2).

Clearly the bulk of the divine figures had their names (and presumably basic functions) in place at the end of the Mycenaean period and were thus in essence creations of the Helladic era of fusion between indigenous and intrusive elements. That age of interaction also marks the onset of the great dichotomy in Greek religion, the contrast between "olympian" (heaven-centered) and "chthonian" (earth-oriented) forms of cult, the former upward looking and brightness prone (white animals offered up on elevated altars), the latter soil bound and infernally inclined, with black victims sacrificed in underground pits. At some point systematizing mythopoeists arranged the "olympian" crew into a neatly genealogized divine clan, perhaps not unlike a Mycenaean dynast's court, and in due course diffusionary eastern motifs supplied the "time depth" of divine dynastic history (descent from Ouranos and the Titans, and the rest) that we studied in chapter 2. Yet the whole, for all its brilliant elaboration, still shows its seams and remains a somewhat rickety hodgepodge, as we can see from sketches of the principal actors.

Zeus is the head of the clan, clearly a patriarchal *despótēs* (= Sanskrit *dámpati-*) 'housemaster', husband (*pósis* = Sanskrit *pátis* 'lord') of Hera, with whom he performs sacral intercourse conducive to vegetal luxuriance. He is in name identical with the old Vedic sky-god Dyaus (Indo-European **Dyḗws* 'Bright Sky'). As we saw in chapter 4, Dyaus sank to insignificance in India, keeping mainly his mythical mating with Earth. In Greece the entire primal Heaven : Earth mating has been shunted to the ancestral track of Ouranos : Gaia, but the hierogamy of Zeus and Hera still replicates it to a point. Zeus has kept the heavenly eminence (one is tempted to say "identity") of his Indo-European prototype and annexed atmospheric dominion as well. He is the cloud-gathering wielder of the swift thunderbolt (*argikéraunos*), the rainbringer (*Zeùs húei* 'Zeus rains'; Aristophanes in his burlesque made him urinate through a sieve), and his own heavy-handed enforcer, but he is also (along with all-seeing Helios) the oath-god who sanctifies swearing and punishes perjury. Even in the desacralized Homeric environment, beyond the divine comedy of the crude bully and wife beater with his rough-and-ready "justice," we can glimpse a more dignified dispenser of fate lots to humankind, a god who weighs on golden scales the fates of heroes and relates to *díkē* 'justice' and *thémis* alike; the former is identical with Sanskrit *díśā* 'direction' and entails man's dues (cf. Latin *directum* > French *droit* 'law'); the latter goes with Vedic *dhắman-* (Varuṇa's law) and implies doing right by the gods.

This is the Indo-European side of Zeus. But there is also the "Cretan Zeus," the divine child sheltered in a mountain cave, nurtured by bees and suckled by a goat, worked by Hesiod into the myth of divine generations, but in truth a reflection of the Minoan-type cyclical vegetation deity or dying god whose tomb was still shown to uncomprehending mainland tourists in classical Greece. Some were offended by the notion that Zeus, that epitome of immortality, could have died, and the poet Callimachus branded the Cretans liars for claiming so. Finally, straddling the contradiction, Zeus Katakhthonios 'Zeus the Subterranean' was a standard allonym for Hades, the infernal consort of Persephone. As we saw in chapter 6, Hades (< **Hawidās* < **Sm̥-wid-*) simply meant 'Uniter, Reunionist'; much as the Indo-Iranian *Yama developed into both the Iranian worldly sovereign and the Vedic otherworldly potentate, the Greek Zeus figure was bifurcated in the olympian : chthonian dichotomy, as ruler of the bright skies on the one hand and of post-mortem murk on the other.

Zeus's sister-wife Hḗrā seems to originate in Argos on the Eastern Peloponnesus and is cognate in name with *Hṓrā* 'Season' and with English *year* (Indo-European **yēr-*), either as the consort (*páredros*) of the year-god (*eniautòs daímōn*) or simply as the 'yearling' cow or heifer. Her propensity for bovine theriomorphism (*boôpis*) matches that of the "Cretan Zeus," who in bull shape abducted Europa and founded the dynasty of Minos, in whose line taurine features persisted down to the Minotaur. As first lady of Olympus, she patronized matrimony. An annual ritual bath in a sacred spring restored her virginity, thus reinforcing the year pattern.

Poseidon (like Hades billed as Zeus's "brother") is the invocational form of 'husband of Dā' (as in **Dā-mātēr* > Demeter; frozen vocative case **pósei* = Sanskrit *páte*). In Arcadian myth he figures as the consort of Demeter; together they produced Despoina ('Lady', i.e., Persephone) in a hippomorphous mating reminiscent of the coupling of Vivasvat and Saraṇyū in India (see chap. 4). Poseidon had a knack for siring famous horses (Areion, Pegasos) and was associated with underground waters and earthquakes (as 'earthshaker', literally 'shake earth': *ennosígaios, enosíkhthōn,* Doric *ennosídās,* Mycenaean *e-ne-si-da-o-ne*); the sea association is secondary, overriding ancient Aegean sea-gods such as Nereus and Proteus. Like Zeus (-Hades), Poseidon combines a clear Indo-European component (horse mythology) with assorted underground associations; he may be an individualized allomorph of Zeus, spun off as theologians detached the latter from the old earth mating (as in Vedic *Dyā́vā-Pṛthivī́*), syncretized him with the "Cretan Zeus," and paired him off with the Argive year-goddess; all this took place well before the eastern intrusion of the Ouranos : Gaia theogony. Let us recall that in standard myth Zeus (not Poseidon) and his "sister" Demeter produced Persephone. Poseidon's ascendancy may have occurred in the Peloponnesus during the second millennium, judging from Arcadian myth and the prominence of Poseidon in the Mycenaean records from Pylos.

Hermes was the son of Zeus and Maia, one of his many extramarital liaisons. The name is not clear. Hermes is the god of roads and travel, trade and transport (including soul escort to Hades), cattle and pasture; but he is also a trickster, a sharp trader, and a cattle thief, compromising what he is supposed to patronize. I pointed out in chapter 4 that the basic positive traits of Hermes resemble those of the Vedic Pūṣan, and that in name Pūṣan is an etymological match for Hermes' Arcadian son *Pā́n* (< *Pāṓn* < **Pāusṓn*) 'Nourisher', perhaps abstracted from his compound allonym *Aigí-pān,* meaning originally 'goat breeder' (cf. Mycenaean *ai-ki-pa-ta-* = *aigipástās* 'goatherd') but subsequently alluding to the god's own goatlike characteristics. Thus the Olympian Hermes and the provincial Pan reflect separate elaborations of the same inherited Indo-European material. Hermes' tricksterism evolved as part of the epic desacralization of the Olympian pantheon, whereas Pan, protected by the earnest folk beliefs of the backwoods, was slated for a remarkable and pervasive para-Olympian cultic career. He was the god at once of the torrid noonday stillness of the Arcadian rangeland and of the sudden stir of unexplained "panic" in cattle, of disquieting woodland visions and the sounds of untamed nature. His Panhellenic (no pun intended) popularity was secure after his reported reassuring epiphany to the Athenians on the eve of Marathon. Plutarch's tale of the "Death of Pan" has become the folkloristic paradigm for the widespread motif of a mysterious hallucinatory voice from nature requesting a death announcement at a designated spot, with lamentations heard as the request is carried out. Folk etymology (*pân* 'all') has helped make this goat-god a paradoxical symbol of pan-theism through the ages, as in John Keats's great hymn to Pan in book I of *Endymion:* "Be still a symbol of immensity, a firmament reflected in a sea!" The fascination of scholars with this ever-relevant mythical figure is seen by such works as Patricia Merivale's *Pan the Goat-God: His Myth in Modern Times* (1969) and Philippe Borgeaud's *Recherches sur le dieu Pan* (1979).

Ares and Hephaistos are strictly minor Olympians, with obscure, presumably substratal names. They were sons of Zeus and Hera, in itself a sign of triteness (Zeus usually picked extracurricular mates for more important sirings). They are involved in those obscure bits of myth mentioned above (the bottling up of Ares, the hurling away of Hephaistos). Ares as war-god has on the whole little "personality" apart from alleged savagery, while Hephaistos is the typical smith-god found in many mythologies, congenitally deformed yet skilled and mostly good-natured, operating in a subterranean or submarine forge and related to such submythological craftsmen as the Kabeiroi of Samothrace and the Telkhines of Rhodes. Both seem to be headquartered to the northeast of Greece proper, Ares in Thrace and Hephaistos on the northern Aegean island of Lemnos (where a pre-Greek population lingered in classical times). Homeric storytelling ties both in with Aphrodite (Ares as her lover, Hephaistos as the cuckolded husband). Ares typically supports the Trojan side in the war, as do other deities with "eastern" attachments (Apollo, Artemis, Aphrodite).

Athena is in origin the Aegean "palace goddess" proper to Athens (Homer calls her *Pallàs Athēnaíē* 'Maid Athenian'). Myth presents her as born from Zeus's aching head under the obstetric ministrations of Hephaistos's sledgehammer, after Zeus had swallowed her pregnant mother Mêtis 'Counsel'. She was virginal (Hephaistos once attempted to rape her) and martial, wearing the Gorgon's head on her breastplate and carrying a goathide shield (*aigís*). She does, however, perpetuate traces of the Indo-European transfunctional goddess in her string of Panathenaic epithets, *Poliás, Níkē, Hugíeia* 'Protectress, Victory, Wellbeing,' a sequence that is elsewhere parceled out over a triple set of goddesses, as in the Judgment of Paris, where Hera offers the Trojan prince sovereignty, Athena promises glory, and Aphrodite successfully holds out the prospect of sex with Helen of Sparta. The names of the three Kharites, Euphrosyne 'Well-mindedness', Aglaia 'Glory', and Thaleia 'Bloom', are echoed in Pindar's evocation of these "Graces" (*Olympian Ode* 14.3–7), employing the adjectives *sophós* 'wise', *aglaós* 'glorious', *kalós* 'beautiful'. Such survivals of tripartition can be found randomly throughout Greek tradition, as when the description of the shield of Achilles (*Iliad* 18.483–608) conjures up a societal triptych of legislation, warfare, and harvest or a fragment of Hesiod (Merkelbach-West 203) details Zeus's gifts to three families of heroes: valor (*alkḗ*) to the Aiakidai (Achilles and Aias), intelligence (*noûs*) to the Amythaonidai (Adrastos and Amphiaraos), and wealth (*ploûtos*) to the Atridai (Agamemnon and Menelaos).

Apollo (obscure in name) is the most complex of Greek gods; his spheres include divination, healing, lustration, legislation, incantation, and poetry. He is both the Python killer in charge of ecstatic mantics at Delphi (with seasonal absences among the "Hyperboreans" in the north, almost a shamanistic trait) and the insular twin of Artemis at Delos, born of Zeus and Leto, whose ancestry lies in Lycia in Asia Minor (indeed, the Lycian Sarpedon in the *Iliad* prays to his native Apollo). He is definitely a Trojan ally, which also marks him as heavily Asianic. That he came to be the epitome of luminous "Greekness" is one of those creative surprises in which Greek mythology abounds. His Trojan role includes his most significant comparativistic dimension. There he appears as the far-darting archer who shoots plague into the Greek host, beasts and men alike (*Iliad* 1.48–52), even as Rudra did in Vedic India; like Rudra, he is also appeased into a healer (*Paiḗōn*) on the ethnomedical principle *ho trṓsas iásetai* 'he that wounds shall make whole'. Like Hermes with Pan, he had his positive side institutionalized in a provincial "son" who in due course made good in the Panhellenic orbit without passing through Olympus. This was Asklepios, born of Apollo and the maid Koronis from Thessaly in northern Greece, a daughter of the Lapith Phlegyas. Before term, Koronis consorted with another man, and the insulted god shot her dead, extracted the fetus, and had Asklepios raised by the pedagogically skilled Centaur Kheiron, who tutored him in the healing arts. Asklepios became a famous physician, equally adept at spells, potions, herbs, and surgery, a comprehensive set of medical abilities that curiously replicates the combined roles of Varuṇa, the Aśvins, and Rudra as patrons of brahmin, vaiśya, and kṣatriya healing in India, and of the Avestan classification of medicine into knife, herb, and incantation specialties (*Vidēvdāt* 7.44). This accordance, however, hardly underpins an Indo-European tripartite comparison; more probably it reflects a spread of Indo-Iranian tradition westward by Greek physicians such as Ktesias, who attended at the Achaemenian court. In the end Asklepios succumbed to hybris by reviving the dead and provoked divine nemesis in the form of Zeus's bolt. This is how Pindar tells the tale in *Pythian Ode* 3, adding the moralistic exhortation that man should not strive for immortal life but rather should exhaust the devices of the feasible.

Asklepios is thus a demigod from Thessaly who has been attached to the Apollinian healing tradition. An entire structure emerges: Apollo as the plague bringer is known as Smintheus (from *smínthos,* denoting a ratty type of mouse), while *Asklēpiós* is derived from *skálops* or *(a)spálax* 'blind rat, rat mole'. This reflects an animal symbolism of the plague rat as the disease spreader and the mole as the blind, beneficent healing animal. Ancillary symbolism abounds: Apollo has the epithet Loxias 'the one with the oblique gait', a reference to the typical movement of mice. The *thólos* or circular underground incubation structure of Asklepios's great healing sanctuary at Epidauros on the eastern Peloponnesus had the interior layout of a molehill, with an inner chamber surrounded by concentric corridors. In Argos, archaic (ca. 700 B.C.E.) terra-cotta figurines of mice or rats have been found, wearing blindfolds or lying on their backs with bellies slit and eyes bandaged, pointing to some kind of sacrificial ritual involving noxious rats and their symbolically neutralized sightless permutations.

The Vedic Rudra had as his animal *ākhú-* '[rat] mole', as did his son Gaṇeśa, who is sometimes depicted as *ākhu-ga-* 'riding on a rat', even as Apollo Smintheus was *bebēkȍs epì tôi muȋ* 'mounted on a mouse' (Strabo 13.48). Rudra was known as *Vañkú-* 'totterer, waverer', also a reference to the typical gait of rodents. Gaṇeśa was a minor figure specialized as a patron of poetry, a hypostasis of Rudra with an epicletic name ('Lord of the Troop'). Rudra's medicinal role disappeared in later times and Gaṇeśa did not inherit it, nor was the rat : mole distinction sharply maintained. Yet the similarities are striking and specific enough to postulate as prototype an ambivalent archer-god who could either hurt or heal and whose animal manifestation was either rat or mole, with the jerky gait characteristic of the species. His hypostases could appear either as pure healer (Greece) or as a patron of incantation and by extension poetry (India), in either case purged of potentially noxious ambivalence.

Is this a separately inherited Indo-European mythologem? If so, there is no third independent witness. It can hardly reflect diffusion from India to Greece, or vice versa, or from a third, common source, for the dates are early (*Rig-Veda* and *Iliad*), and nothing of the kind is attested in the interspace between the Aegean and the Indus valley.

Artemis was Apollo's twin in the Delian birth myth and was mildly coordinated with him in some functions, for example, shooting down females while Apollo's arrows make short work of males, as in the case of the unfortunate sons and daughters of the hybristic Niobe. Otherwise they have little in common. Artemis is another typical example of Greek religious dichotomy. There is the virgin huntress, especially prominent among the Dorians of western Greece, the cruel kind who changed the innocently peeping Theban prince Aktaion into a stag to be devoured by his own pack of hounds. She had theriomorphic propensities of her own: although she expelled from her band the nymph Kallistō, who had been impregnated by Zeus with the eponymous son Arkas (ancestor of the Arcadians) and was subsequently changed into a she-bear by the jealous Hera, her own epithet Kallistē 'Fairest' and her name reveal that she herself was once prone to ursinity, since Artemis and Arkas alike are dialectal cognates of *árktos* 'bear'. On the other hand there is the Artemis of Asia Minor, especially of Ephesus, whose polymastic iconography bespeaks a typical exaggerated fertility goddess, a variant of the lion-throned Cybele of Anatolia who in a wider sense matches the Cretan "Lady of Beasts" (*Pótnia Thērôn*). That this particular Artemis reflects ill-applied Greek nomenclature is clear from the fact that the import name Aphrodite was appended with equal infelicity to the Mistress of Animals on Trojan Mount Ida, who in the "Homeric Hymn to Aphrodite" conceived Aeneas by Anchises in an epiphany attended by mating wolves, lions, bears, and leopards. No wonder both "Artemis" and "Aphrodite" supported Troy during the war.

Dionysos, that presumed latecomer who does not seem to be quite integrated into the Homeric pantheon but unexpectedly crops up in Mycenaean inscriptions, reflects yet another composite divine character. Classical myth depicts him as Theban, conceived by Semele but later sewn into and ultimately born from father Zeus's thigh. Semele is passed off as a daughter of King Kadmos but is in name the Thracian word for 'Earth' (cf. Slavic *zemlja*) and thus stands for a non-Greek deity.[1] There is also the tradition of Dionysos's arrival from abroad, from Phrygia and Lydia in Asia Minor or from Thrace in the north, and of the string of "resistance myths" that stretch from Thrace (Orpheus and Lykourgos) via Boeotia (daughters of Minyas at Orkhomenos, Pentheus at Thebes) down to the Peloponnesus (daughters of Proitos at Tiryns). In these stories, attempts to shun, repress, or suppress outbreaks of Dionysiac frenzy end up in frequently homicidal madness experienced by or victimizing the resisters (sometimes both, as when Pentheus

1. Semele may provide a glimpse of lost Thracian (or Thracian-Phrygian) myth: the earth-goddess struck and consumed by the heaven-god's lightning in the course of bearing Sabazios (Thracian name of Dionysos), literally 'self-being' (**swo-bhwo-dyos*; cf. Slavic *svobodĭ* 'free', and for meaning Latin *Līber* 'Dionysos'; see chaps. 9 and 12).

dons drag and joins the maenads but is torn apart by his own mother). This is the standard Dionysos, also known by the Lydian name Bakkhos, the ivy-strewn, thyrsus-bearing, effeminate instigator of instinctual orgies, whose cultic outbreaks especially affected women and sent them to the hills to lacerate live victims in hallucinatory fury, thus filling the police blotters of well-run, patriarchally orderly Greek communities. But there is also "Dionysos the Cretan," who merits separate attention. Unlike the patron of land-based orgiastic import cults, this Dionysos is strictly a "dying god" from the Minoan substratum. He is in fact a younger, "recycled" version of the "Cretan Zeus," and the name fits, for **Dios-nusos* means 'the nurseling [or the like] of Zeus'. He is associated with a female divine type known iconographically as the "tree goddess," whose myth included episodes of abduction and sometimes death by hanging, reflected variously in such divine or saga figures as Persephone, Helen, Erigone, Phaidra, and especially her sister Ariadne (the last two being daughters of Minos). One tradition is that Ariadne hanged herself (presumably right in Crete) when jilted by Theseus, whom she had helped to kill the Minotaur. In others she died, abandoned by him, on Naxos, or was wind driven to Cyprus, expired from issueless birth pangs, and was venerated there as a syncretistic Ariadne Aphrodite. Homer (*Odyssey* 11.320–23), however, describes her death on the island of Dia at the hands of Artemis on the instigation of Dionysos, before Theseus could sexually possess her. Elsewhere (e.g., Hesiod, *Theogony* 947–48) Dionysos figures as her divine consort, which superficially points to a love triangle similar to that of Apollo, Koronis, and her nondivine lover. More in depth, however, we have here the saga remnants of Minoan myth: Dionysos as the rejuvenated "Cretan Zeus" is a manifestation of the same bull-god who with Europa founded the dynasty of Minos. Minos's wife Pasiphae, in another taurine mating, was blessed with the Minotaur, which the uncomprehending Greeks twisted into bestiality compounded with teratology. The Minotaur was the Lord of the Labyrinth (it was, after all, custom built for him), while Ariadne presumably was the Lady of the Labyrinth, the *da-pu$_2$-ri-to-jo po-ti-ni-ja* (= *Daburínthoio Pótnia*) recorded in Mycenaean Greek as worshiped at the Palace of Knossos. When she betrayed her lord to a stranger it amounted to deicide, for the Minotaur was a genuine, albeit somewhat misconstrued, form of the Cretan bull-god; Dionysos, the surviving "straight" version, merely got even. Artemis, who did the killing, stands for more than the routine targeter of errant women in classical myth; she may in fact represent the Eleuthia of Amnisos (harbor of Knossos), a dionysiac maieutic goddess attested in the Mycenaean inscriptions at Knossos and appearing as Eileithyia in Homer (with a grotto at Amnisos) and in later Greek tradition, where she becomes syncretized with Artemis. Thus Ariadne's divine career was at an end; she never made it into Greek religion proper except as a saga heroine, while Dionysos's godhead was preserved through absorption into the Bacchic cults that had in the meantime engulfed the mainland.

This survey of the Greek pantheon affords rather slim pickings for comparative Indo-European mythology. Bits of Zeus and Poseidon, traits of Hermes-Pan and Apollo-Asklepios, a piece of the transfunctional goddess, and little else. Diffusion from the east fares a little better—there is Aphrodite, a part of Dionysos, and especially much of the pre-Olympian divine-generational material, although here, too the basic Ouranos-Kronos-Zeus pattern is filled out with substratal lore (Hekatonkheiroi, Titans, Tartaros, etc.). The pantheon is, however, a hotbed for the study of typology, of superimposition, juxtaposition, combination, fusion, and multiplication, as are other materials not even mentioned yet, for example, such icon figures of our Western culture as Prometheus and Pandora, or the single Muse of Homer later exponentially expanded to nine, or Hesiod's Ages of Mankind, or the Orphic and Eleusinian mystery religions with their own esoteric transmutations of the myths of Dionysos, Demeter, and afterlife, or the vast saga cycles that fueled epic and tragic literature. In Otherworld traditions and in sagas, however, possible Indo-European survivals also need to be investigated.

I noted above and in chapter 6 that the Homeric Hades in the Odyssean *Nekyia* or "Book of the Dead" (book 11) is something of a contradiction. It is not strictly a hell straight down (underworld access comes later, one such alleged point being Cape Tainaron, a southern tip of the Peloponnesus), but rather somewhere in the northern mists, on a shore at the ends of the Ocean, among the Cimmerians on whom the sun never shines. (As was noted in chap. 3, the Norse *Hel* was also in the *north*, cognate with Greek *nérteros* 'pertaining to the netherworld'.) There Odysseus performs chthonian necromancy to gain access to the ghosts, who seem doomed to an open-ended, suspended shadow life, regaining the power of communication with the living only at the taste of sacrificial blood. Yet there is vegetation in those halls of Hades (a *leimṓn* or watery meadow to grow asphodels), and in the *Iliad* Hades is repeatedly termed *klutópōlos* 'famous for colts', thus requiring horse fodder. We have seen that the name itself etymologically relates to Indo-European family reunion in the hereafter, matching Vedic *saṁ-vid-* 'find [each other]' in the funeral hymns. It clearly was an irrigated place, with a river system first described by Circe in *Odyssey* 10.513–14, elaborated in later times, and cataloged for us by Milton (*Paradise Lost* 2.577–84):

> Abhorred *Styx* the flood of deadly hate,
> Sad *Acheron* of sorrow, black and deep;
> *Cocytus,* nam'd of lamentation loud
> Heard on the ruful stream; fierce *Phlegeton*
> Whose waves of torrent fire inflame with rage.
> Farr off from these a slow and silent stream,
> *Lethe* the River of Oblivion roules
> Her watrie Labyrinth.

The Vedic Yama likewise had to make his way along great watercourses (*pravát-* in *RV* 10.14.1) while settling the Otherworld, ending up with a *gávyūti-* 'pastureland' (*RV* 10.14.2). But Greek tradition also knew the different Otherworld of the Isles of the Blessed (*Makárōn Nêsoi*), home of happy heroes in Hesiod (*Works and Days* 168–73) and of righteous dead in Pindar (*Olympian Ode* 2), a place likewise in the far Ocean, but warmed by soft winds rather than smothered in sunless fog. Homer is silent on this elitist resort of afterlife, except in the one late passage of the *Telemachy* (Odyssey 4.561–69) where Proteus prophesies that at the end of his life Menelaos will be transported to the Elysian Field at the ends of the earth, a place of easy living without extreme climate or precipitation, with zephyrs wafting off the Ocean. Being Helen's husband and Zeus's son-in-law is his ticket to this preferential retirement. The term *Ēlúsion* (*pedíon*) can be reconstructed as Indo-European **wl̥nutiyom pediyom* 'meadowy field' and compared with the Hittite word *wellu-* (< **welnu-*) 'meadow', which describes the goal of the departed in mortuary rituals for Hittite royalty:

> And this meadow, O Sun-god, have rightfully ordained for him!
> Let none sequester it from him or contest it!
> Let there graze for him in this meadow cattle and sheep,
> horses and mules!

Hittite religion and mythology generally are heavily derivative in substratal (Hattic) and adstratal (Hurrian, Mesopotamian) ways and, despite their early attestation, have little to offer for Indo-European comparison. Yet in the funerary texts such traditions seem to survive, not only with respect to the meadow but also in the exhortation against its expropriation, which exactly matches *RV* 10.14.2: *naíṣā gávyūtir apabhartavā́ u* 'this pastureland is not to be taken away', even as its 'rightful ordination' is reminiscent of Proteus's assurance that the Elysian Field is Menelaos's by divine commitment (*thésphaton*). All told, then, Hades and Elysium are two discordant Greek centers of afterlife, but they are in truth complementary, showing joint similarities to Vedic and Hittite tradition, which also explains how a sunless or subterranean Hades is still capable of sustaining horse-breeding meadows. The bleakness of the Homeric conception seems to be an extreme of the fatalistic heroic ethos, countervailed even then by more optimistic views. The on-the-spot segregation of the dead upon arrival, the forked road leading to punishment or reward, in short, posthumous judgment with a view to damnation or bliss (parallel to Zoroastrian Iran), is first sketched by Orphism, that chthonian salvation religion that via Plato's *Republic* and Vergil's *Aeneid* helped Western culture formulate its Dantesque view of infernal goings-on. Already a late interpolation in the *Nekyia* describes a Department of Cruel and Unusual Punishments (Tityos pecked by vultures, Tantalos thirsting and starving, Sisyphos pushing his boulder) and mentions Minos as the judge of the dead; Cretan heroes had some sort of inside track to otherworldly leadership, for Rhadamanthys comes to share the same bench, besides being billed by Pindar as the magistrate of the Isles of the Blessed.

In the vast reaches of Greek saga some patterns can be discovered that transcend the typology of international folktales and seem to reflect inherited Indo-European structures. The typical Indo-European myth-based chronicle-epic strings out in diachronic sequence a succession of rulers or heroes starting with anthropogonic and societal founders, religious and legal establishers, followed by warrior types, and ending up with initiators and maintainers of peace and economic prosperity, thus roughly matching the basic Vedic formulas of Mitrā-Varuṇā, Indrā-Vāyū, and the Vasus or Aśvins. Such a structure is palpable even in the *Shāh Nāma,* where the "founders" starting with Gayōmart are followed by the warlike rule of the Kayanids, who in turn are suddenly replaced by the peace era of Luhrāsp and Gushtāsp with their Aśvinic characteristics (see chap. 7). It is, however, especially rife in Roman, Celtic, and Slavic tradition, as later chapters will show. In Greece something similar is found in the dynastic saga of Orkhomenos, an old Mycenaean city of northern Boeotia. The founding king is Andreus, a real "first man," followed by Eteokles, the religious establisher who instituted the worship of the three Kharites, whose triple transfunctionality was discussed above. Then followed Phlegyas, a crude warrior whose very name has incendiary connotations. Finally came Minyas, who had great revenues and built a treasury. There was no filial succession between the last three, with a dynastic break at each transition point between the levels, as is typical of the *Shāh Nāma* and other chronicle-epics. Significantly, an archaic pattern of this kind survives in local saga rather than in the limelight of Greek culture.

By contrast, the vast agglomerated Panhellenic saga cycles seem least amenable to such archaism. An exception is, however, the Herakles cycle, which does contain important comparative material for the study of the Indo-European warrior, embedded though it is in an accretional mass and touched by the slippage and sea change to which Greece has subjected its heritage (see chap. 13).

There remains one tradition that illustrates to perfection the complexity of Greece for comparative mythology. It is distinctly local and yet Panhellenic, rooted in religion and yet secularized in saga, anchored in the soil and still reflecting Indo-European inheritance. It concerns the *Dióskouroi* 'Zeus's boys' of Sparta, Kastor and Polydeukes, with their sister Helen, all hatched somehow from an egg fertilized in the encounter of Leda (wife of king Tyndareus) and the Swan (= Zeus), pointing to some original ornithomorphous hierogamy. Helen is clearly in part a pre-Doric version of the "tree-goddess," not unknown to local cults in classical times, sometimes named Dendritis (cf. *déndron* 'tree') and occasionally reported as hanged (Pausanias, *Description of Greece* 3.19.10). Her original myth may be autochthonous to Laconia (the part of the Peloponnesus closest to Crete), including her consort Menelaos, who had a shrine to his name (Menelaion) at the ancient Spartan cult site of Therapne. I noted before that the tree-goddess was abduction prone; this feature of her myth probably triggered her induction into saga, both in the simpler story of her childhood kidnapping by the Athenian Theseus and his Lapith boon companion Peirithoos, with rescue by the Dioskouroi, and in the more serious elopement with the Trojan Paris that launched a thousand ships (Menelaos had been somehow promoted by saga genealogy to be the brother of King Agamemnon of Mycenae). Over at Troy, as she and her new father-in-law Priam contemplate the Greek host beneath the topless towers of Ilium, Helen does not spot her own brothers and erstwhile rescuers, thinking that they may be too embarrassed by her adultery to show their faces, whereupon the all-knowing poet sagely comments (*Iliad* 3.243–44):

> Thus she spoke, but them already the grain-growing soil held down
> right in Lakedaimon, in their own native land.

The implication that the brothers had died back home must be qualified against the background of local sagas. Kastor was killed in a cattle raid against the Arcadians Idas and Lynkeus, whereupon Zeus split the difference by allotting to the twins half-time immortality, as described by Odysseus in the "Catalog of Heroines" in the *Nekyia* (*Odyssey* 11.298–304):

> And Leda I saw, the bed-mate of Tyndareus,
> who to Tyndareus bore a pair of strong-minded boys,
> Kastor the horse tamer, and Polydeukes handy with his fist,
> whom both, live, the grain-growing soil holds down.
> And they, below, as an honor granted by Zeus,
> alternately live every other day, and alternately again
> are dead. The honor granted them equals that of gods.

All this boils down to chthonian cyclicity, transmuted by epic whimsy from year-god to day-god, showing that the Dioskouroi, like Helen, have roots in the substratum.

Yet spread over all this we find unmistakable traits of the Indo-European Divine Twins in association with a solar female, comparable to the Vedic Aśvins : Sūryā and the Latvian *Dieva dēli* : *Saules meita* pairings (see chaps. 4 and 12). *Diòs koúrō* (or *koûroi,* with dual number supplanted by plural) matches in meaning *Divó nápātā,* the borrowed Latin dvandva *Castores* for the horse tamer and his brother parallels *Aśvínā,* and Polydeukes' success in the cattle raid is comparable to Sahadeva's prowess with bovines (cf. chap. 5). More in unison, the Dioskouroi were called horsemen (*leúkippoi, eúippoi, leukópōloi*) and sometimes hippomorphously *leukṑ pṓlō Diós* 'white colts of Zeus'; they were also termed *Sōtêre* 'Rescuers' (cf. Nā́satyā) and were credited in mariners' traditions with airborne epiphanies heralded by Saint Elmo's fire, averting shipwreck and death by water. In Christian transposition they turned into Saint Nicholas and Saint Damian as patrons of seafarers, but their roots are clearly in the same Indo-European well from which the Aśvins pulled Bhujyu and Rebha. Helen appears as the sister rather than bride of the Dioskouroi, while they consorted with the daughters of a certain Leukippos; but her name does suggest the Vedic Sūryā (*Helénē* perhaps from **Swelenā,* cognate with *Hḗlios* < **Sāweliyos* 'Sun' and with Avestan *xvarənah* < **swelnos* 'solarity'), and there is nothing to preclude the idea that the Indo-European background of Helen was as the sexual partner of the Dioskouroi, with the birth myth and sibling relationship attributable to syncretistic adjustment to the Laconian substratum.

Thus Greece in its inimitable way has managed to meld elements that can be rolled back to components only by the kind of scholarly struggle waged in this chapter. This is a task requiring thorough familiarity with both the immense store of Greek myth and the vast secondary literature as well as the external comparands, a combination rarely possessed by either specialists in classical studies or generalists in mythology. Hence Greece remains an extreme challenge to the comparativist, a hard nut that we have merely dented.

Recommended Reading

Kerényi, Carl. *The Gods of the Greeks*. London: Thames and Hudson, 1951.

———. *The Heroes of the Greeks*. London: Thames and Hudson, 1959.

Better than other contemporary handbooks, which are often mostly summations or collages of ancient mythographers, these works convey a sense of Greek myth in all its creative and confused richness, without resorting to overinterpretation.

9 · Ancient Rome

Roman myth usually appears as an appendix at the back of handbooks of classical (i.e., Greek) mythology. The moderns have it on good authority, for Ovid himself filled up his *Metamorphoses* with Greek matter, adding a few native tales at the end. Rome was in fact the first big external consumer of Greek myth, bequeathing it to Western literary posterity. When Roman tradition encountered strange gods, be it in Greece, Gaul, or Germania, they were subjected as far as possible to a Roman interpretation and tagged with the names of Roman deities. Hence the standard identifications (really renamings) Zeus : *Jūpiter,* Hera : *Jūnō,* Poseidon : *Neptūnus,* Hermes : *Mercurius, Ares* : *Mars,* Athena : *Minerva,* Artemis : *Dīāna,* Hephaistos : *Volcānus,* Demeter : *Cerēs,* Aphrodite : *Venus,* Dionysos : *Bacchus* or *Līber,* Kronos : *Sāturnus,* Hestia : *Vesta*. Only one major god (Apollo) slipped through with no change of name, and some lesser figures suffered phonetic mutilation in being filtered from the Greeks to the Romans via the Etruscan interstratum (*Hēraklês* > *Herc*[*u*]*les, Asklēpiós* > *Aesculapius, Persephónā* > *Proserpina*). There was from early on a compulsion to nativize, as when the earliest preserved Roman poet, Livius Andronicus, began his translation of the *Odyssey* by invoking not the Homeric Muse but the obscure Latin goddess *Camēna*.

Roman legendry dated the founding of the *Urbs* to 753 B.C.E., a date more than two centuries before the earliest attested inscriptions in the Latin language. At that time the Greeks, newly literate with their Phoenician-origin alphabet, were busy colonizing the coasts of Sicily and southern Italy, though not settling farther north on the west (Tyrrhenian Sea) coast than the Bay of Naples. But their influence did reach, for the west side of central Italy (both coastal and hill towns) was inhabited by the Etruscans ("Tyrrhenians" to the Greeks), a nation of unknown origin, perhaps a mix of autochthons and earlier substratal migrants from the Aegean basin. A language similar to theirs was still spoken on Lemnos in the northern Aegean in classical Greek times; lest there be doubt of its non-Indo-European character, here are the numerals 1–10 in the Etruscan language: *thu, (e)sal, ci, śa, makh, huth, semph, cezph* (cf. Mons Cispius, the "Eighth Hill" of Rome), *nurph, śar* (20 was *zathrum,* but, e.g., 18 was *eslem zathrum* 'two from twenty', recalling Latin *duo-de-viginti,* and 17 was also subtractive, *ciem zathrum*). The Etruscans, with their maritime connections, were prompt in assimilating Greek literacy and culture, which they gradually passed on to their less adept neighbors in the hinterlands of the Apennine peninsula, the bulk of whom spoke Indo-European Italic dialects. Those included Umbrian in north-central Italy (east of the south-flowing Tiber, with Etruria [modern Tuscany] to the west) and Oscan in the south-central interior all the way to Campania (the back country of Naples) and beyond. Latium was in those days a small area at the southern tip of Etruria, and what was to become Rome lay only a few kilometers from major Etruscan cities such as Veii and Caere. The natives spoke Latin, a minor form of Italic rather different from Umbrian and Oscan, and were strictly in the shadow of Etruria, culturally and politically (*Rōma* and *Tiberis* are themselves Etruscan names). Roman annalism readily allows for Etruscan domination during the sixth century B.C.E., down to the "liberation" and founding of the Republic in 509, while filling in the early period with legendry of little historical (but considerable mythological) significance. But even that was probably more of a symbolic event, smacking of warlord-type rivalry between Etruscan and Etrusco-Latin factions (the Tarquin dynasty was in legend expelled by the first pair of consuls, of whom Junius Brutus was a Tarquin on his mother's side, while Collatinus's gentilic name was Tarquinius!). Rome remained heavily Etrusco-Latin through the fifth century, and only with the incipient regression of Etruria about 400 did purely Roman expansionist tendencies seriously assert themselves. Roman cultural identity is hence indebted to the Etruscans, and the "Western" form of the Greek alphabet that the Romans adapted and that we still use shows the influence of Etruscan (gamma becoming *c,* later new *g*-letter created, etc.).

The Etruscans had their own set of deities who, like the Roman ones, did double duty in native cult and as covers for the imported Greek pantheon, seen especially on the backs of inscribed Etruscan mirrors: Tinia (Zeus), Uni (Hera), Nethuns (Poseidon), Turms (Hermes), Maris (Ares), Menrva (Athena), Sethlans (Hephaistos), Thesan (Eos), Turan (Aphrodite), Fufluns (Dionysos). Apulu was simply imported, like Apollo in Rome, while some lesser Greek names suffered more extensive corruption and were on occasion taken up into Latin (e.g., Bellerophontes > Melerpanta; Ganymedes [Zeus's pederastic cupbearer] > Catamitus); others were translated (*Tinas clenar* 'Sons of Zeus' for Dioskouroi, *Thevrumines* 'Bull of Minos' for Minotaur). But the names of several important Etruscan deities were clearly borrowed from Latin (Uni < Juno, Nethuns < Neptunus, Maris < Mars), or formed from Italic elements (Fufluns < **Poplōno-*; cf. Latin *populus*). Conversely, a Roman deity may have a name that sounds like and matches an Etruscan one (Minerva) or has an Etruscan appearance (Mercurius, Sāturnus).

To a degree, then, Etruscan religion did have a bearing on Roman culture, most notably in the composition of the so-called Capitoline triad of deities (ensconced on the Capitol, one of Rome's seven hills), Jupiter, Juno, and Minerva, so unlike ancient Indo-European structures in combining one god with two goddesses. Our task, however, is not so much to follow up as to pierce that interaction, in order to isolate it and arrive at the "pure" Roman tradition.

It is sometimes starkly stated that "Rome has no myth." This is true to a point, but a corollary of such a bald assertion has been the tendency of many scholars to view Roman religion in terms of primitivism, as composed of vague powers, *numina,* rather than personified deities. It is more prudent to assume that at some point Roman religion was stripped of sacred narrative, demythologized yet not desacralized. Why this occurred can only be speculated upon, preferably in terms of what remains. That includes a large body of archaic and conservative cultic religion, feasts and rituals, which so cluttered the Roman calendar that every odd-numbered day was a religious festival of some sort, often opaque to us and perhaps sometimes already to the celebrants. Ovid's great poetic religious calendar, the *Fasti,* regrettably covers only January–June (his banishment by Augustus cut it short); hence we are better informed about the first half of the year than the rest. The guiding light for the early Romans was ancestral precedent, *mōs maiōrum,* with an inordinate fixation on societal rather than cosmic concerns. Rome indeed started as its own center, with subsequent outward radiation as an expression of its vitality and all roads still proverbially leading back to it; it was its own axis mundi, unlike the Greeks, who were scattered in advance and in sporadic search of a center. The founding of Rome was the pivotal "original" event, with the result that cosmogony and anthropogony appear transmuted to legendary urban beginnings. Hence the writers on Roman antiquities, such as Livy in Latin, Dionysius of Halicarnassus and Plutarch in Greek, were in a way mythographers, and the lost annalists they in turn drew upon composed in a real sense prose epics on urban beginnings (Vergil, the arty epopoeist with his imperial commission, belongs to a different, poetic literary sphere).

The profusion of obscure cults and opaque rituals also means that somewhere in the shadows there lurk cult myths, either forgotten or perhaps likewise translated to "history." Their recovery is a prime task of comparative mythology, either by internal reconstruction or, failing that, by comparison with such related Indo-European traditions as that of ancient India, where myth and ritual were perpetuated in tandem.

If proto-Roman myth has to be recovered by a combined excavation of cult and "history," Rome in its own stolid fashion was at least mildly creative in some other paramythical ways. Roman law, to which the West owes much of its jurisprudence, was evolutionary in the limited sense that legal lore can be, but it too harbors a basic societal conservatism with roots deep in the Indo-European past. Comparison with ancient Indic law is once again apposite and, granted sacral origins, with Old Iranian corpora such as the *Vidēvdāt* 'Anti-Demon Law' as well (after all, Mosaic law is part of the Pentateuch in the Old Testament). Even in Hittite tradition, where religion and myth are heavily sub- and adstratal, a healthy amount of Indo-European antiquities survives in the laws, for example, the legal verb **sark-* (infixed *sar-ni-k-*) 'make restitution', which matches Latin *sarcīre* 'repair', also used in a legal sense (*damna* [or *iniuriam, noxiam*] *sarcire* 'make good damages').

Rome also evolved, maintained, and bequeathed a distinct symbolism, very different from the broadly humane heritage of the Greeks. The latter left us 'myth' and 'tragedy', 'hybris' and 'nemesis', 'eros' and 'psyche', 'catharsis' and 'charisma', Achilles' heel and Nessos's cloak, Sisyphos's rock and Tantalos's blend of lure and frustration, the binary quandary of Scylla and Charybdis, the idols of the cave and the song of the Sirens. Athenian Greeks devised democracy (away from tyranny and oligarchy), but to Rome the state was simply "the people's business" (*res publica*), even as religion was "the gods' business" (*res divina*). On top of such symbols as the *fasces* that still adorn the chamber of the United States House of Representatives on Capitol Hill, Rome handed down a lore of patriotic anecdotes. Such was the story of the sudden chasm that had opened up in the Roman Forum, a divine *prodigium* to be propitiated only by precipitating "Rome's best," which Marcus Curtius took to mean himself; he jumped in and caused the hole to close, vindicating his good opinion of himself and sacrificially saving the city. Another concerned Genucius Cipus, whose sudden sprouting of horns presaged royal power, causing the good republican to choose self-imposed exile, lest the prediction come true. Or Cincinnatus in his conspicuous hurry to shed the trappings of office and get on with his plowing, a tale applied to the citizen-soldiers of George Washington, whose chopped cherry tree sprouted a similar legend of his own. The Founding Fathers were so steeped in Roman lore that the great seal of the United States bears three legends from Vergil: *"Novus Ordo Seclorum"* (*Eclogues* 4.5: *Magnus ab integro saeclorum nascitur ordo* 'The great succession of ages is born anew'); *"Annuit Coeptis"* (*Aeneid* 9.625: *Jupiter omnipotens, audacibus annue coeptis* 'Almighty Jupiter, beam on bold beginnings!'); *"E Pluribus Unum"* (*Moretum* 103: *color est e pluribus unus* '[When you mix a salad,] there is one color out of many'). Perhaps unwittingly but certainly appositely, Jefferson picked the image of the melting pot from a Vergilian salad bowl.

The legacy of the ancient Roman priestly establishment (organized into *collēgia* or 'colleges') also extends forward and backward in time. The elective lifetime chief curator of religious affairs, a position held by Julius Caesar, was the pontifex maximus, a title still borne by the pope. The antiquity of the term is clear, for it means literally 'way maker, pace setter, expediter' (cf. *arti-fex* 'skill practicer', *carni-fex* 'meat maker, executioner') and matches the Vedic *pathi-kṛ́t-* as a religious title applied to both gods and priests; *pons* here still reflects the Indo-European meaning 'passageway' (land-based, watery, or even airborne), which lingers on in Indo-Iranian, Slavic (Russian *put'*), Baltic (Old Prussian *pintis*), and Greek (*pátos*) as 'way, road, path' but has developed into 'sea[lane]' in Greek *póntos,* into 'ford' in Armenian *hun,* and into 'bridge' in Latin *pons*. The offices of the pontifex maximus were in the Regia, the old royal palace in the Forum, a building of great import in Roman religion (cf. chaps. 14 and 15).

The cult of a particular deity was directed by a *flāmen,* a priestly title comparable etymologically with Sanskrit *brahmán-* (or possibly alternatively with the Old Norse verb *blōta* 'to sacrifice'). The *flāmines maiōres* were the flamen dialis or high priest of Jupiter (assisted by his wife the flaminica dialis), the flamen martialis, and the flamen quirinalis. This set is important by revealing the structure of the "pre-

Capitoline" Roman pantheon, before the Etruscan intrusion of Jupiter-Juno-Minerva, to have been anchored on Jupiter, Mars, and Quirinus, a canonic set comparable to the Vedic tripartition of gods into Ādityas, Rudras, and Vasus.

Diālis is the adjective derived from *Diēs(piter)* or *Diūs,* the original name of *Jūpiter* (Indo-European **Dyḗws,* Vedic *Dyaús,* Greek *Zeús*), which latter is the vocatival invocation form (matching Greek *Zeû páter;* cf. *Posei-don*). Jupiter's nature and function closely resemble those of Zeus; he has of course taken on some iconographic and anthropomorphic trappings of the latter, but basically he too is the personification of the bright daytime heavens (cf. *sub Jove* 'out in the open'), who also holds sway in the airspace as the thunder-god (Jupiter Tonans) and punishes perjurers with his bolt. At the apex of the pantheon both the Greek and the Italic religions (cf. Oscan *Diovem,* Umbrian *Juve*) have this homologous figure, at variance with both Indo-Iranian and Celtic-Germanic-Baltic-Slavic. This is a remarkable piece of parallel development, not matched by much else in the two traditions. As patron of trothkeeping (*fidēs*), Jupiter has the faded allomorph Diūs Fidius, somewhat as the Vedic Mitra of covenants barely lingers on by the side of his dvandva partner, the great oath-god Varuṇa.

Mars (Mavors, Mamers, Mamars, etymologically obscure) was the war-god minus the storm-god function, but still a much greater figure of Roman religion than his Greek opposite number Ares. Unlike his stock image in modern cartoons, his "agrarian" aspect as patron of the husbandman almost outweighs his "martial" role. In *De agri cultura* Cato addresses to this god the farmer's prayer for deliverance from a threefold set of sufferings, even as the Old Persian kings from their perspective requested similar favor of Auramazda (chap. 6): Mars is to "ban, repel, sweep away" (*prohibessis, defendas averruncesque*) respectively "seen and unseen illnesses" (*morbos visos invisosque*), "depopulation [and] devastation" (*viduertatem vastitudinem*), "blights and bad weather" (*calamitates intemperiasque*). As a warrior Mars also "is in charge of peace" (*praeest paci*) in the same sense that War Departments are preferentially titled Defense (*defendas*), and the motto of the United States Strategic Air Command reads "Peace Is Our Profession." The hardheaded Roman proverb said, after all, *si vis pacem, para bellum* 'if you want peace, prepare for war'. A kind of downward pressure of hierarchies seems to obtain in the Roman pantheon: the heavenly ruler has invaded the airspace, pushing the war-god out of the thunder-god role and toward the "third estate"; in Greece, on the other hand,

Zeus's similar expansion as the *tamíās polémoio* 'dispenser of war' left Ares little to do but alternately rage and dally with Aphrodite.

Quirīnus was the divine embodiment of the Romans (*Quirītes*) at peace, reflecting **Co-Virinos* (altered by analogy of *virīlis*), even as the collective noun **co-viriā* yielded *cūria* 'assembly' (see further chap. 17). He was the patron of men as producers, as progenitors, which is a sense that Indo-European **wiro-* tends to have when juxtaposed to the quasi-synonym **ner-,* as in Vedic *vīrákarma-* 'doing a man's work' = 'penis' versus, for example, *nṛmánas-* 'keen minded, heroic spirited'. In Latin only *viro-* lingered, in Oscan only *ner-,* in Greek only *aner-,* but the difference lived on in Roman religion, where *Nērio* was the wife of Mars while *Virites* (and *Hora*) were the consorts of Quirinus. In the Umbrian triad corresponding to the Latin, *Juve* and *Marte* are joined by *Vofione* in the dative case, reconstructed as **Lewdhyono-,* from **lewdhyo-* 'freemen' (cf. Russian *ljúdi,* German *Leute* 'people'; also **lewdhero-* 'free' in Latin *līber,* Oscan *loufro-,* Greek *eleútheros*). We may compare further the parallel **Poplōnos,* which yielded the Etruscan Fufluns, called in Latin Līber. The "augmentative" *-no-* suffix in Italic and the rest of Western Indo-European raises a common noun to the status of a theonym (e.g., Gaulish *Mātrōna* 'Mother', Old Norse *Ōðinn* < **Wātónos* 'Furious').

Such suffixes and the use of declensional endings at least allow one to segregate the *numina* by gender, as does of course the approximation of the better-known ones with Greek opposite numbers. Otherwise, in the absence of myths, it sometimes might not greatly matter (in Hittite, for example, in the absence of a formal masculine : feminine gender opposition, the sex of a deity can be in doubt). Of the remaining Roman gods, some are probably Etruscan in name (Mercurius and Sāturnus/Saeturnus, despite the folk-etymological echoes of Latin *merx* 'wares' for a god of tradesmen, and of *satus* 'sown' for a harvest deity). Volcānus, the god of fire and especially of wildfires, is cognate with Sanskrit *ulkā́* 'flame' and *várcas-* 'effulgence' and may have an Iranian parallel in the Ossetic epic figure *Kurd-alä-Wärgon* 'Smith-Aryan-Wärgon'. A curious tie to Vedic Agni lore is present in the ritual sacrifice of small live fish to the fire at the *Volcanālia* festival on 23 August, which recalls Agni's deadly enmity toward fish, attested in both Vedic and epic tradition. Neptūnus's name, cult myth, and Indo-European origin are unraveled in chapter 16. Other figures had nonce names: the two-faced *Jānus* was literally 'Gateway', the *numen* of entrances and beginnings, *Portūnus* (from *portus,* cognate with Avestan *pṛtu-* 'bridge' and English *ford*) similarly patronized harbors, and *Cōnsus,* the god of the harvested grain, meant simply 'Storage' (= *conditus*).

Numina tend to be abstract, and abstract nouns are either neuter (like *numen* itself) or feminine in gender (Liberty is a miss!). Hence there are inordinate numbers of Roman feminine deities, in addition to the better-known Juno, Diana, Vesta, Venus, and Minerva. Of those five, Minerva may be of Etruscan provenance, and Venus is in origin an abstract neuter noun (= Sanskrit *vánas-* 'desire'), subsequently feminized under the stimulus of the Greek Aphrodite. Vesta represents the deified domestic hearth fire (cf. Greek *Hestíā* 'Hearth', a "sister" of Zeus like Hera and Demeter), with associations to the Old Indic Agni cults (unique circular shrine in the Forum, with the vigilant Vestal virgins guarding the fire). *Dīāna* reflects **Diviānā* (cf. *dīus* < **diwios,* as in *Dea Dīa*) and is thus root connected with Jupiter, although it may mean little more than 'Divine'. She was billed as a huntress in syncretism with the Greek (and perhaps Greco-Etruscan) Artemis, but she may be in origin a maieutic figure more like the Greek Eileithyia, patroness of menstruality and the birth process, hence with the same moon associations to Lūna as in the assimilation of Eileithyia-Artemis to the Greek Selēnē 'Moon'. *Jūnō Lūcīna* had the same function; by syncretism with Hera, Juno had been promoted to Jupiter's wife and patroness of marriage (*Prōnuba*), but her earlier history may well be akin to that of Diana. The name *Jūnō* is derived from the root of *iuvenis* 'young' (cf. *iūnīx* 'heifer', Sanskrit feminine *yūnī́-* of *yúvan-* 'young', and the month name *Jūnius* or *Jūnōnius*), reminiscent of the possible meaning of Hera as 'yearling' (cf. chap. 8). The stem *Jūnōn-* seems to be secondary in relation to an earlier *Jūni-,* judging from *Jūnius* and the borrowed Etruscan *Uni*. Under the name Uni lurked a great goddess of the Etruscans, one that was syncretized as Uni-Astarte in the Etruscan-Phoenician symbiosis at coastal towns like Pyrgi (Caere's harbor), and who was of course readily assimilated to Juno once Roman expansion began, starting with the sack of Veii in the early fourth century B.C.E.

But Juno also bears the inherited marks of the Indo-European transfunctional goddess, with especial affinity to the Old Iranian Arədvī Sūrā Anāhitā. The name implies youth, even as Anāhitā was described as a "lovely young maiden" (chap. 6). At the cult site of Lanuvium in Latium Juno bore the epithets *Seispes Māter Regīna,* where Seispes (= *sospes*) means 'safe and sound, immune to attaint' (cf. *Anāhitā* 'Immaculate'), Regina signifies the warrior-class aspect (cf. *Sūrā* 'Heroic', and Vedic *rājanyà-*), and Mater refers to the fertility function of the transfunctional goddess (cf. *Arədvī* 'Moist', and the Russian *Máti Syrá Zemljá* 'Mother Moist Earth'). In Vergilian epic the career of Dido, Juno's tool in thwarting Aeneas, looks like a diachronic hypostasis of the triple mythic nature of Juno herself, in her progression from a virginal *intacta* (*Aeneid* 1.345) to an amazonal *dux femina* (ibid. 364) to a would-be mother (*Aeneid* 4.33), albeit abortively, as the plot finally required. Dido herself may have been in origin a heroicized replica of the Carthaginian Astarte (or Tanit), the same Phoenician-Punic great goddess who was syncretized with the Etruscan Uni at Pyrgi. Thus the epicized features of Juno as the Indo-European transfunctional goddess seem to have been grafted onto a saga version of the Semitic Astarte.

Some of the lesser goddesses have the same type of nonce names as Janus, Consus, and Portunus; for example, *Bellōna* (cf. *bellum* 'war'), *Pōmōna* (cf. *pōmus* 'fruit tree'), *Flōra* (Oscan *Fluusaí* [dative case]; cf. *flōs* 'bloom '), and *Ops* 'Plenty' (with her harvest festivals, *Opālia* and *Opicōnsīvia*). Others are opaque in name and known mainly from the scraps of ritual that still attach to them. In several such instances Vedic myth and ritual offer salient points of comparison, proving how deeply rooted in the Indo-European past such Roman petrifacts can be.

Māter Mātūta (cf. *mātūtīnus* 'of the morning') is a cover name for the dawn-goddess (Aurora); her festival, the *Mātrālia* on 11 June, was close to the summer solstice. This in how Plutarch is his *Life of Camillus* (section 5) describes her ritual: "Women lead a female servant into the sanctuary and beat her with rods, thereupon they drive her out and take into their arms their sisters' children rather than their own." A couple of other brief passages in Plutarch's *Moralia* and an allusion in Ovid's *Fasti* refer to the same events. This puzzling activity becomes intelligible with reference to the mythology of the Vedic dawn-goddess Uṣās, discussed in chapter 4, where the young sun-god is nurtured by his maternal aunt, and where the tarrying dawn is violently chased from the morning scene. Camillus, who dedicated the temple of Mater Matuta at Rome, figures in Livy and Plutarch as the great Roman military figure of about 400 B.C.E., who in the course of a long career defeated the Gaulish onslaught on Rome and fought to a successful conclusion the dragged-out war against the neighboring Etruscan city of Veii, thus setting Rome on the path of expansion. Many of Camillus's victories were won by sudden onslaughts and sallies at daybreak, something not reported of other Roman general commanders, which makes him suspect as a transposed epic replica of the sun-god himself, making his triumphant entry from the care of his patroness (really aunt) Mater Matuta. That Camillus was indeed a "solar" warrior is visible from other details of his career, such as the triple accusations brought against him (see chap. 13), the most serious of which was, according to Livy (5.23.6), a sacrilegiously excessive triumphal procession more fit for a sun chariot. In this manner a modicum of sun-related myth, once made anathema by Max Müller's excesses, can be cogently restored to its proper place in Indo-European comparative mythology.

Another obscure goddess, *Dīva Angerōna,* described mainly by Macrobius, was at the calendaric opposite pole from Mater Matuta, with her festival on the winter solstice, 21 December. This was the *brūma* (< *brevissima*), the shortest day of the year, when the daylight was "narrow" (*lux angusta, angusti dies*). *Angustus* is derived from **angus* (= Vedic *áṁhas-* 'narrowness, constriction'; see chap. 4), even as *augustus* 'mighty' is from **augus* (= Vedic *ṓjas-* 'might'), and *venustus* 'charming' is from **venus* (= Vedic *vánas-* 'desire'); *Anger-ōna* has the "augmentative" suffix added to the stem **anges-* of **angus-* (with intervocalic "rhotacism" of *s* to *r*), even as Venus might as well have appeared as **Venerōna*. It is known that Angerona's statue had its mouth bandaged and sealed and that it held a finger to its lips in a gesture commanding silence. Clearly Angerona had something to do with the solstitial constriction of the source of light; with her gag she was the very image of distress. The silence emanating from her, and which she requested of celebrants, must have contained the key to the efficacy of the ritual: by silence, rather than the usual cultic verbiage, would the cosmic crisis be alleviated (a song about the mystery of that same season is still called "Silent Night"). Something similar is found in Vedic lore, involving the priest (*brahmán-*) Atri, whom the Aśvins pulled from a fire pit. When the sun had been blacked out by the eclipse demon Svarbhānu, Atri (*RV* 5.40.6) "found the sun hidden by darkness . . . by means of the fourth formula [*bráhman-*]." Elsewhere it appears that this mysterious "fourth" was silent meditation, as opposed to varieties of the articulated word (*vāc-*), and that Atri thus rescued the sun by the mystic power of silence. Clearly the same unique inherited mythical theme has found two distinct articulations in Rome and in India.

Then there is the matter of the pedigree of *Fortūna Primigenia,* the Lady Luck whose cultic headquarters at Praeneste (modern Palestrina) became a gambling mecca for the Romans. *Fortūna* is derived from a noun **fortu-* (cf. *fortuītus*), besides *forti-* seen in *fors* 'chance, luck'. Cicero (*De divinatione* 2.85–86) described her cult statue, holding the infant Jupiter and Juno on her lap, which would indicate that she was conceived as the primordial (*primigenia*) mother of the gods. And yet preserved inscriptions record dedications *Fortunae Jovis puero* 'to Fortuna child of Jupiter' or *nationu cratia Fortuna Diovo fileia primocenia* 'as thanks for childbirth to Fortuna, Jupiter's firstborn daughter'. There is a paradox here of the chicken-and-egg kind, which again finds its parallel in Vedic, where the divine ancestress Aditi was said to be both mother and daughter of Dakṣa (*RV* 10.72.4 'of Aditi Dakṣa was born, and conversely from Dakṣa Aditi'). Whatever the exact theological implications, singularity has been pulled from isolation and can be ascribed to common heritage.

Lūa Māter, who was the "consort" of Saturnus, and to whom victorious Roman armies dedicated and burned captured enemy weapons (Livy 8.1.6, 45.33.2), is in name a variant of *luēs* 'blight, decay', in modern medical jargon 'syphilis' (cf. Greek *lúō,* Latin *solvō* < **se-luō* 'dissolve'). She has a better-documented parallel in the divinized feminine abstract noun *Nír-ṛti-* of the *Rig-Veda* and *Atharva-Veda,* from the verb *nir-ṛ-* 'dis-array, de-compose' (cf. *ṛtá-* 'order'). One of the rejuvenation miracles of the Aśvins involved a certain Vandana, whom they "fixed up as craftsmen do a chariot" when he was ruined by old age (*nírṛtam jaraṇyáyā, RV* 1.119.7). The goddess Nirṛti is for the most part a sinister figure whom other deities are asked to neutralize; she is rarely invoked directly and then only apotropaically, being more often wished on one's foe in the third person. Here again an ancient conceptual match between Rome and India seems to obtain, further abetted by the Avestan demoness *(Astō-)Vīdātu* '[Bodily] Decomposition' who appears beside Nasu 'Dead Matter'.

Finally there is *Carna,* whose name is derived from *carō, carn-* 'meat', as, for example, *Flōra* is from *flōs, flōr-*. Mentioned by Ovid and Macrobius, she had her feast day on the Kalends (first day) of June and was connected with Junius Brutus, the legendary first consul and hero of the Republican War. Carna seems to have been the deity favoring digestion and alimentary metabolism and may have patronized the meat that supplied vigor to the youthful (*iuvenis* : *Junius*) warrior. A Vedic counterpart is the hymn in praise of the personified Nourishment, *Pitú-* (*RV* 1.187), who conferred the *ójas-* that enabled Trita and Indra to overcome the dragon.

Turning from deities to rituals as such, the Etruscan element again deserves its due, for Etruscan ritual "science" was renowned, acknowledged, and pervasive. The *Libri rituales* of the *Etrusca disciplina* were still available in ancient Rome and were studied by generations of Roman scholars (the emperor Claudius himself wrote a multivolume treatise on Etruscan antiquities). Especially famous were the *Libri fulgurales* and *Libri haruspicini,* dealing with matters of lightning and extispicy respectively. Etruscans were especially adept at divination from entrails and the liver in particular; the hepatoscopy they practiced and the liver models that have been found greatly resemble Mesopotamian counterparts, tying in with the eastern origin of the Etruscans. The Romans adopted much, though using homespun terminology (*haruspex* 'gut-watcher'; cf. *auspex* 'bird watcher' in the practice of augury). Their preoccupation with *prodigia* (unnatural happenings), their horror of ritual pollution, and their compulsive concern with lustration resemble the situation in ancient Iran, as was noted in chapter 6. Indo-European terminological and formulaic matches were also discussed there, involving such key expressions as Latin *crēdō, iūs,* and *iūsta facere* 'perform funeral rites'. In Latin, *iūs* as human right (codified as *lēx*) was contrasted with *fās* as 'divine law', somewhat as in Greek *díkē* (cf. Latin *iū-dic-*) differed from *thémis*. *Fās* and *thémis* (and Vedic *dhā́man-*) reflect the Indo-European root **dhē-* 'set, put' (with a secondary side meaning 'do'); thus divine law was 'laid down'. Such common Latin verbs as *interdīcere* 'forbid' and *interficere* 'kill' also have ancient ritual uses with Indo-Iranian matches:

Latin: *interdicere alicui aqua et igni* 'forbid one water and fire'.

Avestan: *antar3 vīsp3ng dr3gvatō haxm3ng mruyē* 'to all followers of the Lie I forbid communion' (*Yasna* 49.3)

Inter-dīc- : *antarə mru-* express priestly excommunication, literally 'say in'.

Old Latin: *interficere aliquem vita (et lumine)* 'put someone out of life (and light)'; *interficere aliquem siti fameque* 'do away with someone by thirst and hunger'; *interficere panem* 'put away [gobble up] bread'.

Vedic: *antár mṛtyúm dadhatām* 'may they do away with death!' (*RV* 10.18.4); *prátyauhan mṛtyúm . . . antardádhānā duritā́ni víśvā* 'they repulsed death, having done away with all ills' (*AV* 5.28.8); *antár árātīr dadhe* 'I have done in the demons' (*YV, Maitrāyaṇī Saṁhitā* 1.2.1).

Inter-fic- : *antár dhā-* [same root **dhē-*] mean literally 'do in' or 'put away', in the sense of 'do away with, kill, consume, devour'. This was the warrior's way of handling matters on and off duty, as with Thor alternately killing giants and gulping down oxen with mead, whereas the priestly class could do you in with verbiage alone.

We are still not through with archaic ritual fallout from the root **dhē-*. There was the college of priests called *fētiāles* who gave religious sanction to Rome's external relations: they consecrated both declarations of war and treaties of peace, handled border disputes, and formally annexed newly conquered territory. The **fēti-* in their name matches the Vedic noun *dhā́tu-* 'setting, base, foundation' (cf. *forti-* beside *fortu-*) in the adjectives *su-dhā́tu-* 'well-founded', used in *RV* 7.60.11 of rendering territory fit for settlement (*kṣáyāya*), and *tridhā́tu-* 'triple-founded', describing the universe staked out by Viṣṇu in his primordial three steps (see chap. 4).

The most remarkable set of Roman-Indic ritual accordances involves the tabus which the Indic *brahmán* and the Roman *flāmen diālis* (F.D.) had in common. These strengthen the somewhat shaky etymological identification of the two as an Indo-European **bhlaghsmen*. Culled from various Roman sources (Plutarch, Gellius, Livy, Pliny, Appian) and mainly from the *Laws of Manu,* the prohibitions involved the following:

1. The F.D. cannot be forced to swear an oath.
   The brahmin cannot be subpoenaed as a witness.
2. The F.D. must not set eyes on an army.
   The brahmin must stop religious activity in the proximity of warfare.
3. The F.D. must not mount or even touch a horse.
   The brahmin must not pursue religious study on horseback or on any other conveyance.
4. The F.D. must not go near a funeral pyre.
   The brahmin must avoid smoke from a funeral pyre and stop religious activity at the passage of a funeral procession.
5. The F.D. must avoid intoxicants and fermented substances.
   The brahmin must not ingest alcohol.
6. The F.D. must not rub himself with oil outdoors.
   The brahmin, after rubbing his head, must not get oil on other parts of his body.

7. The F.D. must not touch raw meat.
   The brahmin must not eat nonsacrificial meat nor take any alms from a butcher, brewer, or operator of oil press or brothel.
8. The F.D. must not touch or even mention a dog.
   The brahmin must not read the Veda when he hears a dog bark or eat food that has been in contact with dogs or their breeders.
9. The F.D. must never, not even at night, doff entirely the insignia of his priesthood, and his wife the flaminica must ascend only by a closed staircase lest bystanders below glimpse her lower anatomy.
   The brahmin must never be stark naked, and he must not see his wife in the nude.
10. The person of the F.D. is sacrosanct, hence laying hands on him (*flamini manus iniicere*) is an aggravated crime.
    The killing of a brahmin is the supreme felony, which even reverberates into the supernatural realm (witness Indra's troubles over Triśiras).

Many such priestly tabus, whether legal, visual, tactile, dietary, or sexual, are commonplace in the world (cf. e.g., Mosaic law), but the set of precise matches obtaining here clearly points to a common cultural inheritance, which in the circumstances can only be called Indo-European.

A similarly close-knit congruence exists between the various types of marriages attested in ancient Rome and ancient India. There was a provision in Roman law whereby a woman upon marriage passed into the *manus,* under the *potestas* of the husband, who thus came to have rights over her in loco parentis. In two marriage procedures, the solemn religious *confarreatio* in the presence of the flamen dialis, and the *coemptio,* which was a charade of a sales transaction, the husband acquired power over the wife at once by the very act of marriage. On the contrary, the third form of marriage, by *ūsus,* did not grant *manus* to the husband until one year after the beginning of cohabitation, and then only if the wife had not left the conjugal domicile during three successive nights. Thus she had the option to postpone *manus* indefinitely, simply by going away for three consecutive nights every year. This was called *ūsum rumpere* 'break the habit', and the attendant expression *usurpatio trinoctii* reveals the true meaning of *usurpāre:* she acted as a **ūsurupa* 'habit breaker' (cf. *legirupa* 'lawbreaker'). In the midst of the patriarchal severity of Roman law such a common-law loophole for women's liberation looms strange indeed. Since *confarreatio* was obviously priestly in kind, and *coemptio* fictitiously venal, it seems that by exclusion the Indo-European scheme would point to the warrior-class origin of marriage by *ūsus*. This can be tested on the *Laws of Manu,* where eight forms of marriage were listed, but the first four were mere variants of brahmin religious ceremony (*brāhma, daiva, ārṣa, prājāpatya*) and the last one (*paiśāca,* named after demons) involved stealthy rape of a sleeping, drunk, or mad woman rather than legal wedlock. The remaining kinds were *āsura* (marriage by purchase, most proper for vaiśyas; cf. Bhīṣma's buying Mādrī as Pāṇḍu's second wife), *gāndharva* (defined as *icchayānyonyasaṃyogaḥ* 'union by mutual desire'), and *rākṣasa* (marriage by abduction, *hatvā chittvā ca bhittvā ca* 'attended by killing, wounding, and breakage'). The last two were either explicitly or implicitly for the warrior class, although some legal writings denounced both *āsura* and *rākṣasa* as *anārya* for their venality or violence. A combination, stylization, and "toning down" of *gāndharva* and *rākṣasa* produced the epic Indic *svayaṁvara,* which involved free choice on the woman's part but also rivalry among the males and could on occasion end in mock or real abduction. *Gāndharva* stands out here as the free-will union of the parties, without parental involvement, seemingly as anomalous in India as *ūsus* was in Rome. This is where the epic Indic story of Duḥṣanta and Śakuntalā comes in, told in chapter 5. When the king learns that the maiden he has just met is of kṣatriya extraction like himself, he proposes instant marriage, to be consummated on the spot, and persuades her that this is lawful for their class and that she is mistress of herself (*ātmanaḥ prabhuḥ*) and competent to make a gift of her body. She states her terms and then freely consents. The explanation for such marital practices in both India and Rome lies in the self-willed, autonomous nature of the Indo-European warrior, which was discussed with reference to Indra's and the Maruts' *svadhā́* in chapter 4. The warrior class members and their gods both "did their own thing" differently from the rest of the ordered society. That a reminiscence of this trait lingers in Roman law is proof positive that the Indo-European tripartite class structure, submerged beyond recognition in historical Rome, was once ancestrally present in pre-Roman society as well.

Pieces of Roman ritual, obscure in themselves, can find some measure of elucidation in the Vedic texts. Thus the *Fordicīdia,* the killing of a pregnant cow on 15 April, has a close match in the Vedic ritual of the *aṣṭāpadī* 'eight-legged one', that is, cow with calf, whose slaughter had similar connotations of promoting fertility; the Vestals would burn the extracted calf and use the ashes for lustration at the *Parīlia* (or *Palīlia*) six days later. The latter was the festival of the rural goddess *Palēs* and involved the mutilation of a horse, whose blood was used for fumigation along with the ashes of the Fordicidia and empty beanstalks; the etiology of this event was closely tied to the childhood legend of Romulus and Remus as "pastoral twins" first nursed by a she-wolf. In Vedic lists of the Aśvins' miracles (see chap. 4), the mare *Viś-pálā* (= *Palā* of the *viś-*, i.e., of the vaiśyas) had a leg severed in the finale of a race but was promptly fitted by the Aśvins with a metal prosthesis, to enable her to compete for the posted trophy (*RV* 1.116.5). In the very next verse the Aśvins restore eyesight to Ṛjrāśva (blinded by his father) on the insistence of a she-wolf whom he had favored with a hundred edible rams. The several elements (*Palēs* : *Palā,* the mutilation, the twins, and possibly the ancillary she-wolf theme) once again indicate some degree of affinity. Related to both cattle and horses there was the augural rite of *iūges auspicium,* described as *cum iunctum iumentum stercus fecit* 'when a yoked beast makes excrement'; this occurrence was considered inauspicious, to be obviated by unyoking. In the Vedic Mudgala hymn (*RV* 10.102) the name hero and his wife enter a contest, driving a chariot with a yoked bull. In the course of the race the animal stales and farts, and his droppings strike Mrs. Mudgala, but they hang in there and emerge victorious. The text is unclear on many points, but here too concern with the excrement of a yoked animal is somehow essential to the outcome. In this manner both Roman and Vedic religion seem to contain matching pieces of a larger Indo-European puzzle.

There was a real Roman chariot race on the Campus Martius at the Equirria (< **Equi-curria* 'Horse Run'), celebrated around the original New Year (27 February and 13 March) and reputed to have been founded by Romulus in honor of Mars. Johannes Lydus (*De mensibus* 4.20) has preserved the tradition that the participants were divided into three "tribes" and that their colors were red, white, and green respectively. These are of course still the colors of the flag of Italy, and with the frequent green/blue variation also of, for example, France, the Netherlands, Norway, Iceland, Britain, and the United States. In fact there is much evidence that white, red, and green/blue were the canonic colors of the Indo-European three social classes, white for the priests, red for the warriors, and green/blue for the productive class. White and red were in fact the two "privileged" colors, produced by costly treatments (bleaching of linen and red/purple dyes), while the rest (green, blue, yellow, black, etc.) were more or less "natural" hues. In Mycenaean Greek textile inventories only *leuka* 'white' and *porphureia* 'purple' cloth is expressly attested by color, and Spanish *colorado* still means 'red' above all. Thus the *equirria* preserve another reminiscence of the prehistoric tripartite class structure, and Johannes Lydus clinches this by stating that the *russati* (red) belonged to Mars, the *albati* (white) to Jupiter, and the *virides* (green) to Venus, thus to patron deities typical of the warrior, priestly, and commoner orders. But this is not the only archaism, for the *equirria* resembles the Old Indic *vājapeya* 'victory toast' race, which seems to have been originally an open free-for-all for brahmin, kṣatriya, and vaiśya alike but was gradually stylized into a prearranged ritual whereby the predictably victorious kṣatriya king symbolically consolidated his hold over the total society and especially over the vaiśya multitudes.

A race of another kind was involved in the *Lupercālia* on 15 February. A band of celebrants called Luperci (perhaps *lūpus* 'wolf' + *hircus* 'he-goat'), wearing only goatskin loincloths and brandishing goathide whips called *februa,* gathered at the Palatine hill and ran about Rome in a mitigated form of flagellant ritual, striking especially women as a magical aid to procreation. This is a widespread form of folkloristic practice in fertility cult, in the Roman instance under the patronage of the Italic woodland deity Faunus. The etiology Ovid offers (*Fasti* 2.425–52) relates to the Rape of the Sabine Women under Romulus (of which more below). When the forcibly obtained wives proved barren because of divine displeasure, appeals to Juno resulted in a divine voice proclaiming "Let a sacred goat penetrate the women of Italy!" Rather than go through with such bestial abomination, however, whipping with goathide proved to be enough of a symbolic compliance to ensure fecundity. But the Lupercalia interests comparative mythology on a different account. A scant month before the fatal Ides of March, Julius Caesar was reviewing the Lupercalia from his seat of eminence when the consul Marc Antony, one of the Luperci, broke the race, ran up to Caesar, and tendered him a crown. The crowd disapproved; Caesar waved him off, and the incident passed. It seems certain that Caesar and Antony themselves staged this testing of public opinion with a view to a planned restoration of the monarchy after nearly five centuries. Caesar as pontifex maximus was well versed in Roman religious antiquities and must have picked the occasion as opportune, as one that would positively galvanize the multitude. But he miscalculated, and a few weeks later he was slain. What was it about the Lupercalia that advocated its use for a test coronation? Another tradition involving Romulus supplies part of the answer. There were two groups of Luperci, one alleged to go back to Romulus, the other to Remus (Caesar added a third, Luperci Julii, composed of his own henchmen, another sure sign of political machination). The legends of those companions of the founding twins concern their pastoral youth and the cattle-related phase of an incipient rivalry that would end up in the removal of Remus and the consecration of Romulus as *rex*. Thus at the back of the Lupercalia there may lurk an ancient rite of royal installation that Caesar and Antony still knew, but whose persistence in folk memory they perhaps overestimated. A parallel is found in the Old Indic *rājasūya* 'kingmaking' ritual, really a coronation (the kind Yudhiṣṭhira arranged for himself in book 2 of the *Mahābhārata*), but one where the crucial sprinkling ceremony was attended by a staged mock elimination of family rivals, particularly in the form of regaining a herd of cattle.

A footrace also was involved in the *October Equus,* the great sacrificial rite of 15 October. After a horserace on the Campus Martius, a winning horse was sacrificed to Mars with a spear, followed by a struggle of two factions over its head, and the tail was rushed by runners to the Regia (just under a kilometer away), so that blood from it could drip onto its hearth. This important ritual, and its comparison with the Old Indic *aśvamedha,* the horse sacrifice that turned a king into an overking, is treated in chapter 15. Further rites relating to the Regia and the cults housed there are discussed in chapter 14.

Unlike the horse, which was offered only to Mars at the October Equus observances, other sacrificial victims appear in a wider range of structures. The best known of these is the *suovetaurilia,* performed *su, ove, tauro* 'with a swine, sheep, and bull' (or better with a *verres, aries,* and *taurus* 'boar, ram, and bull') on the Campus Martius. Although technically the sheep was sacrificed to Jupiter, the bull to Mars, and the swine to Tellus ('Earth'), Mars was somehow the overriding recipient, the umbrella deity of the whole, just as Cato's old tripartite rustic prayer for protection (quoted earlier) was addressed to Mars alone as part of the *suovetaurilia*. Similarly in ancient India the *sautrāmaṇī* sacrifice consisted of a ram, a bull, and a he-goat, dedicated to Sarasvatī, Indra, and the Aśvins respectively, but the entire rite derives its name from Indra *Sutrāman* 'Good Protector'. Sarasvatī as the somewhat faded transfunctional goddess received the sheep, while her Iranian counterpart Anāhitā in full triple glory claimed wholesale quantities of stallions, cattle, and sheep (see chap. 6). Juno is somewhere intermediate; at the Regia she got a *porca* and *agna* (female pig and lamb), and on the Capitol she was given a *bōs fēmina* (cow), but as Juno Curitis (or Quiritis) at Falerii she had a range fully worthy of a transfunctional goddess, with the sole exception of the horse: heifers, bullocks, pig, ram, and goat (Ovid, *Amores* 3.13.13–18). Jupiter received a sheep at the Regia but a *bōs mās* (male bovine) on the Capitol, distinct from the breeding bull (*taurus*) reserved for Mars. Ancient hierarchies are still at work here, with sheep at the priestly level, stallion and bull in complementary distribution for the warrior deity, and cattle, goats, and swine in the third-estate slot. Similarly in Greece the triple sacrifice called *trittús* originally comprised a ram, a bull, and a boar (*kriós, taûros, kápros*), but these could be offered to almost any deity, and the strict choice and ordering of victims was also collapsing. Thus the bond between ritual and theology, so precious in India, Iran, and Italy, had been broken, which is one reason Greece so often remains the odd man out in this kind of comparative mythology.

Turning from theology and ritual to legendary history as a Roman source of myth, certain ingredients have already been anticipated: Camillus, a general of about 400 B.C.E., figures in the solar myths surrounding Mater Matuta, and Romulus, with his legendary *floruit* of about 750, occurs in the founding etiologies of various rituals described above, which in reality must go back to very archaic levels of religion, as shown by comparison with Old Indic parallels. Romulus is the most complex, most difficult figure of Roman myth, both by himself and in association with his twin Remus. As was remarked earlier, Roman foundation myth replicates world creation, and hence Romulus as a "twin" is potentially comparable to the Indo-Iranian *Yama 'Twin' in terms of Indo-European anthropogony; this study is carried out in chapter 17. Childhood traditions about Romulus cast him with Remus as a pastoral pair of twins more in the cattle-raising Dioskouric mold, with clear conformity to the typical "Raglanian" hero pattern (divine siring, exposure, etc.). The life span of Romulus from conception to apotheosis is spaced in terms of the "pre-Capitoline" divine triad Jupiter, Mars, and Quirinus, since Mars was his father and Jupiter his protector, and after his mystical departure in a thunderstorm he was believed to have become Quirinus (the mechanism of the transfer is discussed in chap. 17). In the list of Roman rulers, however, Romulus stands out as the initial magician-king, the mysterious establisher who is the epic projection of his mentor Jupiter. By contrast, his successor Numa Pompilius was the very model of the humanely oriented lawgiver, who organized priesthoods and instituted the annual ceremony dedicated to *Fides* 'Troth', at which the priests officiated with their right hands swathed to the fingers. His hallmark was his *tutela pacis,* his guardianship of peace (*Livy* 1.21.5). He is clearly a projection of Diūs Fidius, the legalistic (as opposed to magical) allomorph of Jupiter, and resembles the Vedic Mitra versus Varuṇa (Mitra's name is etymologically cognate with Russian *mir* 'peace').

After Numa there was a characteristic break and interregnum, and suddenly the scene changes to the next king, Tullus Hostilius, who is consumed by lust for action and military adventure. The central event of his reign is the war against Rome's sister city Alba Longa under its commander Mettius Fufetius. In the course of the war the outcome is decided by a duel between two sets of triplets, the Roman Horatii and the Alban Curiatii, and when the one surviving Horatius slays all three Curiatii, Alba is by agreement defeated. Then the victorious Horatius returns home in triumph; but seeing the tears of his sister, who had been betrothed to one of the Curiatii, he is overcome by fury and stabs her. The slaying of kin had to be expiated in religious ceremonies that were thereafter traditional in the *gens Horatia,* whose name is derived from that of Hora, wife of Quirinus. Soon thereafter Tullus and his reluctant new subject ally Mettius of Alba were to join in a common military operation, but at a crucial moment Mettius withdrew from battle in order to await the outcome and then side with the winner, thus leaving Tullus in mortal danger. Praying for strength to Quirinus, Ops, and Saturnus, Tullus managed to extricate himself and prevail, then seized Mettius and had him dragged to pieces between horses.

All this is a miniature warrior epic founded on ancient mythic themes. The parallels are found in Vedic myth (see chap. 4), where Indra makes Trita (literally 'Third') Āptya kill a triple adversary, the 'three-headed' Triśiras, a kinsman whose murder had to be expiated by the Āptya family (cf. the *gens Horatia*). Indra's other analogous misadventure involved the demon Namuci, with whom he had a compact of nonkilling, which the demon violated by a ruse, imperiling Indra. The god recovered with the help of the Aśvins and Sarasvatī (cf. Quirinus, Ops, and Saturnus, "third-estate" deities all) and resorted to trickery of his own, decapitating Namuci. Clearly Tullus's career is the Roman epic projection of Indo-European warrior myth. Like Indra, he is soiled by impious kin killing and unwarriorlike contract breaking, yet without completing Indra's triple roster of misdeeds by sexual villainy. This is in the nature of the Roman heroic "ethic," which condoned blasphemy, cruelty, and even cowardice but excluded lechery or baseness, reserving it for the "foreign," Etruscan Tarquins, culminating at the end of the kingship in the Rape of Lucretia.

As soon as Tullus's reign blew over there was another break, and subsequent rulers such as Ancus Martius and the Tarquins were concerned mainly with matters of public works and economic policy, building sewers to the Tiber, consolidating the treasury (*fiscus*), and instituting the *census* or property ranking of the population. The last measure is attributed to Servius Tullius, a strange, magically endowed ruler intercalated between the two Tarquins, whose birth tales involved a flaming halo bursting around his head and his being sired by a divine phallus that mysteriously erected itself out of the royal hearth fire (these traditions smack more of sprightly Indic birth legends or of the Old Iranian *xvarənah* with its combined igneous and spermatic connotations than of the usual dour Roman *gravitas*).

Specific episodes of Roman saga-history mirror well-defined Indo-European mythical themes. The Rape of the Sabine Women under Romulus (capturing wives from the "rurals" ruled by Titus Tatius, occupying the neighboring Quirinal hill) corresponds to the conflict or theomachy between third-estate deities and those of the other two classes that is observable in India (Indra vs. Aśvins; see chap. 4), Ireland (Tūatha vs. Fomoire), and Scandinavia (Äsir vs. Vanir). At the conclusion of the feud the two antagonistic groups are integrated into a tripartite pantheon/society, the latter made up in Romulus's Rome of Ramnes (Romans proper), Luceres (Etruscans), and Titienses (Sabines, a more Oscan-like rustic component).

The Republican War, including the siege of Rome by the Etruscan king Porsenna and the battle of Lake Regillus, exhibits elements that may point to another epicization of Indo-European eschatological battle myth, the same that was discussed with reference to Kurukṣetra and Ragnarök in chapter 5. The personalities of that war seem to form a structured ensemble not unlike the protagonists of the *Mahābhārata*: Horatius Cocles ('Cyclops', i.e., one-eyed) with his paralyzing gaze, and Mucius Scaevola 'Lefty', who burns off his right hand to back up a heroic trickery, are epic exemplars of Jupiter and Diūs Fidius, with bodily mutilations matching their Scandinavian counterparts, the one-eyed host paralyzer Odin and the legal guardian Tȳr who lost his right hand as a pledge in the maw of the cosmic wolf Fenrir (significantly, Diūs Fidius had a temple on the Collis Mucialis, and the priests of Fides, installed by Numa, symbolically bandaged their right hands). Brutus and other early consuls such as Publius Valerius ("Publicola") were the warrior elite, while Larcius and Herminius acted as supply masters and the *virgo* Cloelia, who helped save Rome from Porsenna with her *fides,* bravery, and concern for the young, played the part of transfunctional female, comparable to Draupadī in the *Mahābhārata*. In this way it is conceivable that, as in the *Mahābhārata,* the passing of the old order and the establishment of the Republic were cast in the epicized mold of the old eschatological myth of destruction and regeneration of the world order, with Pāṇḍavas versus Kauravas and Patriots versus Tarquins playing the roles still reserved for gods and demons in Iran and Scandinavia.

Recommended Reading

Dumézil, Georges. *Archaic Roman Religion*. 2 vols. Translated by Philip Krapp. Chicago: University of Chicago Press, 1970.

———. *Camillus: A Study of Indo-European Religion as Roman History.* Edited, with an Introduction, by Udo Strutynski. Berkeley and Los Angeles: University of California Press, 1980.

10 · Celtic Myth

"The Dead prevailed in testimony over the Living, since preference was given to the written word." This denunciation of the dead letter as against vivifying live speech occurs in an Irish tale about the falsification of the inscribed name on a famous sword, a forgery that impressed the judges more than the rightful owner's oral testimony. It is a late reflex of the well-known druidic aversion to writing mentioned by Caesar in *De bello Gallico,* a priestly attitude not unlike that of the Vedic brahmins. Both cultures had early access to writing (India from age-old contacts with Mesopotamia, Gaul since the founding of Massilia [= Marseilles] and other Greek colonies on the "French Riviera" about 600 B.C.E.) but chose not to make large-scale use of it until a later period (Epic India and the coming of Christianity respectively; in the wake of Saint Patrick, Irish monks would scribble furiously all over western Europe, as if to make up for centuries of self-imposed Celtic illiteracy). This tabu against writing may be based on dogma that lingered in the farthest east-west reaches of the Indo-European continuum, as did the archaic items of vocabulary discussed in chapter 3 (Vedic *rāj-* : Gaulish *rīg-* 'king', etc.). Caesar reports druidic teachings of metempsychosis, and India was of course the prime and expanding locus of transmigrational lore. Perhaps the transmission of the sacred text was held to be analogous to the progress of the individual and collective soul, with each successive generation rejuvenating and reincarnating the Word. Such sanctification of orality contrasts with the codificational trends first in evidence in the ancient Near East. Likewise the evidence for open-air divine service makes an impression of expansiveness, as opposed to an ever more centripetal focusing on some boxed-in holy of holies. In this latter respect the northern peoples (Celtic, Germanic, Baltic, Slavic) hewed to a seemingly old pattern, while Italy and Greece had already been strongly internalized by their Mediterranean–Near Eastern exposure.

Chapter 3 outlined the main phases of Celtic protohistory. It was the first great Indo-European migration traceable by historical as well as archeological means, but owing to its own essential illiteracy it remains hazily penumbral. Although the Celts managed to disperse themselves as far afield as Galatia (the old Hittite heartland in central Asia Minor), they were essentially ensconced in central and western Europe, with evanescent excrescences into Italy and Spain and more durable migrations into the British Isles. Pressed by Romanization and Germanic migrations, they were gradually squeezed to the northwestern fringes of Europe. The Celts are thus truly "marginal"; there were never other early Indo-Europeans to the west or north of them, and they were shielded by geography and choice against the impact of Mediterranean civilization. If sedentariness had been their virtue, coupled with early literacy, they would have been an extraordinary source for Western Indo-European archaism. As it is, one must arduously forage for scraps of their early traditions.

In moving westward through the Indo-European continuum, it appears that the social class divisions of priests, warriors, and cultivators, so pronounced in Vedic India in conjunction with pantheonic structures, and subsequently rigidified, played a much less pervasive part in Iranian tradition and were hardly in evidence in Greece and Rome. Despite some echoes here and there in religious, legendary, ideal, or real patterns, neither Greek (Dorian, Ionian, later Athenian) "tribal" divisions nor the Roman patrician : plebeian dichotomy preserved much of the prehistoric setup. Not so among the Celts, where Caesar separated the Gauls into *druides* (priests), *milites* (warriors), and *miserrima plebs* (wretched masses), or early Ireland, where the druids (cf. Vedic *brahmán-*), the *flāith* ('dominion'; cf. Vedic *kṣatrám*), and the *bō airig* ('cow freemen'; cf. Sanskrit *ārya-ka-* and Avestan *vāstryō-fšuyant-*) are uncannily reminiscent of the Indo-Iranian kind. Unlike Germanic society, where the system had been broken by the virtual disappearance of the priestly class, the tripartite societal pattern lingered on in its insular Celtic holding tank, and by the end of the first millennium it experienced a remarkable recrudescence in Anglo-Saxon England. About 900, in his own Old English version of Boethius's *Consolation of Philosophy,* King Alfred the Great divided a ruler's subjects into *gebeðmen, fyrðmen,* and *weorcmen,* which Aelfric and Wulfstan echoed a century later by *oratores, bellatores,* and *laboratores.* Just as the Celtic-Germanic symbiosis in England had saved the tradition, the Norse superstrate on both sides of the Channel (culminating in the Norman invasion of 1066) facilitated its spread to the north of France during the eleventh century, whence it expanded to form the basis of the medieval European and later three estates, which in France lasted as the basis of society down to the revolution of 1789. This is another illustration of the insidious power of Celtic persistence, not unlike its substratal ability to overhaul a seemingly triumphant Latin into subsequently unintelligible French (see chap. 3).

Our written knowledge of the Gaulish pantheon begins with Caesar (*De bello Gallico* 6.16–17), who credits the Gauls with plenty of religious practices and enumerates their gods in Roman interpretation, with brief characterizations: "Of gods they worship Mercury most" as the *omnium inventorem artium* 'inventor of all skills', next Apollo (dispelling disease), Mars (in charge of war), Jupiter (holding sway in the heavens), and Minerva (originator of arts and crafts). This is a strangely unhelpful grab bag, notable for the low ranking of "Jupiter" and the preeminence of "Mercury," whose functions seem to overlap with Minerva's at the end; but Caesar was not doing systematic ethnography; he was merely padding an otherwise meager annual military report to the Senate with curious detail about the natives of Gaul. Caesar's account acquires some systematic meaning only by comparison with subsequent sources. A century or so later the poet Lucan (*Pharsalia* 3.399–425) depicted a blood-spattered sacred grove at Massilia and (1.444–46) described human sacrifice among the Gauls:

> immitis placatur sanguine diro
> Teutates, horrensque feris altaribus Esus,
> et Taranis Scythicae non mitior ara Dianae

> harsh Teutates is cruelly propitiated with blood,
> and dread Esus on savage platforms,
> and the altar of Taranis, a match for that of the Scythian Diana[1]

Later commentators on Lucan supplied their own Roman interpretations for Teutates, Esus, and Taranis, either Mars, Mercurius, and Jupiter or Mercurius, Mars, and Dispater (the ruler of the Otherworld,

1. That is, the Artemis Taurica of the Crimea, to whom strangers were sacrificed, as in Euripides' play *Iphigenia in Tauris*.

whom according to Caesar the Gauls claimed as their ancestor). Caesar also mentioned huge wickerwork dummies inside which human victims were burned, which chimes with the information of Lucan's commentators that Teutates' victims were drowned in casks, those of Esus were hanged and lacerated, and those of Taranis were burned. At this point the names begin to be informative:

Teutātes (Toutates, Totates, Tutates) is derived from **tewtā́* 'people' (Old Irish *tūath,* Oscan *touto,* Gothic *thiuda*) and thus resembles in meaning the Umbrian Vofione and the Roman Quirinus.

Ēsus may mean simply 'Lord' and be cognate with Latin *erus* 'master' (with rhotacism); yet there is also the variant form *Aesus,* pointing to an original diphthong.

Taranis is cognate with the *u*-stem **taranu-* seen in Old Irish *torann,* Welsh *taran* 'thunder' (Taran is a man's name in the Welsh *Mabinogi,* and there was a Christianized Saint Taran in Brittany). The Celtic *taran-* is metathetic for *tanar-* (= Germanic **thunar-* 'thunder'), as seen in the inscription *J(ovi) O(ptimo) M(aximo) Tanaro* (Chester, England, 154 C.E.; *Corpus Inscriptionum Latinarum* 7.168).

People's god, lord, thunderer—this descriptively named triad does not sound very compatible with the Roman Jupiter, Mars, Quirinus, which explains the wretched results of the Roman interpretation. Teutates may somehow fit the third-estate or "collective" slot of Quirinus, but the relatively low estate of Caesar's "Jupiter" shows that Taranis is no head of the pantheon, rather a thunder-god with either wheel (= thunderball) or spiral (= thunderbolt) as emblem, of the order of the Norse Thor (< **Thunaraz*). Equating Esus with Mars makes no particular sense either, once it is clear that Taranis is no match for Jupiter. But the alternative interpretation of Esus as "Mercury" is interesting on several counts:

1. In Tacitus's Roman interpretation of the Germanic pantheon, too, "they worship Mercury most," and there "Mercury" reflects with certainty the great god *Wōðanaz, the Norse Odin (see chap. 11).

2. Esus is homologous with the Norse Odin in receiving human sacrifices by hanging, whereas the victims of Teutates were drowned, in the manner of offerings to the Germanic fertility deities, for example, Tacitus's Nerthus (see chap. 11) or the man being plunged headlong into a vat in a cultic scene depicted in high relief on the inside of the Gundestrup cauldron, a Celtic silver-plated copper vessel found in a Danish peatbog (first century B.C.E.; see figure 6).

FIGURE 6. Gundestrup cauldron. (Courtesy of Nationalmuseet, Copenhagen. Photograph by Lennart Larsen.)

3. Granted "Mercury's" pride of place on Caesar's list, it is possible that "Mercury" = Esus is the high god of the Gaulish pantheon, above Taranis and Teutates.

Esus has mythologically significant iconography. The "Paris Altar," datable to the time of Christ and found in 1711 under the choir of the cathedral of Notre Dame de Paris (now in the Musée des Thermes at the site of the Roman baths of Lutetia Parisiorum), depicts on two sides Taranis (inscription *Jovis*) and *Volcanus,* and on a third the bearded, ax-wielding god Esus cutting a tree (see fig. 7). The fourth panel shows a similar leafy tree protruding from behind a bull on whom three birds are perched, surmounted by the inscription *Tarvos Trigaranus* 'Bull with Three Cranes'. On an analogous relief from Trier (now in the Landesmuseum there) a woodcutter is felling a tree with a bull's head and three birds on top of its foliage. At the basis of this depiction may lie some lost myth reminiscent of Indra's killing of Triśiras, as told in Yajurvedic texts and especially in book 5 of the *Mahābhārata,* how Indra struck

FIGURE 7. Esus on the "Paris Altar." Musée des Thermes, Paris. (Photographie Giraudon, Paris.)

down the adversary with his bolt, but then enlisted the services of a woodcutter who completed the slaying by severing the three heads with his ax, whereupon birds (woodcock, partridge, and sparrow) escaped through the three necks. Tricephalic representations are common in Celtic iconography, but in the absence of texts, the full meaning of the Gaulish scene is bound to remain opaque.

The figure of Esus can perhaps be brought together with the theonym *Lugus,* which lurks in toponyms (*Lugu-dunum* 'Lugus town' > Lyons in France, Leiden in Holland, etc.), and with the Irish Lug (discussed further below) who was the all-around man of skill (*samildānach;* cf. "Mercury" as *omnium inventor artium*). Lug was the father of Cūchulainn in Irish saga, even as Odin was the sire of prominent Norse heroes; likewise *Esugenus* 'Begotten of Esus' was a Gaulish name of nobility. When Lugudunum = Lyons became the capital of Gaul, Augustus fixed his own imperial feast day there on 1 August, which was the date of the festival of Lugnasad in Irish lore and presumably had been the holy day of the town's eponym; the emperor "usurped" the antecedent cult, much as later Notre Dame de Paris rose on the emplacement of a sanctuary of Esus and Taranis.

Esus-Lugus, Taranis, and Teutates as a triad receiving human sacrifices may thus roughly match the Scandinavian set of Odin, Thor, and Freyr in pagan Sweden, who were given human victims at Uppsala up to the Christianization in the eleventh century (see chap. 11). They, like Jupiter-Mars-Quirinus, were a stylized Western Indo-European embodiment of the erstwhile tripartite pantheon, thus a match for the Eastern structure first glimpsed at Mitanni (Mitra-Varuṇa, Indra, Nāsatya; see chaps. 3 and 4). Around their axis swarmed the rest of the pantheon. "Mars" takes on more sense in two directions. There is epigraphic attestation of *Mars Teutates* (e.g., *Marti Toutati*) who, like the rural Roman Mars, seems more a patron of peace and fertility than a war-god, warding off plague, invasion, and blight alike. At the same time, "Mars" and "Mercury" alternated in Lucan's scholiasts as interpretations of Teutates and Esus, and in inscriptions both take similar epithets (e.g., Vellaunus, of unknown meaning). Thus "Mars" may hide yet another divine figure, structurally akin to Esus-Lugus and perhaps partially syncretized with him. One thinks here of the faded Vedic Mitra, Roman Diūs Fidius, and Scandinavian Tȳr by the side of Varuṇa, Jupiter, and Odin, thus the god of covenants paired with the magical lord of oaths and bonds but subsequently eclipsed and almost absorbed by him (Mitra practically reduced to Varuṇa's dvandvamate, Diūs Fidius as an "allomorph" of Jupiter, Týr "militarized" along with Odin in Scandinavia). "Mars" was likewise the Roman interpretation of the Germanic god **Tīwz* (> Old Norse *Týr*), as "Mercury" was of **Wōðanaz;* a Latin inscription from northern England (third century C.E.) mentions Mars Thingsus, thus the Germanic god Tīw, the protector of the judicial assembly held on Tuesdays, even as the Scandinavian Týr originally patronized the *thing* (Latin *Martis dies* came out in Germanic interpretation as *Tuesday;* see chap. 11). The Gaulish name of such a "Mars" is not known, but he appears in Ireland as Nūadu beside Lug (see further below).

The rest of the Gaulish divine inventory can be characterized more in list fashion. "Apollo" does duty for both Borvo or Bormo (god of thermal healing waters; cf. the French name Bourbon) and Belenus 'Bright' or Grannus 'Sun' as solar deity (cf. Old Irish Beltene 'Bright-fire', name of the Mayday feast, and *grīan* 'sun'). "Vulcanus" is attested in Gaul, but his native name is not; it may have been based on the word for 'smith' (as his Irish counterpart, the divine smith Goibniu, reflected *gobae* 'smith'; cf. MacGowan 'Smithson'). "Hercules" characterized the Gaulish Ogmios, according to Lucian (*Herakles,* chap. 1) an aged, baldish, sun-blackened champion who literally held men spellbound by the ears with golden-tongued eloquence, matching the Irish 'sun-faced' strongman Ogma, who was credited with devising the Ogam notch script; elements of his myth may have resembled those of the Indo-European warrior hero embodied by both the Greek Herakles and the Norse Starkaðr (the former met up with Gêras 'Old Age' and was known as *Hercules Musarum;* the latter was both a *senex* and a great skaldic poet; cf. chap. 13). "Dispater" (*Dīs,* the Latin name for Hades, from *Dīves* 'Rich' translating Greek *Ploútōn* = "Pluto") cropped up in Lucan's scholiasts as the alternative cover for Taranis but more plausibly reflects a death-god. The Gaulish deity Sucellus 'Good Striker' or Silvanus 'Woodsman', depicted with mallet and cask, sometimes with wolfskin and dog, may be a representation of this "ancestor" figure, who can perhaps be thought of as a "first colonizer" on the lines of the Vedic Yama or as the otherworldly replica of the ruling deity, in the manner of Zeus Katakhthonios or the Norse Odin, who extended his dominion to include Valhöll. In any event belief in an afterlife was strong, for Gauls would lend money on terms of postmortem reimbursement.

"Minerva," with the epithet Belisama 'Brightest', is the cover term for a great goddess. Powerful female types stand out in Celtic mythical lore at both the divine and the saga levels. The transfunctional goddess has here come into her own. "Minerva" had a temple with "eternal flame" in third-century C.E. Britain and is identifiable with the British Celtic theonym Brigantia, formally identical with the Sanskrit feminine adjective *bṛhatī́* 'great, lofty' and with the Irish Brigit, the later saint with her feast day of Imbolc (1 February) and her monastery with perpetual fire at Kildare. (Unlike the usual overlay, e.g., with the Virgin Mary superimposed on the sanctuary of Aphrodite at Cypriot Paphos, the Celtic deity was simply Christianized, name and all.) Triplicity or triunity is in evidence among the Celtic mythical females: Brigit herself had two synonymous "sisters," there was the triad of Irish Machas, and Gaul had the triple Mātres or Mātrae or Mātrōnae. Just as the Greek three-by-three Muses did not perturb Homer's Muse, the Matronae did not preclude a single great Matrona, embodied in a river (Matrona > Marne), whereas in Ireland the mother-goddess was the land itself (*Ēriu;* cf. the Indic Sarasvatī [river] vs. the Iranian Harahvaiti [land]). Matrona was the mother of the 'Divine Son', Maponos, matching Modron and her son Mabon in Welsh saga and the river-goddess Bōand (> Boyne) and her 'Young Son' (Mac Ōc = Oengus) in Irish lore. In addition the Gaulish male deities had "consorts," somewhat as in Roman or Indic religion (Rosmerta 'Foresighted' for "Mercurius," Nemetona 'Shriner' for "Mars," Damona 'Cow' for Borvo, Sirona 'Star' for Grannus, Nantosuelta 'River-?' for Sucellus, and so forth).

There were the taurine Tarvos Trigaranus and an antlered god Cernunnos 'Horned One', the latter sitting cross-legged in the inside of the Gundestrup cauldron with a ram-headed snake in his left hand and torques in his right hand and around his neck, surrounded by a wolf, a stag, and a bull (see fig. 8). But females were more prominent among the theriomorphic type, though their animal nature tended to be mitigated: Epona 'Mare' (surnamed Regina 'Queen') had shed her presumable original hippomorphism and was depicted riding sidesaddle, much like her Welsh saga version Rhiannon (< **Rīgantōna* 'Queen') in the *Mabinogi*. Like many Celtic deities, she was not free of an otherworldly tinge; horses appear to have been important to that place, as they were in Greek and Hittite myth (see chap. 8). Dea Artio was a bear-goddess (cf. the Greek Artemis), and Dea Arduinna rode on boarback. Cathubodua (*Corpus Inscriptionum Latinarum* 12.2571) is matched by the ornithomorphous Irish *Bodb (catha)* '[Battle] Crow' and such other bird-shaped battle-goddesses as Morrīgan 'Great Queen'. A kind of animal totemism is also discernible (names like Boduognatus 'Crowson'),

FIGURE 8. Detail of the Gundestrup cauldron. (Courtesy of Nationalmuseet, Copenhagen. Photograph by Lennart Larsen.)

reaching over into Ireland (Cūchulainn [*cū* 'dog'], Oisīn [*oss* 'stag']), although it need be no stranger than Leo, Wolf, or Björn as men's names in the Latin and Germanic orbits.

The bulk of the Gauls seem to have belonged linguistically to the branch later known as "British" (still surviving in Welsh and Breton), whereas the Irish (and Scottish) represent the "Gaelic" variety (the differences resemble those between the Oscan-Umbrian and Latin types of Italic, e.g., in the treatment of original labiovelars [*qu* sounds], which developed into labials [*p* sounds] in British and Oscan but were retained in Gaelic and Latin: Welsh *pump,* Oscan *pompe,* but Irish *cōic,* Latin *quinque* 'five'). Apart from names, the records of insular myth postdate Christianization. Ireland has the edge here for several reasons. It was a backwater of tradition, escaping Roman invasion and sheltered from Christianity until the mission of Saint Patrick (who died in 461). On the other hand, its monastic converts fast developed a zealous literacy that was pious and antiquarian-minded at the same time, leaving a record the Welsh material from the High Middle Ages (such as the *Mabinogi*) can only remotely emulate. The separate developments were conditioned by geographic isolation and linguistic split alike (Irish and Welsh were no longer mutually intelligible).

Ireland had its own "mythic geography," made up of the five *cōiced* 'fifths', comprising Ulster in the north, Connaught in the west, Munster in the south(west), and Leinster in the (south)east, all in relation to Mide

'Middle' (county Meath, the site of Tara, seat of the *ard-rī* 'high king'). This is an inherited structure with a clear parallel in ancient India, where the 'five tribes' (*páñca kr̥ṣṭáyaḥ* or *carṣaṇáyaḥ*) typically express the *ārya* or even human totality (*páñca* equaling *víśve* 'all'; cf. the Hittite *pankus* 'plenary assembly', and English *fist* < **pn̥kʷstis* 'a fivefold', namely the sum of the *five fingers* [< **pénkʷe penkʷrṓs*]). Presumably in India, too, the ethnocentric seat of power and the four outlying cardinal divisions formed the basis of the quinary system (cf. the Chinese "Kingdom of the Middle"). The fivefold division of the community survives elsewhere, too, especially with tribes that have recently emerged from the obscurity of prehistory—for example, the five demes of Sparta or the Philistine pentapolis of Gaza, Askalon, Ashdod, Gath, and Ekron. The partition of the Irish year into quarters, punctuated by the great feasts of Samain (1 November, New Year, Day of the Dead, later All Saints' Day), Imbolc (1 February), Beltene (Mayday), and Lugnasad (1 August), may be at least proto-Celtic, for *Samonios* is attested also on the Gaulish "Calendar of Coligny"; in this system the "markers" fall in the interspaces of the solstices and equinoxes, thus in the "center" of each quarter.

Central to the Irish myth tradition are the epic reflections of the old Celtic gods, the Tūatha Dē Danann 'People of the Goddess Danu'. Traditions about them can be culled from various antiquarian texts, such as the *Dindshenchas* ('Place Traditions') or *Cōir Anmann* ('Fitness of Names', dealing with onomastic etymology), but especially in the *Lebor Gabāla Ērenn* ('Book of Conquests of Ireland'), a legendary history compiled in the twelfth century, and the *Cath Maige Tuired* 'Battle of Mag Tuired'. The monkish redactors have fitted the Tūatha into a whole string of legendary invasions of Ireland, starting biblically with a certain Cessair, a granddaughter of Noah, and antedating the Flood. The only survivor of the flood was Cessair's husband Fintan, who led a subsequent ichthyo- or ornithomorphic open-ended life as an observer of Irish history. The next settler was Partholōn with his followers, a culture hero who cleared the land and instituted custom and also had a first conflict with the Fomoire, monstrous archenemies each with a single arm and leg who loom large in the sequel. Partholōn and his folk perished in a plague and were succeeded by Nemed and his people. After their leader's death the Fomoire imposed on them crushing tribute, leading to revolt, decimation, and emigration of the remnants to the south and the north. The descendants of the first group ultimately returned as the Fir Bolg, who are credited with the division of Ireland into *cōiceds* and a golden age reminiscent of Hesiodic and Avestan descriptions (soft showers, plentiful harvest, no falsehood). The northern emigrants, equally descended from Nemed's people, returned later as the Tūatha and defeated the Fir Bolg in the First Battle of Mag Tuired. Besides the mother figure Danu (or Anu), they comprised her brother Dagda 'Good God' (also known as Ollathair 'Allfather'), the latter's daughter Brigit, Ogma the champion, Goibniu the smith, Dian Cēcht the healer, and Nechtan (onomastic match of the Latin Neptūnus, whose story is elaborated in chap. 16). Their king was Nūadu, who lost his arm in the battle against the Fir Bolg. They brought along four magical objects: the spear of Lug, the sword of Nūadu, the cauldron of Dagda, and the Great Fāl. The first two were talismanic weapons that ensured victory, the cauldron guaranteed a full meal at all times, and the Great Fāl would cry out whenever mounted by the true king of Ireland (matching in kind the Scottish Stone of Scone under the coronation chair of the British sovereign).

At this point the Fomoire reappear. They seem to be a shadow presence all along—the perennial foe and yet linked intimately to the society they antagonize; in chapter 7 we were reminded of them in the context of the ambivalent relations of Iran and Turan. When Nūadu abdicates the kingship because of his physical handicap, Bres ('Beautiful'; son of a Fomoire father and a Tūatha mother) is elected to succeed him on the urgings of the women; here one is reminded of the Etruscan period in Roman legendry down to the Republican War, when even Brutus the Liberator was (conversely) a Tarquin on his mother's side (even as in Iran Khosraw's mother was the daughter of the king of Turan). Bres turns out to be a poor choice, for he favors the Fomoire, forces menial tasks on the Tūatha champions, and lacks the generosity essential to a successful Irish king. Culinary abundance and other entertainment decline under his niggardly regime, and he draws the fatal ancient equivalent of a poor press, namely lampooning by the poets of the Tūatha. When his resignation is demanded, Bres with his twisted loyalties musters his Fomoire allies for assistance.

The stage is thus set for a showdown. The Tūatha regroup against their own failed king. Nūadu has a new prosthetic silver arm made by Dian Cēcht and the latter's son Miach and is hence rehabilitated to resume the kingship with the epithet *Argatlām* 'Silver Hand'. At this point the young Lug arrives at Tara (he too was part Fomoire, daughter's son of Balor, the Fomoire champion) and impresses everyone with his range of expertise, to the point that Nūadu cedes his leadership to him. Seven years of preparations culminated in the great Second Battle of Mag Tuired. During the slaughter Dian Cēcht and his three children used magic arts (singing spells over corpses thrown into a healing well) to revive the dead of the Tūatha, thus furthering their victory. Lug circumambulated the enemy host on one foot and with one eye closed, a magic circuit that mimed the single-leggedness of the foes in general and Balor's "evil eye" in particular. The latter shared with Cūchulainn and assorted Norse berserks the contortionist trick of sucking in one eye and expanding the other to a monstrous, paralyzing gaze, only in Balor's instance it took four men to raise the resulting heavy lid. At that instant Lug shot a sling stone through the opening and forced the eye backward through Balor's head, so that its evil was vented instead at the Fomoire themselves. Thus died Balor (having earlier slain Nūadu), and the Tūatha triumphed. This marked the end of the Fomoire, while Bres was reprieved in return for becoming a governmental advisor in matters of agriculture. But the peace era of the Tūatha was not to last either, for a final invasion by the "Sons of Mīl," that is, the Irish under their king Eremon, forced them to retire to the *sīde,* the fairy mounds, and thus perpetuate their influence from a subterranean spirit world. This is a unique tandem approach by levels to ethnogenesis and Christianization. The gods once held sway over the land, and in a sense they still do, despite yielding the surface of the Hibernian soil to the folk and to a new cult and being retired to what is sometimes called the "lower mythology." In subtlety the Irish solution outshines downright demonization of the onetime pagan gods in Christianized cultures.

Sound method requires that this material be confronted first with other Celtic, in this instance Welsh, traditions before resorting to extra-Celtic comparisons. Our main sources are the *Four Branches* of the *Mabinogi* and such other tales as *Lludd and Lleuelys* and *Culhwch and Olwen*. Far more than Irish tradition, this literature is caught up in the more cosmopolitan world of medieval romances and international folktales, nor did its authors have the same feeling for native myth that still guided the Irish compilers. The frequently fantastic narrative rarely yields systematic matter for comparison but can nevertheless be probed for incidental relevant lore.

Clear parallels to the Tūatha occur in the Welsh material. The *Fourth Branch* concerns the family of Dōn (cf. Danu) with her brother Math (cf. Dagda), ruler of Gwynedd (North Wales). Math could live only if his feet were held in a maiden's lap, except in time of war. Through the machinations of two sons of Dōn the incumbent foot holder was disqualified for loss of maidenhead. At length Math interviewed a new candidate, Dōn's daughter Aranrhod, who had to step over a magic wand as proof of her virginity, but in doing so dropped a male child (the sea-god Dylan) and a second object that was put in a chest. The latter turned out to be another son whom Aranrhod would not name until tricked to do so, and he became Lleu Llawgyffes 'Lleu the Deft-Handed', a match for the Irish Lug Samildānach 'Lug the Many-Skilled'. Aranrhod likewise swore to deny him weapons and spouse but was also induced unwittingly to countermand this ban. Lleu eventually became lord of Gwynedd. Gofannon 'Smith' (cf. Goibniu) and Amaethon 'Plowman' (both with the "augmentative" *-*no*- suffix) were further sons of Dōn. Amaethon is mentioned in *Culhwch and Olwen,* which is also the attested source for Lludd Llawereint, the Welsh match for Nūadu Argatlām (*Lludd* < *Nudd* by alliterative assimilation to the epithet *Llaw-ereint,* literally 'Hand [of] Silver'). The tale of *Lludd and Lleuelys* tells of Lludd, king of Britain (popular etymon of London, known in Welsh tradition as Caer Lludd 'Lludd-town'; cf. names like Ludgate), and his brother Lleuelys who had married his way to the throne of France. Three calamities afflicted Britain under Lludd: the advent of a people called the Coraniaid, armed with such advanced eavesdropping capabilities that no secrets were safe, a terrible dragon fight every Mayday, attended by a blood-curdling cry that debilitated people, animals, and nature at large, and an ongoing mysterious disappearance of provender from the royal larder. Brother Lleuelys (in whose name we recognize Lleu), "a man of great and wise counsel," supplied the remedy: a poison specifically calibrated to exterminate the Coraniaid, a means of talismanic entombment of the dragons for ever after, and the arrest of the magical purloiner of food and drink, who not only made restitution but reformed to become the king's faithful retainer (in modern times he might have become his castle security consultant). Thus Lleuelys helps Lludd overcome a tripartite set of afflictions, the kind we have seen from India to Iran to Rome, consisting of miscarriage of language or violation of verbal sanctity (botched formulas, lies, spells, oath breaking, eavesdropping), breach of communal peace (invasion, armed attack, mayhem, unsettling screams), and loss of physical resources (blight, plague, famine, theft). The regime of Bres in Ireland, relieved by the intervention of Lug taking over from Nūadu, was likewise characterized by breakdown of verbal trust (Bres plotting with the Fomoire against the Tūatha), debilitation of warriors (Ogma reduced to carrying firewood), and shortage of victuals (unfair tribute of crops and produce to the Fomoire, the stingy foodways of Bres himself). The formula seems to be inversely replicated in the series of invasions, where Partholōn's and Nemed's people were decimated by plague and famine, the Fir Bolg and the Tūatha were conquered by force of arms, and according to druidic prophecy, the Sons of Mīl will perish by fire and water after a breakdown of law and social order. In the principal Old Irish legal corpus, the *Senchus Mōr,* disease/famine, warfare, and breach of covenant are singled out as the threefold causes of calamity, even as in Plato's *Republic* (413b–14a) Socrates lists theft, spells, and violence as reasons for alienation from truth. Underlying the stories of Nūadu (genitive Nūadat) and Lug and that of Lludd and Lleuelys we may thus discern a Celtic myth of Lugus bringing relief to Nōdons; the latter is attested in dedications from Lydney (cf. Lludd!) in Gloucestershire bordering South Wales (*Deo Nodonti*) and seems to mean 'Fisher' (cf. Gothic *nuta* 'fisherman', from **nudōn*[*s*]), the probable ancestor of the Arthurian "Fisher King" of the Grail legend, whose maiming resulted in the Waste Land.

Other *Branches* of the *Mabinogi* are less amenable to comparison, but the mythic background is still palpable. In the *First Branch,* Pwyll, lord of Dyfed (South Wales), whose name means 'Wisdom', also mysteriously acquires condominium in the Otherworld (Annwn; cf. the Arthurian Avalon) before meeting and marrying the Lady on the White Horse, Rhiannon 'Queen' (who was compared above to the Gaulish horse-goddess Epona Regina). Their son Pryderi was kidnapped at birth and was found and reared by Teyrnon (< *Tigernonos 'Lord'), the events being linked with the birth of a horse. The *Second Branch* deals with the brood of Llȳr 'Sea', notably the giant Brān ("The Blessed", *Bendigeid-fran*), Manawydan, and their sister Branwen, and the misadventures resulting from the latter's unhappy marriage to the king of Ireland. Here the Irish connection is felt in more than the plot, for the main characters match in name the Irish god Manannān Mac Lir ('Son of the Sea') and such Otherworld-farers as the hero of the "Voyage of Bran" (cf. Saint Brendan). Sea voyages and Otherworld notions are often interlinked in Celtic lore, implying Elysian isles or sunken paradises in the West (*Mag Mell* 'Field of Pleasure', *Tīr na n-Ōg* 'Land of the Young', Land of Lyonnesse, City of Is, etc.), but in fairytale fashion the Otherworld can also be entered by a kind of on-the-spot enchantment—through the looking glass, so to speak—without any visible or distant boundaries. In the *Second Branch* battle between the Welsh and the Irish, the latter made good field use of their "Cauldron of Rebirth" to revive the casualties, a close parallel to Dian Cēcht's restorative well in the Second Battle of Mag Tuired. Only seven Welshmen survived, including Manawydan; Brān's severed head was buried as a talisman at London, facing the Continent, where it has warded off invasion of Britain at least since 1066. The *Third Branch* ties together the first two (Manawydan marrying Pwyll's widow Rhiannon, whose son Pryderi is now lord of Dyfed; together they have to fight off an evil spell cast on the land by a certain Llwyd), while in the *Fourth Branch*, in addition to the family saga of Dōn, Pryderi's death is told, tied to a gift of horses, a last leitmotif alluding back to the mythology of his mother Rhiannon. In this way the *Mabinogi* still yields vague echoes of Celtic myth, in confirmation of the Irish and even Gaulish material.

Essaying extra-Celtic comparisons for the insular tradition, we find the Irish pair Nūadu and Lug (or their Welsh counterparts Lludd and Lleu) homologous with Scaevola and Cocles of the Roman Republican War, marked by loss of a hand and one-eyed battle magic respectively. On the divine level this means comparability with the Germanic pair *Tīwz and *Wōðanaz, in Old Norse terms Tȳr and Odin, the former having given up his right hand in order to bind the wolf, the latter sacrificing an eye to gain magical powers. The ascendancy of Lug over Nūadu parallels the eclipsing of Tȳr by Odin in Norse tradition. Ogma seems to embody the warrior level, with his club matching Thor's hammer (and Feridun's *gurz*), while the third estate is reflected by Bres, the agricultural expert and popular favorite elected king by the women's vote. That he has to be put in his place by a violent conflict indicates that the Second Battle of Mag Tuired contains elements of the Indo-European myth of the "war of the divine classes" (Indra vs. Aśvins, Romans vs. Sabines, Äsir vs. Vanir, discussed in chaps. 4, 9, and 11). Yet while the Fomoire in addition to Bres himself seem to be to a degree "Sabinic" (soil oriented, intermarrying with the Tūatha, etc.), as a group they are not integrated by the conflict but rather are eliminated from the scene. Hence more than a divine skirmish and conciliation took place at Mag Tuired. The Fomoire also have a definite demonic tinge, that of a monstrous and oppressive archenemy who is yet too close for comfort and sooner or later requires a showdown with eschatological overtones. The Indic and Iranian gods versus demons, the Norse gods versus giants, the Roman patriots versus Tarquins, and such modern mutations as communism versus capitalism are all fair parallels (cf. the "end struggle" of the Internationale). Dian Cēcht's resurrective battlefield well has its analogue in ancient India, where Kāvya Uśanas, serving as sorcerer of the demons, kept reviving the dead in the ongoing conflict against the gods. But while Ragnarök and communism hold out a postconflict millennium, India eschewed eschatology, contenting itself with a mere epic resolution in the *Mahābhārata* (see chap. 5). In Ireland too the epicized triumph of the Tūatha proves transitory. Even as the Pāṇḍavas move on to posthumous heaven, the Tūatha are retired to the mounds in favor of a new set of men. But Ireland is not yet through with mythological surprises. The king of the Sons of Mīl, Eremon, is etymologically the equivalent of the Gaulish Ariomanus, reflecting the same personified **aryomn̥* 'Aryanness' as is seen in the Vedic Aryamán and the Iranian Airyaman. In addition, very specific traits connect Eremon with both of the latter. The dossier of Eremon in the *Lebor Gabāla* involves his role as builder of causeways and royal roads. In the *Historia Britonum* of Nennius, the *Book of Leinster,* the *Book of Lecan,* and some other sources, Eremon arranged a protection against poisoned enemy arrows that consisted of pouring cow's milk into furrows on the battlefield. He also provided wives to his allies and arranged for hereditary succession in favor of the Irish, his own people. All three features are distinctly "Aryamanic" in Indo-Iranian terms: Aryaman is connected with roads and pathways from the *Rig-Veda* onward. Airyaman invented the *gaomaēza* ritual of decontamination and healing, consisting of filling furrows with bovine excretions, specifically urine. Aryaman, Airyaman, and Vidura (the epic transposition of Aryaman; see chap. 5) are all connected with marriage rituals. The Indo-Iranian *Aryaman was clearly a satellite of *Mitra, a kind of hypostasis of the Mitra type proper, an abstraction expressing the self-sense of the community and championing the operation of communal welfare and health, especially in terms of marital compacts and rituals of healing. In Celtic tradition, a linear downward projection has replaced the "timeless" level of coexistence of figures such as Mitra and Aryaman. Eremon is in fact a diachronic hypostasis of Nūadu as king of the "next" layer of settlers, appropriately closer to mankind proper, even as Aryaman was in contrast to Mitra. Thus Celtic theology seems to have perpetuated, at the far end of the Indo-European continuum, a match for the Mitra-Aryaman structure at the other extremity—a notable instance of the "archaism of the fringe."

The perceptive mythological ear may pick up further Celtic : Indic echoes. Aranrhod's triple withholding of name, weapons, and spouse from the young Lleu recalls Devavrata's renunciation of kingship and marriage in the *Mahābhārata* in return for a new name (Bhīṣma; see chap. 5); since Bhīṣma incarnates Dyaus, something of the Indo-European sky-god *Dyēws may still lurk in the Celtic Lugus-Lug-Lleu (he was worshiped on mountaintops, for example, at the Lugnasad in Ireland, and with the colossal statue erected by the Gaulish Arverni on the peak of Puy de Dôme in the Massif Central range in the Auvergne). Students of ancient India are reminded of the Vedic three-stepping world measurer Viṣṇu in the triple-leaping Irish Saint Moling, and of the all-encompassing Kṛṣṇa-Viṣṇu of the *Bhagavadgītā* when the bard of the Sons of Mīl, Amairgin, takes possession of the soil of Ireland with a lay in which he equates everything with himself. The death-god Donn, first of the Tūatha to die and the post-mortem receiver of mankind, has traits in common with the Vedic Yama. The nine or so forms of marriage listed in Irish and Welsh traditions resemble the *Laws of Manu* by several varieties of family-centered and wealth-related "honorable" union at the beginning and stealthy rape or "mockery" at the end, separated by free-will and abduction marriages closely resembling the Indic *gāndharva* and *rākṣasa;* in this instance the Indic and Celtic multiplicity contrasts with the reductionistic tripartite stylization seen in Roman law (chap. 9).

In the *Lebor Gabāla* the female figures (Danu, Brigit) are in the background; this is a man's world, perhaps owing to skewing by the monkish compilers. Important women are more to the fore in the Welsh tales (Modron, Rhiannon, Aranrhod), but they hardly do full justice to the notable goddesses of the Gaulish pantheon either. To find proper insular reflections of the female component in Celtic myth one must turn to the Irish sagas and to folklore. Danu-Anu, Brigit, Ēriu, Bōand, the three Machas, Bodb, Morrīgan have flitted past in the pages above. They, augmented by Medb, reflect aspects of the Indo-European trans-functional goddess, but with specific Celtic emphases. Sacrality, "untaintedness" is not much in evidence. Instead there is embodiment of "sovereignty" in the secular sense, and nary a virgin in sight. There is hypertrophy of the "amazonal" and fertility components, but these have often been tucked under the umbrella of "sovereignty" to yield domineering warrior-harridans and fountains of sexuality alike. Some figures were a bit "provincial" (Bōand local to Ulster, Medb in Connacht with a "double" in Leinster, Brigit in Leinster, Anu in Munster with her two breasts embodied by the twin hills of county Kerry known as *Dā Chīch Anann* 'Paps of Anu'; see fig. 9), but names like Medb (< **Meduā*), Bodb (< **Boduā*), and Brigit (< **Brigantia*) are paralleled in Gaul and Britain; they all reflect a pan-Celtic type. Those that have more "myth"

FIGURE 9. Paps of Anu, County Kerry, Ireland. (Courtesy of Hamlyn Publishing Group, Ltd. Photograph by Donal Macmonagle.)

to their name, such as Medb, the Machas, and Bōand, will have their stories told in chapters 14, 15, and 16.

The world of Irish saga in its imaginative and anarchic fluidity is even harder to explore for comparative mythology than the lucubrations of the "Mythological Cycle" centered on the *Lebor Gabāla*. But while the latter may with reservations be called a "chronicle-epic" on the lines of Livy, the sagas of the "Ulster Cycle," with their alternating prose narrative and direct-speech verse, and the story and ballad versions of the "Fenian Cycle" can be characterized as remnants of heroic epic art. Folktale motifs proliferate, stock themes abound,[2] and yet the sagas have an ancient flavor that makes one suspect their core of a mythical residue. What they lack in direct mythological concern is compensated

2. Some of these have parallels in India, such as the magically potent "act of truth" in Irish lore and the analogous *satyakriyā,* resorted to by Damayantī and Sītā (for the latter, see chap. 5), or even the romantic commonplace of the "love sight unseen" (*sercc ēcmaise* : *adṛṣṭakāma*) afflicting the likes of Nala and Damayantī, Oengus, and Findabair (in the *Tāin Bō Froich*).

for by sheer untouched native archaism and by the absence or mitigation of any clerical distortions.

The "Ulster Cycle" purports to be "tribal," involving the Ulaid (Ulstermen) with their king Conchobor Mac Nessa residing at Emain Macha ('Twins of Macha'), near the later Christian capital of Ard Macha ('Hill of Macha', Armagh). It is a reflection of Celtic Iron Age warrior society, untainted by Roman, let alone Christian, influences. It bears notable resemblance to the heroic late Bronze Age traditions depicted in the Homeric poems. Conchobor's courtiers included the druid Cathbad, the conciliatory sage Sencha, the oversexed champion Fergus Mac Roich with his outsized phallus, and the trickster and troublemaker Bricriu. The old king grew himself a young wife, Deirdre ("of the sorrows"), whose elopement with Noise brought death to Noise and his brothers and desperate suicide upon herself; the story is of a Celtic triangle type also seen in the Fenian (Finn : Grāinne : Finn's nephew Diarmaid) and Arthurian traditions (Mark : Yseult : Mark's nephew Tristan; Arthur : Guinevere : Lancelot). Underlying it is the willful, strong female divine figure of Celtic myth, epitomized in saga form by Queen Medb, who takes and discards mates at will but whose power play no longer matches her sex drive in courtly intrigue, so that she trails "fate" and disaster in her wake. The chief driving forces in this company were aristocratic honor and the craving for fame, and the main pastimes included feasting, feuding for primacy over the "hero's portion," and intertribal fighting, especially with Connacht under Medb over a great bull whom the latter coveted (*Tāin Bō Cuailnge* 'Cattle Raid of Cooley'). Into this circle was born Conchobor's nephew Sētanta, sired by Lug and synchronized with the birth of twin foals (cf. Pryderi in the *Mabinogi*). Tutored and trained by the best teachers (Amairgin, Cathbad, Sencha, Fergus), Sētanta took on the name Cūchulainn ('Culann's dog') in atonement for one of his "boyhood deeds" (killing the hound of the smith Culann). Like Achilles, he alacritously chose a short life of fame and in short order developed into a full-blown berserk, complete with contortions (*riastrad*: eye trick, mouth stretched from ear to ear, hair standing on end as if by static electricity, magic halo [*lūan lāith* 'warrior's moon'] over his head), but also subject to the multiple *geis* or tabu that shadows the Irish hero. He killed a murderous triple adversary (three sons of Nechta Scēne) but thereupon in his frenzy attacked Emain Macha itself (shades of Horatius slaying the three Curiatii then turning on his own sister). Conchobor confronted him not with champions but with a phalanx of naked women; when this vanguard embarrassed his youthful modesty, the men grabbed him and cooled him off in successive tubs of cold water (one burst, one boiled, the third merely warmed). Now a full-fledged champion, he had to ward off single-handed Medb's cattle raid into Ulster, until the other men could recover from their annual "childbed sickness" (a couvadelike travesty of travail induced by a curse of the Third Macha; cf. chap. 15). Later he enrolled for some adult education from the divine instructresses Scāthach 'Modest', her daughter Uathach 'Terrible', and Aife 'Fair', who sound suspiciously trifunctional on the pattern of the Greek Euphrosyne, Aglaia, and Thaleia (it must be an ancient set, for 'modesty' is not otherwise a notable component of Celtic transfunctional triads). Uathach advised Cūchulainn to wring from her mother Scāthach at swordpoint a triple set of boons: instruction in warfare, Uathach's hand in wedlock, and a foretelling of his future, for Scāthach was also a prophetess. Instead the hero ended up begetting upon Aife a son Conlae, whom he later unwittingly slew in combat, in enactment of the Rustam : Sohrab pattern of filicide (cf. chap. 7). His own end came by being caught between two *geasa* when his enemies served up roast dog on his passage: he could neither pass up a meal nor eat dog, which might be his totem. A statue of him collapsing, with the death crow perched on his shoulder, adorns the main post office in Dublin. His head was retrieved by his brother-in-arms, Conall Cernach, chiming with the well-documented Celtic cult of human heads (cf., e.g., Brān's head buried at London).

Even this quick glance at some salient points of the "Ulster Cycle" points up the scattered but palpable mythical elements in the heroic narrative. The same is true of the "Fenian Cycle," but with a difference. It is not "localized," though mostly southern (Leinster and Munster), not centered at some heroic court; in fact it is almost extrasocietal with its free-roaming band (*fiana*) of fighters and hunters beholden only to themselves, an epic-romantic Irish body of tradition about ancient initiational warrior brotherhoods still marked by a free-will autonomy resembling that of Indra and the Maruts. First codified in the *Acallam na Senōrach* 'Parley of Oldsters' in the twelfth century and fueled by James Macpherson's Ossianic fancies in the eighteenth, it has proved durable with storytellers and balladeers until modern times, especially in the southwest (Munster). Much nature lyricism enters into the epic material, Finn-Fingal himself (with his son Oisīn-Ossian and grandson Oscar) being not only a warrior but a seer (*fili*) and a bard (*fāith*, cognate with Latin *vātēs*). He had his "boyhood deeds" like Cūchulainn, and like Conchobor he suffered marital infidelity at the hands of his willful wife and his nephew Diarmaid, the fellow with the irresistible 'love spot' (*ball seirc*); when the latter was mortally gored during a boar hunt in Sligo, Finn begrudged him his magic healing waters, thus declining to save him (even as Kay Us withheld his elixir from the dying Sohrab in the *Shāh Nāma*). Despite the folktale aura, Finn's divine origins are probable (**Vindos* 'White', cf. the Welsh Gwyn son of Nudd as a magical hunter and fighter, and theophorous continental placenames like *Vindobona* 'Vienna'); he may in fact be an allonymous saga version of Lug, and so may Cūchulainn, the "son of Lug." Lugus-Lug-Lleu is, as we have seen, homologous with the Germanic *Wōðanaz, the patron of the Germanic warrior bands, who had part demonic (giant) ancestry, even as Lug was part Fomoire. It would be nice to report that *Lugos means 'Bright', as is sometimes alleged, beside *Vindos 'White', but more probably it matches Gaulish *loûgos* 'raven' and thus provides another analogue to *Wōðanaz with his ravens. But the intra-Irish similarities of Lug and Finn are themselves patent; just as Lug the spear wielder killed Balor with his evil eye, the eight-year-old Finn with the help of a magic spear vanquished a one-eyed fire-breathing marauder who would burn down Tara on every Samain; thus he secured his position within the brotherhood, but he had to deal even later with an antagonist Goll ('One-Eyed') Mac Morna (also called *Aed* 'Fire'), who before his birth had killed his father Cumaill. Lug was of consummate skill, while Finn had his "thumb of knowledge" that imparted preternatural insight (even as Odin had his magic of runes). Altogether Finn strengthens the case for a Celtic magician-god *Lugos, in many respects (part-demonic ancestry, secret knowledge, one-eyedness, magical warrior character, perhaps raven connection) similar to the Germanic *Wōðanaz; his saga reflections are not only Lug and Lleu but Cūchulainn and Finn, and even Arthur (the boar hunter of *Culhwch and Olwen*), who resembles Finn in many respects.

The "Historical Cycles" deal with royal persons who sometimes interact with figures such as Medb (e.g., Ailill, Lugaid, Conn, Art, and Cormac); these are dealt with in chapter 14. In other instances, such as Suibhne Geilt 'Sweeney the Madman', the saga itself is of direct relevance to Indo-European warrior myth (see chap. 13).

Recommended Reading

Cath Maige Tuired: The Second Battle of Mag Tuired. Edited by Elizabeth A. Gray. Irish Texts Society, 1982.

Dillon, Myles. *Early Irish Literature*. Chicago: University of Chicago Press, 1948.

Early Irish Myths and Sagas. Translated, with an introduction and notes, by Jeffrey Gantz. New York: Penguin Books, 1981.

Knott, Eleanor, and Gerard Murphy. *Early Irish Literature*. New York: Barnes and Noble, 1966.

The Mabinogi and Other Medieval Welsh Tales. Translated, with an introduction, by Patrick K. Ford. Berkeley and Los Angeles: University of California Press, 1977.

MacCana, Proinsias. *Celtic Mythology.* Feltham, Middlesex: Hamlyn, 1970; New York: Peter Bedrick Books, 1985.

Rees, Alwyn, and Brinley Rees. *Celtic Heritage*. London: Thames and Hudson, 1961.

11 · Germanic Myth

The Germanic emergence from prehistory was late compared with that of the Celts, and it was also protracted and gradual. From Brennus's sack of Rome in 387 B.C.E. to the martyrdom of Vercingetorix (the Arvernian "superwarrior king") in Caesar's dungeons in 46 B.C.E., Rome had been dealing with Celts for centuries, whereas the Germanic tribes were quaint, restless, and remote barbarians whose midwinter swimming in the Rhine made Caesar shudder. When occasional tribes such as the Teutones and Cimbri had tried migrating into Gaul they were crushed by the Roman general Marius around the modern Aix-en-Provence and Vercelli in 101 B.C.E. Yet soon after Caesar, Germania became the all-too-crucial northern frontier of the empire, etched deep into Roman consciousness by the defeat of Varus's Augustan legions in the Teutoburgerwald (northwest Germany) in year 9 of the common era. In the late first century Tacitus in his *Annales* graphically commemorated this tragic debacle, and in his *Germania* he sketched a concise, insightful, and in many ways sympathetic ethnography of the unspoiled "noble savages" who were beginning to pose a serious threat to the increasingly decadent Roman Empire. Tacitus is in fact our main source on the early Germanic tribes, supplemented by stray materials in other historians such as Dio Cassius and Ammianus Marcellinus. Although a form of Etruscan alphabet had seeped northward through the Alps and been adapted into Germanic runic script well before the common era, its Continental remnants are sparse and mostly micromonumental inscriptions on objects; nor did the late elaboration of runic writing in Viking Scandinavia get beyond the tombstone stage. Germanic peoples attained essential literacy only in the context of Christianization, and thus it is not surprising that the first large written record in any Germanic language is the Gothic (East Germanic) Bible translation by the Visigoth Wulfila, made in the northern Balkans in the early fourth century. (That the Visigoths also ended up in Spain is an indication of the mobility of the Germanic migrations.) Nonpious native material picks up only in the second half of the first millennium: Frankish and Langobard laws from France and northern Italy (in Latin!), the Anglo-Saxon literature in England (notably *Beowulf*), but precious little from Germany proper (*Hildebrandslied*, *Merseburg Charms*), where conversion was still going on (partly by Irish monks) and even engaged Charlemagne, who forcibly converted the Saxons in the late eighth century. Germany, once fully Christianized, was drawn into the orbit of Continental medieval culture, with relatively little antiquarian preoccupation. Not so Scandinavia, which remained essentially heathen through the first millennium until the Viking era (ninth to tenth centuries) drew it out of its isolation, providing interculturation with Britain, Ireland, Normandy, Russia, and down to Byzantium and creating in 874 new but fruitful insularity by the settlement of Iceland (previously the refuge of Irish anchorites). The seepage of Christianity began quite early (Saint Ansgar's mission to Sweden in 830) but needed two centuries to take root (Denmark was decreed Christian by Harald Bluetooth in 985, Iceland officially converted in the year 1000, Saint Olaf imposed the new religion on Norway about 1015, but Adam of Bremen (*Gesta Hammaburgensis Ecclesiae Pontificum,* ca. 1070) still reported human and animal sacrifices at Uppsala in Sweden. In that period the colonial cranny of Iceland saw a flowering of antiquarian culture, with its Eddic and Skaldic poetry and saga literature (both heroic *fornaldar* and family sagas) culminating in the *Prose Edda* (*Gylfaginning* + *Skāldskaparmāl* + *Hāttatal*) and *Heimskringla* (especially the *Ynglinga Saga*) of Snorri Sturluson (1178–1241). About the same time, Saxo Grammaticus in Denmark produced his *Gesta Danorum,* a "history" of the Danes from the beginning to 1185, whose first nine books constitute a chronicle epic in prose with heavy mythical undercurrents (in chap. 5 Saxo's account of the Battle of Brāvellir was compared with the *Mahābhārata*). These works are the basic fund of Germanic mythic tradition, while the German materials from the High Middle Ages, such as the *Nibelungenlied* (ca. 1200), show heavy contamination by Continental literary convention.

Owing in large measure to the Icelandic material, Germanic myth, especially as it served the Viking Age, has remained a living part of

Western civilization, abetted by the centrality of such modern cultural movements and ethnic trends as German romanticism and nationalism. The relatively bare shelves of German heathen myth proper were restocked with adapted Icelandic material (as in Wagner's *Ring des Nibelungen*). Names such as Thor keep company with Apollo, Nike, and Saturn in the panoply of American rockets and warheads, whereas nobody in the Pentagon has thought of naming another death dealer Vṛthragna (or even Lug). Because of its richness and relative archaism, and despite the lateness and antiquarian (rather than primary) nature of the main sources, coupled with diffusionary influences from classical cultures, Germanic myth ranks with Vedic and Roman as the third mainstay for triangulated Indo-European reconstruction. As in Rome, myth-based saga is an important source. Unlike Rome, however, ritual is poorly attested, whereas divine myth proper flourishes in the *Poetic Edda* and Snorri's prose compilations alike. The subarctic, volcanic, insular environment of Iceland was conducive to otherworldly contemplation; even nowadays most Icelanders report having had preternatural experiences, especially seeing revenants and zombies (*draugar*). Germanic at large is an exceptional form of Indo-European language, subject to wholesale yet systematic and structured slippage in phonology (the so-called sound shifts that made English *father* out of **patḗr*) and extreme stylization in verbal morphology (with "principal parts" like *sing, sang, sung*). Both tendencies are replicated in Germanic myth. Thus, compared with ancient India and Iran, or Celtic Gaul and Ireland, the tripartite social system has slipped a notch by the virtual disappearance of the priestly class; Caesar noted (*De bello Gallico* 6.21.1, 6.22.1) that the Germans had no equivalent to druids and cared little for ritual. Hence, instead of priests, warriors, and peasants, early Germanic legal sources speak of *nobiles, ingenui, serviles,* thus aristocrats, freemen, and slaves, more like a decapitated Vedic system (minus the brahmin) of *rājanya, vaiśya,* and *śūdra*. That this scheme reflects a true shift is suggested by the Eddic poem *Rīgsthula* 'Lay of Rīgr'), where the god Heimdalr (called *Rīgr,* borrowed Celtic for 'King') on his wanderings visits three households on a rising socioeconomic scale and sires a son on the lady of each house: Thräll 'Thrall, Slave', Karl 'Churl, Yeoman, Peasant', and Jarl 'Earl, Aristocrat'. That we have here an "updated" Germanic version of the birth of the social classes is clear from color symbolism: Jarl is white-blond in hair and complexion, Karl is ruddy, and Thräll is black. The Indo-European priestly white, military red, and third-estate blue/green (further subdivided in India into yellow for the vaiśya and black for the śūdra) have slipped along with the structure, so that white now marks the warriors, red the peasants, and black the slaves. Jarl's youngest son Konr Ungr 'Young Noble' ended up as a magician-king, thus symbolizing the fusion of the remnants of the priestly function into the warrior aristocracy (cf. Old Norse *konungr* 'king' < Proto-Germanic **kunungaz* or **kuningaz,* preserved as a borrowed petrifact in Finnish and Estonian *kuningas* 'king', Russian *knjaz'* 'prince').

If systematic slippage marks the social structure, a trend to reductionistic stylization is observable in the pantheon. Tacitus (*Germania* 9) makes short work of the latter: *Deorum maxime Mercurium colunt* (echoing verbatim what Caesar said of the Gauls); this "Mercury" qualified for human sacrifice, while "Hercules" and "Mars" had to make do with animals, and some tribes also worshiped "Isis" (shades of the Eastern mystery cults rampant among Rome's legionnaires). In fact this short list covers the linchpins of Germanic theology, and its Roman interpretation parallels the converse Germanic one in weekday names:

Martis dies: Tuesday, Old English Tīw (= Old Norse Tȳr)

Mercurii dies: Wednesday, Old English Woden (= Old Norse Odin)

Jovis dies: Thursday, Old English Thunor (= Old Norse Thor)

Veneris dies: Friday, Old English Frige (= Old Norse Frigg)

Tacitus's substitution of Hercules for Jupiter is a subtle one (with Hercules' club rather than Jupiter's bolt matching Thor's hammer), for Tacitus must have sensed that in this system, unlike the Roman one, the thunderer was not the supreme head of the pantheon. Such structured Germanic sets stayed in place to the very end of paganism, becoming even more strictly triadic: what Adam of Bremen related about the temple of Uppsala about 1070 included a sceptered Thor flanked by an armed Wodan (= Odin) and an ithyphallic Fricco (= Freyr). Not that there were no sectarian tilts: in rural Swedish Uppland, in the valleys of Norway, and among the landholders of Iceland, Thor the enemy of marauders and husbandman's friend became central, while the warhawk Odin dominated in more footloose Viking society and Tȳr had faded. On the Continent, on the contrary, some tribes were Wodan oriented even in name (e.g., the Franks; cf. *francea* 'spear'), while others were just as clearly votaries of Tīw, especially the Saxons (named after a type of sword, *saks*), whose version of Tīw was called *Saxnōt* (Anglo-Saxon *Saxnēat*), that is, 'Sword-**Nauta-*' (cf. the Irish Nūadu with his talismanic sword, besides Lug with his spear). Correspondingly there were two early Germanic leadership types, one a warlord with his band of followers, typical of migratory tribes and quintessentially beholden to Wodan/Odin, the other elective, consecrated, and sanctioned. The latter kind was the **kuningaz* 'head of the kin group' or **thiuðanaz* 'head of the people' (Gothic *thiudans,* Old English *thēoden*), the former a **druhtinaz* 'head of a warrior band' (Old Norse *drōttinn,* Old English *dryhten;* borrowed as Finnish *ruhtinas* 'prince'; cf. Swedish *drottning* 'queen', Russian *drug* 'comrade, friend', *družína* 'warrior band, bodyguard of a prince') or a **harja-tugan-* 'host leader' (Old English *heretoga* [also *folctoga*], German *herzog* 'duke'). The two were not necessarily mutually exclusive, and each had his qualifications (cf. Tacitus, *Germania* 7: *reges ex nobilitate, duces ex virtute sumunt,* adding that the *rex* did not have unlimited power, and the *dux* led by brave example and inspiration rather than by command).

Wodan/Odin is the towering god of the Germanic pantheon, whether the latter appears reductionistic in the early manner of Tacitus and the late fashion of Adam of Bremen or expansive and well stocked as in the *Eddas*. Any sectarian leanings, whether toward Tīw or Thor, tend to be away from Wodan/Odin, even thereby stressing his intrinsic importance.

The name of the god (Old Norse *Ōðinn* < Proto-Germanic **Wōðanaz* < **Wātónos*) is formed with the "augmentative" suffix **-no-* from the adjective **wātós* attested in Gothic *wōths,* Old Norse *ōðr* 'raving, possessed' (cf. Old Norse *ōðr,* German *Wut* 'rage, possession, fury'), cognate with Latin *vātēs* and Old Irish *fāith* 'ecstatic bard'; Adam of Bremen (4.26) glossed Wodan with 'Furor'. Granted the martial emphasis of Germanic tradition and the centrality of the warlike element, this "rage" seems to refer primarily to warrior fury, the same as Cūchulainn's *ferg*. But there are important qualifications, for Odin is extremely complex. He does not "embody" martial ecstasy, he dispenses it, being himself devious and manipulative. He is in fact a magician rather than a champion, an orchestrator of conflict rather than a combatant. Odin is the master of arcane ("runic") wisdom, poetry, and magic (*galdr*, *seiðr*), having given up an eye to quaff the essence ("mead") of Mīmir's wellspring and left the eye on deposit in the well

(*Poetic Edda, Völuspā* ['Sibyl's Prophecy'] 28).[1] With his one-eyed paralyzing battle magic (*herfjöturr,* literally 'host fetter') and spear Gungnir he resembles the Irish Lug, but the external appearance of the young Celtic whiz kid could not be more unlike the old man with his slouch hat that was Odin's common epiphany (although he was prone to disguises and a shape changer; according to Snorri [*Ynglinga Saga* 7], he could lie in cataleptic trance as if dead while roaming abroad in animal shape). This shamanic aspect of Odin (including intimations of sexual inversions and androgyny) is encapsulated in the "supreme mystery" of Germanic theology, Odin's primordial self-sacrifice on the world tree (the Old Norse Yggdrasill, the axis mundi of many mythic traditions, literally 'Ygg's [= Odin's] horse', a kenning for 'gallows,' which the victim "rode"):

> I know that I hung on the windy tree
> for nine full nights,
> wounded with a spear, and given to Odin,
> myself to myself,
> on that tree of which no one knows
> where the roots run.
>
> (*Poetic Edda, Hāvamāl* 138)

This is partly a validation myth wherein the god as the founding initiate "charters" a centerpiece of his own cult, namely the sacrifice (including self-immolation) by hanging and stabbing that was practiced by his votaries (cf. Starkað's sacrifice of King Vīkarr to Odin in chap. 13). But Odin's "passion" (consisting mainly, it seems, of hunger, thirst, and loneliness) and the illumination that ensued ("I got a drink of the precious mead" [*Hāvamāl* 140]) also resemble Finnic shamanic rituals, where a nonlethal nine-night suspension in birch branches was conducive to otherworldly experience.

Odin is described as a necromancer in the *Völuspā* and elsewhere. He is the god of the hanged (*hangaguð*; see fig. 10) who leads the wild hunt, the ghostly riders in the sky (Old German *Wutanes her*). His

1. 'Eye' and '[well]spring' are curiously interchangeable in the lexica of many Indo-European and Semitic languages: Hittite *sakui-*, Armenian *akn*, Akkadian *īnu(m)*, Hebrew and Arabic *'ayn* have both meanings, Persian *čäšm* 'eye' and *čäšmä* 'spring' both reflect Old Iranian *čašman-* 'eye', and Latvian *aka* 'well' matches Russian *oko* 'eye'. The connection might reside in mythical traditions about fiery substances deep in water on the one hand, attested from India and Iran to Ireland (cf. chap. 16), and in prescientific speculations about sight as an intraocular form of fire, found for example in Plato's *Timaeus* (45b–d) and in the Old Indic *Sūtrasthāna* (21.7) by Suśruta.

FIGURE 10. Odin as *hangaguð*. Stave church of Hegge, Norway. (Courtesy of Universitetets Oldsaksamling, Oslo. Photograph by M. Blindheim.)

countless Norse poetic epithets include Herjann 'Lord of the Host' (< **Koryonos*, an etymological match for the Homeric *koíranos*, title of Agamemnon as the Greek supreme commander). The "host" that Odin commanded became "militarized" from the souls of the hanged to the *valr*, the battlefield dead, the posthumous Odinic warriors (*einherjar* 'elite troops') whom the god entertained in a vast hall of his Otherworld (*Val-höll*). There they kept in fighting trim for the upcoming eschatological battle, and after a hard day's jousting they were attended to by the Valkyries 'Corpse pickers', comparable to the Celtic battle-goddesses, who supplied Valhöll with newcomers in tandem with worldly carnage but also performed as serving wenches or barmaids; in some of its catering aspects the establishment prefigured the Hofbräuhaus or après-ski facilities at a winter resort.

Whether in pre- or postmortem status, a true Odinic warrior was infused with a generous helping of the god's *furor*. Odin's contorted martial ecstatics (cf. Cūchulainn in chap. 10) underwent metamorphoses ranging from bestiovestism (animal disguise) to lycanthropic transformation, appearing as *berserkir* 'bear shirted' or werewolfish *ūlfheðnar* 'wolf skinned'; either way, the result was homicidal mania and murderous menace to one and all, graphically depicted by Saxo and Snorri (see fig. 11). In Saxo's book 7, the berserk Harthben from Swedish Hälsingland goes into a fit, takes bites out of the rim of his shield, gulps down live coals, runs through fire, and ends up slaughtering six of his own champions. Snorri (*Ynglinga Saga* 6) describes Odin's men who shunned mailcoats and *varu galnir sem hundar eda vargar* 'were mad as dogs or wolves', "bit their shields, and were as strong as bears or bulls. They slew men, and neither fire nor iron bit on them. This is called going berserk [*berserksgangr*]." They would carry on *ululantium more luporum* 'like howling wolves' (Saxo, book 5), and in more ordered forms of society were treated accordingly: the Old Icelandic law code (*Grāgās* 1.23) proscribed *berserksgangr* and outlawed berserks and their accomplices, even as other "wolfish" behavior made an *ūtlägr* out of a *morðvargr* (clandestine killer, literally 'murder wolf') or a *vargr ī vēum* (temple robber, literally 'wolf in sanctuary'). Werewolfish killing (biting through the windpipe) was practiced by Odinic heroes, as when Sigmundr so dispatched Sinfjötli (*Völsunga Saga* 8) or Egil disposed of the berserk Atli on whom weapons would not bite (*Egils Saga* 65). The Old Norse words for 'wolf', *ūlfr* and *vargr*, are paralleled elsewhere in Indo-European as terms for 'mad rage' (Greek *lússa* < **wl̥k*^{w}*ya*, literally 'wolfishness') or criminality (Vedic *vṛ́ka-* 'barbarian

FIGURE 11. Odinic warrior and *ūlfheðinn*. Sixth-century C.E. helmet-plate die from Torslunda, Öland, Sweden. (Courtesy of Antikvarisk-topografiska arkivet, Statens Historiska Museer, Stockholm.)

enemy, brigand'; Hittite *hurkil* 'capital sex crime', and 'wolf' as a juridical expression for a killer not qualified to offer wergeld in atonement).

Odin himself was accompanied by the wolves Geri 'Greedy' and Freki 'Ravenous', in addition to his ravens Huginn 'Thought' and Muninn 'Memory', and rode the eight-legged gray death mount Sleipnir. Not a little in his complex makeup smacks of demonic enormity, and he has notably close ties to the giants, the Norse parallels to the Indic demons and the Irish Fomoire, or epically the Indic Kauravas, the Iranian Turanians, and the Roman Tarquins. These hostile foils are more like rival clans than polar opposites and are strangely woven into the ancestral fabric (Kauravas being cousins of Pāṇḍavas; Lug, Khosraw, and Brutus born of "enemy" mothers). Even so Odin is descended from the primordial giant Ymir on his father's side, and his mother Bestla is a giant's daughter. Although he occasionally prevails over giants in contests of wits and by trick questions, he is remarkably cozy with the demonic archtrickster Loki (technically a god) and strangely tolerant of even the most obnoxious giants.[2] In such instances the straight arrow Thor, giant killer without fail or compunction, has to save the situation, and he has plenty of other opportunity to remind Odin of the latter's underhandedness and marginal morality. In a way Odin is in a bind; in Germanic theology he epitomizes what is called in German *die Not der Götter,* the cosmic crisis that foreshadows the world end cataclysm, which he foresees and tries to stave off by increasingly desperate and deviant expedients. In his hour of need (the etymological cognate of *Not*) he is even a figure of some nobility and certainly of pathos, at least in the modern German Wagnerian representation (*h-e-i-l-i-g-e N-o-t* is impossible to replicate in English; 'holy distress' would sound too much like Batman).

The Norse profusion of data on Odin helps shed light on the spare and obscure Continental material as well, such as that of Tacitus, the Latin master of compressed and elliptic laconism. In *Germania* 39 he mentions a sacred grove of the Semnones, the cream of the Suēbi (modern Schwaben), where gruesome human sacrifice occurred. Anyone entering the grove had to be bound with a chain, in deference to the *regnator omnium deus* 'ruling god of all' who was inherent there. Everything points to Wodan, especially the parallel with Odin's host fetters in general, and in particular with the *fjöturlundr* 'fetter grove' where Dagr slew Helgi with a spear lent to him by Odin (*Poetic Edda, Helgaqviða Hundingsbana* 2.24).

In contrast to the immense amount of material on Odin and his ramifications deep into heroic saga (with "Odinic" heroes like Helgi, Sigmundr, and Sigurðr),[3] Tȳr's dossier is limited. In chapter 10 mention was made of the Mars Thingsus of Germanic Roman legionnaires at Hadrian's Wall in England in the third century, thus the Continental Tīw, patron of the judicial assembly (the Norse *thing;* cf. the medieval Low

2. But giants could be wisdom figures as well as lecherous rowdies; besides the rapist kind there was in the *Völsunga Saga* Sigurð's noble tutor and foster father Reginn, brother of the dragon giant Fāfnir (one is reminded of the Greeks' Centaurs: Kheiron who taught heroes versus Nessos who molested women). Reginn is a giant in the *Fāfnismāl* but a "dwarf" in the *Reginsmāl,* which shows that the two kinds (as complementary types of "enormity") were sometimes interchangeable (Alvīss, a dwarf defeated by Thor, "looked like a giant").

3. These tend to be progeny or descendants of Odin. They often act out Odinic role patterns, for example, Sigurðr matching wits with Fāfnir or questing for the drink of wisdom from Reginn and Sigrdrīfa, even as Odin did from Suttungr and Gunnlöðr. The parallel with the Indic epic heroes as saga transpositions of their divine fathers is palpable.

FIGURE 12. God (Týr?) binding monster (Fenrir?). Sixth-century C.E. helmet-plate die from Torslunda, Öland, Sweden. (Courtesy of Antikvarisk-topografiska arkivet, Statens Historiska Museer, Stockholm.)

German *dingesdach,* modern German *Dienstag* 'Tuesday').[4] He has been eclipsed by Odin and tritely assimilated to him, routinely credited with runes, wisdom, and victory. The name perhaps reflects **Dyēws* (rather than the generic **deywos* seen in Latin *deus,* Sanskrit *devá-,* Old Norse plural *tīvar,* Lithuanian *diẽvas* 'god') and thus matches the Latin Diūs (Fidius), the patron of troth with his temple on the Collis Mucialis (see chap. 9). Týr's one important myth has already been compared above (chaps. 7, 9, 10) with traditions about Jamshid in Iran, Mucius Scaevola in Rome, and Nūadu in Ireland. He loses his right hand as a pledge in the maw of the wolf Fenrir, forswearing himself so that the beast can be bound until Ragnarök (see fig. 12), thus rendering an im-

4. The calendrical importance of this institution is seen also in Baltic, where the Old Prussian word for 'council [day]', *savaite* (cognate with Russian *sovjet*), has come to mean metonymically 'week' (cf. *possisavaite* 'midweek', i.e., Wednesday, like German *Mittwoch*), even as in Russian *nedelja,* originally 'inactivity' (day of rest, Sunday) has developed to denote 'week'.

portant service to Odin's scheme for averting or postponing the twilight of the gods.[5] As Snorri tells the story in the *Gylfaginning,* he comments that *Tȳr* is *einhendr ok ekki kallaðr sättir manna* 'one-handed, and is not called a peacemaker'. This is a curious negative statement; why *not* a peacemaker? It makes sense only in terms of a disqualification; Tȳr had really been a peacemaker but had been disbarred because of his perjury-based mutilation, even as Nūadu was deposed as a consequence of his disability. In Scandinavia he is a sunken god in the heyday of the Odinic death cult, but his intrinsic eminence is not in question; witness the lingering importance of the Continental Tīw-Saxnōt (in a ninth-century Old Saxon baptismal vow the convert renounces allegiance to Thunär, Woden, and Saxnote).

As a pair, *Tīwz and *Wōðanaz have Western Indo-European traits in common with Nūadu and Lug, Scaevola and Cocles. It is less easy to compare them to the high gods of the priestly level in Rome and India, and not only because of the martial hypertrophy of the Germanic tradition. Tȳr recalls in name and function the Roman Diūs (Fidius), but an attendant comparison of Odin with Jupiter would make little sense. There is more congruence between *Tīwz and *Wōðanaz and the Vedic Mitra-Varuṇa pair as the benevolent contractual patron coupled with the devious and sinister binder-god. There may even be a Germanic parallel to Mitra : Aryaman (and Nūadu : Eremon in chap. 10) in the Saxon coexistence of Saxnōt and Irmin (a god whose name occurs in *Irminsūl,* the cultic pillar razed by Charlemagne, and in Old Saxon *irmintheod* 'mankind', literally 'Irmin's people'; cf. *aryamán-* in chap. 4).

Yet this is still mainly schematic and typological. The Indic god with whom Odin has most in common is not Varuṇa but Rudra-Śiva. Both are to a degree demonic, both are morally ambivalent, even evil and destructive, both require human sacrifice, both have their sworn bands of votaries and possess arcane magic knowledge. There are even more specific "personal" traits: ocular enormity (Odin minus one eye, Rudra with an extra one), distinctive headgear (Odin's slouch hat, Rudra's turban), a passion for disguises and incognito appearances, a tendency to roam. Rudra is mainly a kṣatriya god in India, but he reflects the "chaotic," antisocial, morally ambiguous aspect of the warrior in a

5. The entire theologem is a melancholy reflection on the Germanic view of rule and justice at the "highest level": The divine chief executive operates by a combination of charismatic "magic" and Machiavellian manipulation, while the chief law enforcement officer perjures himself to perpetuate the regime.

no-man's-land between raw nature and civilized society, as opposed to the more integrated (though still self-willed) Indra and especially Viṣṇu. Similarly Odin seems to be in origin the semidemonic patron of the warriors, and in consequence the same is true of the Celtic Esus-Lugus (and whatever deity underlies the Roman saga figure Cocles). In warlike Germanic and Celtic society a homologue of Rudra ascended to the pinnacle of the pantheon, assimilating or supplanting whatever pristine god may have kept company there, Varuna-like, with the trothkeeper/ peacemaker.

The Odinic fusion of the intellectual and the instinctive, of the clairvoyant and the ecstatic, of poet and berserk was a volatile one that required its own counterfoil in any ordered religion and society. In the Germanic, and especially the Norse, instance this balancing figure was Thor, who was as predictable as Odin was fickle, as trustworthy as Odin was treacherous. His cult was typical of entrenched rather than free-booting circles, of conservative settlers rather than land grabbers and seafarers. The Icelandic colonists, who had fled southwestern Norway to escape the depredations of such Odinic ruler types as Harald Fairhair and his son Erik Bloodaxe, had brought with them no love of Odin, but fully a fourth of the thousands of early settlers recorded in the *Landnāmabōk* bore theophorous names of the type Thorsten or Thorolf (Odinic toponyms are absent in Iceland and rare in Norway, being common only in southern Sweden and Denmark [e.g., Odense]). Thor was a reassuring supernatural presence in both divine and human crises, be they encroachments by giants on gods, or petty tyrants on peasant freeholders, or overzealous Christian missionaries on idols of the old religion; no wonder he had eclipsed Odin in the temple at Uppsala and elsewhere in the twilight of paganism (cf. the many place-names like Torshälla or Torslunda in Sweden, Tollund in Denmark).

The name means simply 'Thunder' (*Thōrr* < **Thunaraz;* cf. the Gaulish Taranis in chap. 10), and Thor's "hammer" *Mjöllnir* (< **meldhniyos;* see fig. 13) is etymologically cognate with Russian *mólnija* and Welsh *mellt* 'lightning' (cf. Russian *mólot* 'hammer'). It is thus the bolt, and it can be represented also as an (originally stone) ax, a club (cf. Feridun's *gurz* in chaps. 2 and 7 and the *milna* of the Latvian Pērkōns [chap. 12]), or as a counterclockwise hooked cross symbolizing a thunderball, resembling the Indic *svastika-* 'good luck sign' (from Vedic *su-astí-* 'well-being, good fortune'). It was a tool that the god used to 'hallow' (*vīgja*) beings in a positive vein (consecrate a bride, revive his own goat team, sanctify the dead; cf. Indra's *vájra-* cognate with Latin *vegeō* 'arouse, quicken'). Its other function was to exterminate giants, indirectly life-enhancing dirty work that had to be done, related with gusto by the skald Vetrliði, himself murdered by Christian missionaries in the year 999:

> You smashed the legs of Leikn,
> thrashed Thrīvaldi,
> stomped on Starkaðr,
> trod to death Gjölp!

Monster and demon fighting is characteristic of thunder-weapon wielders (Indra, Thraētaona), and Thor did his share in tackling the Miðgarðsormr or Jörmungandr, the sea serpent whose coils encompassed the world of men (Miðgarðr). His fishing for the creature was unsuccessful, however, partly thwarted by the sea giant Hymir, until Ragnarök, when the two killed each other. Unlike this eschatological note of gloom, routine giant bashing is the occasion of high good humor in the Old Norse sources, often verging on the burlesque and laced with folktale motifs; the Icelanders were comfortable with Thor and his enormous appetite and not above making a buffoon of him as well as the boastful and intemperate ogres whose skulls he ended up crushing. This provided good poetic entertainment, as in Snorri's account (in *Skāldskaparmāl*) of Hrungnir's bragging about wrecking the divine residence and ravaging its goddesses and his subsequent duel with Thor. Obscure myth can lurk in such tales: a piece of a whetstone hurled by Hrungnir had penetrated Thor's head, and a sorceress Grōa 'Growth' was called in to dislodge it by magic. During the procedure Thor chattered on about how he had carried Grōa's husband Aurvandill back from Giantland (Jötunheimr) in a basket, but Aurvandill's toe had stuck out and frozen, so Thor had amputated it and tossed it into the sky to become a star. The news distracted Grōa so that the operation miscarried, and the piece remained embedded in Thor's skull. Astral etiology aside (there is also Old English *Earendel* for 'Morning Star'), who was Aurvandill? Saxo (book 3) tells of (H)orvendillus, father of Amlethus (Hamlet); the latter cohabited in a remote swamp with the prototype of Shakespeare's Ophelia, and in his account of it (Saxo 3.6.10) refers to the names of various bog plants. *Aur-vandill* seems to mean 'bog wand', and Vandill alone is found as a man's name, an ethnic term (Vandals), and a toponym (the ancient site of Vendel in Swedish Uppland). 'Wand, Staff, Stick' as a man's name is a phallic metonym (cf. Hittite *pesna-* 'man' cognate with Latin *pēnis*), and Aurvandill was hence some kind of wet-

FIGURE 13. Thor with Mjöllnir, ca. 1,000 C.E. (Courtesy of the National Museum, Reykjavik, Iceland. Photograph by Gisli Gestsson.)

land-related fertility figure, husband of 'Growth'; the Germanic fertility deities were involved in the kind of magic (*seiðr*) practiced by Grōa. Perhaps the astral "toe" legend is a euphemistic one, and what Thor really broke off was Aurvandill's frozen male member. Norse tradition teems with such brittle, confused, and opaque mythical matter.

The story of Thor's extermination call on the giant Geirröðr is likewise told in the *Skāldskaparmāl* (and revamped as "Thorkillus" and "Geruthus" in Saxo's book 8), including the episode of how the giant's daughter Gjālp tried to drown Thor by straddling a torrent and urinating into it until the god, commenting that "a river must be dammed at the source," plugged her orifice with a well-aimed rock. Thor was saved by grabbing hold of a rowan tree, a significant detail, considering that the tree name figures as Thor's wife in the borrowed Lappish Ravdna (consort of Hora Galles < **Thunra-karlaz* 'Thor fellow') and in the Finnish Rauni, wife of Ukko, the 'Old Man' thunder-god (cf. Norwegian *raun,* Swedish *rönn* 'rowan'; but in Norse tradition proper Thor's wife was Sif).

Sheer burlesque obtains in the *Poetic Edda*'s *Thrymsqviða,* where the giant Thrymr has stolen Thor's hammer and will restore it only in return for marrying Freyja. Instead Thor dresses in bride's clothes, goes to Jötunheimr, and when the hammer is brought out to hallow the supposed bride, grabs it and breaks the giants' heads. This debased transvestism recalls Arjuna's masquerade at Virāṭa's court (chap. 5) and similar episodes of donning female garb in the careers of Greek heroes (Herakles, Achilles).

The general adherence of Thor to the Indra pattern is striking, but so are the differences, for Indra is a generalized, all-round warrior-god, whereas Odin holds down much of that slot and has relegated Thor to being a solitary champion with a much more down-to-earth, not to say rural constituency. Perhaps the early Vāyu was in some regards a more specific character mate of Thor. The remaining Indic kṣatriya god, Viṣṇu, also resembles Thor in some respects, such as serial demon killing. But Viṣṇu's specific Norse comparand is the "silent god" Vīðarr, who according to Snorri's *Gylfaginning* "has a stout shoe and is almost as strong as Thor. The gods rely greatly on him in all difficult situations." Of the latter kind is Ragnarök itself: when Fenrir has swallowed and killed Odin, Vīðarr will stride forward, plant his well-shod foot on the wolf's lower jaw, and with his hand force the upper jaw open until the beast's throat is torn asunder. This is the ultimate mythical exhortation 'Wider!' which inheres in Vīðar's name as well as Viṣṇu's, only here it is carried out eschatologically and in retribution rather than primordially in mapping out the universe (cf. chap. 4). Typically much of Norse myth gravitates away from creation and toward Ragnarök: Thor's showdown with the serpent, Vīðar's exploit of the wide step.

Freyr was the third member of the triad reported by Adam of Bremen and used in Norse religious formulas until supplanted by Father, Son, and Holy Ghost. Unlike Odin and Thor, however, Freyr is not a solitary eminence but rather an epitome of his own kind, the Vanir deities who form a distinct subgroup within the divine community and were at primordial loggerheads with the bulk of the pantheon (the Äsir, from singular *āss* 'god'). Typified by his exaggeratedly phallic iconography at Uppsala, Freyr patronized peace, prosperity, and fecundity (see fig. 14). But he was himself part of a Vanic subtriad composed of Njörðr (< **Nerthuz*), Freyr (< **Fraujaz* 'Lord'), and Freyja (< **Fraujō* 'Lady'). Njörðr was the father of the brother-sister pair Freyr-Freyja, but this seems merely a weak attempt to bring order to the sexual ambiguities and incestuous proclivities of the Vanir.

*Nerthuz is even etymologically ambivalent, cognate not only with Old Irish *nert* 'strength' and Greek *andro-* but with Vedic *sū-nṛ́tā* 'good vigor, vitality' (used especially of Uṣās, thus gender ambivalent). Tacitus (*Germania* 40) gives a famous description of the *goddess* Nerthus whom he glosses by 'Terra Mater'. She had a sacred grove on a (Danish?) island, and an enclosed ox cart in which she periodically journeyed through the land, attended by a priest and accompanied by peaceful festivity with 'all iron locked up' (*clausum omne ferrum*). On her return the conveyance and, 'if you would believe' (*si credere velis*), the goddess herself were lustrated in a secluded lake, followed by the immediate drowning of the slaves who had done the bathing and thus witnessed the mystery.

Even granted the difference of gender, all this resembles not Njörðr but rather Freyr as worshiped especially in Sweden, where he occurs in many place-names (e.g., Frösö), had a cultic journey in a covered wagon in the company of a female attendant, and received human sacrifices at Uppsala (according to Adam of Bremen, there was a well next to the temple, into which live victims were plunged). His worship included degenerate features that offended macho heroes such as Starkaðr. Effeminacy and passive homosexuality were touchy matters in Old Germanic society; according to Tacitus (*Germania* 12), perverts were sunk in mudholes and marshes, as perhaps corroborated by the hundreds of well-preserved corpses impregnated with tannin that have been found in

FIGURE 14. Ithyphallic Freyr from Södermanland, Sweden. (Courtesy of Antikvarisk-topografiska arkivet, Statens Historiska Museer, Stockholm.)

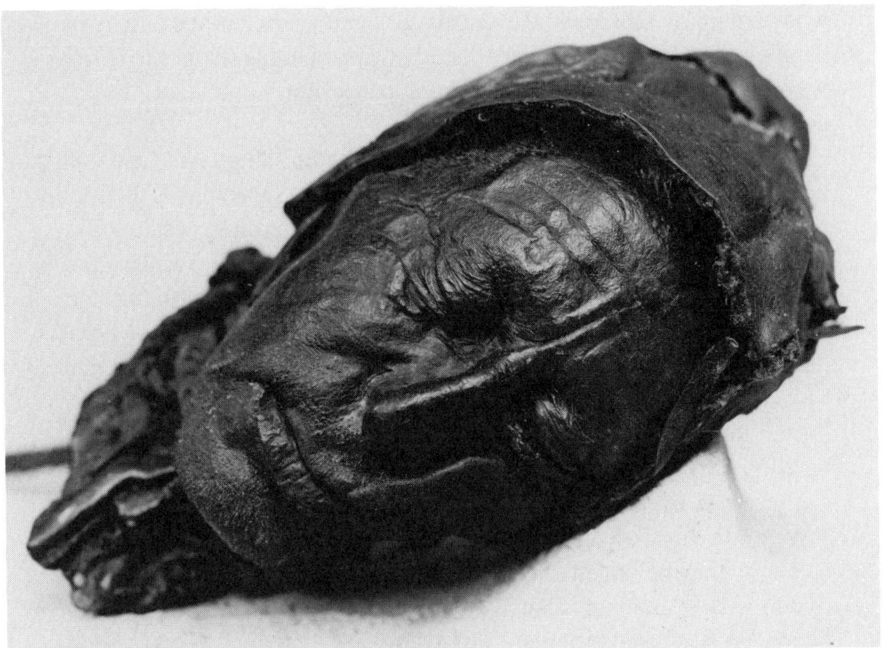

FIGURE 15. Peatbog corpse from Tollund, Jutland, Denmark. Early common era. (Courtesy of Silkeborg Museum, Denmark.)

Danish and north German peatbogs (fig. 15). The corresponding term *ergi* was the worst opprobrium in Old Norse vocabulary, as was the adjective *argr,* especially when combined with the rhyming "criminal" *vargr* as insult plus injury.

Freyr also figures importantly in the euhemerized account of Snorri's *Ynglinga Saga,* where Odin and his cohorts are presented as immigrants to Scandinavia from Asia Minor (in Snorri's fancy Äsir = Asians!). On arrival in Sweden Odin set up Freyr at Uppsala, where as Yngvi-Freyr 'Lord Yngvi' he later became a legendary ancestral peace king whose dead body in its barrow continued to receive tribute and vouchsafe prosperity. His son Fjölnir followed in his footsteps until drowning in a vat of mead (shades of Vanic sacrifice!), and the Swedish Ynglinga dynasty (known as Scylfingas in *Beowulf,* besides the Scyldingas of Denmark) traced its lineage to him (cf. the anthropogonic, north-coastal Ingaevones of Tacitus [*Germania* 2], discussed in chap. 17). The same typology obtains among the various kings named Frōði (Saxo's Frotho) in the Danish Skjöldunga dynasty, especially Frōði III, who traveled about the land in a ceremonial wagon while alive and whose mummy still made the rounds for three years, propped up by his handlers, lest news of his death disturb the prosperous status quo (*Frōði* was also an epithet of Freyr, whose peace era was called "Frōði's peace").

Njörðr was equally male, at home in Nōatūn 'Shiptown', and with maritime associations to seafarers and fishermen, surviving as the merman Njor in Norwegian folklore. He was also proverbially wealthy and, according to Snorri, succeeded Odin directly as king of Sweden, preceding his son Freyr. The kinkiness of the Vanir is present in him too. After abandoning a sister-wife who in typical Vanic incest had borne him Freyr and Freyja, he married Skaði, daughter of the slain giant Thjazi, in peculiar circumstances. When Skaði sought armed revenge for her father, the gods mollified her by letting her choose a divine husband by looking only at the gods' feet (with echoes from the Roman *Nudipedalia* ritual to foot-fetish fairytale motifs such as Cinderella's slipper). In this male beauty contest Skaði picked the best-looking pair, believing they belonged to Baldr, but ended up instead with Njörðr. The role inversion in this mismatch is reinforced by the general character of Skaði, an amazonal mountain lass who could not stand Njörð's dockside routine any more than the groom would put up with the howling of wolves in the hills. Skaði with her armor, bow, and snowshoes resembles the obscure male deity Ullr, well attested in place-names of central Sweden (Ultuna) and southern Norway (Ulvik), the great skier and bow hunter whose name means 'Glory' or 'Splendor' (Gothic *wulthus,* Old English *wuldor*) and may have had an "augmented" variant form **Wulthunaz,* judging from Norwegian toponyms like Ullinshof. He appears in Saxo's euhemerized saga transposition as the magician Ollerus who usurped Othinus's (Odin's) position for a decade before being overthrown and killed. It may be that, before all the inversions, Ullr-Skaði (the latter perhaps a masculine word meaning 'Injurer') was the male partner of the female earth- or water-deity Nerthus, Tacitus's 'Terra Mater'; since Ullr seems to be a wintry version of the bright sky-god, perhaps we have here in the last analysis a distant reflection of a subarctic mating of heaven and earth. An ancient hierogamy may ultimately be involved also when Freyr sends his retainer Skīrnir 'Bright' to woo Gerðr (daughter of the giant Gymir), who is not swayed by gifts of gold or threats of violence but yields in the end to spells and curses.

Compared with the ambiguous Freyr and Njörðr, Freyja or Vanadīs was a straightforward love-goddess. She was married to a certain *Ōðr* 'Raving' ("unaugmented" name parallel to *Ōðinn*) and wept golden tears while he was away on long journeys. In some ways she is difficult to tell from Odin's consort Frigg, even in name (Frigg appears as Frija in Old German, while conversely Adam called Freyr "Fricco"; Frigg/Frija is cognate with 'free' and 'friend'); they also shared the traits of covetousness and wanton demeanor. Freyja likewise displays some Valkyrie-like features, picking up part of the slain, even as Frey's bride Gerðr resembled the type, being reached by Skīrnir only through a ring of magic fire. Freyja was also Odin's tutor in the vile sorcery peculiar to the Vanir (*seiðr*), which involved both witchcraft and *ergi*.

Vanic myth was particularly prone to transposition, not only into euhemerized dynastic saga but into heroic epic matter as well. Thus the career of the hero Haddingr (Hadingus) in book I of Saxo is in many ways a transmutation of the myth of Njörðr, combined with Odinic elements.

Haddingr, son of Gram of Denmark, father of the future Frōði I (cf. Njörðr as father of Freyr in the Swedish Ynglinga dynasty), was orphaned and reared in Sweden by the giantess Harðgreip (Harthgrepa), a *seiðr* specialist who was both his wet nurse and afterward his "incestuous" seducer and mate. Later on Odin entered his life and guided him on the heroic path, but his Vanic associations persisted, for he founded the annual Freyr sacrifice (Fröblot) in Sweden. He rescued from giants the ravaged Norwegian princess Ragnhild (Regnilda), who later married him after inspecting the legs of various suitors. After a mysterious journey to the Otherworld and more warfare under the tutelage of Odin, the marriage turned disharmonious for the same mariner/mountaineer incompatibility that had bedeviled Njörðr and Skaði. Hadding's end came after his friend, the Swedish king Hundingr, drowned in a vat of beer (cf. Fjölnir above). In grief Haddingr conducted his own public hanging, thus going out in Odinic fashion (Njörðr in the *Ynglinga Saga* also had an Odinic death by receiving the symbolic spear mark that was a form of extreme unction and a shortcut to Valhöll for those unlucky enough to expire with their boots off).

This interlocking of Odinic and Vanic features in the career of a hero is symptomatic of the effected symbiosis of the two kinds of deities, of mythic conflict resolution transposed to saga level. The name *Haddingr* is suggestive, for it is also that of a dual pair attested elsewhere (Saxo's *duo Haddingi,* Icelandic *tveir Haddingjar*), of the Old English *Heardingas* ('East Danes' who worshiped Ing), and of the eastern Continental Vandalic *Hasdingi* led by the pair Raos and Raptos. The etymon is Old Norse *haddr,* Old English *heord* (< _*hazdaz_ < _*kos-dhos_) denoting a feminine hairdo (cf. Russian *kosá* 'braid'). Thus effeminacy creeps in once more; Tacitus (*Germania* 43) reports that the eastern Naharvali worshiped a Castor-Pollux type of couple called Alcis, whose cult was presided over by a priest with womanish insignia (*muliebri ornatu*). Helgi Hundingsbani, one of the Haddingjar, is reported to have on one occasion donned transvestite disguise. We are in the realm of Germanic dioskourism and dual kingship, corresponding to Aśvinic myth in India. The equine aspect is seen in the leaders of the Anglo-Saxon invasion, Hengist and Horsa. The "watery" rescue angle appears in prehistoric iconography (e.g., pairs of superhuman figures hovering over ships in cave drawings) and in what must have been an original twinlike twosome later reflected by the "father and son" Njörðr and Freyr (the former the patron of sailors, the latter the skipper of the good ship *Skīðblaðnir*). The third member of the Vanic threesome must have been in origin the female companion of the Dioskouric pair. But since the Vanir clearly reflect the deities of the original "third estate" (= the Vedic Vasus) at large, the Freyja kind also contains elements of the transfunctional goddess, even anecdotally (Skīrnir on his proxy wooing mission tries to get through to Gerðr in each of her triple aspects, using successively gold, threats of force, and verbal persuasion).

The myth of the "War of the Äsir and Vanir," the primordial conflict that solidified the pantheon, is attested in some obscure allusive verses of the *Poetic Edda* (*Völuspā* 21–24), euhemeristically in the *Ynglinga Saga,* and most importantly in the *Prose Edda* (*Skāldskaparmāl*). In the saga, the conflict concluded with an exchange of hostages, as a result of which Njörðr and Freyr ended up among the Äsir and were made priests by Odin along with Njörð's daughter Freyja, the seiðr teacher, and permanent symbiosis of Äsir and Vanir ensued. In the *Skāldskaparmāl* a truce was concluded by the two parties' spitting into a crock (a well-known primitive means of inducing fermentation), out of which was born the wise man Kvasir (cf. the Russian fermented cereal drink or fruit drink *kvas*). He was killed by dwarfs, who mixed his blood with honey to produce the mead of poetry. The latter fell into the hands of the giant Suttungr, but Odin ultimately ingested it by a trick, flew away in eagle shape, and regurgitated the precious stuff into the vats of the Äsir.

Apart from the general analogues to the Fomorian and Sabine conflicts, the most notable similarities are with the Indra-Aśvin encounter (see chap. 4), where the integration of the "lower gods" also entailed the creation of a figure embodying an intoxicant (Mada), which was subsequently apportioned for its "inspirational" properties; but in India Mada was the monster that forced the issue, whereas in Iceland Kvasir so to speak sealed the peace process. Also, in India alcohol came to have the negative connotation of assorted vices, whereas in Iceland (and also in Ireland) the by-products of the sacred mead were learning, wisdom, and poetic power. A special detail matching the Sabine War may be the role of the female figure Gullveig ('Gold Drunk'), alluded to in the *Völuspā* as sent by the Vanir to corrupt the Äsir, in comparison with Tarpeia, the Roman girl whom the Sabines suborned with gold or sex. In this way bits of random and specific tradition reinforce each other and aid in the reconstruction of an important protomyth, or at least in a better appreciation of the true time depth of the individual versions.

Another important Icelandic-Indic isotheme involves the god Heimdalr, who was singled out above (chap. 5) as the Norse comparand of the faded Indic sky-god Dyaus, whose myth is lost in Vedic lore but survives in his incarnation as Bhīṣma in the *Mahābhārata*. Earlier in this chapter Heimdalr appeared as the father of Thräll, Karl, and Jarl and as grandfather of Konr Ungr, who embody prototypes (almost eponyms) of the social classes. At the outset of the *Völuspā,* the seeress solicits the attention of her audience for the prophecy to follow:

> Hljōðs bid ec allar helgar kindir,
> meiri oc minni mögo Heimdalar!
>
> Hearken I bid all hallowed kin groups,
> larger and lesser sons of Heimdalr!

Heimdalr is hence somehow primordially ancestral (born *ī ārdaga* 'of yore'), and through generations, for the *Rīgsthula* describes his serial sirings as involving visits to couples named successively "great-grandparents" (Thräll), "grandparents" (Karl), and *Faðir oc Mōðir* (Jarl) respectively. Elsewhere in the *Völuspā* Heimdal's own *hljōð* is described as hidden under the evergreen holy tree (i.e., the Yggdrasill), perhaps as a pledge in the well located there, in the manner of Odin's eye, possibly in the form of an ear (*hljōð* matches Avestan *sraotam* 'hearing' and Sanskrit *śrótram* 'ear' < Indo-European **k̂lewt*[*r*]*om*). In any event Heimdalr is a great hearkener—he can pick up the sound of grass and wool growing—and he is no visual slouch either, since he can see for a hundred leagues around the clock. In this ever wakeful stance at the high end of the Rainbow Bridge (Bifröst), he guards the access to heaven, ready to sound the alarm on the Gjallarhorn at the first sign of

Ragnarök. Vigilance is the watchword for this strange god, who is not only primeval but also ultimate, for he will be the last to perish in the cataclysm, in an internecine duel with Loki. His birth myth is peculiar, involving as joint mothers nine sisters who are sometimes listed as giantesses. His name is obscure, perhaps **heim-dalthu-*, literally 'world tree' (*heimr* means 'habitat, world', and **dalthu-* may be reflected by the later Icelandic *dallur* 'fruit-bearing tree', cognate with Greek *thállō* 'to bloom'); hence the watchman at the top of the rainbow could be ultimately identical with the axis mundi that points to the center of the firmament. Heimdalr has neither wife nor weapon, but he does possess certain theriomorphic associations to the ram (*heimdali* being a poetic term for 'ram', whose offensive weapon is his butting head; hence kennings describe a sword as 'Heimdal's head', or conversely a head as 'Heimdal's sword'; his epithets Gullintanni 'Golden-Toothed' and Hallinskīði 'Bent Sticks' refer to the discolored teeth and head-hugging horns of an old ram).

His nine mothers resemble the nine daughters of the sea-god Ägir, who are more than a poetic conceit for sea waves, since they occur also in Celtic (Welsh) maritime folklore, where whitecaps were termed the "sheep" of the mermaid (*morforwyn*) Gwenhudwy 'White Sorceress', but the ninth, magically powerful breaker was called the "ram." This may provide an inkling of why Heimdalr was known both as Vindhlēr 'Gale Sea' and as the 'white god' (*hvīti āss*). But more remotely, away from northern seas and deep into prehistory, the birth myth of Heimdalr and its Welsh analogue resemble the story (chap. 5) of Dyaus incarnated as Bhīṣma in the amniotic plenitude of the great river-goddess Gangā, with eight of his preceding brothers drowning in her birth waters (cf. the eight waves that peter out before the ninth, decisive breaker, and Heimdalr described as born of "one and eight mothers," as if only one really mattered). We may thus have in Dyaus and Heimdalr a primordial Indo-European myth of heaven born of a great water deity, the only survivor (or perhaps mystical "sum") of nine births.

The parallelism of the birth myths extends to the "careers" of Heimdalr and Bhīṣma. Both are in a sense "sideliners" from an early start to a belated end, unmarried avuncular or "grandfatherly" types who attend to procreation matters and sponsor successive generations (Jarl and Konr Ungr, Pāṇḍu-Dhṛtarāṣṭra and their sons) without overt paternity, performing as watchful counselors and observing guardians without occupying center stage. In this way Heimdalr remains one of the most enigmatic and fascinating divine figures of Norse myth. His associations are with the Vanir more than the Äsir (one of Freyja's allonyms, Mardöll, resembles Heimdalr in the second element), even as the Vedic Dyaus was the ancestor of the Aśvins and of Uṣas. It seems that elements of the Indo-European *Dyēws live on in Germanic tradition in triple guise: in the patron of troth *Tīwz, in the bright wintry sky-god *Wulthuz, and in a water-born heaven sustainer and ancestral type realized in Heimdalr.

In contrast to Heimdalr, the story of Baldr is more all of a piece. He is the son of Odin and Frigg, husband of Nanna and father of Forseti (the great arbitrator of men's lawsuits). He is bright and beautiful, wise, just, and merciful—in short, too good for this world or the flawed regime of the Germanic gods ruled by the devious Odin, with the serpent Nīðhöggr gnawing at the roots of Yggdrasill and Heimdalr keeping a round-the-clock watch for signs of Ragnarök. His premonitory dreams of death caused Frigg to exact from all nature a pledge to do no harm to her son, which made Baldr handy as a live dart board for divine sport. Loki, whose powers of demonic shape change exceeded even Odin's, took on feminine guise and in the course of womanly chit chat learned from Frigg that she had neglected to pledge the puny mistletoe. Therefore Loki picked the mistletoe, placed it in the hands of the blind god Höðr, ostensibly to help the handicapped to a piece of the action in the divine dart game, and aimed it at Baldr, who when hit fell dead. Loki thus became Baldr's *rāðbani,* the planner of his murder, with Höðr as the *handbani,* the actual killer, and an unwitting one at that (this well-known motif of the blind shot occurs also in Irish lore, where the jealous Ailill caused his blind brother Lugaid to shoot Fergus Mac Roich as the latter swam in a lake with Ailill's wife Medb). Snorri in the *Gylfaginning* gives a powerful account of divine grief and of Baldr's obsequies. Odin's son Hermōðr is to ride Sleipnir to Hel to attempt a recovery, while the gods set out to give Baldr a blazing ship funeral at sea. They cannot move the vessel without the help of a monstrous giantess Hyrrokin, who arrives on wolfback with snakes for reins and launches the large ship with one seismic shove while four berserks restrain her mount. Thor, who is allergic to giants, tries to crack her skull but is restrained. Nanna dies of grief and is laid by Baldr's side. Thor hallows the ship pyre with Mjöllnir, trips up a dwarf Litr who gets in his way, and kicks him into the blaze. Odin lays on the pyre his magic ring Draupnir, and Baldr's harnessed horse joins his master in death. This cremation draws not only the grieving parents attended by Valkyries and ravens, and the various gods in their characteristic conveyances (Freyr drawn by his boar, Heimdalr on his horse, Freyja driving her cats), but also a great crowd of frost ogres and rock giants, showing that on such a traumatic occasion the feuding clans of Āsgarðr and Jötunheimr would band together despite the enraged mutterings of the likes of Thor.

Meanwhile Hermōðr rode for nine nights through dales deep and dark, crossed the river Gjöll, where a maiden directed him "downward and northward" (cf. chap. 3, note 1), and finally cleared the gate of Hel, finding Baldr there in the high seat. Hel (the goddess ruler of the place, daughter of Loki) agreed to let him go if universal nature would lament his death. Everything did except the giantess Thökk (Loki in disguise), whose refusal thwarted it all. Baldr stayed dead, and in some traditions Odin's son Vāli by Rindr was to be his avenger. Baldr (and Höðr) would emerge from Hel only in the rebirth following Ragnarök.

This myth of the god of light and goodness done to death by evil counsel, abortively resurrected but returning for good at an eschatological renewal, has been compared to everything from Adonis and Orpheus to Christ and Lemminkäinen, the great lover of the Finnish *Kalevala* who was shot by a blind herdsman and ended up piecemeal in the river of death, Tuonela, whence his mother reassembled and resurrected him with spells. Whatever diffusionary motifs may have spread back and forth, it is remarkable that a magic incantation for rejoining broken bodies, first attested in the *Atharva-Veda* (4.12), occurs almost verbatim also in the *Kalevala* (Runo 15) and in the ninth-century German *Second Merseburg Charm* ("bone to bone, blood to blood, limb to limb"), describing how *Balderes* horse sprained its foot and various deities charmed it back to health (this is almost all we know about an extra-Norse Baldr; in parallel Germanic folklore the horse involved with this kind of spell is usually Christ's).

Baldr's name is etymologically unclear, perhaps akin to the stem denoting 'brightness' in Gaulish Belenus and Belisama (cf. Old English *bealdor* 'lord'). The name Höðr, however, clearly reflects *höð*, matching Old Irish *cath* 'battle' (cf. Gaulish *Catu-rix,* Old High German *Hadu-brand*), and is thus onomastically fitting for an Odinic warrior type. He appears as such in Saxo's story of Starkaðr (see chap. 13), Latinized as Hatherus, and in the variant form Hötherus in Saxo's book 3. There the myth of Baldr and Höðr has been nearly reversed and transmuted into a chevaleresque novella of romantic rivalries for the hand of Nanna, pitting the hero Hötherus against a wholly unsympathetic and largely villainous *semideus* Balderus, with no blindness and no Loki in sight (Balderus is still the son of Othinus, whom Saxo euhemerized into a confidence man promoting his own fake divinity, with his wanton and profligate wife Frigga). Hötherus ended up killing Balderus after many vicissitudes of warfare, but Othinus sired on a Russian princess Rinda the avenger Bous, who slew Hötherus.

The blind Höðr (cf. Odin's epithet Tvīblindi 'Double Blind', besides his being one-eyed) may be a spin-off, a subsidiary allomorph of Odin himself in his "fatal" aspect. Odin's two sons Baldr and Höðr then stand for contradictory strands of Odin's own nature, his better self versus his blind spot abetted by his evil genius Loki. For all his preternatural foresight he could not stave off Ragnarök, but once the evil was burned away his dual hypostases were spared for regeneration. This is a Germanic reconstruction predicated on Odin's own ambivalent nature. In Indo-European terms, however, Baldr and Höðr in their eschatological aspects recall the brothers Vidura and Dhṛtarāṣṭra of the *Mahābhārata* (chap. 5), in the epic transposition uncles (rather than sons) of the chief figure (Yudhiṣṭhira), one a discreet mediator of quarrels (cf. Baldr's son Forseti), the other the pathetic tool of blind fate, with both pairs surviving the supreme crisis that destroys the archvillain (Loki, Duryodhana) and functioning effectively in the "renewal." In Vedic theological terms (where the eschatology is not preserved), Yudhiṣṭhira-Vidura-Dhṛtarāṣṭra match Mitra-Aryaman-Bhaga, and in epic tradition Yudhiṣṭhira and Vidura were both incarnations of Dharma (with Vidura "fusing himself" into Yudhiṣṭhira at death). In Scandinavia Baldr (who would do justice to Yudhiṣṭhira's epithet Dharmarāja) instead procreates out of himself the mediator Forseti and is placed in limbo in Hel until after the showdown by the treacherous dart game of Loki using a blind agent, even as in India Yudhiṣṭhira is exiled from his kingdom until final victory as a result of the crooked dice game arranged by Duryodhana with the connivance of a blind weakling. All this is prelude and aftermath of the cataclysmic holocaust, thus of the Indo-European eschatological myth attested in Ragnarök and epicized in the *Mahābhārata*. The rise of Odin and the fading of Týr have made Baldr and Höðr sons and seeming "aspects" of Odin, whereas Aryaman and Bhaga were "satellites" of Mitra.

Mythic epitomes of evil tend to become polar and unmitigated, as Cousin Duryodhana did in the *Mahābhārata* and as Loki (also called Loptr and perhaps Lōðurr) ended up doing in the interval between Baldr's murder and Ragnarök. During this time Loki underwent a combination of Promethean punishment and Chinese torture, being tied to rocks with the guts of his son, with viper venom dripping onto his head (though it was caught for the most part in a cup held by his loyal wife Sigyn). But for most of his career Loki was a sort of honorary *āss,* a tolerated mixture of trickster, jester, and resource person in the divine company, despite being the son of a giant Fārbauti and himself the sire of a monstrous brood (Fenrir, Miðgarðsormr, Hel) by the giantess Angrboða 'Grief Boding'. He had a special affinity to Odin, sharing giant ancestry, common fosterage, deviousness, shape changing, and sexual ambivalence. He befriended the obscure Hönir (< **K̂ukniyos;* cf. Sanskrit *śukrá-* 'shiny') and even got along with Thor after a fashion, but he was the mortal enemy of Heimdalr, with whom he had once struggled in seal shape over a mysterious 'sea kidney' (*haf-nȳra*) and who would be his terminal opponent at Ragnarök. He had also incurred the enmity of Skaði over the death of her father Thjazi, to the point that Skaði supplied the viper for Loki's "martyrdom." Loki had under duress delivered into Thjazi's clutches (literally, for the giant had assumed eagle shape) the goddess Iðunn (wife of Bragi, an obscure god of poetry), who held the apples that kept death away. The gods, suddenly gray and wizened, forced Loki wearing Freyja's falcon dress to recover Iðunn, whereupon Thjazi in pursuit crashed into a fire lit by the gods (thematic shades of the Greek Hesperides and the Irish Garden of Hisberna with their apples, and of Odin's mead theft and Indra's soma acquisition in the form or with the help of eagles). The gods not only let the bereaved Skaði choose a divine husband by his feet but met her challenge that they make her laugh despite her grief. Loki arranged this by tying his balls to a billy goat's beard and tugging away until both god and goat squealed with pain and Loki tripped onto Skaði's knee. The gods also made stars out of Thjazi's eyes (cf. Aurvandill's toe above). Yet in spite of all, Skaði's grudge would remain long-lasting.

Loki typically tricked the gods into a fix, then when cornered used ingenuity to extricate them. When at the beginning a contractor was retained to build a giant-proof wall around the divine residence, the terms for completion in one winter stipulated the sum of Freyja, sun, and moon. Loki arranged for the builder to use his stallion to drag large boulders, so that a timely finish was imminent. In panic at the price, the gods then coerced Loki into sabotaging the work. He turned into a mare, distracted the stallion into mating, and thus effectively interrupted the project. The *jötunmōðr* ('giant wrath') of the enraged contractor revealed his home address, and Thor was called in to exterminate him, while Loki as a mare gestated and bore Sleipnir.

While Odin's (and the largely "Odinic" Hönir's) closeness to Loki is expectable, Thor, considering his curtness toward giants, also is surprisingly involved with this false and fickle friend. Loki can be of real help, for example, as Thor's quick-thinking "bridesmaid" in the expedition to Thrymr; but more often he acts true to type, inveigling the god into carelessness (setting out for Geirröð's place minus hammer and power belt) or shearing the locks of Thor's wife Sif and being forced by the irate husband to procure a golden wig from the dwarfs (characteristically cheating the latter in the process). Loki also accompanied Thor in Snorri's satirical account of the visit to his near-namesake, Ūtgarðaloki, in fact a folkloristic alter ego, as is shown by Saxo's Utgardilocus (book 8), a fettered and fetid giant to whom Thorkillus trekked looking for treasure (actually Loki chained until Ragnarök in "Ūtgarðr," i.e., outer darkness). Loki's way with dwarfs also accounts for the curse on the gold of the Niflungar in the *Völsunga Saga,* for he robbed the dwarf Andvari among the Dark Elves of his treasure in order to pay wergeld for killing an all-too-human salmon-eating otter, down to a last ring on which the distraught victim of the robbery pronounced a malediction.

Folktale looms large in all this, as it does in Loki's diffusionary typology. His comparands range from the trickster Bricriu of Irish saga (*Fled Bricrenn* 'Bricriu's Feast') to an earthquake demon of Georgian folklore (not to mention the Christian Satan chained in hell). Loki does resemble the quarrelsome Irish spoilsport, when at a banquet in Ägir's sea lodge he cleverly insults every divine colleague in sight (in the *Poetic Edda*'s *Lokasenna*) and in fact convulses seismically at every drop of venom whenever Sigyn is not quick enough with her cup. The Caucasian demon, attacked by an eagle, is ancient and diffusive (Prometheus was chained there in Greek saga), and with external influences gave the Zoroastrian and later Christian devil his due (identified as Amirani < Ahriman); his tracks can be followed in folktales across Europe, from the Balkans to the Baltic. Loki does, however, have his very specific, genetically significant counterpart in the trickster Syrdon of the Ossetic *Nart* epic, who is a hanger-on among the divine heroes and a devious shape changer who on occasion extricates the group from tight situations but also treacherously causes the death of the beloved hero Soslan, who is invulnerable except for a weak spot in his knees (which Syrdon deviously discovers in disguise). In a seemingly innocent game (rolling a saw-toothed wheel down a hill for the sport of seeing it bounce off Soslan's invulnerable anatomy), Syrdon inspires specific aim at the knees, and Soslan is cut down. Here, then, is another piece of Indo-

European eschatological myth (Ossetic < Scythian < proto-Iranian < Indo-Iranian) matching Old Norse tradition, this time centered on Loki and Baldr, even as above the Baldr : Höðr axis found its Indo-Iranian counterpart in the *Mahābhārata*.

Few significant deities remain to be mentioned. Gefjon and Fulla were two virgin goddesses, a rare type among the Äsir, as Loki acerbically notes in the serial obloquy of the *Lokasenna,* where he accuses Gefjon of selling her body for a gem, in the manner of Freyja. Precisely by being atypical, they are suspect of archaism, as chapter 14 will show. There were both a god Fjörgynn (Frigg's lover or father) and a female Fjörgyn, mother of Thor and possible allonym of Jörd 'Earth'; they may be in origin a divine sky-earth couple, with a name cognate in the Lithuanian thunder-god Perkū́nas (cf. chap. 12). The Norns Urð, Verðandi, and Skuld in the *Völuspā* were a threesome of the type of the Greek Fates, Klōthō 'Spinster', Lakhesis, and Atropos taking the place of a single Moira. In the Norse case the "original" Norn was Urð, with her well Urðarbrunnr under the Yggdrasill, hard to distinguish from two other fountains, Hvergelmir and Mīmisbrunnr. Other multiple females were the Dīsir (also Fylgja, Hamingja), tutelary goddesses or guardian spirits reminiscent of the Celtic Matronae and the Iranian Fravaši and Daēnā (chap. 6). Considering the survival of specific mythic eschatologies in Iran and Iceland, this last accordance may also be a joint archaism.

Yggdrasill was known alternatively as Mīmameiðr 'Mīmi's tree'. Mīmir, Mīmr, Mīmi are variant names of the mysterious god in whose well Odin pawned his eye (and perhaps Heimdalr his ear). Mīmir was a strange source of arcane wisdom, for in crisis (as before Ragnarök) Odin would commune necromantically with his preserved head, which had been severed by the Vanir while Mīmir (along with the not-so-bright Hönir) served as peace hostage in the enemy camp, in reciprocity for Njörðr and Freyr. His namesake, the smith Mīmir, figures as Sigurð's foster father in *Thiðreks Saga* (corresponding to Reginn in the standard versions), whereas the dragon (Fāfnir) is called Reginn. Mīmir may also lurk under the kenning "renowned son of Bölthorn, Bestla's father," from whom Odin "took nine mighty songs" in the course of his shamanic suspension on the "windy tree" (*Hāvamāl* 140; Bestla was Odin's mother, and Bölthorn's son was hence his maternal uncle, perhaps his foster father; Germanic avunculate is mentioned by Tacitus, *Germania* 20).

Alone among the ancient European traditions Germanic myth preserves comprehensive cosmogony, cosmography, anthropogony, and eschatology. These may be one-sidedly transmitted (mainly by Snorri using Poetic Eddic materials) and not immune to diffusionary influences from the general direction of the Near East, but they are nevertheless one of a kind and very relevant to Indo-European reconstruction.

In the beginning was Ginnungagap 'Yawning Abyss' or 'Gaping Yawn', cognate with Greek *kháos* 'yawn' as the primordial entity in Hesiod's *Theogony* (and with the verb *khaínō* 'yawn' and English *yawn*), thus the imagery of an expanding buccal cavity at the start of the universe. Next came Niflheimr 'Fog World', with a well Hvergelmir at its center and rivers flowing from it. But even before it there existed a fire world Mūspellsheimr in the Southern Hemisphere (identical in name with the eschatological term meaning 'world end' or 'last judgment' in the Old High German *Muspilli* poem and the Christian Old Saxon *Heliand*), guarded by the demon Surtr 'Black'. Out of condensation vapors (as the two worlds interacted) was formed the primordial giant Ymir (< **Yumiyáz*) 'Twin' (alias Aurgelmir), who sweated out the ancestors of the giant tribe and was himself nurtured by a frost-born cow Auðhumla. The latter got her own dubious nutrients from an icy salt lick, finally shaping the ice blocks into a man who was animated as Būri. He begot Bor, who married Bestla and begot the trio of brothers Odin, Vili, and Vē. These slew Ymir and formed the world from his body (details in chap. 17). The same gods (or according to the *Völuspā* Odin, Hönir, and Lōðurr) also animated the first pair of humans, Askr and Embla, from trees found on a seashore, a trite tale of a current kind that differs from the more profound Germanic anthropogony of Tacitus (*Germania* 2), involving Tuisto 'Twin' born of Earth, his son Mannus 'Man', and the three tribal ancestors born of the latter (more in chap. 17). The world of men was Miðgarðr, in the center of which lay Āsgarðr, the divine compound, the whole overhung by Yggdrasill with its spring(s). Giant country (Jötunheimr) lay to the east or northeast, and in the north was Hel, reachable across mountains, dark dales, and turbulent rivers. Unlike Celtic tradition, the West does not figure importantly in mythic topography.

Ragnarök 'Gods' fate' (misperceived as Ragnarökkr 'Gods' twilight', hence 'Götterdämmerung' in German rendering) is presaged by Odin's premonitions, preceded by an awesome winter (*fimbulvetr*), and powerfully prefigured by visions in the *Völuspā:*

Brothers will fight and fell each other,
siblings will spoil their own kind;
hard times at hand, whoredom is rampant,
ax-age, sword-age, shields will be cloven,
wind-age, wolf-age, ere the world perish.

When the attack comes, it is to be concerted. Fenrir (and his allomorph Garmr) will break the bonds and advance with jaws agape, the Miðgarðsormr will lash the shore and spew venom, the ship of the dead (Naglfar) will cast off from Hel, piloted by the giant Hrymr, Loki and the giants will approach from the east as Surtr and his crew arrive from the south and cross the Bifröst, which collapses under them. As they all rally on the battlefield named Vīgrīðr, Heimdalr will sound the alert while Yggdrasill groans and creaks, Odin consults with Mīmir, and finally the *einherjar* ride out of the many gates of Valhöll to face the enemy. In the showdown Surtr will kill Freyr and Garmr and Tȳr dispatch each other, as will Thor and the Miðgarðsormr, and Fenrir will swallow Odin, who is immediately avenged by Vīðarr. Loki and Heimdalr will engage in reciprocal slaughter while Surtr casts fire upon the world. The sun and stars will go out, and the flaming earth will sink into the sea.

A rebirth will follow, in a kind of paradise called Gimle, after a green earth is raised again out of the sea. Vīðarr and Vāli will be there at Iðavöllr where Āsgarðr used to be, as will Thor's sons Mōði and Magni with the heirloom Mjöllnir. Baldr and Höðr will come from Hel, and (according to the *Völuspā*) Hönir will "read the auguries." They will sit and go over the lore of bygone times. As with the postconflict *Mahābhārata,* life has gone out of the story, for paradises, posthumous or postcataclysmic, are almost by definition dull places of marginal mythic interest. For better or worse, men's mythopoeic minds are stirred by conflict rather than composure and by yearning for eventual rather than immersion in actual ataraxy. Norse cosmology begins with fire and ice, as befits volcanic Iceland, where a Surtsey rose from the ocean as late as 1964; it culminates with a bang in fire and water and ends as divine epigones whimper about the days that are no more.

Recommended Reading

Davidson, H. R. Ellis. *Scandinavian Mythology.* Feltham, Middlesex: Hamlyn, 1969.

Dumézil, Georges. *From Myth to Fiction: The Saga of Hadingus.* Translated

by Derek Coltman. Chicago: University of Chicago Press, 1973.
———. *Gods of the Ancient Northmen*. Edited by Einar Haugen. Berkeley and Los Angeles: University of California Press, 1973.
Glob, P. V. *The Bog People*. Ithaca, N.Y.: Cornell University Press, 1969.
Poems of the Vikings: The Elder Edda. Translated by Patricia Terry. Indianapolis: Bobbs-Merrill, 1982.
Saxo Grammaticus. *History of the Danes*. 2 vols. Translated by Peter Fisher, edited by Hilda Ellis Davidson. Totowa, N.J.: Rowman and Littlefield, 1979–80.
Snorri Sturluson. *Heimskringla*. Translated by Lee M. Hollander. Austin: University of Texas Press, 1964.
———. *The Prose Edda*. Translated by Jean I. Young. Cambridge: Bowes and Bowes, 1954; Berkeley and Los Angeles: University of California Press, 1964.
Turville-Petre, E. O. G. *Myth and Religion of the North*. New York: Holt, Rinehart and Winston, 1964.

12 · Baltic and Slavic Myth

Item 1: In his 1963 novel *Hundejahre* ("Dog Years"), the German writer Günter Grass (born in 1927) weaves a fanciful, many-dimensional tapestry of his native Danzig-Gdansk, a multinational historic East Prussian city on the Baltic, forced between the two world wars into an unnatural "free town" status between the "Polish Corridor" to the sea and the sundered pieces of the German Reich. A main character in the novel is an artist, Eduard Amsel, who makes a living creating and selling symbolic scarecrow images rooted in the folkloristic and mythical past of this ancient land of the Baltic Prussians. The extinct heathen culture of the latter, submerged in the millennial German/Slavic tug-of-war, starts making phantasmagoric sallies from the collective psyche of the Danzigites, as the rising wave of neopagan nationalism crests in their very hometown and unleashes the Second World War. In addition to the parallel lives of the novel's characters and a line of pedigreed black shepherds (culminating in Hitler's favorite dog, Prinz), Amsel's line of rag dolls progresses from rustic realism to ominous folklore to gruesome recreations of heathen gods, ending up in robot figures programmed only to march and salute. The gods involved are Perkunos, Pikollos, and Potrimpos, depicted as fiery red, deathly pale, and youthfully joyous respectively. Out of this Old Prussian triad, the "mortuary-nuptial" Pikollos turns out to be the biggest marketing success, not surprisingly in the heyday of the Nazi love affair with death and the silvery skull emblems on the black uniforms of the storm troopers. Throughout, Amsel is coached and counseled by a mysterious aged local character named Kriwe. The modern reader may be excused for puzzling over the author's antiquarian erudition.

Item 2: In 1545 the rector of the University of Königsberg (chief city of East Prussia), Georg Sabinus, son-in-law of Luther's famous collaborator Philipp Melanchthon, addressed a verse epistle in Latin distichs to Cardinal Pietro Bembo:

> There is a savage race of rustics under the North Star
> that has as yet no notion of true religion
> but worships as deities blue-green snakes
> and performs unspeakable rites of ram slaughter.

What subpolar primitives was he speaking of? Not the Tungus, not the Lapps, but the peasants of his own East Prussian countryside.

Item 3: In 1458 Enea Silvio Piccolomini, later Pope Pius II, published his book *Europa*. Chapter 26 contains an account of a sojourn in Lithuania in 1432 of a Bohemian monk Hieronymus from Prague. He encountered snake worshipers and sacred fires with oracular ministrations by priests. Farther in the interior he came upon a tribe of solar cultists who had a huge hammer fetish and told a myth of the onetime capture of the sun and its liberation with the help of such an object of veneration. Hieronymus also found sacred groves and with misplaced zeal proceeded to cut them down; he soon wore out his welcome and was expelled from the country.

Lithuania was the last place in Europe to be Christianized (from Poland), merely officially and from the top, during the early fifteenth century; and as we saw above, more than a century later the ecclesiastical authorities in East Prussia still had their hands full stamping out rampant heathen practices. Latvians to the north had been forcibly and nominally converted by the Teutonic Knights in the early thirteenth century, and the Grand Duchy of Lithuania stretched for a while from the Baltic to the Black Sea under a succession of notable rulers starting with Mindaugas in the thirteenth century, via Gediminas, Algirdas, and Kestutis in the fourteenth, to Vytautas in the early fifteenth century. Its nonliterate character resembled that of ancient Gaul and did not preclude the existence of an influential native religious establishment. In his Latin-language *Chronicle of Prussia* (1326), Petrus von Dusburg speaks of a pagan "pope" called Criwe at the site of Romowe, who was held in great awe by king, noble, and commoner alike. Entrenchment is in fact a key characteristic of Baltic culture, and linguistically this branch is the most conservative and archaic of all surviving Indo-European subgroups.

Of Baltic myth proper next to nothing has survived, but some idea can be formed of deities and cults. Assorted Russian and German chronicles starting with the thirteenth century supply divine names, notably that of the thunder-god Perkun(as). Others include the obscure Andaj, Teljavel' (divine smith who forged the sun; cf. Lithuanian *kálvis* 'smith'), Diviriks (cf. Old Prussian *deiwas* 'god'), Žvoruna, called "bitch" (cf. Lithuanian *žvèris* 'beast'), and Mějdějn (a woodland goddess; cf. Lithuanian *medainis* 'silvestris'). A memorandum of 1419, addressed to the pope on behalf of the sagging Order of Teutonic Knights, extolled the labors of the latter in exterminating assorted Baltic devil worshipers, notably votaries of Patollus, Natrimpe, and other disgraceful figments of the pagan mind. Jan Długosz's *Polish Chronicle* (in Latin) of about 1460 listed the Lithuanian objects of worship as fire, lightning, woods, and snakes, adding sacrifices to the dead and essaying various Latin interpretations (Vulcanus, Jupiter, Diana, Aesculapius), with a significant gloss: "In worshiping the thunderbolt they called Jupiter in their own language Perkunus, which would mean 'Striker' [*quasi Percussorem*]." He went on to describe how female Vestal types tended his perpetual fire and paid with their lives [*capite expiabant*] for its extinction.

In the early sixteenth century the onset of antiquarian quasi-history both enriches and complicates the material. The most notable document is Simon Grunau's German-language *Prussian Chronicle* of about 1520, which details the purported ethnogenesis of the ancient Borussians. A band of Cimbrians led by a certain Witowudi and his brother Bruteno had emigrated from Sweden and settled on the Vistula River soon after 500 C.E. They must have impressed the local population, for Witowudi was made king, while Bruteno became high priest with the title Crywo Cyrwaito, in the service of a divine triad, Patollo, Potrimpo, and Perkuno, whose idols were in a place called Rickoyto, the headquarters of Bruteno and his priesthood, whom Grunau calls *waidolotten*. Witowudi's banner was emblazoned with the iconography of this triad. Potrimpo's depiction is described as a beardless young man crowned with ears of grain and glad of mien. Perkuno's likeness is that of an angry-looking middle-aged fellow with a fiery face and curly black beard. Patollo appears as an old man with a long green beard and deathlike pallor, wearing a white cloth like a turban and gazing up at the others from below. The icons of the gods were installed in three equal niches of an evergreen oak tree. Perkuno had his perpetual fire, maintained by the priesthood on pain of death, Potrimpo had a snake in a jar covered with sheaves of grain and fed milk by the *waidolottinnen* (priestesses), while Patollo's sacred objects were skulls of man, horse, and cow. Grunau claims that the triad was introduced by the Cimbrians and replaced earlier solar cults. He calls Patollo the highest Prussian deity, a terrifying god of the dead, and characterizes Potrimpo as a patron of good fortune, adding that both had an inordinate taste for human blood. Perkuno gets rather brief notice as the oracular thunder-god. Grunau also mentions two rustic deities, recipients of fish and fowl offerings respectively, and especially Curcho, a harvest-god who figures already (as Curche) in the peace treaty of 1249 between the Teutonic Knights and the Old Prussians.

Interest centers on the triadic structure of Grunau's Patollo, Perkuno, and Potrimpo. It bears some resemblance to the Uppsala trio of Odin, Thor, and Freyr (war-god, thunder-god, phallic bestower of pleasure), but emblematic discrepancies dominate (Odin had weapons rather than skulls, Thor was sceptered rather than fiery, and it takes a confirmed Freudian to relate Frey's overgrown priapus to Potrimpo's milk-fed serpent). Therefore, despite the attempts of Wilhelm Mannhardt and others to discredit Grunau's information as imaginative garble based on Adam of Bremen, it must be taken seriously as reflecting Old Baltic theological realities. Although Grunau may have known Adam's as yet unprinted *Gesta,* either in a manuscript copy or in some renarrated version, and despite his own ethnogenetic claims of Scandinavian origin, coupled with some proven Viking inroads into East Prussia (ship burials and the like), it is more reasonable to appraise the material against the backdrop of specifically Baltic data. The Prussian Criwe of Romowe (or Grunau's Crywo of Rickoyto) and his counterparts at cult centers in Lithuania must be thought of as establishment theologians during the thirteenth and fourteenth centuries, and the presence of a stylized triadic Indo-European priestly paganism just before conversion is no more implausible than that of Uppsala itself a few centuries earlier. Whether the pantheon had undergone any Germanic diffusionary influences is ultimately a moot question. In the absence of strong evidence it is sensible to regard the Baltic traditions as essentially indigenous.

Grunau may thus be regarded as a transitional figure between the eyewitness era and the antiquarian one. However distortedly, he transmitted a piece of the pagan establishment that by the sixteenth century was irretrievably lost. His followers were reduced to repetition or to amassing whatever folk religion remained, and it is not surprising that they record a confused and manifold crew of divinities. One is reminded of the difference between a chronicler such as Adam of Bremen and an encyclopedist like Snorri in relation to Scandinavian tradition.

A great variety of ecclesiastical documents, antiquarian treatises, ethno-, geo-, and historiographic compendiums, and linguistic works stretching from 1530 to almost 1700 contain divine names such as Occopirmus ('Very First', the sky-god), Suaixtix (sun-god), Auschauts (a healer), Autrimpus (sea-god), Potrimpus (river-god), Bardoayts (seafarers' god), Pilvitus (harvest deity), Pergrubrius (god of the spring), Puschkaytus (earth-god, possibly etymologically connectible with the Vedic Pūṣan and the Greek Pan), Percunus (thunder- and rain-god), and Pecullus (with many variant spellings), explained variously as 'Pluto' or 'Furiae' or 'god of hell and darkness', or 'god of airborne ghosts'. Many other names and epithets patently of "lower mythology" crop up in those writings, but the listing above is representative of some kind of postconversion underground pantheon. Apart from some expectable traces of solar cult and a contingent of sea deities, it is reducible to healing and fertility figures (including Potrimpus), plus Percunus and Pecullus.

The name of Potrimpus is onomastically integrated, not only with Autrimpus but with the fifteenth-century Natrimpe. Granted prefix variation, the theonymic stem *trimp-* (in itself obscure) points to a watery fertility connotation.

The Old Prussian equivalent of the Lithuanian Perkū́nas and Latvian Pērkōns was understood as 'Striker' by Długosz, but in Old Prussian *percunis* had come to mean 'thunder', and in Lithuanian *perkū́nas* and *perkū́nija* are the common terms for thunderstorm. The root **per(kʷ/g)-* means 'hit', seen in Lithuanian *peȓti* 'whisk, birch [in a sauna]', Russian *prat'* 'beat', Armenian *har(k)-* 'strike'. A nominal protoform **per(kʷ/g)o/u-* meant 'stroke' and by extension 'striker', expanded by the "augmentative" theonymic suffix **-no-* to **Per(kʷ/g)o/u-no-* '[Thunder]stroke' or '[Divine] Striker', with a derivative adjective **per(kʷ/g)o/u-n-yo-* 'prone to thunderstroke'. Thus are subsumed not only Lithuanian *Perkū́nas,* Old Norse *Fjörgynn,* Vedic *Parjánya-,* and Old Russian *Perunŭ* (on whom see further below), but also Gothic *faírguni* 'mountain', Old Russian *peregynja* 'wooded hill', and Celtic-Roman *Hercynia* 'Oak Ridge, Oakwood', as well as Latin *quercus* 'oak' (< **perkʷu-o-*), involving highlands with rocks and trees that attracted lightning and were in consequence sacred to the god 'Percussor'.[1]

1. Other possible cognates are Hittite *peruna-* 'rock' and Sanskrit *párvata-* 'mountain, boulder'. Thunderstroke would in folk belief "impregnate" certain rocks (silex,

Pecullus has obviously supplanted Patollus. The latter may mean something like 'underground' (cf. also Sanskrit *pā́tālam* 'underworld'), whereas Pecullus is identical with Lithuanian *pikùlas* 'devil' and Latvian *pīkals* 'heathen god, demon' and connectible with Lithuanian *pìktas* 'angry', *pỹkti* 'be wroth'. In his *Deliciae Prussicae* (1690), Matthias Praetorius (chap. 4.4) closed his long list of assorted deities by remarking that "all these are not equally renowned in their sources; before all others incontestable preference goes to those three whom they have worshiped above all others at Romove, by the names Pykullis, Perkunas, and Padrimpus"; thus "Pykullis" has taken the place of Grunau's (and earlier) Patollus, while the historical Romove is back in place, in preference to Grunau's variant "Rickoyto."

Indo-European structure of the Baltic pantheon hinges heavily on a correct appreciation and interpretation of Patollus-Pecullus. Christian demonology found him exploitable yet did not quite know what to do with him. He was a demon of the underworld and leader of the host of the dead in the skies, hellish and aerial at the same time. This hesitation helps piece together his original nature. He has a Lithuanian allonym Vẽlinas (Vélnias, Véls, nowadays 'devil'), which is cognate with *vẽlės* 'ghosts' and with the ancestral goddess Veliuonà; Szyrwid's dictionary of 1629 already equates Velnias with 'Piktis'. In Lithuanian folklore

---

flint) and trees (oak, fir) with igneous potential, apt to produce fire by friction. Hence a verb 'to strike' could have noun derivatives meaning 'hill', 'rock', and 'oak', and conversely lithonyms became terms for divine firearms (Thor's Mjöllnir, in origin perhaps a grindstone [cf. English *mill*], was a *hamarr* 'hammer', but Old Norse *hamarr* also meant 'rock' or 'cliff', cognate with Russian *kamen'* 'stone'; these words are related to Greek *ákmōn* 'meteor; anvil', Lithuanian *akmuõ* 'stone, rock', Vedic *áśman-* and Avestan *asman-* 'stone, rock; [stony vault of] heaven', Old Persian *asman-* 'heaven'; Indra, who 'engendered fire between two rocks', *áśmanor antár agním jajā́na* [*RV* 2.12.3], would use on demons both *áśman-* and *párvata-* as throwing weapons on top of his *vájra-* [*RV* 7.104.19]). Firestones and firesticks with their striking and rubbing action afforded numerous coitional and generative associations: Mjöllnir placed in a bride's lap was patently phallic (cf. chap. 11). The fiery Iranian Xvarənah embodied ejaculate and sperm (cf. chap. 6). Vedic *pásas-*, Greek *péos,* and Latin *pēnis* are all derived from an Indo-European root **pes-* 'to rub', attested in Hittite as a living verb and in the derivative *pesna-* 'man, male'. In Homer and Hesiod, a proverbial expression 'from [or about] oak or rock' alluded to anthropogonic procreation (*Odyssey* 19.163) and by extension meant 'back at the start, not going anywhere' (*Theogony* 35), in short, 'not getting anywhere, it's no use' (*Iliad* 10.126). The Thracian myth of Semele 'dead from the thunderstroke' (Pindar, *Olympian Ode* 2.25–26) or 'midwifed by [Zeus's] lightning-born fire' (Euripides, *Bacchae* 3; cf. chap. 8, note 1) was a fulgural hierogamy that "got out of hand"; Danae's golden shower represents a more moderate effusion of divine sexual effulgence. In myths of the thunder-god there lingers the basic tension of an electrical storm: deadly discharge combined with fructifying moisture.

Velinas is the one-eyed, prophetic, treacherous, raging god of the *vẽlės* who fight, hunt, and march in the skies; he is also the lord of hanging and the hanged. This dossier is ample to permit a typological comparison with both the one-eyed Hangaguð Odin and the Old German *Wutanes her.* Beneath the death-god described by Simon Grunau and revived by Günter Grass and the devil of demonology and folklore, we find a principal figure of the Baltic pantheon, whose name Pecullus has the same "rage" meaning that inheres in Odin, and whose parallel name Velinas is best connected with Old Norse *valr,* denoting the host of the slain. The presence of such a magical, death-oriented high god in close complementarity with the ruling thunder-god seems to be typical of several contiguous northern European subgroups (cf. Odin : Thor and perhaps Esus : Taranis); Patollo's white headcloth may indeed be the missing link connecting Odin's floppy hat with Rudra's turban in India (cf. chap. 11).

In general, Latvian tradition takes a backseat to East Prussia and Lithuania in the antiquarian and folkloristic dimensions, with one exception: the large store of Latvian lyric folk songs (*dainas*), recorded as late as the nineteenth century, makes a unique contribution to the otherwise skimpy Baltic preservation of Indo-European lore. It affords a crucial third dimension to the myths of the Divine Twins, otherwise attested mainly in Vedic India and ancient Greece (cf. chaps. 4 and 8). In those lays two (or sometimes multiple, the dual number having disappeared in Latvian) horsemen called *Dieva dēli* 'sons of Dievs' woo the Sun's daughter (*Saules meita*) and save her from death by water, which latter feature may well be a trait of the original mythologem (based on which the Aśvins and Dioskouroi were "franchised" as routine rescuers). Some typical verses from the considerable bulk of *dainas* are as follows:

Div' svecītes jūrā dega sudrabiņa lukturos; tās dedzina Dieva dēli, Saules meitu gaidīdami.	Two candles burned at sea in silver candelabra; sons of Dievs lit them, waiting for Saule's daughter.
Saules meita jūru brida, vaiņadziņu vien redzēja. Iriet laivu, Dieva dēli, glābiet Saules dvēselīti!	Saule's daughter waded in the sea, they saw only her crown. Row the boat, sons of Dievs, save Saule's[2] soul!

2. *Saules meita* is alternatively referred to simply as *Saule* ('sun' is a feminine noun in Baltic), even as *Sū́rya*'s daughter in Vedic myth is *Sūryā́* (beside *Duhitā́ Sū́ryasya*), with grammatical feminization.

Dieva dēli klēti cirta,	Sons of Dievs built a barn,
zelta spāres spārēdami;	fixing rafters of gold.
Saules meita cauri gāja,	Saule's daughter walked through,
kā lapiņa drebēdama.	trembling like a leaf.

This is the oldest pattern, dislocations of which shy away from mythical polyandry (presenting a single *Dieva dēls,* or conversely two or more sun-maids) or otherwise identify a single suitor (Morning or Evening Star [astral interpretations of *Dieva dēli*], Moon, Perkun), even as in Vedic variants Sūryā sometimes ends up with Soma (*RV* 10.85) or Pūṣan as her mate (*RV* 6.58.4). Lithuanian tradition also knows of *Diẽvo sūnẽliai* and *Sáulės dukterȳs,* without, however, a comparably cogent body of archaic mythic accordances (what is clear is that underneath the generic Baltic *Deivas 'God' lurks in this instance the Indo-European sky-god *Dyēws). There may be other Indo-European matter as yet undiscovered in the Latvian songs; Baltic tradition, with its inherent archaism but late attestation, is still a kind of last frontier of comparative mythology.

The Slavs became "Europeanized" almost a millennium before the Balts, simply by intruding in the sixth century into Central Europe and penetrating the Balkans all the way to Greece, in migrational waves replicating the earlier Celtic and Germanic thrusts at half-millennium intervals. They are still in Bohemia, and the current German-Polish border on the river Oder is only moderately east of their maximum expansion to the Elbe (Berlin and Dresden are Slavic names). Their conversion lingered awhile and for geographic reasons engaged Byzantium more than Rome: the apostles Cyril and Methodius started with Moravia in 863; Bulgaria became "officially" Christian in 885 and Russia in 988. The Roman church gained a foothold in western areas all the way to Poland (formally converted in 966), whereas in North Germany West Slavic paganism lingered deep into the twelfth century. Such splintering of subsequent culture (epitomized to this day by the Croatian : Serbian split) had a deleterious effect on the literary preservation of pre-Christian lore. The Western church exerted a Latinizing influence conducive to classicist garble, as in the Slavic pseudo-Olympus created by Długosz in his fifteenth-century chronicle; only some early chroniclers (Thietmar of Merseburg [ca. 1015], Adam of Bremen [ca. 1075], Helmold [ca. 1170], three biographers of Bishop Otto of Bamberg [ca. 1150], Saxo [book 14], *Knytlinga Saga* [ca. 1265]) transmitted genuine scraps of information on West Slavic cults. In the Balkans matters were not helped by the subsequent Islamic overlay. Russia was relatively shielded from Europe and did develop a significant ecclesiastic, monastic-annalistic (especially the Kievan *Primary* [Nestor's] *Chronicle*, up to the year 1110), legal (*Russkaja Pravda*), and heroic-epic literature (*Lay of Igor's Host* of 1187, *bylínas*) which is the main antiquarian source for Slavic mythic tradition. Such matter is supplemented by the rich store of Slavic folklore, some of which has been brought to modern Western awareness via the musical arts, from forest-maid (*vila*) to firebird to the hallowing of spring.

If Russia was sheltered from Western influence, its early history was yet not immune to penetration. The Slavic homeland itself lay somewhere around the western borders of Russia, and the south Russian steppes were inhabited by a succession of Iranian tribes (Scythians, Sarmatians, Alanians). Balto-Slavic, Thraco-Phrygian, and Indo-Iranian are contiguous Indo-European dialect groupings that participated in the very latest stages of Common Indo-European linguistic changes (especially the palatalizations of velar consonants, as in Russian *slóvo* vs. Greek *kléos*). They share a remarkable amount of social, religious, and legal vocabulary, different in kind from the extreme East-West accordances studied in chapter 3 and later. The latter were by definition Proto-Indo-European archaisms preserved independently in the fringes. The Balto-Slavic and Indo-Iranian isolexemes are instead regional innovations, and specific Iranian-Slavic matches are suspect of lexical borrowing between contiguous cultures or diffusion from Iranian to Slavic. On the other hand, the Russian state with its northern and southern anchors at Novgorod and Kiev was founded in the ninth century as a by-product of Scandinavian Vikings (Varangians) securing their river and portage routes from the Baltic via the Black Sea to Byzantium. Although official Soviet chauvinism takes a dim view of foreign marauders' founding Holy Russia, the names of early legendary dynasts and other data make a Norse ruling component indisputable and likewise raise the specter of a potential Viking veneer on the official religion. The conspicuous Varangian presence is illustrated by the Arab traveler Ibn-Fadlan's account of the shipboard cremation of a "Rus" chieftain on the Volga River in 921, complete with elaborate offerings and animal sacrifices in the Norse manner, and the ritual slaughter of a drugged servant girl by an aged priestess called the "angel of death" (cf. Baldr's and Nanna's joint ship funeral in chap. 11, the "suttee" of Brynhildr on Sigurd's pyre, and Gunnilda accompanying Asmundus in death [Saxo, book 1]). Yet even when viewed with one eye on the Scythians and the other on the Varangians, the spare Russian information remains our mainstay for understanding Slavic cultural antiquities.

Lexical matches between Balto-Slavic, Thraco-Phrygian, and Indo-Iranian have flitted past in preceding chapters: Vedic *Índra-*, Proto-Slavic **jędrŭ* 'strong' (< **indros*); Vedic *svayambhū́-*, Thraco-Phrygian *Sabazios,* Old Church Slavic *svobodĭ* 'self-being, free' (here may belong also the Germanic tribal name *Suēbi*); Vedic *médhira-*, Avestan *manzdra-*, Old Church Slavic *mǫdrŭ,* Russian *múdryj* 'wise'; Avestan *spənta-*, Old Church Slavic *svętŭ,* Russian *svjátyj,* Lithuanian *šveñtas* 'holy'; Vedic *Bhága-*, Old Persian *baga-*, Russian *bog(ŭ)* 'god' (cf. Phrygian *Bagaîos* [epithet of Zeus] : Russian *božij* 'divine'). We saw in chapters 6 and 8 that the Vedic verb *sam̐-vid-*, which describes posthumous family reunion and underlies the Greek *Hades,* is matched by the Russian *svídet-sja* 'meet again'; the common farewell greeting *do svidánija* ('auf Wiedersehen'), uttered in extremis, would mythologically and etymologically amount to 'see you in Hades' (< **Sm̥widā-*). Russian *mir(ŭ)* was described in chapter 9 as cognate with Vedic *Mitrá-*; the peace that it denotes is in origin not the antonym of 'war' but rather a 'peace community' regulated by social compact. In the *Russkaja Pravda, mirŭ* appropriately means 'settlement, township', and in Russian generally *mir(ŭ)* expanded macrocosmically to mean also 'world'. "Disturbing the peace" can be a matter not only for the local police but for the United Nations, as reflected in the Soviet slogan *mir miru* 'peace to the world'. The semantic link ('peace' > 'settlement') is inversely similar to Old Russian *gojĭ* 'peace, trust, friendship' (cf. *iz-gojĭ* 'extra-communal') Vedic versus *gáya-* 'abode, livelihood' ('peace' < 'settlement').

Other comparisons are more controversial. Unlike Baltic and Indic, Slavic matches Iranian in using *bogŭ* as the current word for 'god', in place of Indo-European **deywos*. There is a fossilized trace of **Dyḗws* in the Slavic word for 'rain' (Russian *dožd'*, Old Church Slavic *dŭždĭ* < **dus-dyus* 'bad sky'; cf., e.g., Latin *diū*[*s*] 'under a bright sky, in broad daylight'); otherwise *nébo,* originally 'cloud' (Vedic *nábhas-*, Greek *néphos,* Lithuanian *debesìs*) has moved into the semantic slot of 'heaven', as in many other languages (Hittite *nepis-*, Avestan *nabah-*, Old Irish *nem,* Latvian *debess*). The Slavic term *divŭ* means 'demon', much like the Persian *dīv* (Avestan *daēva-*), and it may be a borrowing from some Iranian dialect. As a mythical figure in the *Lay of Igor's Host* (*Slovo o polku Igoreve*), Divŭ was a watchful deity of the eastern steppe, who stirred resistance to the Russian hero and himself bore down (literally 'threw himself') in conquest on the Russian land (*zemljá*). Even granting petrifaction of epic formulas, any parallel to a Thraco-Phrygian flaming Zeus (Divŭ) pouncing on hapless Semele (Zemlja) would seem far-fetched, since there is nothing remotely hierogamic about having one's territory overrun by a foreign intruder (the frequently juxtaposed *diōs* and *zemelō*[*s*] of Phrygian tomb curses are of little help, since even their sense is unclear ['heaven' : 'earth' or 'god' : 'earthling' = 'man'?]).

Most Slavic deities are little more than names, frequently obscure by themselves, with some iconographic and cultic data but next to no myth. Considering the great linguistic uniformity of the various forms of Slavic during the first millennium, it is disappointing to find very little accordance between West and East Slavic data (for South Slavic there is mostly silence). Best known of the West Slavic deities in North Germany is *Svantovit,* whose temple at Arkona on the Baltic island of Rügen was destroyed by King Valdemar I of Denmark and his archbishop Absalon in 1169. Helmold, Otto's biographers, Saxo, *Knytlinga Saga,* and archeological exploration confirm a temple seventy feet square with carved walls and a statue twenty-eight feet high with four heads—two in front and two in back. Polycephality was rampant also at Carentia on Rügen, where *Rujevit* had seven faces, *Porevit* five heads, and *Porenutius* four faces, with a fifth on the chest (*Knytlinga Saga* called the same trio *Rinvit, Turupit,* and *Puruvit,* where Turupit resembles the god *Tarapita* attested for the Estonian island of Osilia in the *Livonian Chronicle* of Henricus Lettus). All three biographies of Otto of Bamberg refer to a patently three-headed *Triglav* at Stettin and Wollin in Pomerania, and the Icelandic source also knows of a *Tjarnaglofi* on Rügen who resembles Helmold's *Zcerneboch* as 'Blackhead' besides 'Black God'. Ebo's biography of Otto records a *Gerovitus* (= Jarovit) on the Havel River and at Wolgast on the coast between Rügen and Stettin. *Prove* and *Pripegala* are other divine names that occur. Besides temples, open-air idols are attested, and there is repeated mention of a sacred oracular horse at various sanctuaries. Besides purely descriptive terms such as Triglav, a theonymic segment *-vit* combines with adjectives such as *svętŭ* 'holy' (Svantovit) or *jarŭ* 'impetuous' (Jarovit). It seems that in these late sources original proper names had been supplanted by descriptive epithets. By contrast, Thietmar of Merseburg (6.23) about 1015 recorded the only deity with an East Slavic onomastic counterpart, *Zuarasici* at Riedegost in Mecklenburg, where he was foremost among the inscribed and armor-clad idols of diverse gods. That this figure was truly prominent among the West Slavs around the turn of the millennium is confirmed by a letter from Saint Bruno of Querfurt to the German emperor (later saint) Henry II in 1008, chiding the pragmatic monarch for his alliance of convenience with the heathen Slavs against the Christian Polish king Boleslaw the Brave and averring that "Zuarasiz diabolus" and the king's chief patron saint Mauritius made strange bedfellows. Adam of Bremen (2.21) referred to Riedegost as Rethra and to the god as *Redigast,* with *Radigast* also in Helmold (1.21 and 1.52); clearly the latter was an epithet of the god ('Joyous Host' or the like) that could both attach itself to his cult site and supersede his original name.

The eastern counterpart of Zuarasici appears a century later as *Svarogŭ,* identified as "Hephaistos," father of *Dažĭbogŭ* ("Helios") in Old Russian addenda to material from the Byzantine chronicler Johannes Malalas; the diminutive form *Svarožičĭ* of later sources matches Zuarasici. But this apparently fire-related or solar-tinged god of obscure name was not the chief deity and was absent among the pantheon whose idols Vladimir erected on a hill outside Kiev in the dying days of official Russian paganism (980): *Perunŭ, Khŭrsŭ, Dažĭbogŭ, Stribogŭ, Simarĭglŭ* (all male), and a goddess *Mokošĭ.* In the north, Perunŭ's wooden idol (with silver head and golden whiskers) had a counterpart on an elevation outside Novgorod called Perynja (or Perynĭ, Perunĭ). Upon Vladimir's baptism in 988, the Kiev idols were toppled, smashed, and burned. Perunŭ, attached to a horse's tail, was beaten, dragged, and dumped into the Dniepr, and the Novgorod variety similarly landed in the local Volkhov River.

Vladimir's list is notable for the primacy of Perunŭ, the appearance of the female Mokošĭ at the end, and the absence of the remaining important Old Russian god, Velesŭ or Volosŭ. Of the other names, Khŭrsŭ and Simarĭglŭ have the look of latter-day borrowings from Persian Xoršīd 'Sun' and the wonder bird Sīmorg. Dažĭbogŭ and Stribogŭ share the element *-bogŭ;* the former is perhaps a compound epithet of the "spoilsport" type, literally 'Give Fortune' (< **Dādhi-bhagos*), where *-bogŭ* does not mean 'god' (< 'apportioner') but has the alternative original sense of 'portion' (cf. *bogatŭ* 'endowed with fortune, rich', *ubogŭ* 'poor', and Vedic *bhága-*); Slavic *Daždĭ-bogŭ* would thus resemble the Vedic divine epiclesis *dā́tā vásu* 'giver of goods'. *Stribogŭ* may similarly mean 'Scatter Goods' or 'Spread Wealth'. Other etymologies are possible (e.g., *Stribogŭ* < **P[a]tri-bhagos* 'Father God'), but each in its uncertainty merely prejudices what are basically unknown quantities.

The *Lay of Igor's Host* called the Russians poetically 'grandsons of Dažĭbogŭ', while winds were 'grandsons of Stribogŭ'. As in West Slavic, epithets have come to conceal the basic names of such gods.

Mokošĭ 'Moist' (cf. Russian *mókryj* 'wet') is an allonym of Máti Syrá Zemljá 'Mother Moist Earth', a Slavic counterpart of the water-related fertility goddess, semantically akin to both the name *Harahvaiti and the epithet Arədvī of her Avestan opposite number Anāhitā.

Velesŭ/Volosŭ (the latter from **Velsŭ*) appears as Volosŭ in the *Primary Chronicle,* where he joins Perunŭ as divine witness of several state treaties between Russia and Byzantium during the tenth century; he is characterized as *skotĭjĭ bogŭ* 'cattle-god' or 'god of riches' (*skotŭ* 'cattle' < 'wealth'; cf. Old Norse *skattr* 'treasure'). As an oath-god of the Varangian overlords he might be suspected of Scandinavian origin, perhaps akin in name to *Völsi,* a sacred horse phallus that was manipulated in Norwegian fertility magic, much to the displeasure of Saint Olaf. More probably, however, this god is to be compared with the Lithuanian Vẽlinas or VélS. A death-god can in folk religion easily acquire chthonian connotations of "riches," while his deeper "prophetic" nature is seen in the *Lay of Igor's Host,* where a bard is called 'grandson of Velesŭ'. Like his Baltic parallel, **Vel(e)sŭ* must have been somewhat homologous to Odin and could thus become the latter's Slavic interpretation in the Varangian overlay.

Perún is the only Slavic and Russian deity of whom much can be said with confidence. The formal aspects of his name were discussed in connection with the Lithuanian Perkū́nas above. *Perunŭ* reflects **Perawnos,* even as the Latvian *Pērkōns* comes from **Perk*^{w}*awnos,* both with full vowel grade of the underlying *u*-stem, whereas **Per(k*^{w}*/g)ūn(y)o-* (with alternative prederivational lengthening of the *u*) appears in *Perkū́nas* and in Russian *Perynja* (Perún's hill sanctuary at Novgorod) and *peregynja* 'wooded hill'. Already Procopius, secretary to Justinian's general Belisarius (*De bello Gothico* 3.14, ca. 550 C.E.), spoke of the Slavs as having the lord of lightning as their supreme deity, to whom they sacrificed cattle and other animals. Russian folklore has much to tell of Perún, for example, how he slew a serpent on a mountain to release cattle and waters (cf. Indra) or produced thunder and fiery slivers of rock (= bolts) by grinding together huge millstones (cf. the probably etymological origin of Thor's Mjöllnir and cognates as 'millstone[s]' and Hrungnir's tit-for-tat in using a whetstone on Thor's own skull [chap. 11]). No wonder Thor would be equated with Perún in any Varangian-Russian syncretism, while later Christianized folklore masked him under the biblical rainmaker Elijah (Ilja) with his fiery chariot. Rain magic was important in Perún's folk ritual, surviving especially among the Balkan Slavs (and in adjacent Romania, Albania, and northern Greece) as the *Perperuna* rite centered on a dervishlike rain dance by a naked, garlanded, prepubescent flower girl. An alternative name for the performance was *Dodola,* which recalls not only Perkū́nas's allonym Dundulis but Zeus's oak oracle at Dodona in Epirus. Perperuna as a (reduplicated) feminine derivative from Perún's name parallels the Norse *Fjörgyn* (< **Perk^{w}ūnī́*) besides *Fjörgynn* (< **Perk^{w}ū́nos*), the Lithuanian *Perkū́nija* from *Perkū́nas,* and the Greek *Keraunίā* as an allonym of the ivy-wreathed Semele (Sophocles, *Antigone* 1139; Euripides, *Bacchae* 6), besides *Zeùs Keraunós* 'Zeus the Bolt' (*Inscriptiones Graecae* 5.2.288, Arcadia, fifth century B.C.E.). A relationship of *Perunŭ* and Greek *keraunós* 'thunderbolt' has long been suspected, with the initial *p* : *k* discrepancy blamed on "tabuistic variation." *Keraunós* can be explained with reference to the verb *keraḯzō* 'smash, destroy', but both the Dodona and Semele links argue for the extra-Greek comparison. A clue may be seen in Zeus's epithet *terpi-kéraunos,* seemingly 'delighting in the bolt', where one would have expected **terpsi-kéraunos* (cf. *Terpsi-khórē* 'Delighting in Dance'). *Terpi-kéraunos* parallels *argi-kéraunos* 'having a darting [or gleaming] bolt', which is a possessive compound, not of the "spoilsport" type. We may similarly start with an alliterative, quasi-reduplicative **perk^{w}i-peraunos* 'having a striking bolt', metathesized to **k^{w}erpi-peraunos* by the same *p* : *k* transposition that produced, for example, Greek *sképto-* (< **spekyo-;* cf. Latin *specio-*) or Lithuanian *kèpti* 'to bake' (< **pek^w-*; cf. Sanskrit *pac-*) and *kùmstė* 'fist' (< **k^{w}m̥pst-* < **pn̥k^{w}st-*). Realliteration accompanied the metathesis, producing **k^{w}erpi-keraunos*. The subsequent gradual formal shift of the labiovelar to *t-* (cf., e.g., *téttares* 'four' besides Mycenaean *qe-to-ro-* and Latin *quattuor*) yielded *terpikéraunos,* with the new compounded variant *keraunós* prevailing. Thus Greek seems to partake here of a theonymic and typological continuum that stretches via Thraco-Phrygian to Slavic and Baltic and reaches more distantly into Germanic and Indic alike.

An addition to the dossier of Indo-European myth transposed to saga in terms of diachronic dynastic projection is found in the *Primary Chronicle*. The history of the Kiev state, from the calling of the Varangian princes from Scandinavia in 862 to the baptism of Vladimir in 988, is wrapped in a legendary haze reminiscent of Livy's account of Roman kingship. In Nestor's sequence the shadowy Rjurik (understudied by

Sineus and Truvor) is succeeded by his partner and clansman Oleg (< **Helgi*), who assumes total rulership and serves as regent for Rjurik's son Igor. Oleg's standard epithet is *věščij* 'wizard'; he is not a fighter but a military manipulator, and his treaties are sacrally sworn covenants. As a saga figure he matches in name and type the Vol'ga of epic, likewise a sorcerous kind (*volkhv;* see below). He displays both "Odinic" and "Romulean" traits, which may have partly devolved from Rjurik, and at the same time resembles the "peace king" Numa, capping his career in 912: *I živjaše Olegŭ mirŭ imĕa ko vsĕmŭ stranamŭ* 'And Oleg dwelt at peace with all nations'. By contrast Igor, whose name is also Varangian (< **Yngvarr*), was a brutish and cruel warrior recalling Tullus Hostilius, whereas his successor was the noble and chivalrous warlord Svjatoslav. These two reflect disparate strands of the warrior class, the same as are epicized in Bhīma and Arjuna of the *Mahābhārata,* sons of Vāyu and Indra respectively. Svjatoslav is succeeded by Jaropolk, in whose story famine, a beautiful wife, and her abduction by Jaropolk's subsequently sainted brother Vladimir suggest transposed mythical third-estate ambience and what corresponds to Dioskouric woman trouble. It appears that, up to the cutoff of the pagan tradition by the sudden Christianization of 988, the dynastic "history" of the Russian state is no history at all but chronicle-epic in the manner of Livy and Firdausi's *Book of Kings*.

Saga transposition of myth is also observable in the Russian epic tradition. The *bylínas* ('past events') are oral epyllia recorded from the seventeenth century to modern times, surviving especially in the far north of Russia. They know a set of *stáršie bogatýri* or 'elder champions' from the mythical, prehistoric past, notable among whom are Volkh (or Vol'ga) Vseslavjevič, Svjatogor Kolyvanovič, and Mikula Seljaninovič. The patronymics are not to be taken literally; they are more in the nature of name doubles or type epithets. *Seljanín* means 'villager, peasant', and Mikula is the superhuman plowman who clears the land and peacefully promotes agriculture. Kolyvanovič reflects a Slavic form of the name of the Finnish-Estonian mythical strongman Kalev(a), to whom the mountain giant Svjatogor has apparently been assimilated; the huge, heavy, and dense Svjatogor earned his name ('Holymount') by literal postmortem petrifaction. Volkh (cf. *volkhv* 'sorcerer') is in origin a title attached to the proper name Vseslav but secondarily assimilated to the allonym Vol'ga (< **Olĭg-;* cf. Oleg above). Possessed of occult knowledge, a shape changer, characterized by *khítrost' múdrost'* 'craftiness [and] wisdom', he was the noncombatant magical provider and master strategist of his own private army (*družína*). With his preternatural siring by a dragon father, prodigious birth attended by seismic and ecliptic phenomena, and early mastery of animal language, he resembles not only the Norse Odin but "Odinic" heroes such as Sigurðr and Helgi. Many accordances are areally diffused folktale material rather than specifically anchored in either native Russian or imported Varangian tradition, but some are structurally significant, such as Volkh being not only a magician but also a manipulator of warriors, to the exclusion of the lumbering strongman Svjatogor. The latter was beset from both sides of the social spectrum, for he was actually banned from treading the earth, since Máti Syrá Zemljá (the patroness of the plowman Mikula) could not sustain his bulk. Svjatogor is a kind of *miles otiosus,* a warrior figure put out to pasture in a "rejuvenation" of champions. He supplies the link to the group of younger *bogatýri* around the Kiev court of Vladimir (Dobrynja Nikitič, Alёša Popovič, et al.), above all to the greatest of them, Ilja Muromec. Ilja alone keeps company in the bylinas with the usually solitary Svjatogor. As the latter is about to die by fusion into a mountain, he transfuses his might and weight into the junior partner by the breathing, foaming, and perspiration that attend his passing, which the initiate either inhales or licks up. There is also the bylina of Ilja's healing, how as the longtime crippled son of humble peasants he was cured and made heroic by a miraculous draught administered by three roving pilgrims, who then instructed him to take on allcomers but to beware of confronting Svjatogor, whom Earth could barely sustain, Mikula the darling of Mátuška Syrá Zemljá, and Vol'ga with his *khítrost' múdrost'*. This episode looks like a relic of some initiatory enjoining against offending the three levels of society, of becoming a triple sinner in the manner of Indra—in short, a tripartite "loyalty oath" for the warrior. A bylina about the last three forays of Ilja's old age places him at triple crossroads where a signpost points to being slain, getting married, and becoming rich respectively. Taking the first route, Ilja instead mows down his attackers. On the second, he outwits a dangerous seductress whose bed is a trapdoor to a dungeon, making her take the plunge and freeing a collection of czars who had earlier fallen for the ruse. On the road to riches, he uses these to build a glorious cathedral at Kiev and dies in blessedness. He thus evades the perils and temptations of the champion (death, seduction, subornation), instead turning the challenges to heroic virtues: eradication of miscreants, punishment of treachery, restoration of sovereigns, and pious works. All this classifies Ilja as a specimen of the warrior type, perhaps even an epic vessel for traits pertaining to the god Perún; like the latter, he was drawn to mountains and fired oak-splitting shafts, riding the skies in the manner of his saintly eponym Ilja, the Christianized Perún, and disposing of monstrous adversaries, notably Solovéj Razbójnik or 'Nightingale Robber'. While he did not escape the barnacles of international folktales, enacting with his son Sokol'nik the Rustam : Sohrab, Hildebrand : Hadubrand, and Cūchulainn : Conlae pattern of filicide, Ilja is indeed the Slavic epic exemplar of the Indo-European warrior who will occupy us in chapter 13.

III · THEMES

13 · God and Warrior

At the end of chapter 12, the initial and terminal high points in the career of Ilja Muromec appeared to be couched in tripartite social symbolism. He was cautioned against taking on any of the senior heroes—Volkh the sorcerer, Svjatogor the strongman, and Mikula the plowing champion—in short, against challenging the entrenched establishment of priestly, political-military, and economic power. At the end of his life he had nobly met the test and even channeled his last trials to positive ends, eschewing the lures of carnality and gold, exterminating evildoers, restoring to temporal power the czars caught in the seductress's sex trap, and contributing heavily to the building fund of the church. Despite the folktale aura and the intrusion of Christian piety, Ilja's career is steeped in Indo-European warrior myth.

Basic to that myth is a profound anomie of the human and societal condition, rooted in the use and abuse of power. Order, security, peace—positive conditions all—tend to depend for their preservation on the readiness of something that is inherently destructive, such as "security forces" or a military machine with the attendant mentality. If boosters of law enforcement like to describe their favorite agents of public order as a thin phalanx protecting civilization from anarchy, there is an even thinner line separating champion from berserk, police action from police riot. Those trained as agents of aggression and repression may experience difficulty functioning as normal human beings under great stress, or conversely when the pressure is off. Such abnormality also induces clannishness vis-à-vis the general society, "fraternal" orders, "protective" associations, gangs, juntas, and other forms of structured apartness.

FIGURE 16. The Lapis Satricanus. Latium, ca. 500 B.C.E. (Courtesy of the Netherlands Institute in Rome.)

This kind of perennial tension is reflected in the ancient myths. Warlike exaltation, martial ecstasy where fury gets out of hand, is displayed by the Third Horatius, by Cūchulainn, by the *berserkir.* The Maruts, *sodāles, fiana,* or *einherjar* constituted bands with their own inner structure and interactional dynamics, with a collective *svadhā́* or "ethos" (the two cognates meaning etymologically 'self-law, autonomy') that was only capriciously at the call of a commanding figure such as Indra, Publicola,[1] Finn, or Odin. The warlord himself could be an equally self-willed individualist and from inspired and inspiring leader shade over into a lone-wolf kind of martial toiler (Indra led the Maruts, and yet he was also *éka-* 'one, alone, unique', acted *yathāvaśám* 'as he chose', and had a *svadhā́* of his own). The warrior thus had an ambivalent role as single champion or part of a self-centered corps or coterie, both a society's external defender and its potential internal menace.

Royalty appears to originate in the warrior class (cf. Vedic *rājanyà-,* and Indra as king), but the sovereign seems to have become early on detached from narrow class characteristics as the "complete man" in charge of the total society, either symbolically wedded to the transfunctional goddess as in Ireland or required to be on top of things across the board (rune-master, conqueror, crop promoter rolled into one in Norse tradition). He was also translated into reaches where sacrally tinged "nobility" could lead to a thinning of the blood royal, to the point where he needed a true warrior as mentor, troubleshooter, rescuer, and tutor in regal worth (Rustam's role vis-à-vis the Kayanid kings comes to mind).

1. Cf. the Old Latin dedicatory inscription of ca. 500 B.C.E. from the temple of Mater Matuta at Satricum: *steterai Popliosio Valesiosio suodales Mamartei* 'the *sodāles* of Publius Valerius set [this] up for Mars' (see fig. 16).

But as the king could fail, so could the champion. Royal downfall is epitomized by the Iranian "first king" Yama Xšaēta, whose one tragic flaw coincided with the supreme sin of his religion. Instead of living by the royal prayer that climactically (after invasion and blight) craved surcease from falsehood, he began consorting with the Lie, thereby compromising his regal glory, which left him in staggered tripartite installments, to be seized by other, more specialized mythical type figures. Thus the complete ruler was dismantled back into the portions he had summed up as the embodiment of the whole community. A somewhat different scenario obtained when a warrior-god (and "king" of gods) such as Indra succumbed to malfeasance: he was successively guilty of impious, treacherous, and lecherous demeanor and was in consequence divested of his religious, forceful, and sex-related attributes, which were reassembled under other auspices to breed compartmentalized heroes. Thus his losses match the transgressions point by point, rather than his undoing being triggered by a single overriding compromising of sovereignty. Like the true sovereign, he had tripartite qualities deserving of piecemeal reinvestiture, but he was not the synthesis of them, merely an aggregate of compartmentalized characteristics. A third type was the warrior who was not divine but a saga hero manipulated by deity, not a king but merely in the royal service. This is the kind most marked by a tense relationship to the environment where he operated, to his divine and human patrons and his social constituency at large. He had no agglomeration of transfunctional attributes to lose, but he nevertheless managed to offend (or was perceived as offending) all segments of the social order by a structured set of misdeeds. With his flawed willfulness (or perhaps rather his "programmed," predestined, predictable nature) he compromised his career by nadir episodes that involved impious/unjust/sacrilegious, cowardly/underhanded/unwarriorlike, and covetous/venal/adulterous acts respectively. This type is the main topic of this chapter. The varieties described are found in epic, saga, and folklore, from the fells of Scandinavia to the jungles of India, from the Bay of Bengal via the Gulf of Argos and the Tiber to Galway Bay. These kinds are not extinct—they were spotted not long ago on both the Mekong and the Potomac.

An epitome of the warrior figure is presented as "Starcatherus" by Saxo in books 6–8 of his *Gesta Danorum,* but the early stages of the hero's life and career are elaborated upon in the Icelandic *Gautreks Saga*. There was a first Starkaðr, a giant with eight arms, who abducted a girl and got her pregnant and was for this himself extirpated by Thor (as mentioned in Vetrliði's poem quoted in chap. 11). The dark-haired offspring, a powerfully built normal man Stōrvirkr, in turn had a son whom he named Starkaðr after the grandfather. Early orphaned, this young Starkaðr had a shifting and complicated fosterage, in part jointly with an equally fatherless young prince Vīkarr, much of it under the tutelage of a mysterious mentor Hrosshārsgrani ('Horsehair Grani'). As a young man he helped Vīkarr regain his father's kingdom and remained Vīkar's trusted associate. Grani, however, still hovers around the pair. He is none other than Odin in human disguise, who early on has selected Vīkarr to be sacrificed to him, with Starkaðr as the offerant, and is biding his time. During a sailing expedition a prolonged calm strands Vīkar's fleet near an island, and remedial divination indicates Odin's desire for a human victim (shades of Iphigenia at Aulis). When lots are drawn, Vīkarr himself is chosen, much to the consternation of the members of his party. The next night Grani takes Starkaðr over to the island to witness a phantasmagoric assembly in a forest clearing, with the gods in their high seats and Odin presiding over fixing the destiny of Starkaðr. The proceedings boil down to parliamentary infighting between Odin and Thor. Thor leads off in a negative vein, citing Starkað's giant ancestry, recalling how he, Thor, had killed the eponymous grandfather and complaining that the girl he had rescued, Alfhildr, "chose as father of her son a crafty giant rather than Thor of the Äsir (*hundvīsan jötun heldr enn Āsathōr*)"; he thus hints at a sexual triangle rather than Thor's having been called in merely as a professional exterminator by Alfhild's outraged father. In consequence Thor condemns the young Starkaðr to be childless. Not to be outdone, Odin counterbalances this by awarding him three human lifespans. Thor tries to sour this by decreeing the commission of a criminal act (*nīðingsverk*) in each span. And so it goes for a while: Odin promises a steady string of victories, Thor an attendant series of serious wounds. Odin confers the gift of poetry, Thor adds an impairment of memory, which is crucial to an oral skald. Odin makes Starkaðr appealing to noble folk, Thor impairs his relations with commoners. One god cannot cancel the other's gifts, but he waters them down by contrary "counterboons." In the end the assembly summarily concurs in the total package and adjourns. As the vision vanishes, Starkaðr realizes what he owes Odin and gives in to Grani's insistence that he expedite Vīkar's immolation. He is given a spear disguised as a harmless reed, and in the next day's crucial council he outlines the plan of a mock hanging with calf guts from a slender twig. The king goes along with this seeming charade, but in the implementation Odinic magic works its transformation: as Starkaðr symbolically pokes the king with the reed, with the consecrational formula "Now I give thee to Odin," it reverts to a spear and pierces him, the gut stiffens into a sturdy withy, and the twig hardens and flies up to serve as a functional gallows. The sacrifice is complete, but it does not endear Starkaðr to Vīkar's men. He is exiled from Hordaland (western Norway) to Sweden, where he is credited with putting the final skaldic touches to the *Vīkarsbālkr,* leaving the following unsparing self-portrait: "They think they see on me the giant's mark [*jötunkuml*], eight arms, where [Thor] . . . robbed [my grandfather] of his arms. Men laugh when they see me, ugly jaw, long snout, wolf-gray hair, hanging arms, scarred neck, wrinkled skin." With that he peters out of *Gautreks Saga,* for he interested the author only because of Vīkarr.

Saxo is more comprehensive. He describes Starcatherus as renowned for physical and mental prowess, a favorite of the Danish king Frotho, a brilliant adventurer whose achievements were celebrated "even today" and way beyond "our own country" (i.e., Denmark). Saxo states that he came from lands east of Sweden, inhabited by Estonians and other "savage hordes." (Giantland also lay in the East in Norse mythic topography!) Then he tells a story he calls "fictitious, unreasonable, and downright incredible": Starcatherus was born of giants, with an extraordinary number of hands. Thor tore off four of these, thus reducing the six-armed monster to human normality by a rough form of remedial surgery (rather than, as in the saga, murderously lopping off the limbs of his eight-armed grandfather, with the grandson still exhibiting hereditary vestigial stumps of supernumerary arms). Next Saxo recounts how Starcatherus was induced by Othinus (a notorious wizard and impostor masquerading as a god) to become friendly with the Norwegian king Wicarus in order to murder him (Odin also outfitted him with three mortal life spans, "so that he might perpetrate a proportionate number of damnable deeds"). Once upon a piratical foray the king and hero were long stranded by storms and at length resolved that only human sacrifice would break the meteorological deadlock. Wicarus was picked by lot, and Starcatherus fitted him with a noose made of osier, promising a merely symbolic momentary suspension. At the crucial juncture, however, he tightened the knot, strangled the king, and finished him off with his sword. With his curious half-baked euhemeristic rationalism Saxo rejects the version that the osier might have hardened of itself; Odinic immolation, so well conveyed by the saga, was already beyond his comprehension. Nor did Saxo sense the extent to which the hero is buffeted in a theological tension field between the gods Thor and Odin, the former the implacable foe of giantkind, the latter himself part giant and manipulator of kings and heroes alike. Instead of this opposition, demonstrated by the fate-fixing night assembly of the gods, where Thor is the single-minded antagonist and Grani reflects the full "fatality" of Odin, Saxo's Thor acts like a humanitarian plastic surgeon, while the confidence man Othinus performs like a mafioso godfather: Thor's intervention is isolated and out of character, while Odin is the fountainhead of favors and felonies alike.

After the ritual murder Starcatherus finds a home base at Frotho's Danish court but spends his time on extensive forays, especially in eastern lands from Finland and Russia to Byzantium, as a matchless and admirable warrior in sporadic service to both Danish and Swedish kings. His gift of three lives seems offset by an accelerated and premature aging process, for Saxo starts calling him *senex* soon after the death of Wicarus. The rest of his career in Saxo brings to pass many of the fate fixings of the *Gautreks Saga*: his great victories are won at the cost of terrible wounds, and his allegiance to royalty is matched by a deep antagonism toward the lower orders whom he heartily despises, with the exception of tillers and armorers. Central to his character is an almost mystical reverence for kingship as such. He acts on occasion as a tough-minded enforcer of royal dignity, notably in "straightening out" the decadent and dissolute children of Frotho, punishing their lowlife accomplices, and in a flood of poetic eloquence tutoring them in regal behavior. Yet, tragically, he is already a regicide, and his remaining two shortcomings also involve deaths of kings. In the service of the Swedish ruler Regnaldus he, the quintessential brave champion, panics and flees just as his master is being cut down on the battlefield. In a final villainy he accepts from conspirators 120 pounds of gold for stabbing in his bath the Dane Olo of the piercing gaze, a cruel king but his sovereign and friend nonetheless. Having thus betrayed, forsaken, or murdered rulers of Norway, Sweden, and Denmark, this disquieting ultraroyalist has completed the three crimes decreed to go with his three lives, and by implication has exhausted his extended term. All of a sudden his vigorous old age is at an end, and Saxo portrays a horribly disfigured, nearly blind, deeply remorseful cripple on crutches. He is still able to kill anyone who gets too close, but he has none of his former ease of locomotion, when he seemed to shuttle between Uppsala and Denmark faster than SAS could nowadays fly him. His one thought is of an honorable end in the Norse manner, spurning death from age or illness. Out of remorse for his last crime he resolves to use the proceeds from Olo's murder to hire a killer for himself. Fate once more brings across his path a preordained agent in the person of the young nobleman Hatherus, son of Lenno, one of those who had suborned the old hero to kill Olo and whom he had himself later slain in frustration over his crime. Urging the young warrior to avenge his father and accept the blood money, Starcatherus induces Hatherus to behead him, promising magical invulnerability if the executioner will jump between the decapitated head and the collapsing torso (which Hatherus warily refrains from doing, lest he be crushed by the bulk of the body). Piercing Saxo's clumsy novelistic motivations, Hatherus can be unmasked as Höðr, who was described in chapter 11 as a subsidiary allomorph of Odin himself in his role as fate-god. Thus another manifestation of Odin attends to the hero's death and cremation, even as Grani fostered, tutored, and guided his childhood and youth. **Stark(h)aðr* itself is a theophorous name similar in kind to the Hebrew *Gabriel* 'Strong as God', and the hero is thus even onomastically a spin-off from the divine orbit of Odin-Höðr. But he is not a "positive" Odinic hero such as Sigurðr; instead he acts out an ancient myth of the warrior as a pawn in divine infighting, as an admirable champion who is yet ancestrally burdened and fatally programmed to perpetrate villainies against all orders of society, to end up as a serial evildoer guilty of ritual regicide, battlefield cowardice, and contract murder.

Starkaðr's career strongly resembles that of Śiśupāla, touched upon in chapter 5, in the context of book 2 of the *Mahābhārata*. Śiśupāla is billed as king of Cedi, but also as the field marshal (thus military subordinate) of the overking Jarāsaṁdha of Magadha, hence as less than a sovereign. He was born with four arms and three eyes; multiarmed deities are common in India, but triocularity is a mark of Rudra-Śiva, and the name *Śiśu-pāla-* itself is a takeoff on the god's Vedic and later epithet *Paśu-pati-* 'Master of Animals'; Śiśu-pāla is 'Young Master', thus in essence a 'Junior Śiva'. His parents wanted to do away with their teratogenic brood, but a disembodied voice dissuaded them, saying that he was fated to live—and die otherwise. In whosever lap his abnormalities would vanish, that person would also in the end be his slayer. "Thousands" of curious kings came to observe the prodigy, and the parents let each hold the child, but in vain. At length the Yādava brothers Kṛṣṇa and Balarāma (cousins of Śiśupāla) dropped by, their paternal aunt placed her son on Kṛṣṇa's knees, and the instant normalization occurred. The mother then begged Kṛṣṇa to promise to be tolerant of her son's potential derelictions, and Kṛṣṇa readily agreed to forgive up to a hundred capital offenses. Thus a "Rudraic" hero with a theophorous name and excessive anatomy was pared down by Kṛṣṇa-Viṣṇu, who also set the limits of his transgressions, even as the "Odinic" Starkaðr with a theophorous name and multiple arms was "reduced" by Thor, who likewise stipulated the roster and extent of his crimes.

Śiśupāla's mature career is not elaborately spelled out, for most of what is known of him is told at his death scene in book 2 of the *Mahābhārata,* with such flashback narrations (the birth tale) and dialogue references as the participants provide. His service to Jarāsaṁdha looms large in his military record. Jarāsaṁdha himself has traits in common with Śiśupāla, and his story on several points replicates and complements the latter, starting with his birth: His father, king of Magadha, married twin princesses of Kāśi, promising to honor them equally. When neither conceived, he secured from a hermit a mango of supposed efficacy, to be divided equally between his queens (a difficult task, considering the clinging meat and huge pit). He succeeded. The queens became pregnant, but each bore a live half of a baby. The midwives discarded this pair of complementary monstrosities, but a cannibalistic demoness Jarā 'Old Age', foraging for food, found them, packed them together, and saw them miraculously fuse into a whole, well-formed, strong infant boy. Spared by the ogress, gratefully received by the parents, and prophesied by the eugenic mango supplier to be a great ruler who would behold Rudra Mahādeva, Jarāsaṁdha 'Joined by Jarā' thus entered life as another Śivaistic miracle baby in need of corrective adjustment, albeit suturing rather than amputation. As a mature conqueror he was irresistible, defeating "a hundred" kings (nothing less will do in hyperbolic India) and sequestering them in his fastness of Girivraja ('Mountain Corral') as a pool of victims for his patron Rudra-Śiva. Just like his general Śiśupāla he was fatally ill disposed against the Yādavas, and it was Kṛṣṇa who finally persuaded the Pāṇḍavas to eliminate him, as described in chapter 5. As a sacrificial offerant of kings to Rudra-Śiva, Jarāsaṁdha complements Śiśupāla by filling in a gap in the latter's similarities to Starkaðr, for Śiśupāla's list of outrages, while climbing rapidly toward the hundred mark set by Kṛṣṇa, stopped short of regicide. In the final settling of accounts Kṛṣṇa recited a sampling of five felonies by his fiendish cousin: burning down the Yādavas' capital city behind their backs and sneakily attacking rājanyas at play (unethical warfare); stealing Vasudeva's sacrificial horse intended for an aśvamedha (sacrilege); and twice abducting betrothed women, once disguised as the groom (sexual offense resembling Indra's impersonation of Gautama). After Bhīma's killing of Jarāsaṁdha events move rapidly towards a climax for Śiśupāla as well. The kings freed by Kṛṣṇa from Girivraja's death row are told to hie themselves to Yudhiṣṭhira's rājasūya; Śiśupāla will be there too as the ruler of Cedi, with his credit of forgiveness down to zero. In the preliminary ceremonies guest gifts are handed out, and Bhīṣma proposes a special award to the worthiest visitor. Yudhiṣṭhira agrees and names the old great-uncle himself as a one-man jury. Bhīṣma chooses Kṛṣṇa, providing a well-founded Viṣṇuite rationale for selecting an incarnate god. This provokes Śiśupāla to loud protests, claiming that a nonking as guest of honor in a gathering of kings is an insult to the majesty of royalty. His demagoguery sways a portion of the audience, and the escalating logomachy threatens to disrupt the ceremony. Bhīṣma remarks that Śiśupāla is out to "lead all the kings to the seat of Yama," unconsciously acting out a death wish on the royalkind he purports to extol. After another harsh tongue-lashing directed at Bhīṣma by Śiśupāla, Bhīma is about to attack the latter, but Bhīṣma restrains him and recounts the birth tale of Śiśupāla, noting sagely that the Cedi king appears to be swayed by fate, that he, like everyone else, is but a scintilla of the universal godhead, and that Kṛṣṇa himself must be orchestrating the recovery of this recalcitrant particle into the Whole. He deflects the rage onto Kṛṣṇa, and Śiśupāla challenges the latter to a fight, but Kṛṣṇa merely lists the five sample misdeeds and declares that the account of a hundred is overdrawn, that Śiśupāla must now be courting death. Kṛṣṇa adds that Śiśupāla was once betrothed to marry Kṛṣṇa's wife Rukminī but could no more win her than a śūdra can get to hear the Vedas (Kṛṣṇa and Rukminī had been lovers, but her father and brother, urged by Jarāsaṁdha, had given her to Śiśupāla, only to be rescued and spirited away from the wedding by Kṛṣṇa). Śiśupāla hurls back the terminal insult that if he were Kṛṣṇa he would not broadcast too loudly that he had a secondhand spouse, whereupon Kṛṣṇa promptly beheads him with his discus. A radiance rises from the corpse, salutes Kṛṣṇa, and enters into him, as the errant part is reabsorbed into divine grace.

Vaiṣṇava mysticism aside, this climax lends itself to comparison with Starkaðr. The surprising trading of sexual slurs at the end, with Kṛṣṇa's old rancor making his rage spill over, recalls Thor's reprisals against Starkaðr the Elder, with swift revenge but long-harbored grudges still boiling over in the third generation. Thor's visiting of the grandfather's sins on the grandson resembles Viṣṇu's serial pursuit of his demonic adversary through successive incarnations, as Hiraṇyakaśipu, Rāvana, and Śiśupāla. At the same time Thor had better reason to remain aggrieved, for Alfhildr had spurned him, whereas Kṛṣṇa got his willing girl after all. Thor and Kṛṣṇa-Viṣṇu are clearly homologous in the two narratives as the ancestral foes of the demonic warrior, as are Odin and Rudra-Śiva as his divine "sponsors," but in the "here and now" of Viking Scandinavia and Epic India their relative systemic roles had shifted. As epitomes of the tormented hero, Starkaðr and Śiśupāla needed catharsis rather than mere extermination, something that Thor with his one-track mind and Śiva in the sectarian hostility of Viṣṇuism were quite incapable of supplying. Fortunately for Starkaðr, Odin had risen to the top of the pantheon and was able to take care of his own. Śiśupāla had no such luck and could be redeemed only by the metaphysical leap of a Vaiṣṇava salvation miracle. Hence the Norse version is intrinsically sympathetic to the hero, whereas the Viṣṇuite *Mahābhārata* cannot but paint Śiśupāla in dark colors, down to the theological coup de theatre at the end. The mana of invincibility that flowed from the severed anatomy of Starkaðr (but that Saxo's wary Hatherus failed to collect) must have matched in origin the emanation radiating from the dying Śiśupāla, which Viṣṇu's reservoir of allness was only too ready to absorb and reintegrate. The theological sea change is clearly more sweeping in India than in Scandinavia, and hence the Norse version, despite its chronologically late attestation, is probably more faithful to a putative Indo-European prototype.

The Greek Herakles turns such binary comparison into a triangulated construct. Especially as told by Diodorus Siculus (book 4), his life story resembles that of Starkaðr. Zeus (impersonating Alkmene's husband, Amphitryon) stretched out the night of insemination to threefold length, "signaling by the amount of time spent on the begetting the supranormality of the offspring being engendered" (cf. Starkað's triple life span). Herakles was named theophorously for Hera, consort of the supreme godhead, even as Starkað's name incorporated that of an allomorph of the chief god Odin. Early on Herakles was caught in the antagonistic machinations of Hera and Athena, with Hera's jealous hostility counterbalanced by Athena's solicitude. Herakles becomes a toiling wanderer, whose labor-studded career is punctuated by three crimes: defiance of Zeus, leading to madness and killing of his own children (impiety, infanticide); ruseful hurling down of Iphitos (unwarriorlike sneak assault); and adultery with Iole. These misdeeds resemble most closely the "three sins" of Indra, and the sexual component also matches Śiśupāla rather than Starcatherus; the reasons are cultural, for lechery was as alien to Starcatherus as to Tullus Hostilius, and hunger for cash gold entered into complementary distribution with the sexual lures of "golden Aphrodite." Each crime marked a downward turn in Herakles' life and career, plunging him into bondage under Eurystheus, transvestite slavery with Omphale, and insufferable pain from Nessos's poisoned garment, which drove him to seek death on the pyre on Mount Oeta. Like Starcatherus offering return of blood money and invulnerability to Hatherus, Herakles arranged his own death as a direct consequence of his final misdeed, with the help of the young warrior Philoktetes, whom he rewarded with the fatal bow and arrows dipped in Hydra venom that had already recoiled on their wielder via the poisoned blood of Nessos. The reconciliation of the deified Herakles to his eponym Hera is depicted by Diodorus as an adoption rite entailing a mock birth, with the hero dropping through the goddess's clothes to the ground. Engravings on Etruscan mirrors also show the adult Herakles suckled by Hera in a scene of adoption supervised by Zeus (see fig. 17). On the whole, including the fact that both Starcatherus and Herakles have poetic abilities (one a skald, the other associated with the Muses), the Greek saga ties in with the Norse one, while (apart from the venal/sexual complementarity) there are next to no binary isothemes between Greece and India. Once again the Scandinavian version seems prototypical, for most of its features are matched in either India or Greece, while many traits of the latter two lack a parallel elsewhere.[2]

Just as in India, the discrepancies in Greece are culturally conditioned innovations. Unlike Starcatherus and Śiśupāla with their innate enormities that require surgical intervention, Herakles conforms to the Greek norm that eschews congenital monstrosity in Olympian heroes, reserving hand-related and ocular irregularities for the former gods of the Titan generation (Hekatonkheiroi, Kyklopes). Instead of decapitation, Herakles has an apotheosis by fire on a mountain, in conformity with the classical heroic pattern. Unlike the royalist fanatics and regicides of Scandinavia and India, Herakles has no extreme proclivities, despite the strain inherent in the "precedence" of Eurystheus and his expiatory servitude under Eurystheus and Omphale; furthermore, the immolation of kings was obsolete in classical Greece, unlike the per-

2. In all three places the hero is problematically involved with old age: Starcatherus as a protracted geriatric case, Jarāsaṃdha as welded into normality by Jarā, and Herakles through his pathetic encounter with Gêras as depicted in Greek art (cf. also the ancient-looking Gaulish champion Ogmios discussed in chap. 10).

FIGURE 17. Hera suckling Herakles. Engraving on back of Etruscan bronze mirror from Volterra, ca. 300 B.C.E. Museo Archeologico, Firenze. Gerhard-Körte, *Etruskische Spiegel,* 5, no. 60 (1884–97). The inscription held by Zeus reads "This picture shows how Hercle became son of Uni (= Juno, Hera)."

sistence of ritualistic murder in pagan Scandinavia and its lingering traces in Vedic and later India. The divine tug-of-war over the hero's fate, best reflected by the Odin : Thor pattern in Scandinavia, suffered serious sectarian dislocation in Viṣṇuite India, converting the tormented hero to villain and reconciliation to savioristic wonder; in Greece Herakles remains a positive hero and conciliation prevails, but the pantheonic oppositions have become obfuscated: Zeus tries to take care of his son through the proxy of his head-born daughter and inveighs against his pernicious "better half" for her persecution of Herakles (*Iliad* 15.24–28), with Olympian household tensions replacing inherited Indo-European antagonisms.

These antagonisms involve an opposition of demonic and life-enhancing deities within the warrior class. It is the difference between a figure of monstrous ancestry or attachments and one who makes the world safe against monsters, a kind of nature : culture tension in which the warrior is caught up. Rudra with his three eyes and four arms, one-eyed Odin of giant ancestry riding an eight-legged horse, Hera born of Titans and parthenogenous mother of the monster Typhoeus—all these fit the demonic slot, to which the hero has definite onomastic associations. The contrasting deity is one who prunes the wild by holding down the monstrous (Indra or Trita Āptya slaying Triśiras, Thor cutting back on giants, Athena wearing the Gorgon's head on her breastplate) and furthering normal nature (releasing waters, nurturing vegetation, protecting the young). The warrior hero is somehow genetically and inherently demonic, and his career is marked by the drama between this ancestral burden and the rehabilitational and "civilizing" efforts under the figurative (and in Athena's case literal) aegis of the opposing deity.

Stray pieces of this complex epic myth have survived elsewhere, most notably the theme of the structured misdeeds. Remembering the Indraic characteristics of Rāma, it is not surprising to find the pattern in that epic paragon as well (chap. 5). In the Ossetic *Nart* epic the hero Batraz manages to savage successively the pastoral Boratä, the martial Äxsärtägkatä, and the religious powers (angels, spirits), until his death reconciles him to God. In Irish saga (*Buile Suibhne*), Suibhne Geilt ('Sweeney the Madman') was a poet-warrior whose life was dramatically highlighted by his unprovoked outrages against Saint Rōnān, his strange cowardly flight from the battle of Mag Rath, and his violent death in the house of Saint Moling on an accusation—albeit false—of adultery, accompanied by last rites administered by the saint who had long expected Suibhne's coming and was thus fatally foreordained to attend to the final stages of his life. Rōnān the church builder is clearly the "constructive" authority figure here, and Suibhne's frenetic hatred of him has much in common with Śiśupāla's onslaught against Kṛṣṇa. Moling, on the other hand, figures as the ingatherer of the spent soul of this Sweeney Agonistes in the manner in which Odin arranges for the return of his own: reconciliation of the hero to his god rather than miraculous transfusional salvation, in line with Scandinavia and Greece rather than India. An inverted variant of the theme in the *Bōrama Laigen* has Saint Columb describe three Irish kings who went to heaven: Daimīn Damargait who never harassed the church, Ailill who in the nick of time thought better of fleeing from battle, and Feradach who was beguiled by gold but repented his hoarding on his deathbed. Here the pitfalls the first two "saved" rulers avoided match the first two sins of Suibhne, whereas Feradach's last-minute immunity to gold looks like an antidote to Starcatherus's third sin, with the same gold/sex complementarity that contrasted the latter to Śiśupāla and Herakles.

Akin to the "three sins" is the theme of the three charges against the warrior-statesman, as when the Romans Coriolanus (a sometime renegade) and Camillus (a Starcatherus-like populace hater according to Plutarch) were accused of usurpation/sacrilege, irregularities in the disposal of military spoils, and opposition to populist measures (such as lowering the market price of grain). Echoes of this pattern continue to reverberate. An Associated Press dispatch from Saigon on 6 September 1971 reported that Vice President Nguyen Cao Ky had talked four hunger-striking disabled war veterans out of incinerating themselves at a protest rally in Nha Trang (a fifth set himself on fire but was saved). Their complaint? "The one-man presidential election Oct. 3, the rising price of rice, and alleged official mistreatment of veterans." And similar charges reechoed a few years later in James J. Kilpatrick's syndicated column of 24 July 1974: "A melancholy time is approaching. . . . Our President . . . is about to be impeached. . . . The articles of impeachment . . . will boil down to . . . the abuse of power, the abuse of justice and the abuse of money." From Coriolanus and Camillus to Thieu and Nixon, *nil sub sole novi*. Mythic formulas refuse to die because they encapsulate enduring verities.

Recommended Reading

Dumézil, Georges. *The Destiny of the Warrior.* Translated by Alf Hiltebeitel. Chicago: University of Chicago Press, 1971. In French, *Heur et malheur du guerrier.* 2d ed. rev. Paris: Flammarion, 1985.

———. *The Stakes of the Warrior.* Translated by David Weeks. Edited, with an Introduction, by Jaan Puhvel. Berkeley and Los Angeles: University of California Press, 1983.

14 · King and Virgin

Royal needs vary in the ancient myths. Kay Us had to be saved from himself and his harebrained enterprises by the hero Rustam, and Frotho's dissolute children required discipline from the Dutch uncle Starcatherus. The Welsh Math's peacetime existence depended on a maidenly foot holder, even as king David's retainers procured him a fair damsel to keep him warm in old age in a chaste kind of closeness, for "the king knew her not" (1 *Kings* 1:1–4). The dependence of the king on virginal support is a theme attested in the three mainstays of Indo-European comparative mythology—India, Rome, and Scandinavia—and, with a curious twist of the virginal angle, in Ireland as well.

In this instance Indic tradition is paradigmatic. It involves the family of the ancient *samrāj* Yayāti, whose career in book 1 of the *Mahābhārata* was summarized in chapter 5, and whose posthumous downfall was compared to the "sinning" of Yama Xšaēta in chapter 6. Yayāti was inordinately dependent on his progeny in various seemingly unique ways that comparative mythology can elucidate. The "good" youngest son Pūru temporarily took on Yayāti's premature old age (to which he had been cursed by his wrathful father-in-law Kāvya Uśanas) and gratified his lust for an extra millennium of vigorous life, thereby earning the kingship, while Pūru's older, unaccommodating brothers Druhyu and Anu and equally obdurate half-brothers Yadu and Turvasu were banished to outer parts to breed alien tribes and foreign peoples. This story parallels the ultimogenitures and "world divisions" in Iranian tradition (sons of Feridun and Targitaos) and resembles the tale of the drunken Noah and his sons (told in garbled fashion in *Genesis* 9:18–29), where Shem the respectful one covered his father's nakedness and won approbation on home turf, while Ham and Japhet were destined to beget southern and northern races. Yayāti's reprieve involved role bartering with vigorous youth rather than merely protracting senility (something Tithonos in Greek myth failed to insist upon), but otherwise it recalls the life extensions the Swedish king Aun or Āni of Uppsala (in Snorri's *Ynglinga Saga*) granted himself on the installment plan by sacrificing his sons to Odin (sixty years for the first, ten each for the next eight, until he was too decrepit to carry through with the tenth and last one). In his posthumous life Yayāti needed the company of his four grandsons in order to regain salvation after his "fall," but book 1 of the *Mahābhārata* is strangely silent on how he acquired this posterity, and the quartet of worthies seems unaware of the relationship until Yayāti unmasks himself as their grandfather when they all take off for heaven in golden chariots. The missing link, Yayāti's daughter Mādhavī, appears instead in book 5. Even here her genealogical integration is unstated and mysterious; unlike the five sons (here reduced to two, Yadu and Pūru) who were born to Yayāti's successive wives Devayānī and Śarmiṣṭhā, Mādhavī is just there, without any overt mother. She is part of an exemplary tale incidentally told, with no integrated role in the epic (Yayāti's earlier presence in book 1 was at least a link in the genealogical chain).

In the passage the seer Nārada warns Duryodhana to mend his aggressive ways before it is too late, the moral being that excessive obduracy can backfire, for "look what happened to Gālava." We are treated first to another installment in the protracted shenanigans between Vasiṣṭha and Viśvāmitra, those two ancestral gurus whose priestly clans are credited with the authorship of mandalas 7 and 3 of the *Rig-Veda* respectively. Viśvāmitra, the ambitious kṣatriya, who early on had tried to rustle Vasiṣṭha's magic wish cow, was now doing exaggerated penance in order to gain promotion to brahmindom. He was still in postulant status and fair game for hazing by Vasiṣṭha (Dharma incarnate, otherwise son of Varuṇa, the same who cursed Dyaus to be born as Bhīṣma; cf. chap. 5). Vasiṣṭha turns up hungry at Viśvāmitra's hermitage and asks for a meal. In deferential solicitude, the latter fusses too long over a hot rice dish, and when he is ready to serve it, Vasiṣṭha tells him to hold it awhile, for he has already eaten elsewhere. As the guest leaves, Viśvāmitra remains holding the serving dish on his head, and so he stays immobile for a whole century, with his own needs catered to by his devoted ascetic disciple Gālava. Finally, Vasiṣṭha returns, hungry once more, finds the food still piping hot and delectable, and in gratitude for such devotion dubs Viśvāmitra a brahmin. The latter in turn rewards the patient Gālava by instant (though hardly accelerated) graduation. When the grateful student offers the teacher some tuition gift and insists once too often, the temperamental sage snaps back that he should bring eight hundred moon-white horses with one black ear. This was apparently an inside joke in Viśvāmitra's family; his father Gādhi had married off his daughter to a brahmin, asked for a thousand such thoroughbreds as the bride-price, and actually taken delivery from the bridegroom, thanks to Varuṇa's favor at a place called Aśvatīrtha 'Horseford'.

Now it is the earnest but impecunious Gālava's turn to lose his appetite. In his anorexic desperation he is befriended by the wonder bird Garuḍa, who takes him under his wing and ultimately steers him to the potential wealthy donor Yayāti. After learning of their errand, the king is flattered to be asked to contribute to such a worthy brahmanic cause but confesses that he is a bit down on his revenues and short of cash. Instead he proffers as a gift his virginal young daughter Mādhavī, intimating that she will be a means to Gālava's end via the avenue of procreation. Kings would give whole kingdoms for her, she is destined to perpetuate four lineages, and Yayāti is eager to have grandsons. Garuḍa then departs, and Gālava sets out with his young protégée to sell her to some childless royal prospect in return for a bride-price of eight hundred moon-white steeds. The first customer, Haryaśva of Ayodhyā (in Rāma country), is amenable but has only two hundred of the kind and offers these in return for a single night with the girl. When Gālava hesitates about such piecemeal pandering, Mādhavī herself helpfully pipes up that (like her sisters under the skin, Satyavatī, Kuntī, and Draupadī) she is gifted with renewable virginity and has no objection to being an incubation vessel in stepwise progress toward the august ascetic's noble goal. When she has borne the son Vasumanas ('Wealth Minded'), Gālava collects his ward and they move on to Divodāsa of Kāśi (Banaras), who has already heard of the arrangement and also signs up in return for another two hundred moon-white horses. The begetting is elaborately likened to a multitude of well-known mythical couplings, and its issue is Pratardana, destined to be a great warrior. The strange pair of pimping ascetic and saintly virgin next try to exact the balance of four hundred from Auśīnara of Bhoja (on the lower Yamunā) in return for two births, but he only has two hundred like the others, and the usual bargain is struck. The bouts of love making, in caves, by waterfalls, in woods and gardens, on terraces and rooftops, in palaces and boudoirs result in the son Śibi, later to be renowned as a good king who never told a lie. At this point Gālava, who has sat out three pregnancies in nearby forests and boarded his three horse herds with their former owners, is still two hundred short, but the reappearing Garuḍa informs him that there is no use looking further, that he has collected all living specimens of the breed. Instead they jointly approach Viśvāmitra and offer him the girl for one begetting in lieu of the remaining 25 percent of the debt. Viśvāmitra, that kṣatriya in brahmin's clothing, whose lustful encounter with the Apsaras Menakā was told in chapter 5, takes one look at Mādhavī and asks Gālava where he has been all along; he is glad to accept but would rather have taken the girl four times instead of some stupid horses, which he turns loose about the hermitage. And so he begets on Mādhavī the son Aṣṭaka, who is to become a great religious offerant and will also inherit the stud farm of moon-whites. Gālava's debt is hereby settled; before retiring to the forest he thanks off Mādhavī: "You have borne one son who is a lordly giver, a second who is a hero, another who is fond of truth and right, and yet another who is a sacrificer. Therefore go, full-hipped woman, you have saved your father with sons, you have saved four kings and myself as well, slim-waisted Mādhavī!"

Back home as a *virgo intacta,* Mādhavī deserves a *svayaṁvara.* She is driven by Yayāti and her two brothers to a hermitage at the confluence of the Ganges and Yamunā, where a huge human, semidivine, and animal throng has gathered. She passes up all suitors and instead pledges her troth to Vana 'Forest', walking off into the woods, and on a reducing diet of green grass and spring water she fasts herself down to a doelike existence, out of sight of mankind in general and men in particular.

With time thus on hold in Mādhavī's woodland nunnery, the outside world moves on. Yayāti's grandsons grow up, and he himself, after living for "many thousands" of years, passes on to heaven, where he spends further millennia in choice company, sampling assorted paradises and posthumous retirement havens. But one day he squanders his store of virtue by a fatal onset of pride: in what looks like a momentary aberration, a stray lapse of modesty, he succumbs to self-admiration and contempt for the merits of others, thereby compromising his salvation beyond repair. Indra orders him out of heaven in disgrace, his celestial friends disown and jeer him, and with garlands faded and divested of his glory he is shown the door. In his discomfiture he keeps a cool enough head to essay an earthly landing "among the good" (*satāṁ ma-*

dhye) and plots his descent by a pillar of smoke that he takes to come from a pyre of sacrifice. And rightly, for he plummets down into the midst of a *vājapeya* offered jointly by four kings, Vasumanas, Pratardana, Śibi, and Aṣṭaka. As an ancient revenant from heaven, not of human form, he introduces himself to his unknown and unknowing grandsons. At that moment a doe emerges from the woods, in whom the sons recognize their mother Mādhavī, who salutes her father and makes the introductions. These grandsons shall restore him, she declares to Yayāti, starting the contributions rolling with one-half of her own ascetic merits, to which Gālava (who also materializes out of nowhere) adds the more modest donation of one-eighth of his store of virtue, to further Yayāti's return to heaven. Next the grandsons chip in with their specialties: wealth, heroism, truth, and worship are stockpiled by these specialized paragons, and as a result their grandfather is levitated back into posthumous bliss. This vicarious reassembling of Yayāti's merits and restoration of his *tejas* are inversely parallel to the dismantling of the tripartite regal store of virtues and the loss of *xvarənah* of his Iranian congener Yama Xšaēta (cf. chap. 6).

For all its sprightly and pathetic detail, this tale has serious mythical meaning. There is nothing lewd here, since everyone is busy trying to live piously: Gālava to honor his teacher, Yayāti to observe hospitality, and Mādhavī to do her filial duty as a necessary but in the end inconsequential interlude to her true vocation of virginal purity. But in a deeper sense this phase is part of her vocation, for by the disinterested series of births she saves her father from damnation and rescues four royal lines from dynastic extinction. The overlays of egomaniacal holy men and bargaining ascetics cannot obscure the mythical kernel: the salvation and perpetuation of kings and kingship by the bodily, carnal intercession of a virgin. The remarkable feature in the Indic case is that Mādhavī is somehow extragenealogical, without explanation of how she was begotten and reared. It is as if Yayāti had thought her up as the need for grandsons arose, that he took counsel and brought her forth himself, even as Zeus swallowed Mêtis ('Counsel') and produced a virgin from his head. Just as the latter happens to be named after a place (*Athēnâ* 'Athenian'), Mādhavī seems to mean 'the Mādhava woman', an ethnic adjective derived from an eponym Madhu (there are several other women named Mādhavī in the *Mahābhārata*). And yet, because she is created so to speak ex nihilo, almost, as a Jungian would put it, as the *anima* of Yayāti's self, and has no further "dossier," such random local attachment makes little sense unless Madhu was a suppressed allonym of Yayāti himself and Mādhavī thus a hidden patronym. In the latter case the name begins to make mythological sense. **Médhu* is an ancient Indo-European *u*-stem noun denoting honey and specifically a fermented alcoholic drink (*mead*) made from it,[1] thence also 'ritual beverage' and by metonymic extension 'libation, sacrifice'. As a personified abstract noun it could secondarily mean 'Libator, Sacrificer' (cf., e.g., *Bhága*- 'Portion' > 'Apportioner').

These deliberations find support at the far western fringe of the ancient Indo-European world, in Gaul and Ireland. The man's name *Medugenus* is patronymic from **Medus* (cf. *Esugenus* from *Esus*), and there was a Gaulish goddess *Meduna* with the "augmentative" *-*no*- suffix. The Arvernian royal name *Epomeduos* reflects an **Ekwo-medhu*- with a compound-marker *-*o*-, meaning 'Horse Sacrifice[r]', similar to the Vedic princely name *Áśva-medha*- (*RV* 5.27.4–6; *médha*- 'sacrifice' < *miyédha*- 'oblation'; cf. Avestan *myazda-*, from **m*[*i*]*yas-dha*- 'satisfying', and Vedic *máyas*- 'enjoyment'). The Irish queen's name *Medb* < **Meduā* can be (like Mādhavī) a patronymic from **Medus,* or it may represent a short form of **Ekwo-medu-ā* (cf. the Irish *Bodb* beside the Gaulish *Cathu-bodua*).[2] In the latter case she ties in even onomastically with the horse mythology discussed in chapter 15, but her involvement with horses was in any event equal to her taurine fixation on the Donn of Cooley, even as Mādhavī did her considerable best to help in the acquisition of vast numbers of special equines. The traditions surrounding Mebd offer many parallels to those of Yayāti, his sons, his grandsons, and Mādhavī. While specific parts of the Yayāti legend (rejuvenation, downfall) have been seen to have at least Indo-Iranian antecedents (with reference to the Iranian Kay Us and Yama Xšaēta in chaps. 7 and 6), the total tale of Yayāti and his progeny transcends Indo-Iranian levels of comparison and goes to the heart of Indo-European kingship, even as the ancient name of the king, **rēg*-, survives only in India, in Rome, and among the Celts, the same branches that preserved

1. Vedic *mádhu* 'honey, honey drink', secondarily 'sweet beverage, soma, milk', Avestan *madu* 'berry wine', Greek *méthu* 'wine', Old Irish *mid,* Old Icelandic *mjöðr,* Old English *meodo* 'mead', Lithuanian *medùs,* Old Church Slavic *medŭ,* Tocharian *mit* 'honey'; cf. also Finnish *mete-*, Japanese *mitsu* 'honey', and the parallel term **melit*- 'honey' in Hittite *milit,* Greek *méli,* Latin *mel,* Old Irish *mil,* Gothic *milith.*

2. Medb is formally similar to the Welsh adjective *meddw* 'drunk, besotted' (< **medwo-*) derived from *medd* 'mead', literally 'meady', and is often interpreted as 'Intoxicating' or 'Drunkenness', as the dispenser of a draught that accompanies the conferral of sovereignty (such as the mead or "red ale" of Irish tradition); but her etymological roots in comparison with Mādhavī seem to go deeper.

ancient priesthoods (brahmins, flamens, druids) capable of elaborating and articulating theologies and theories of royalty.

The Irish material aptly involves the *ard-rī* of Tara, the counterpart of the Indic *samrāj,* occupying the central *cōiced* of Mide, even as Yayāti (and his designated successor Pūru) ruled the heartland as opposed to the outlying "four corners." This high king is Eochaid (short form Eochu) Feidlech, with a compound name derivable from **Ekwosāti-* 'Horse Winning' (cf. Rig-Vedic *arká-sāti-* 'gaining of light', and Indra with his *máda-* 'drunkenness' as *aśvasā́tamaḥ* 'most horse winning' in *RV* 1.175.5; the verb is seen in Old Irish *con-suī* 'try to win, strive for', Welsh *cynyddu* 'conquer, acquire'). As recounted in the *Cath Bōinde,* Eochaid son of Finn had four sons, including a set known after their grandfather as the Findeamna 'Finn Triplets' (plural of *emain* 'twin'), who on the night before they fought their own father begot on their sister a son known as Lugaid Three Red Stripes. Eochaid slew the triplets and then proscribed direct filial succession to the throne of Ireland. The fourth son, Conall, in consequence did not become high king. A second text, the *Rennes Dindshenchas,* adds interesting detail. As the sons crossed the countryside to confront their father, they were sought out at Mag Cruachan by their sister Clothru, who tearfully entreated them to relieve her childlessness. As a result they jointly begot Lugaid Red Stripes. The text somewhat enigmatically adds that Clothru acted thus to keep the brothers from gaining "truth of battle" from their father Eochaid. A big showdown the next day, which Eochaid vainly tried to postpone, resulted in thousands of deaths. When the sons' heads were delivered to the father at day's end, he decreed that no son should henceforth take the kingship of Tara in direct succession to his father. Still a third source, *Aided Medba* in the *Book of Leinster,* elaborates further. Clothru is said to have been the predecessor of Medb at Cruachan (thus in fact her anterior allomorph) and to have tried to talk her triplet brothers (with no mention of a fourth) out of attacking their father. Failing, she instead announced her fertile period and inveigled them to cohabit with her one by one, thus conceiving Lugaid Red Stripes. Then, flinging at them the accusation of incest, she enervated them and thwarted their action against their father.

The analogues to Yayāti's case are palpable: the high king has multiple sons who compromise his welfare and are in consequence consigned to the ultimate individual exile of death or the generational banishment of nonsuccession. His daughter averts his undoing by thrice-repeated carnal interventions that produce the "complete," tripartite grandson who can perpetuate him and his line: Lugaid's "three stripes" (according to the *Cōir anmann*) were in fact two, one around the neck and one around the waist, thus dividing the anatomy into three parts (head, torso, abdomen + legs). His head resembled his father Nār 'Modest', his torso took after the second triplet, Bres 'Tumult', and below the belt he was the spitting image of the third sire, Lōthar 'Trough' (i.e., 'Belly'). Not only are the names of the fathers tripartite, reminiscent of those of Cūchulainn's set of tutoresses Scāthach 'Modest', Uathach 'Terrible', and Aife 'Fair' (cf. chap. 10), but the motif recalls the Vedic Puruṣa hymn (*RV* 10.90; see chap. 17) with its anthropogonic story of caste creation (brahmins from the mouth, kṣatriyas from the arms, vaiśyas from the thighs, śūdras from the feet), or the Indic aśvamedha (chap. 15), where the sacrificial horse is anointed on the head, back, and crupper in order to yield to the royal offerant *téjas* 'majesty', *indriyám* 'force', and *páśu* 'livestock', or the Irish story of Bōand (chap. 16), whose piecemeal anatomical dismantling at the murderous well of Nechtan involved the loss of a thigh, a hand, and an eye. The one Lugaid thus comprehensively matches Yayāti's pious, truthful, brave, and opulent grandsons. The Irish version of events is sketchier, more elliptic, and less religiously tinged than its Indic counterpart. The exceptional role of the one "good" son (Conall; cf. Pūru) is not differentiated or elaborated upon and is even suppressed entirely in most texts. Eochaid needs to be rescued only once, from his aggressive brood, unlike Yayāti, who had to contend with uncooperative sons in life and to be saved posthumously from his own moral foibles. Clothru's "mission" involves one-time group incest rather than serial "sacral" prostitution, and Lugaid is more notable for his external characteristics than for any helpful actions. But the main thrust is clear: the king was threatened by his sons, his upcoming dynastic rivals, while his daughter physically bought him security and further progeny.

This daughter looms larger in Ireland than in India. Unlike Yayāti's single, mysterious virgin, the *Cath Bōinde* credits Eochaid with six female offspring. This is uncharacteristic proliferation (India normally scores infinitely higher in the numbers game), but by pruning of patent multiplication it can be drastically reduced. At least four of the daughters (Mumain, Eithne, Clothru, Medb) are said to have been given as wives to King Conchobor of Ulster, and we already saw that Clothru was a replicate of Medb. Medb is herself a type figure, for Irish tradition knows two provincially differentiated Medbs, Medb of Cruachan in Connaught (daughter of Eochaid Feidlech) and Medb Lethderg of Leinster (daughter of Conān Cualann).

Medb daughter of Eochaid bears little external character resemblance to Yayāti's self-effacing virginal Mādhavī. She is a "strong" woman, in the blatant sense, and the marrying kind. Her initial stint with Conchobor ended when "through pride of mind" she returned to her father at Tara. She was next wooed by Fidech of Connaught (cf. Fidach, name of one of the "thirds" of tripartite Connaught), who pressed his claim to be king with the high king at Tara and tried to cement it with a dynastic marriage. Another claimant, Tinde, waylaid Fidech in the Shannon valley, and in the skirmish Fidech was slain. In punishment for such murderous rivalry, the high king inflicted on Tinde *anfīr flātha* 'untruth of rule' (= removal from power; cf. "truth of battle" = military success), banished him to the wilds, and installed Medb at Cruachan "in place of a king," as a kind of satrap over unruly Connaught. This curious arrangement took root, or rather seems to have much deeper roots, because Cruachan came to figure right away as a center for royal activity in its own right, with Medb as a magnet for multiple further suitors from all over Ireland, including once again Conchobor, who waylaid and raped her as she bathed in the Boyne back home at Tara. It seems almost an afterthought that she chose to marry the exiled Tinde, who, however, soon fell in battle and was succeeded in Medb's favors by Eochaid Dāla, another petty king of a "third" of Connaught. This Eochaid had rescued Medb from military jeopardy and been chosen as king of Connaught by the nobility. But the real kingmaker was Medb, for she would agree to it only if he could marry her, and she would marry him (or anyone else) only if he was free of jealousy, fearless, and without greed (*cen ētt cen omun cen neoith*), for such was her *geis*. Eochaid Dāla qualified, but it was not to last either, for Medb grew herself a young boyfriend in Ailill, son of king Rus Ruad of Leinster, who early on was found to have neither jealousy nor fear in his heart. Eochaid Dāla had the bad taste to stoop to jealousy and was then finally dismissed and killed in battle by Ailill. Ailill figures as Medb's consort and king of Connaught in the context of the *Tāin Bō Cuailnge* and as the father of their three sons, all named Maine. Nor was this a happily-ever-after, for further legendry concerns Medb's involvement with the much-too-virile Fergus Mac Roich and the jealous husband's scheme of having the latter shot by Ailill's blind brother Lugaid during an erotic swim. As Medb herself aptly put it about her serial polygamy early in the *Tāin,* "never was I without one man by me in another's shadow."

Medb of Cruachan started out at Tara but was translated to the provinces, whereas the Leinster version of this femme fatale, Medb Lethderg ('Redside'), is presented first as a queen of Leinster, wife of Cū Corb (in the line of Ailill's father Rus Ruad) and the mother of his two children. When Cū was killed by Feidlimid Rechtaid, son of a high king of Tara, she ended up with the killer who was the father of the famous Conn Cētcathach ('Hundred Battles'). Thenceforth "exceeding great was the might and main of this Medb over Eire's menfolk, for she brooked no king at Tara unless he took her for his wife." She thus became the transgenerational mainspring of royal power at Tara, marrying in succession Conn's son Art and later Art's son Cormac. It was she, rather than dynastic filiation, that conferred and assured the succession; nor was it matrilineal descent, for she was the mother of none, merely a lateral validator who married each king rather than producing progeny. This Medb thus appears as an allomorph of Ēriu herself, as the land-goddess to whom each king of Tara was symbolically wedded in a conferral of sovereignty, less "amazonal" and less blatantly oversexed than her namesake in Connaught.

How did the Irish counterpart of the holy virgin Mādhavī end up like this? Neither she nor the Medbs was "motherly," and childbearing was merely a technical duty to Mādhavī and incidental to the Medbs. But even the Welsh Math's foot maiden shows that the king needed a virgin to keep him safe and warm, not a browbeating harridan who outranked him and tested his immunity to jealousy. In short, Irish tradition has suffered a perversion of the protomyth. The king as the regal "complete man" needed to be magnanimous, valiant, and generous. The first requirement could be violated by excessive possessiveness in the field of power, by fear of rivals, paranoia about competition, and the like, all inducements to obsessive and erratic use of prerogative. Irish myth has redefined this aspect as debased to jealousy in the sexual sphere. It has also recast the virginal component, not so much as chastity versus promiscuity or asceticism versus sensuality as in terms of "power": virginity is in essence a holding back of potential, of procreative (and by extension salvational) storage, but the Irish Medbs operate instead by sexual squander. The reason seems to be that two mythic themes have been crossbred here: one is the salvation of the king by a maiden, the other the validation of kingship by the transfunctional goddess. Because of the leveling of divine and human strata in Irish myth, the latter theme came to connote actual sexual mating and invaded the former, while in other cultures intercourse with a goddess is rarer and usually not very healthy for the mortal man (e.g., Purūravas, Anchises). Thus behind the Medbs there lurks not only the virgin Mādhavī but a fortiori the strong goddess Ēriu who has usurped the myth, the conferror of Flāith 'Dominion' and herself its personification. In Irish legendry she tends to appear disguised as an old hag (even Grāinne in the Fenian tradition meant 'Ugliness'), as in the story of Niall, who alone of several brothers had the fortitude to kiss an ancient sorceress and saw her change into a radiant beauty who revealed herself as Flāith and pronounced him king of Tara. The similar tale of the sons of Dāire tells of a prophecy that his son Lugaid would be king of Ireland. To better the odds he named each of his five sons Lugaid (a common name, borne above by Clothru's striped son and Ailill's blind brother). At a horse race a druid told Dāire that the lucky candidate would have to catch a fawn with a golden fleece. When the animal appeared and was pursued, the five Lugaids were sheltered by a magic mist, and one of them, Lugaid Lāigde, caught the fawn. Surprised by a snowfall, the brothers made their way one by one to a well-appointed hut where a repulsive hag offered board and especially bed and intimacy. Only the last brother, Lugaid Lāigde, took her up on everything and saw her change into glorious Flāith in his arms. Obviously in this conflation of myths the doe Mādhavī has her Irish counterpart in the fawn of Flāith. Unlike Ireland, India kept Mādhavī "pure," distinct from the transfunctional goddess in her various manifestations, be they Sarasvatī or Śrī-Lakṣmī or her epic incarnation as the polyandrous Draupadī.

If the Irish traditions are elaborate, conflated, transmuted, and confused, those of Rome and Scandinavia are by contrast straightforward but fragmentary and elliptic. In piecemeal fashion they do retain the tradition of rulerish dependence on virginal females. In Roman legend, Numitor of Alba Longa was divested of his kingship and restored at long last only after his virginal daughter Rhea Silvia had miraculously conceived and borne the "complete" grandson Romulus, begotten by Mars, having Jupiter as a mentor, and turning into Quirinus. Long after the end of kingship, republican Rome still had the Regia (domus) in the Forum that housed the offices of the pontifex maximus. This old royal palace continued to reflect in its layout and religious function the ancient character of the king as the embodiment of the social and sacral totality, even as the pontifex, who had inherited most of the religious roles of the king, still did in contrast to the specialized flamines. In the main part, the cult of Jupiter was attended to by the flaminica dialis. But there were also two secret chapels, *sacraria,* dedicated to Mars and to Ops. The first contained the sacred shields and spear of Mars, which a commander-in-chief was allowed to visit and touch on investiture, while pronouncing the words "Mars vigila!" Otherwise the cult of Mars in the Regia was in the hands of the Salian Virgins, dressed like warriors. The chapel of Ops was accessible only to the Vestal Virgins and to the sacerdos publicus, that is, the pontifex maximus, who in this instance acted in succession to the obsolete *rex,* even as the *imperator* did in assuming military command. Once a year the Vestals are reported to have approached the *rex* with the words "Vigilasne rex? Vigila!" which Vergil paraphrased in *Aeneid* 10.228–29: *Vigilasne, deum gens, Aenea? Vigila!* Watchfulness was clearly the ritualistic watchword of the royal wardens of military preparedness and stored-up harvest alike, and these day-to-day guardians were virginal women, themselves symbolic reservoirs of untapped, ripe, stockpiled human potential. Thus the cults of all three levels of deity in the onetime house of the king were in the hands of women, of the wifely high priestess for the day-to-day affairs of the king of gods, and of two virginal orders for those spheres of life where readiness, timeliness, ripeness, and seasonality were of the essence. The king had departed, but his female/virginal support structure stayed in place, in typical tribute to Roman religious conservatism.

Unlike such ritual survivals in Rome, the Scandinavian remnants, chiefly in Snorri, pertain to myth and saga. According to Loki's astute observation, virgins were few and far between in Āsgarðr, but when found they were strictly in the service of the divine king Odin. His auxiliary corps of Valkyries was (in Saxo's term) composed of *virgines,* apart from such sporadic lapsed specimens as Brynhildr; these helpmates were crucial to his recruitment of *einherjar* and hence to his grand design of eschatological salvation. As mentioned in chapter 11, two goddesses are characterized as virgins by Snorri. One is Fulla, quite literally 'Plenty, Ops', not one of the Vanir as one might expect but an associate of Odin and Frigg, and something of a lady-in-waiting to Odin's consort (carrying her box, caring for her shoes, sharing her secrets). When Hermōðr went to Hel, Baldr sent back precious gifts to Odin, Frigg, and Fulla. The other one, more directly tied to Odin, is Gefjon, whom Snorri calls a virgin goddess served by women who die unmarried. Her euhemerized myth is told both at the beginning of the *Prose Edda* and in chapter 5 of the *Ynglinga Saga:* When Odin, on his way from Asia to Scandinavia, arrived at the Danish straits, he sent

Gefjon ahead to king Gylfi in Sweden to ask for land. He granted her all that four oxen could plow in a day and a night. She then went to Giantland, had a giant father four sons on her, turned these into oxen, yoked them to a plow, and in twenty-four hours managed to slice off a piece of Gylfi's kingdom, which became the Danish island of Zealand (where Copenhagen is situated), Odin's first possession on his way to the conquest of Sweden. Thus Gefjon physically and physiologically secured Odin his dominion. Here once more the similarity to Yayāti and Mādhavī is striking. The four sons of Gefjon are not differentiated, but with Odin's three types of virginal helpmates they add up to the same kind of transfunctional, tripartite set of assets as was stockpiled by Mādhavī and her four sons: Fulla as the "rich," the Valkyries as "valiant," and Gefjon with her sons as consecrators, validators of the king by bodily procurement of his realm. Clearly an Indo-European myth lies at the base of such notable parallel traditions.

Recommended Reading

Dumézil, Georges. *The Destiny of a King*. Translated by Alf Hiltebeitel. Chicago: University of Chicago Press, 1973.

15 · Horse and Ruler

Diverse layers of mythic equinity have flitted by in the preceding chapters. On the level of name giving alone there are the Indic, Iranian, Greek, and Celtic types Bṛhádaśva 'Big Horse' and Áśvamedha 'Horse Sacrifice[r]', Vištāspa 'Ready Horse' and Kṛsāspa 'Lean Horse', Agáthippos 'Good Horse' and Hippónīkos 'Horse Win[ner]' (which Aristophanes parodied into Hippóbīnos 'Horse Fucker'), Eochaid 'Horse Win[ning]' and Epomeduos 'Horse Sacrifice[r]'. Some of these are ostensibly "possessive" compounds ("having such-and-such a horse"), but in onomastic usage the line gets blurred, even as "Crazy Horse" hardly evokes the proud owner of a deranged equine. In Germanic tradition the brothers Hengist and Horsa, leaders of the Anglo-Saxon invasion of England, had names meaning 'Stallion' and 'Horse'. Hippomorphism of the divine twins is sometimes patent, from the Vedic Aśvins begotten by the stallion Vivasvat on the mare Saraṇyū (chap. 4) to the Dioskouroi as the "white colts of Zeus" (chap. 8). Alternatively those twins are merely 'horsey' (*aśvín-*) or 'well horsed' (*eúippoi*), even as the Latvian Dieva dēli were horsemen, and one of the pair is especially horse related (Kastor *hippódamos,* Nakula as horse groom). The Arcadian mating of Poseidon Híppios with Demeter Erīnȳ́s produced the horse Areion, and Kentauros split the man : horse difference in the wake of a mating of Ixion and Nephele, with both pairings reminiscent of the doings of Vivasvat and Saraṇyū (cf. chaps. 8 and 4). Poseidon and Medusa engendered the winged Pegasos whom Bellerophontes rode against the Khimaira, and Loki, in a twofold feat of metamorphosis, coupled with a stallion and bore Odin's eight-legged gray death mount Sleipnir (chap. 11). The death connection of horses is patent in Greece (Hades being "famous for colts"). The wind Zephyros sired on the Harpy Podárgē 'Swiftfoot' Achilles' talking horses Xánthos and Balíos, and Xanthos miraculously foretold the hero's impending doom (*Iliad* 19.408–18). The oracular horses kept in West Slavic sanctuaries, without benefit of speech, served for divination by stepping over spears. Their colors (white at Arcona, black at Stettin), coupled with those of Xanthos 'Bay[ard]' and Balios 'Dappled, Piebald', cover just about every shade of horse and frustrate any match-up with function, for example, by specifying white coursers, bay steeds, and grays or blacks for oracle horse, war-horse, and workhorse (or death mount), respectively. I shall attempt rather to extract Indo-European equine tradition from a systematic study of rituals, hoping it will prove to be a horse of a different color.

The horse figures as a race animal in the Roman Equirria, which I compared in chapter 9 to the Indic vājapeya. There was color symbolism in those chariot races, not however of the animals but of the drivers (prefiguring the red-white-green of Italy). Presumably such events preserved atavistic traces of the millennial wheeled expansions and land rushes that were essential to the Indo-European migrations, where the horse chariot outperformed the oxcart (the horse was not yet much of a riding animal). But the horse was also important as the victim of a great sacrificial ritual. Horse sacrifice stands apart from other animal offerings, it is in a class by itself, homologous with the immolation of human beings rather than beasts, with close ties to regal consecration and consolidation. Here again India supplies a profuse matrix, Rome contributes a ritual petrifact, and Ireland affords a seemingly "perverse" variant. A triangulation of these three strands provides ample scope for speculative reconstruction.

The centerpiece of this triptych is the well-documented and much-studied Indic aśvamedha ritual. It is exceedingly well endowed with descriptive and exegetic matter, starting with the *Rig-Veda* (1.162, 163) and stretching through many Vedic texts (especially the *Śatapatha Brāhmaṇa* and numerous *Sūtras* of the *Yajur-Veda*) down to Yudhiṣṭhira's great ritual in book 14 of the *Mahābhārata* (*Āśvamedhikaparvan*). The aśvamedha is a production with a cast of thousands, incorporating many ancillary rites and representing in a sense the sum of Indic sacrificial pageantry. The central proceedings may be summarized as follows:

The start was made in the spring, with the king as patron and the four main priests as officiators. During the preliminary celebrations the king had to spend the night chastely with his favorite wife by the *gārhapatya* or domestic fire. A prize stallion was selected as the prospective victim and subjected to a number of ceremonies, including sprinkling in a pool, at which time a dog was killed and thrown under it. The stallion was then set free to roam, accompanied by a hundred gelded or aged horses and four hundred young men of different castes who were to guide it toward the northeast and keep it from contact with mares and from further immersion in water. This roaming took a whole year, and meanwhile preparations were made back at the ranch. A huge fire altar went up, the king underwent fasting and other observances, a new hearth was built for the domestic fire, and a large store of soma was stockpiled. The main ritual took three days. On the principal, second day of sacrifice the king drove in a war chariot drawn by the stallion and three other horses. The victim was anointed by the king's three foremost wives, and its mane and tail were adorned with pearls. The sacrifice took place at twenty-one stakes, the three principal victims being the stallion, a hornless ram, and a he-goat. All together hundreds of victims were prescribed, but the wild animals among them were released rather than killed. The stallion was smothered to death, whereupon the principal queen symbolically cohabited with it under covers, while the entourage engaged in obscene banter. Then followed the cutting up of the victim, disposal of the parts, further blood sacrifices, ablutions, and disbursement of priestly honoraria.

In the *Śatapatha Brāhmaṇa* and in several sūtras the aśvamedha description is accompanied by what amounts to its summary replication in the form of human sacrifice. This *puruṣamedha* involved purchasing a brahmin or kṣatriya victim from his family for a thousand cows and a hundred horses. After initial rites he was set free for a year and was indulged in everything except sex. The ritual itself took five days. The victim was adorned and throttled on the second day much like the horse, together with a hornless ram and a he-goat. The liturgy was taken mostly from the Puruṣa hymn (*RV* 10.90) and the funeral hymns in *RV* 10. The queen had intercourse with the dying or dead victim. Rather than a menagerie, an accompanying human massacre was prescribed, reaching into the hundreds.

What was the relationship of these two rituals? Some have seen in the puruṣamedha a figmental parallel to the aśvamedha, thus disclaiming its historical reality. It is evident that to the brāhmanic and sūtric compilers the puruṣamedha was a somewhat unreal appendage to the horse sacrifice, almost a theoretical afterthought. In epic and classical literature there is no instance of its performance, except for the preposterous statement in book I of the *Mahābhārata* that Ayutanāyin performed ten thousand puruṣamedhas. It was thus at best obsolete, at worst unreal. A case for its historicity would be as a onetime practical means of begetting a royal heir when the king for some reason was unable to do so. Medical evidence for reflex-caused tumescence and seminal emission in the course of hanging and decapitation would match the circumstances of the cohabitation of the queen and the victim. The aśvamedha would then look like a symbolic substitute. Yet matters are not so simple, for in the aśvamedha the king is triumphantly in charge, as dedicant to Prajāpati, and the whole performance is guaranteed to make him victorious, sinless, happy, and glorious. Even though occasionally childlessness propels an aśvamedha, as with King Daśaratha in book I of the *Rāmāyaṇa,* the cohabitation part starring the queen is somehow extraneous to the central concept. In short, a "hardheaded" practical view of the puruṣamedha, with the aśvamedha as its mere attenuation, cannot do justice to the origin and development of the latter.

Let us turn now to one of the side panels of the "triptych." As pieced together from Polybius, Plutarch, Festus, and Paulus Diaconus, the Roman October Equus may be summarized as follows: After a horserace on the Campus Martius on the Ides of October, the right-side horse of the victorious chariot was sacrificed to Mars by being killed with a spear. The people of Suburra and of the Sacra Via fought over the horse's head; if the former caught it, they fixed it on the wall of the Turris Mamilia; if the latter, on that of the Regia. The tail was raced to the Regia, and drops of blood from it were sprinkled on its hearth.

There are important differences from the aśvamedha, notably the manner of killing. But there are also broad similarities, for example, the dedication to Mars in Rome and the clear anteriority of Indra to Prajāpati as the onetime recipient of the aśvamedha. There are further specific accordances of the curious type that tends to exclude chance, such as the singling out of *equus bigarum victricum dexterior* 'the right-hand horse of the winning team' in Rome and the Indic injunction that the aśvamedha victim must "excel on the right part of the yoke," or the role of the horse's tail in both rituals.

A similar singularity is described by Dio Cassius (43.24.2–4). After a mutiny of troops in Rome in 46 B.C.E., Caesar had one ringleader summarily executed. Two others were ritually killed on the Campus Martius by the pontifices and the flamen martialis, and their heads were deposited in the Regia. It appears that in preparation for restoring the monarchy, Caesar with his antiquarian instincts was reviving an obsolete ritual of human sacrifice that was a replication of the October Equus. It places the relationship of aśvamedha and puruṣamedha in a truer light by indicating that in an Indo-European warrior-class horse sacrifice substituting a human victim for the horse was possible. Thus the horse sacrifice was not a toning down of the human sacrifice; rather, the human victim reflected an exceptional escalation of the practice.

Now for the other side panel. It is best subsumed in the words of the outraged Gerald of Cambrai in his *Topographia Hibernica* (ca. 1185 C.E.), describing something scandalous that was allegedly consummated in the full Middle Ages in the Irish hinterland:

> There is in a northern and remote part of Ulster, among the Kenelcunil, a certain tribe that is wont to install a king over itself by an excessively savage and abominable ritual. In the presence of all the people of this land in one place, a white mare is brought into their midst. Thereupon he who is to be elevated, not to a prince but to a beast, not to a king but to an outlaw, publicly proceeds to bestiality, and with impudence matching foolishness makes profession that he too is a beast. Right thereafter the mare is killed and boiled piecemeal in water, and in the same water a bath is prepared for him. He gets into the bath and eats of the flesh that is brought to him, with his people standing around and sharing it with him. He also imbibes the broth in which he is bathed, not from any vessel, nor with his hand, but only with his mouth. When this is done right according to such unrighteous ritual, his rule and sovereignty are consecrated.

To summarize, the horse sacrifice was a regal consolidation ceremony in India, one that turned a *rāj-* into a *samrāj-*; it is sometimes a little difficult to differentiate in purpose from a rājasūya or royal installation, for the aims of the two could become telescoped, as when Yudhiṣṭhira became *samrāj-* by virtue of his coronation early in the *Mahābhārata* but was reconsecrated with an aśvamedha after the great showdown. In tradition if not in practice, the aśvamedha could be "upgraded" to a puruṣamedha. In Rome the October Equus culminated in the Regia, and a *rex* in-spe was capable of exhuming and implementing its emergency martial law allomorph of human sacrifice. The Irish rite installed and consecrated a king, but there is no visible parallel of human sacrifice (yet the heads of his rebellious sons were delivered to the high king [*ard-rī*] Eochaid; see chap. 14). On the other hand the aśvamedha and puruṣamedha involved coition between the queen and the smothered male victim, and the royal initiate in Ulster cohabited with a live sacrificial mare, whereas the October Equus was decidedly non-erotic. Pudency alone cannot account for the absence of this trait in Rome, for the foundation myth of the Lupercalia (which was compared in chap. 9 to the Indic rājasūya) let copulation thrive as a sacred he-goat was enjoined by divine revelation to penetrate the women of Italy. The October Equus did have connotations of fecundity, being performed *ob frugum eventum* 'on account of successful harvest', and its tail may have involved vegetal symbolism, even as grain sprouted from the wound and tail of the dying bull in Mithraic cult scenes (see chap. 6). But even as to Freud a cigar occasionally was just a cigar, the tail of the October Equus actually was the tail, despite attempts to see in it a euphemism or "attenuation" for the phallus.[1]

The main divergence within the coitional parallel uniting India and Ireland involves the discrepancy of queen and stallion versus king and mare. Mindful of the Irish situation in chapter 14, one might suspect that Ireland is once again innovative here, but this is by no means evident. There is ample reason to suspect a hierogamous mating as the mythical underpinnings of the horse sacrifice. The nature of this mating seems best discernible in the Celtic tradition and involves a representative of the warrior class with the transfunctional goddess figure. As we saw in chapter 10, this figure is preeminent, and in several varieties. The Gaulish Terra Mater and the triad of Matres or Matrae or Matronae are matched in insular tradition by the divine ancestress Irish Danu, Welsh Dōn, and especially by the goddess Ēriu, with whom every king of Tara was symbolically wedded in a conferral of sovereignty. This goddess has manifold horse-related features. The Gaulish Epona (Regina) of mostly iconographic fame, riding or surrounded by horses, and her legendary *Mabinogi* counterpart Rhiannon are suspect of original hippomorphism. The equine associations of Medb were dealt with in chapter 14. The Irish Macha or Ulster, or rather the three so-named figures, is a textbook case of a female deity in triple manifestation. She is found chiefly in the story of the "childbed sickness" of the Ulstermen and in the *Rennes Dindshenchas*. The First Macha was a prophetess and wife of Nemed, a druidic figure connected with the word for "shrine."

1. Even the argument that a severed horse's tail (unlike the penis) was not viscous enough to retain enough blood for sprinkling during the scant thousand-meter race from the Campus Martius to the Regia has been put to rest by tests in the abattoirs of Paris. Cf. Georges Dumézil, *Fêtes romaines d'été et d'automne* (Paris: Gallimard, 1975), pp. 183–87.

The Second Macha was the daughter of Aed Ruad ('The Red'), herself called Mongruad 'Red Mane'. Her father had contracted a triumvirate with two other kings, that each should reign supreme for seven years. On Aed's death Macha claimed for herself his due term of sovereignty and made her claim stick by force of arms. Unlike this amazonal daughter, the Third Macha, wife of Crunniuc, was forced by King Conchobor to race against horses while in the last stages of pregnancy. She won, then immediately gave birth to twins and died uttering a curse on the Ulstermen that led to their annual couvadelike debility.

Among the varied reflections of the transfunctional goddess as the embodiment of dominion, the Third Macha is conspicuous for having outrun horses and borne twins. It may be that a cult myth somewhat resembling that of Vivasvat and Saraṇyū in India, involving hippomorphous flight, copulation, and gestation of twins, belonged to the original inventory of this goddess and hence remained part of the mystique of the Irish Flāith. It was acted out in ritual form in the ceremony of royal installation, with the mare symbolizing the hippomorphous Flāith. Before the monkish Gerald was through with this material, it had deteriorated to bestial abomination, much as Pasiphae's sacral mating with the Cretan bull received bad notices on the Greek mainland (see chap. 8). That the king "made profession of being a beast" may retain a hint of an actual ritual utterance on the lines of "I am **ekwos,* thou art **ekwā,*" recalling the Vedic marriage formula *amo aham asmi sā tvam* 'I am he, thou art she'. In this way the eminence of the transfunctional goddess in Irish sovereignty lore in a sense fossilized the primitive cult myth covering regal consolidation via horse sacrifice.

Accordingly it is India that has innovated in this instance. The reason may be that the aśvamedha has been cut adrift from the myth that once underwrote its significance. In compulsive ancient Rome this was no serious matter, for ritual petrifacts were readily perpetuated there in a vacuum. But the aśvamedha must have floundered, ever since at some point its prototype ceased to depict the ritual union of the king and the transfunctional goddess, owing probably to a downgrading of the goddess (Sarasvatī had paled badly by Vedic times). The king's role as the patron of a sexually tinged horse festival persisted, but the detail was elaborated with the development of new religious typology and incorporated instead a ritual union of queen or goddess and male animal. The Indo-European pattern of theriomorphic hierogamy was clearly King and Mare, the Near Eastern and Mediterranean one Queen and Beast (e.g., Europa, Pasiphae, and the wife of Archon Basileus copulating with bulls; the Roman women ordered to cohabit with Faunus's he-goat). The aśvamedha is thus a halfway house of transformation, keeping the horse but reversing the sexes of the hierogamic actors.

The ritual enactment of the horse sacrifice redounded to the weal of the canonically constituted total society, as subsumed in the priestly whisperings into the ear of the victim during the preparatory ceremonies: blessings were to accrue successively to priesthood (*brahman*), royalty (*rāṣṭram*), cow, ox, horse, woman, chariot fighter, and youth. Similarly in *RV* 1.162.22 the aśvamedha is to yield fine cattle and horses, male progeny, all-nourishing wealth, freedom from sin, and *kṣatrám* or sovereign power. These comprehensive lists resemble Italic formulas such as the Umbrian *nerf arsmo ueiro pequo castruo frif* 'heroes, priesthood, men [and] cattle, fields [and] fruits'. It is highly likely that such pandemic rosters played an ancient part in Italic lore and belonged to the ritual that we still imperfectly glimpse in the October Equus. The across-the-board benefit of the Irish rite is implicit in the "total" attendance and the transfunctional essence of Flāith herself.

Hence the horse sacrifice did for the Indic *rāj-* and the onetime Roman *rēx* what mating with the tripartite Flāith in mare form accomplished for the Irish *rī:* making him the transfunctional sovereign, the "complete man." India inverted the coitional part of the rite, thereby reducing it to ancillary and incidental status; Rome suppressed it, rendering the equine's gender immaterial, while Ireland kept it intact.

Horse sacrifice is known widely in the Eurasian orbit and elsewhere, for example, among the Turkic peoples of Central Asia and Siberia. It often involves a stallion whose phallus plays a role in the ritual, as it does in the Old Norse Völsi tradition (see chap. 12). That in Indo-European tradition the basic myth-sanctioned pattern was rather Man and Mare is made likely also by the Hittite Law Code. Unlike the sweeping injunction against bestiality in sources such as *Lev.* 20:15, the Hittite code expressly exempts from punishment men having intercourse with (presumably female) horses or mules, after sternly meting out capital punishment for such behavior with cattle, sheep, and swine. The only reservation is that the perpetrator "does not become priest," which seems to anchor the practice squarely in the warrior class, that is, among potential candidates for kingship. In this manner a mutually reinforcing study of myth, ritual, and law relating to horses can spread further light on the foundations of Indo-European kingship.

16 · Fire in Water

Fire and water are archetypally antithetical in the physical world and in human perception alike. In the former their incompatibility is relentless, but in the mind of mythopoeic man it has created its own dialectic of conflict resolution that is reflected in ancient tradition. Fire and ice/water were both present in Norse cosmogony and eschatology alike. "Fire in water" is a theme that recurs in Indo-Iranian, Irish, and Roman lore, in a complex mythologem of clear Indo-European relevance.

Central to this theme is the Indo-Iranian deity attested in Vedic as Apā́m Nápāt and in Avestan as Apam Napāt. In Chapters 4 and 6 these names were rendered as 'Offspring of the Waters', but the Indo-European kinship term **nep(ō)t-* is actually both more specific and more ambiguous, denoting either grandchild or nephew/niece, and specifically 'daughter's child' or 'sister's child' (as still in Old Irish, where *niae* is 'sister's son', versus *macc brāthar* for 'nephew' as the son of a brother). This skewing of generations, observable in early Indo-European kinship systems, extends to terms for 'daughter's husband' matching 'sister's husband' (e.g., Greek *gambrós,* Latin *gener*), and likewise upward to 'mother's father' (Latin *avus*) on a terminological par with 'mother's brother' (Latin *avunculus*). In saga **népōt-* was clearly important to a king: **népōtes* included Manushchihr for Iraj (chap. 7), the four grandsons for Yayāti, Lugaid for Eochaid, and Romulus for Numitor (chap. 14). Yet this has reference to a male ego in dynastic context. It is less obvious what exact relationship is implied by "*Nápāt-* of the Waters" (the latter being vague plural feminine deities); the nearest parallel is *Divó nápātā* 'Twin *Nápāt-* of Dyaus' as an allonym of the Aśvins (chap. 4). In Vedic lyricism the Waters are occasionally referred to as "mothering" or fondling Apām Napāt, but there is no clear-cut or even approximate maternity. The expression *apā́m nápāt* resembles above all such figurative, pleonastic, stylistic patro- and metronymy as, for example, *RV* 1.58.8: *sūno sahaso . . . Agne . . . ūrjo napāt* 'son of might, Agni, *nápāt*— of strength'. 'Son of strength' is simply 'strongman', even as 'son of man' is 'man', and Seljaninovič of the bylinas is simply 'Peasant' (chap. 12). Even so Pūṣan is called *vimuco napāt* (*RV* 1.42.1, 6.55.1), literally '*nápāt*- of unharnessing', synonymous with his epithet *vimocana* 'unharnesser' (*RV* 8.4.15, 16). The one difference is that Apām Napāt (rarely Napāt Apām, *RV* 1.122.4, 1.186.5, 5.41.10) is of Indo-Iranian date and thus not merely a feature of Vedic poetic diction. Rather than being a pleonasm for Āptya 'Watery One', it denotes "*Nápāt*- of (i.e., residing among) the Waters." Proximity, intimacy, kinship are implied, not necessarily filiation. Such a mythic feel for *coincidentia oppositorum* also animated Norse skalds like Thjodolf, who in his ninth-century *Ynglingatāl* used the kenning *sävar niðr* for 'fire', literally 'kin of the sea', where *niðr* is cognate either with Gothic *nithjis,* Sanskrit *nítya*- 'relative' or with Avestan *naptya*- 'offspring'.

The Vedic god has no obvious myth, but his characteristics, gleaned from the hymns and summarized in chapter 4, mark him as a fiery deity immersed and inherent in watery depths, giving off light and lightning without visible energy source, and as a power that needs to be ritually placated for proper utilization of waters. In this instance Iran contributes the story. *Yašt* 19 of the *Avesta,* celebrating the Xvarənah as the luminous and fiery hallmark of the duly elect king of Iran, tells of a mythical time when it became a pawn in the tug-of-war between the poles of Zoroastrian dualism (Spənta Mainyu and Angra Mainyu), in the course of which it withdrew from the fray in the direction of the mythical Lake Vourukaša. At that point Apam Napāt seized the xvarənah and deposited it in the safety of the waters of the lake. Ahuramazda thereupon declared open season on the xvarənah as a legitimate goal of striving by qualified humans, holding out sacerdotal, pastoral, and martial rewards. The first pretender, the Turanian Franrasyan, made three nude dives in an attempt to reach the xvarənah, but his efforts were doomed in advance, since it was by definition attainable only by the *airya* and was out of bounds to aliens. Thus the Turanian was forced to desist, but each time he tried the xvarənah recoiled from his grasp and fled in the opposite direction, creating an outflow from the lake. Various rivers were brought about, and one river, Haētumant, still contains the escaped xvarənah; it empties into the mythical lake, which is thus the beginning and end of earthly watercourses.

In Irish tradition, especially the *Dindshenchas,* Nechtan of the Tūatha Dē Danann had a secret well that only he and his three cupbearers could approach with impunity; all others would suffer bursting of the eyes, apparently because of some deadly source of heat or light in the well. Nechtan's wife Bōand once approached the well, either hybristically to disprove the tabu by the force of her beauty or hoping to cleanse herself of her adultery with Dagda, who had fathered Oengus on her. She circled the well counterclockwise three times, upon which three waves rose from the well and broke over her, severing a thigh, a hand, and an eye. Mutilated, Bōand fled with the water pursuing her, creating a river in her wake, until she drowned in its estuary by the sea. This river (the Boyne), which bears her name, then took a submarine and subterranean course, reemerging to form many of the world's great rivers, only to return in the end to Nechtan's mound.

Along with minor differences, a set of common denominators emerges: A deity hoards a fiery and effulgent power immersed in a body of water. His trust is challenged by one who is inherently unqualified to possess this treasure and may in addition have had truck with falsehood (in either a religious or a veridical sense). Three rounds of approach by the usurper result in three countermeasures, either retreats or attacks; in either instance, whether fleeing or pursuing, the advancing waters with their inherent fiery power create a watercourse or courses that after a worldwide circulation revert to their mythical source.

This is a remarkably complex mythologem of extreme east/western distribution. What is more, a reconstruction **Neptonos* for Nechtan (cf. Old Irish *necht* 'niece') provides an onomastic match with the Indo-Iranian *Nap(ā)t-* and brings up the relevance of the Roman god of waters, *Neptūnus* (analogy of *Portūnus*). Evidently in the West a short form of the name without the qualifier prevailed (cf. other "bare" Celtic kinship terms with the "augmentative" suffix serving as theonyms: Gaulish *Matrona*, *Maponos*, *Bratronos*, Welsh *Modron*, *Mabon*). The same trait may have prevailed in later Iran, judging from Greek *Nápas* (glossed by the lexicographer Hesychius as "an oil-producing well in the mountains of Persia") and the borrowed Greek term *náphtha* (cf. Avestan *naptya-*) that we still use for the quintessential flammable liquid substance. Perhaps oil seepage and oil flares on the Caspian shores were not unknown to the Indo-European protohabitat. Fire in water was mythically embodied by the **Nep(ō)t-* of the waters, and the theonym could yield mundane terminology as well.

Rome, too, has preserved a corresponding Neptūnus myth in saga shape in the legend of the prodigy of the Lacus Albanus, as told by Livy (book 5), Plutarch (*Camillus*), Dionysius of Halicarnassus (book 12), Cicero (*De divinatione*), Valerius Maximus, and Zonaras (using Dio Cassius). In the tenth year of the war against Veii, just before Camillus took successful charge of it, the deep crater lake, which is fed only by underwater springs, suddenly rose during the dry season to the very rim of the surrounding mountains (at least a hundred meters above its normal level). According to Dionysius the time was around the rising of the dog star (about 23 July), while to Plutarch it was autumn. Dionysius's early date is more probable, for Plutarch carelessly even places the October Equus on the Ides of December. According to both authors, the swollen lake finally breached the mountain barrier and caused extensive damage in the surrounding countryside. Livy and Valerius Maximus downplay the overflow aspect, while Plutarch and Zonaras tell of waters moving in the direction of the sea.

To ascertain the causes of divine anger that must underlie the prodigy, the Romans sent a delegation to Delphi for oracular advice and also caught an Etruscan soothsayer from whom their interrogation specialists obtained divinatory data (thus in all sources except Cicero, who mentions only the Etruscan). The responses on the whole confirm and sometimes expand one another. The Romans were warned that if the waters were allowed to run wild and reach the sea, Veii would be impregnable (and in consequence a future menace to Rome). To conquer Veii, the Romans must divert the overflow away from the sea into the countryside, where it would be ritually harmless and practically useful for irrigation. Plutarch's and Livy's responses also stress cultic irregularities in the surrounding mountains as the cause of supernatural wrath.

That this is a lost cult myth of Neptūnus is clinched by the fact that 23 July was the festival of Neptunalia in the Roman calendar, an occasion of which little detail is otherwise known. The prodigy occurring on that date is a saga reminiscence of its erstwhile mythic attachment to the feast of Neptūnus. The entire Veian involvement is an obvious consequence of the myth's "historicization" as part of the Veian war, Veii being situated on the opposite side of Rome and in no other way connected with the Alban Lake.

The outline of the myth in Rome casts the Romans themselves as the "usurpers" of the divine powers of the Lacus Albanus, in the guise of their sacrilegious officialdom. As a consequence the lake overflows, running wild to the sea and threatening Rome's survival. Rome manages to expiate the prodigy and to obviate the danger by a combination of ritualistic and engineering procedures (paying reparations and digging channels). This concern for humoring the deity and keeping the waters usable is reminiscent of the Rig-Vedic propitiation of Apām Napāt.

Yet this reconstructed Roman myth differs in several respects from the Iranian-Irish prototype. Neptūnus may be the Lord of the Lake, but there is no reference to fiery powers in his Alban demesne (an extinct volcanic crater). The only radiation-related feature is a seasonal one, blazing summer heat that threatens the water supply itself and thus affects all potential users alike. The Romans are in violation of cults in the hills rather than explicitly of Neptūnus's watery domain. The Romans are not inherently unworthy of possessing the divine favor, they are merely in temporary and remediable default. There are no "three rounds" of anything, and no permanent creation of rivers by the waters, only of irrigation works by the Romans themselves.

The first discrepancy is the most serious. The postulated protomyth involves the **nep(ō)t-* of waters hoarding fire in water, but there is no apparent mention of this in the Roman version, not even a tidal wave, merely a quiet rise and overflow. By contrast the xvarənah was by definition 'solar matter' (< **swelnos*), and Nechtan's well had a murderous radiation in it, both being intrinsic to the body of water itself, as was the Vedic Apām Napāt with his *súar* 'solar element' (*RV* 2.35.6), etymologically cognate with *xvarənah*. The Roman synchronization of the onset of atmospheric canicular solar scorching with the lake's abnormal behavior might at best be an ancillary variant of the protomyth (the eruption being prone to occur as the deity's effulgent powers are being recharged by infusion of solar radiation). But more probably it embodies local climatological accretions in a Mediterranean ambience, expressive of a seasonal crisis in the water-distribution system, which underlines the importance of keeping the deity appeased (logically sun heat should make the lake shrink rather than swell, hence the "prodigy" notion of the demythologized version).

There may, however, be a hint that the Roman myth, before it became attached to pseudohistoric lore, before it was even geographically localized in the topography of Latium, knew of the fiery power inherent in a mythical lake. All the pretended "oracular" (Delphic) and "divinatory" (Etruscan) advice cannot hide the fact that we are dealing with a purely Roman *procuratio* of a prodigy, thus a ritual procedure of a native kind. We might therefore look for formulaic petrifacts relevant to the erstwhile Roman myth. The "Delphic oracle" in Livy (5.16.9–11) is in fact an ancient versified formula in the indigenous Saturnian meter, as betrayed by its rhythmic and alliterative features:

> Romane, aquam Albanam cave lacu contineri,
> cave in mare manare suo flumine sinas.
> Emissam per agros rigabis dissipatamque
> rivis exstingues
>
> Roman, beware of keeping the Alban water confined in the lake,
> beware of letting it flow by its own stream into the sea.
> You shall send it out through the fields to water them;
> you shall scatter it in channels and put it out.

The oracle proceeds to promise victory against Veii and urges resumption of neglected rites once the war is concluded. But the quoted part is self-contained and may well provide the general *procuratio* recipe for the event as it occurred in mythic rather than pseudohistorical time. What it says is that, once "the heat from the lake is on," it is futile to restrain the outflow and dangerous to let it run wild. Instead it has to be "defused," and the safety valve of irrigational diversion will effectively "put it out."

Aquam . . . exstingues is a unique expression in Livy, who elsewhere uses this verb only to mean 'put out [fire]', or figuratively 'stamp out, quash, suppress'. Only in late classical Latin do we find *exstinguere* used as a technical term for 'dry up', in imitation of the Greek verb *sbes-* meaning both 'put out, quench' and 'dry up'. Since it is plain that the Delphic oracle factory never had actual occasion to manufacture this item (the prodigy of the Alban Lake being a mythical event), and since Roman religious law in any event banned the consulting of foreign oracles, a Greek original would have to be a literary artifice first concocted for some Greek-language annalistic source on Roman pseudohistory, with some verb like *(kata)sbes-* subsequently translated by *exstinguere*. It is more probable that *aquam . . . exstingues* slipped through the demythologizing fingers of Livy as a phraseological survival from the ritual of the Roman protomyth, a formula proper to the *procuratio* of a theological prodigy, originally indicating what to do when there was eruptive fiery water pouring forth and running amok from Neptūnus's mythical lake.

Recommended Reading

Dumézil, Georges. "La saison des rivières." In *Mythe et épopée,* 3:18–89. Paris: Gallimard, 1973.

17 · Twin and Brother

Ancient myths teem with trite "first couples" of the type of Adam and his rib-product Eve. In Indo-European tradition these range from the Vedic Yama and Yamī and the Iranian Mašya and Mašyānag to the Icelandic Askr and Embla, with trees or rocks as preferred raw material (cf. chap. 12, note 1), and dragon's teeth or other bony substance occasionally thrown in for good measure. But there are also traces of a much more sophisticated anthropogony in Germanic, Indo-Iranian, and Roman sources.

Before tackling this topic of anthropogony and cosmogony head on, we might consider for a moment traditions concerning the "unwinding" of the world, that is, eschatology. One would expect that Rome would have nothing to say about something that takes place in sacred time, in this instance the future. Lucretius's grandiose prediction of the world's end (*De rerum natura* 5.96–97) was rather a poetic formulation of Epicurean atomism:

> una dies dabit exitio multosque per annos
> sustentata ruet moles et machina mundi

> one day will consign it to an end, and the bulky structure
> of the universe, upheld through many years, will rush to ruin.

To Lucretius's countrymen it was merely a nice conceit by a great poet, and Ovid used it charmingly in *Amores* (1.15.23–24) to pay a compliment to an older writer:

> carmina sublimis tunc sunt peritura Lucreti
> exitio terras cum dabit una dies

the songs of lofty Lucretius will perish only
when one day consigns the world to its end.

Elsewhere, too, eschatologies have been hard to come by. The only exceptions were Iran and Iceland, where such specific traditions are explicitly formulated. Fraškart and Ragnarök are remnants of an apocalyptic myth that survives elsewhere only in transmuted battle saga, be it Kurukṣetra or Lake Regillus or Mag Tuired or Brāvellir. In the showdown of gods versus demons (and by Norse extension giants, monsters, and the dead) the world perishes in a combined holocaust and cataclysm (a hot one at that, considering the molten metal in Iran and the incendiary Surtr in Icelandic geyser country). In the prophecies of the *Bundahišn* and the *Völuspā* the end will come with a bang, and in fire rather than ice, unlike alternative options suggested by two latter-day prophets, T. S. Eliot and Robert Frost.

If there are fire and scalding liquid at the end, ice is not absent in the earlier stages. Yama Xšaēta's *vara* sheltered men from the cosmic winter, but by the *fimbulvetr* matters were beyond redemption, with the "wolf age" at hand. Fire and ice were both present in the Norse creation story, as Niflheimr and Mūspellsheimr pooled their opposites to spawn the primordial 'Twin', Ymir, out of whose carcass Odin and his brothers shaped the world, seas from blood, earth from flesh, mountains from bones, sky from skull, and so forth. Much of this myth smacks of primitive and universal cosmogonic motifs, and other traits have possible remote diffusionary ties to the traditions of the ancient Near East, discussed in chapter 2. A more significant anthropogony is contained in the Continental Germanic myth reported by Tacitus (*Germania,* chap. 2), with an earthborn (*terra editus*) protoancestor Tuisto, his son Mannus, and Mannus's triple and multiple brood, the Ingaevones, Herminones, and Istaevones. Tuisto means etymologically 'Twin', and Mannus means 'Man', and the three tribes in fact denote the social class divisions of ancient Germania, in a manner reminiscent of the Scythian foundation legend discussed in chapter 6. Thus 'Twin' spawned 'Man' and the latter was the immediate ancestor of the total society. Ymir (from Proto-Germanic **Yumiyáz*) is also cogently etymologized as 'Twin'. But whose twin, and why? For the answer we must look elsewhere.

An obvious parallel is found once again at the opposite end of the Indo-European continuum. *RV* 10.90 tells of the primordial being Púruṣa 'Man' who was cut apart to make the world and the class society of men, that of brahmins, kṣatriyas, vaiśyas, and śūdras. Yet behind this figure lies that of the Vedic Yamá ('Twin', cognate with Ymir), the first man to die and to colonize the Otherworld, and of his brother Mánu ('Man') who introduced sacrifice and religious law (see chap. 4). Yamá has been fitted with a twin wife Yamī́, and Mánu likewise acquires a wife Manāvī́ whom he is reputed to have sacrificed. If we strip away such heterosexual excrescences and try to restore the original myth, in the protoversion Yama and Manu were primal twins and Yama was the sacrificial victim essential to the act of creation over which Manu presided. In other words, 'Man' sacrificed his 'Twin'.

In both Germania and India we thus have two versions of the same myth in bifurcated transmission, one involving a primeval creature called either 'Twin' or 'Man' and crudely butchered by "the gods," and a tidier, more societal anthropogonic variety including layers of speculative genealogy (originally collaterally with twin brothers, secondarily diachronically with father and son, as in the case of Tuisto and Mannus, or entailing heterosexual duplication, as with Yama and Manu).

This accordance represents a significant Indo-European archaism that is absent in Greece, for example, where Homer offhandedly refers to Ocean as *theôn génesis* and Hesiod draws his inspiration mainly from the Near East (see chap. 2). Iran, however, has something analogous on the "crude" and "societal" levels alike, both versions being colored by the Zoroastrian reform. As discussed in chapter 6, Yama Xšaēta was turned into a sinner, and the myth of creation was sublimated to involve merely an abstract 'Life' (*gaya-*), only to be remythologized in due course as Gayōmart 'Mortal Life'. According to the *Bundahišn* this first mortal was killed by the evil pole of Zoroastrian dualism, Ahriman, and the world and men were thus created. The other version, preserved in the *Avesta* (*Yašt* 19), tells of Yama's sinning and of his "moral dismemberment" by losing his triple royal halo, which was reapportioned to the patrons of the social classes. Yama himself was cut in two by his own brother and the latter's henchmen. Through all this one can still imperfectly glimpse the same myth that was present in India and Germania.

A myth that is recoverable from India, Iran, and Germania might well be sought also in the remaining mainstay of Indo-European comparative mythology, ancient Rome. Granted the peculiarities of the Roman mythological scene, we should expect it to be not only of the "societal" variety but specifically legendary and "historical." It is well known, especially from the works of such scholars as Mircea Eliade, that legendry surrounding urban beginnings tends to replicate myths of world creation. Therefore the traditions of Rome's founding are the most likely saga transpositions of Indo-European anthropogonic and cosmogonic lore.

Rome was founded by twins, Rōmulus and Remus, which is an old problem for scholarship, since a single founder was obviously called for. Various attempts have been made to explain this complicating trait, for example, the suggestion that it is a fictitious gemination, Remus being an arbitrary and spurious spin-off from Romulus, a latter-day manipulative invention designed to habilitate the two-man consulate of republican times by analogous duplication of the legendary kingship. Or again it has been suggested that the foundation legend is basically of Greek provenance, a literary import drawing on diffusionary twin motifs, which abound in Greek saga. Against all such theorizing the native and ancient character of the legend deserves emphasis. Greek writers call the pair *Rhômos* and *Rhōmúlos*. The former is a trite eponym based on the name of Rome itself, and *Rōmulus* is simply an original adjective meaning 'Roman', even as 'Sicilian' is in Latin either *Siculus* or *Sicānus*. The crux is *Remus,* which is not derivable from *Rōma* and thus seems the least facile and most archaic name.

Remus is the twin who gets killed in the process of foundation. The standard tradition puts this down to a quarrel between antagonistic brothers (the folkloristic Cain : Abel motif) or to a breach of tabu involving the newly completed walls of the city. But there is another possible interpretation of Remus's death as an essential consecrational act for the good of the new urban creation, as a blood sacrifice that hallowed the soundness of the project. This is a well-known pattern in many folklores. Remus literally went into the making of the city, a mythic fact that was no longer understood on religious terms and had to be dealt with on a "historical" and moral basis.

In this way one may comprehend how Rome got stuck with a subsequently inconvenient set of twin founders and had to rid itself of one of them by the clumsy and guilt-laden expedient of legendary fratricide. Rome was floundering in the backwash of its own suppressed mythical inheritance. It was trying to understand what had been sundered in the great Roman separation of myth and ritual. Ritual had lost its myth, which was of little concern in the peculiar atmosphere of Roman liturgical petrifaction. But the severed myth in its turn had become transposed to saga and history, thus purporting to be overtly understood. When this "history" was no longer matched by relevant ritual or theology, it had to make sense on its own terms. Coming to grips with primeval twins suddenly masquerading as city fathers was part of the price Rome had to pay for its peculiar tamperings with the normal workings of myth in societal thinking.

There is also evidence that Remus was in origin somehow the hierarchically primary or senior partner in his twinship with Romulus. Romulus as the actual founder is normally in the forefront, and Remus as the fratricidal victim is a skeleton in the Roman closet throughout the twists and turns of state ideology and moral philosophy. But in ancient formulas the fixed order of the brothers was regularly Remus and Romulus (e.g., *de Remo et Romulo* 'from time immemorial'); it became reversible only with Cicero and Varro and always retained its proverbial rigidity. Likewise, when one brother did double duty for the pair in elliptic turns of phrase, it was regularly Remus, as when Romans were called *Remi nepotes* 'descendants of Remus', or poets referred to *domus alta Remi*. Remus was thus the primary or senior twin who suffered a sacrificial death as part of the creation of Rome, at the hands of his brother who was the actual founder and whose relatively late and surely secondary epiclesis designated him simply 'Roman', Romulus.

Transposed to the mythic level of the Vedic Yama and Manu, or the Germanic Tuisto and Mannus, Remus was thus the original 'Twin', and Romulus was the 'Man'. Remus had to die as part of the act of creation, which led to the birth of the three Roman "tribes" (Ramnes, Luceres, Tities) and the accession of Romulus to his role as first king, who is the saga equivalent of the anthropogonic first man. The seniority of Remus, Tuisto, and Yama to Romulus, Mannus, and Manu is hierarchic rather than chronological, although it can be reprojected into a father : son relationship, as with Tuisto and Mannus. The 'Twin' is senior to the 'Man' because he goes into the cosmogonic inventory, whereas 'Man' stays behind to get history going. Remus, like Tuisto and Yama, behind whom lurk Ymir and Puruṣa respectively, is what is called in anthropology a "dema" figure, the type of being whose murder ends sacred time and who occupies a crucial slot in many cosmologies.

Strangely enough, the "crude" version of the creation myth has also been surreptitiously preserved in the Roman tradition. Parallel to the standard thunderstorm apotheosis of Romulus there is in many sources (Dionysius of Halicarnassus, Plutarch, Appian, Dio Cassius, Livy, Ovid, Florus) the alternative tradition that he was killed by the senators for being a tyrant. The perpetrators then cut up his body and carried away the pieces under their robes. This strange tale is what is left in a "historicized" version of the Roman equivalent of the slaughter of Ymir, Puruṣa, and Gayōmart. It attaches to Romulus rather than Remus because a man can be killed only once, as Remus already was in the preceding foundation episode; this is simply a consequence of the logic of storytelling.

The Proto-Roman names of 'Twin' and 'Man' may have been **Yemos* and **Wiros,* or with the "augmentative" suffix **Yemonos* and **Wironos*. **Yemonos* survives in Old Irish *emain* and in Latin *geminus,* both meaning 'twin'. The word-initial sequence **yem-* has disappeared from the Latin phonetic pattern and by some kind of cross-attraction has been replaced by *gem-* in *geminus*. The mythical name **Yemos,* matching Vedic *Yamá-,* has been similarly transformed to *Remus* by alliterative association with Romulus (cf., e.g., the Welsh Nudd becoming Lludd under the influence of his brother Lleuelys and his epithet Llawereint).

**Wiros* yielded Latin *Vir,* and **Wironos* developed regularly to **Virinus;* one or the other or both may be claimed as the original name of Romulus. **Virinus* became **Virīnus* by analogy with derivatives like *virīlis, virītim*. The name *Quirīnus,* which designates the deified Romulus, is simply a compound **Co-Virīnus* of the same name.

It is usually assumed that the god Quirinus and the deified Romulus were identified at a rather late point in time, on the basis of imported Greek ideas about apotheosis. Instead we witness here another example of the Roman sundering of theology and myth. At some point the mythical figure **Wiro(no)s* was preserved as a ritual numen of collectivity **Co-Wironos,* while its stripped myth was epicized around the hero **Wiro(no)s*. One developed into Quirinus; the other was first epithetized and then supplanted by Romulus. A "historical" hero needed a life story with an end, and the badly misapplied mythical theme of senatorial quartering of the body of the "tyrant" Romulus was hardly what Rome needed. The Greek-based notion of apotheosis via a mysterious vanishing act supplied the means of reestablishing a long-broken tie between the god and the hero.

The cohorts of Romulus were referred to as *Ramnes viri* by the poet Propertius, which formula may be translatable as 'the Romans of the Man', that is, the people of *the* Roman, Romulus. When Juvenal (11.105) called Remus and Romulus *geminos Quirinos,* literally 'the twin Quirini', he used a plural formula reflecting an ancient double-dual coupling of divine names **Yemonō-Wironō* 'Twin [and] Man', on the well-known pattern of the Vedic *Mitrā́-Váruṇā*.

The reconstructed Indo-European creation myth of man and society thus rests on the triple foundation of Yama and Manu in India, Tuisto and Mannus in Germania, and **Yemo(no)s* and **Wiro(no)s* in Rome. In back of these pairs we spot the more primitive cosmogonic giants Puruṣa, Gayōmart, and Ymir, and also the butchered Romulus of the Roman senate house, the same place that saw Julius Caesar done to death. Shakespeare's Brutus even says "Let's carve him as a dish fit for the gods." It may be that this is a real mythological layer cake: underneath the murder of Caesar lurks the dismemberment of Romulus, and deepest down the primordial sacrifice of the Indo-European cosmic twin.

Index

COMPARATIVE MYTHOLOGY

Designed by Ann Walston.

Composed by Graphic Composition, Inc.
in Times Roman with Trajanus display.

Printed by the Maple Press Company
on 50-lb. Warren's Sebago Eggshell Cream
Offset, and bound in Holliston Roxite
with Lindenmeyr Elephant Hide Paper end sheets.